MALRAUX

A Biography
by Axel Madsen

W. H. ALLEN · LONDON
A Howard & Wyndham Company
1977

Printed by Fletcher & Son Ltd, Norwich,
for the Publishers, W. H. Allen & Co. Ltd,
44 Hill Street, London W1X 8LB
Bound by Richard Clay (The Chaucer Press) Ltd,
Bungay, Suffolk

ISBN 0 491 02070 8

Unless otherwise noted, all translations are by the author.

to St. Armand

André Malraux died on November 23, 1976, two weeks after his seventy-fifth birthday. His death wouldn't have interested him. Death was the hemstitch of his life and his thought. As he said a month before he died, "For me death is extremely important—in metaphysical not in human terms. What interests me is what Kierkegaard calls the scandal. The irreducible fact interests me, not the décor." His own death was banal. It came eight days after he had entered the Henri Mondor hospital in Créteil, ten miles from his beloved Verrières-le-Buisson on the southern outskirts of Paris, his native city. The cause was pulmonary embolism. The lung condition was a relapse from a chainsmoker's cancer for which he had been operated on three months earlier.

President Valéry Giscard d'Estaing, in a message of condolence to Malraux's daughter, Florence, spoke of his "life of commitment, marked by an exceptional dialogue between creative work and action." According to Malraux's wishes the burial at Verrières was private. Only two "official" personnages were present, Françoise Giraud, his successor as Secretary for Cultural Affairs, and Philippe de Gaulle. A few days later, the government paid him a "national homage", a memorial service in the courtyard of the Louvre, with President Giscard and Prime Minister Raymond Barre in attendance and Beethoven's *Marche Funèbre* and a recording of his own nervous, snapping voice echoing between the historical walls.

Talking about death, he had said the western fear of death also stemmed from the dying person unconsciously imagining himself reincarnated as a cadaver. "This is something enormous for the white man. For the individual who believes in the passage of the soul from one body to another, this anxiety doesn't exist. The Asian isn't too afraid. Perhaps he doesn't particularly like to come back as a frog, but he can always hope to come back as a canary."

This book, written before the irreducible scandal of Malraux's death, is dedicated to the most important Malraux. The Malraux après Malraux.

A.M., 1977

Part One

To see an aquarium, better not be a fish.

Picasso's Mask

1

"The last meaningful revolution, you ask me?" His gaze is keen and searching. "Modern revolutions are either hangovers from 1917 or they are fascist takeovers, but of course the Russian Revolution, the Chinese Revolution require cobblestones to make barricades against cavalry. With the invention of the tank, revolutionary action really becomes obsolete."

André Malraux is an elegant and slightly bent septuagenarian of extravagant memory and prodigious knowledge who receives his visitor with formidable verbosity and a choice of Scotch or mint tea. He talks about what Mao Tse-tung told him and what he told Trotsky and Kennedy and about History's finer ironies. He recalls camels coming down the Pamirs, bellowing through the clouds, and says that listening to Europe's great composers in Asia makes him feel that the West's deepest emotion is nostalgia. He talks about the next war—a war for diminishing resources—while contrasting his darkening vision with faith in human resilience. He says God *is* dead, but that what ultimately matters is neither material rewards nor even happiness but spiritual dimension. What makes humanity awesome and culture a great adventure is not our own saying so, but our questioning everything.

His spare strands of hair are dark, his eyes green and his face, with its chiseled furrows and nervous twitches, is dominated by the arch of his brow. He examines his visitor's half-finished sentences with intuitive impatience. He has a gift for taking quick and forceful possession of ideas and for formulating them in dazzling propositions. Yet his language is without redundancy or hesitancy. He never seems to feel his way toward ideas, and words flow from him at a rate that is almost the speed of thought. For punctuation, he may lift a long, apostolic forefinger and say, *Mais, attention!* as if to warn of upcoming illuminations. Objections are taken into account and a partner in conversation may come to feel grateful

9

that doubts are entertained at all. Ideals are not defended with asperity but with common sense and a series of *primo, secundo* and *tertio* to keep matters straight until all extensions, consequences and impossibilities of various hypotheses have been disposed of and a cogent conclusion reached. When conversing with Malraux, André Gide has said, one doesn't feel very clever.

"War puts questions stupidly, peace mysteriously. Our history is not a chronicle of ideologies or political abstractions, but of empires, of powers seeking to control events."

He has always felt the tragic dimension of modern man and his novels are peopled with characters who in violent situations fight to create their own transcendental usefulness. He believes our civilization no longer has a clear idea of man and is therefore bound to change or disappear.

"You ask me if the universe has a purpose, if history leads somewhere or whether such questions are senseless. Not senseless, I'd say, unintelligible. The Iranians have given the answer in the Koran a modern twist: 'Does the cricket run over by a truck understand the internal combustion engine?' The cricket may think it has been run over by something very big and very nasty, but not *how* the internal combustion engine works. Nor what the engine thinks, or that it doesn't think at all. Man thinking of himself in biological terms started with Darwin. The idea of a common human fate is very recent, and we don't even know yet whether evolution is divergent or convergent."

Malraux's progression has been from high-pitched radicalism to political agnosticism and art as transcendence rather than beauty. His fiction is a tragic universe where individuals are opposed to society but at the same time draw their forces from it, a world where revolutions fail but justice rekindles justice and where to accept the unknown is to be fully human. A revolutionary movement is fraternal not only because it defends the individual's values but because in revolt the individual exceeds himself. In his books, clear-eyed revolutionaries and magnificent losers die so that others may live with dignity. "What do you call dignity? It doesn't mean anything," a Kuomintang officer asks the captured Kyo in *La Condition humaine,* which in English received the title *Man's Fate.** "The opposite of humiliation," the revolutionary answers. Pages later, he realizes that to die for human dignity is to die a little less alone.

Malraux's last novel appeared in 1943. Since then, he has published over fifteen books, memoirs of his extraordinary life not always written in the first person and volumes about art and the creative process which say that what ennobles Man is what transforms him. "Art is a dialogue we have always carried out with the unknown. We have come to distinguish the contours of the unknown through the unconscious, through religion

* See pages 363 for "Books by André Malraux" in French and in English.

and magic and we may soon begin to understand such totally modern emotions as the feeling that we belong to the future, that our civilization is the sum total of all others."

Five books appeared between 1974 and 1976, all parts of his ongoing life work. *La Tête d'obsédienne,* which became *Picasso's Mask* in English, sees art as its own absolute, freed even of a need to be beauty, and as promise of a universal language that allows modern man to converse across civilizations and time. It is also about Pablo Picasso and the traces the artist leaves behind. *Lazare* is a meditation undertaken in the limbo of critical illness—Malraux's own voyage to the edge of death in 1972 when a collapsed peripherical nervous system threatened him with paralysis of the cerebellum and total amnesia. It is also about the realization that the medical technology that saved him had not existed a few years earlier. Together with other, as yet unpublished texts, *La Tête d'obsédienne* and *Lazare* will form the second volume of the *Antimémoires*—"anti" because Malraux wants the ego talking about itself to yield to what is *created* in life. *L'Irréel* and *L'Intemporel* are the second and third volumes of *The Metamorphoses of the Gods. L'Irréel*—in English perhaps not so much the unreal as the non-real—sees the Renaissance as the stupendous turning point when artists stopped re-creating the world according to sacred tenets and began re-creating it according to imaginary values. *L'Intemporel*—in Malraux's view neither timelessness nor immortality, but the peculiar time warp that allows a work of art to escape its own era—traces the *volte-face* of modern painting since Manet with whom Venus ceased to be both naked woman and poetry to become color arranged in certain forms. With these two big, richly illustrated volumes, Malraux has finished *The Metamorphoses of the Gods,* his reflection on art and its transmutations, started in 1957 as an afterthought to the monumental *Voices of Silence,* his hymn to art as intelligence imposed on matter.

He receives his visitors at the Vilmorin family château in Verrières-le-Buisson on the southern outskirts of Paris where he lives surrounded by the affectionate attention of the sister and family of the last woman in his life. Louise de Vilmorin lies buried somewhere in the park-sized garden under a cherry tree. "The cherries will rain down on my tomb and children will feast on them," the novelist wrote in her will. Verrières is less than ten miles from the city limits and only a last few fields from suburban high-risers. The lovers of Verrières, twentieth-century Chateaubriand and Madame Récamier, found each other late and lived a whimsical if autumnal liaison. De Gaulle didn't exactly approve but when Madame de Vilmorin died, the president sent a rare personal note. A year later, he died.

The modern world is baffling, Malraux says, because our value system is devoid of meaning. "If asked, a thirteenth-century Christian could tell you on the spot what is good and what is evil. To think values today is

11

to undertake a research. What is curious of course is that whereas nearly all civilizations with weak value systems have been moribund societies, ours is the most powerful the world has ever known."

When asked whether he thinks this is a contradiction, he says the modern world *is* contradictory, in technology triumphant beyond the wildest dreams yet without spiritual ferment or direction.

He feels that although the atom bomb must be categorized as a shattering event, the major facts of our times are not events but shifts in concepts. "The relentless way we question our civilization is an example. Earlier societies have had individuals asking questions and wondering about the future. But nobody *announced* the end of Rome. Saint Augustine talked very seriously about it, but when he did Rome had already fallen. We, on the other hand, are engaged in wholesale challenge and are aware of a civilizational crisis."

Modern man, he feels, is both fearful of tomorrow and hopeful, peering into the future for signs, but nobody has ever been able successfully to predict profound spiritual change. "In 200 A.D., thoughtful Romans began realizing that the empire had had it. What would happen next? Nobody really knew, but almost every one agreed—we have those letters from Baiae—that the most probable philosophy of the future would be stoicism. As it turned out, stoicism was to play no role at all because Christianity swept everything away. Nobody predicted the rise of Islam. It's probably in the nature of revolutions of the mind to simply happen. Great religious minds aren't necessarily the harbingers of great truths. To be a prophet, you must discover that soft spot in people that is vulnerable to your prophecy."

Malraux believes that within a hundred years the two main spheres of human endeavor will be science, still advancing at a dizzying pace, and what he calls "the spiritual phenomenon." He finds it curious that there is no real research into religious *change,* no History of Spiritual Movements from a social point of view. "Everybody has studied the origins of Christianity, of course, but no sociologist has studied such profound changes as Franciscanism, which brought into the Church a kind of Buddhism— 'My brother the rain' and all that—which caused an incredible transformation. Likewise, primitive Buddhism was a kind of tragic agnosticism, Gautama Buddha teaching us to try to escape 'the wheel' of suffering, but it's someone else, someone whose name we don't even know, who got the idea that you can be reborn through inward extinction if you pronounce Buddha's name with all the possible commiseration for the distress and misery of this world, in other words that you are in a tragic world but that you *can* move on to paradise. It's as if Luther had said there's no hell. The result was one hundred million conversions in twenty years."

Malraux thinks faster than he speaks and feels terrorized in any language but French. He is without formal education. He reads Greek, has a smattering knowledge of Mandarin and a bookish command of English that allows him to read Shakespeare in the original but not to give directions to a London cabdriver. With the exception of Terence Kilmartin, who translated the *Antimémoires,* he has never been very lucky with his English translators. Stuart Gilbert's translation of *Les Voix du Silence* is curiously archaic while passages of Robert Hollander's rendition of *La Tentation de l'Occident* are downright inaccurate. The most famous of the novels, *La Condition humaine,* has been translated in stilted and heavy fashion by Haakon Chevalier, a University of California, Berkeley professor of Norwegian-French descent (whom Malraux helped during J. Robert Oppenheimer's 1953 "trial" when the Father of the Atom Bomb pointed a hysterical finger at Chevalier as the man who had tried to lead him astray). Not that Malraux underestimates the difficulties involved in transposing his words and thoughts, which often seem to mean more than they state. Before Gilbert started on *The Voices of Silence,* Malraux told him, "You'll find my lyric passages frequent and fatiguing; just do the best you can with them." A former colonial judge from Burma, famous for accomplishing the feat of translating James Joyce's *Ulysses* into French, Gilbert is the translator of four other Malraux books.

It is not one of Malraux's habits to visit a country without adopting its causes and in *La Tête d'obsédienne* he takes up Picasso's struggle against old age and in so doing asks himself what his own creation might weigh in the face of the Big Void. Malraux first met the painter, twenty years his senior, as a tall, pale youth with a romantic lock over one eye trying to crash the clever, anarchic scene of post-World War I dadaism and cubism. In 1937, Picasso's sketches for *Guernica* were to have illustrated the first edition of *L'Espoir (Man's Hope),* the novel about the Spanish Civil War that made Hemingway so jealous he accused André of untimely pullout in order to write "masterpisses."

The title of the Picasso book comes from a pre-Columbian skull carved in volcanic crystal that Malraux first saw at the National Museum in Mexico City in the company of Spain's last Republican ambassador. Seated under his unframed Rouault and Braque paintings in the *salon bleu* overlooking the Verrières park, he explains that the obsidian head is exhibited in a glass case with a mirrored background that fuses the crystal cranium with the onlooker's own reflection, "like in Narayana's temple where the images of the gods on the sacrificial stones have been replaced by mirrors."

Death has been at his shoulder since he was thirteen and, a week after France's first flush of victory in 1914, a patriotic teacher took him and his classmates to visit the Marne battlefield and ashes from a funeral pyre wafted onto their box lunches. The best passages in his novels are descriptions of death up close—Perkins in *The Royal Way,* dying in a Cambodian village, fascinated by his own disintegration, or Katov, the

13

medical student turned revolutionary in *Man's Fate,* giving the cyanide pellets hidden in his belt buckle to wounded comrades in Chiang Kai-shek's prison while he himself is led off to be executed in a manner singularly prescient of the next war's concentration camp ovens—burned alive in a locomotive boiler on a Shanghai railway siding, a detail that lends credence to the oft-quoted remark that history has come to resemble Malraux novels.

Death has always hit close to him—and has not only felled comrades-in-arms. The mother of his two sons and the sons themselves died in accidents. His two half-brothers died in World War II, the elder absurdly during the closing hours of the conflict. His grandfather split his own skull with an ax, perhaps not inadvertently. His father committed suicide. "To reflect upon life—life in relation to death—is perhaps no more than to intensify one's questioning," he wrote on the opening page of his *Anti-mémoires*. "I don't mean death in the sense of being killed, which poses few problems to anyone who has the commonplace luck to be brave, but death that brushes by."

From above the mantel, he takes an exquisite early Braque. He brings it over to the garden window, to show the grain of the painting. "The last time I saw Braque, I quoted Cézanne's phrase: 'If I were sure that my paintings would be destroyed and never reach the Louvre, I'd stop painting.' Braque took a long time answering. Finally in a subdued tone he said, 'If I were sure all my canvases would be burned, I think I'd still go on.' "

When Braque died in 1963, Malraux was France's Secretary for Cultural Affairs and ordered a state funeral in the inner court of the Louvre. It was a blustery, rainy September evening. A military honor guard played Beethoven's *Marche funèbre* and Malraux delivered the eulogy, saying that burying Braque with state honors seemed to avenge a little Van Gogh's suicide in the Auvers asylum, Modigliani's pathetic obsequy and the long record of scorn, poverty and despair that is the history of art. As he finished the oration, the moon came out.

Malraux was Secretary for Cultural Affairs for nearly eleven years and as such tasted what few intellectuals ever come to enjoy—the power to experiment in culture. He sent the Louvre treasures on globe-trotting tours and for scraping centuries of grime off Paris landmarks. He initiated an unprecedented inventory of France's artistic wealth, started new archaeological reserves, had Chagall paint the Opéra ceiling and Coco Chanel decorate a wing of the Louvre. He pushed subsidies for theater, ballet and cinema ("for the price of one freeway," he thundered in the National Assembly, "France can again become a land of culture"). He launched his "Maisons de Culture"—multi-purpose art centers designed not only to extend Paris standards to the provinces but to foster an interpenetration of the arts by combining facilities for drama, music, film and exhibitions. Although budgetary limitations prevented the building of the twenty-one

14

"culture houses" originally planned, a number are in operation—at Bourges, Amiens and, the most grandiose of them, in Grenoble. He had eight thousand delegates attend a theater congress in Bourges and on Picasso's eighty-fifth birthday organized a huge one-man show in the renovated Grand Palais. He created the Orchestre de Paris, had the Chambord, Vincennes and Fontainebleau castles rehabilitated and the Reims cathedral restored. And he traveled, from New Delhi to Brasilia, Cairo to Tokyo, Dakar to Ottawa, as de Gaulle's ambassador to the world. "We all want to take part in life's numerous adventures, but Mr. Malraux beats us all," declared President Kennedy at a White House state dinner. His most spectacular voyage was to China to cement France's early recognition of the People's Republic. It culminated with a remarkable and much-quoted Mao Tse-tung interview, which Malraux was to recall in eighty sonorous pages in his *Antimémoires*.

"Malraux is an expensive minister," said Georges Pompidou. The limits of the "Malraux era" were the limits of the Cultural Affairs ministry itself. Education and telecommunications were not under his control.

Modern industrial societies, he says, must break the stronghold of money on culture and see to it that the majority of citizens aren't always flooded with trash. This holds true not only for bourgeois states without political leadership in cultural affairs, but for Marxist and totalitarian countries as well. Governments, he feels, must try to impose reforms that widen the access to authentic art and promote and preserve culture.

"Concrete suggestions? Not on the level of creation. The state has no business in the artist's studio, but it certainly has in the dissemination of art. The most urgent area is education, which must be reorganized via television and video, a task as important as universal education was a hundred years ago. You must have the best minds teaching their specialty simultaneously in fifty thousand classrooms. Not all great minds are teachers, of course, which is where superior journalism comes in. Sartre put it very well when he said great minds reach their audiences *in stages* and Einstein told me theoretical scientists shouldn't try to explain themselves, just write forewords to popularizing volumes."

His days are busy. Schedules are kept by Sophie L. de Vilmorin and adhered to with reasonable punctuality. A symbol of his ministerial years he has hung on to is a chauffeur and a jet-black Citroën limousine. Sensitive to boredom, he finds things to do in Paris three, four days a week and has himself whisked into town on the flimsiest of pretexts. He has no sense of money but has an acute business sense and is uncompromising when it comes to his contractual due. Gallimard has been his publisher since 1930—he worked there as an editor while he wrote *Man's Fate*—and likes to show up unannounced at the Rue Sébastien-Bottin. Although he lived for years in the nearby Rue du Bac, he is no Left Bank person. Hanging out in cafés never appealed to him. He has an apartment on Rue

15

de Montpensier near the Comédie-Française and with Louise de Vilmorin had plans to buy a house in the restored Quartier des Marais.

He buys his clothes at Lanvin—gray flannels, navy blue serges, herringbones and always wears a tie and an elegant wristwatch. He was in his chartreuse camel hair coat inaugurating the Chagall building in Nice when a man stepped forward, yelled "Down with Chagall!" and splashed him with red paint. Malraux promptly "disarmed" his aggressor and in turn covered *him* with paint. "An esthetic disagreement," he said calmly, "but I resent anyone insulting one of our greatest living painters."

His favorite restaurant is Lasserre's and he has always approached culinary temples with reverence. To outdo Le Grand Véfour's *Pigeon Prince Rainier,* Lasserre's has created *Pigeon André Malraux,* yet he is attached to dishes he learned to like as a child. If served beef stew he will politely eat up all the carrots on his plate. He doesn't care much for fruit, but likes a dessert with his meals, either a pithiviers, his favorite cake, or a napoleon. A reformed chain smoker, he has given up both alcohol and cigarettes, but relapses occur at the sight of an ashtray.

The facial tics, which at moments afflict his composure and impair the flow of words, have long been legendary, psychosomatic proof, so to speak, of his staccato mind. In reality, the twitches are the result of acute sinusitis, neglected since childhood and in recent years complicated by aphasiac apheresis. The only sport he ever indulged in was fencing when, at twenty-five, he edited a newssheet in Saigon.

He has always had a taste for ostentatious living. During the first months of the Spanish Civil War when he commanded a small squadron of foreign airmen he lived at Madrid's Hotel Florida. Whatever the day's bombing mission, he appeared freshly shaven for before-dinner cocktails.

"I remember Stalin at Gorky's house, arriving late, beguiling and farfetched. That was in 1934, just before the purges. I think Stalin was obsessed by statistics: if we kill all those who have known, etc., we *will* end up catching the real culprits."

When asked what the world's leaders he has known have in common, he says a feel for what will resist them and the ability to overcome such resistance. He remembers Trotsky in exile in southern France, his laughter showing his tiny gapped teeth. He remembers Mao as someone hesitating, a man haunted by what he hasn't accomplished, Nehru as a British gentleman with a sad smile who couldn't believe, as Gandhi, that the Ganges was a holy river. He remembers Kennedy asking him what popularity was. His relations with de Gaulle, he says, were not political but historic. When the general was defeated in a referendum in 1969 and resigned, Malraux followed him.

He was late for the general's funeral at Colombey. Family, parishoners and old comrades-in-arms were kneeling in the arched nave when squealing tires were heard. Malraux didn't speak at de Gaulle's funeral.

16

Instead, he wrote *Felled Oaks,* a hallucinatory retelling of de Gaulle's confidences to him a few months earlier. The title comes from a Victor Hugo poem: ". . . oh, what savage noise in the waning light, the oaks felled for Hercules's pyre."

The following year, Malraux discovered a war where *he* could die heroically—Bangladesh. But the war lasted only ten days and Indira Gandhi made him wait. She knew the victory would be India's and had no intention of giving any part of it to any international Malraux brigade.

If he was refused a hero's death at the side of a crucified people in an Asia that had always fascinated him, he was given the satisfaction of being the man the leader of the world's foremost power consulted before meeting the ruler of the world's most populous empire. In February 1972, President Nixon called him to Washington. "He wants to meet someone who knows Mao," Malraux said, taking off from Orly airport. American bombs were raining on Vietnam, and, Malraux tartly told the assembled French press, "to help bring about peace, you can contribute more by making a trip to the White House than by writing articles in *Le Nouvel Observateur.*"

"I told Nixon that nobody would know for fifty years whether his mission would be successful," he says, replacing the Braque on the mantel between a Fautrier and a Poliakov. His newest acquisitions are from Japan, a prehistoric clay dove and a rare eighteenth-century drawing, gifts from admirers in Tokyo. The pigeon, predating Buddhism and the 600 B.C. foundation of the first archaic empire, is a curiously abstract rendition, with the tail prolonging the body without interruption. He explains that such figurines, usually of horses, doves and imaginary animals, were set on high poles around burial sites, apparently as protectors of graves. "What really makes them interesting is that this is the absolute anti-African art because this is the only sculpture executed in continued planes. In African fetish carvings you'd have interrupted surfaces, whereas here the roundness of the body continues into the plane of the tail in a single trait."

He unrolls the Edo period drawing and indicates the delicacy of the pen stroke. "Skill, which plays such a major role in Western art, was less important in traditional Eastern and Egyptian art, perhaps because ideographic writing makes fluent calligraphy a matter of course. It may also explain why caricature is unknown in traditional Japanese drawings."

He has always had far-flung contacts with influential people—Trotsky wrote to Simon and Schuster urging a quick American edition of *Man's Fate,* and the Shah of Iran lent him Babylonian sculptures—but he also knows how to be generous with his person and his time to lesser mortals. To the many doing research on his life or writing about his place in literature, art history or politics he makes gifts of patience and counsel that are magnanimous, even princely. Questions must be submitted in writing in advance, but on the appointed day the interviewer is picked up by the chauffeur in the black Citroën at Antony station, whisked to Verrières and in the *salon bleu* met by a Malraux armed with typed-up key answers. A tape recorder is invited and once it is rolling, the typed sheet in his hand becomes not so much a string of signposts as a series of casual fermatas now and then arresting the flow of ideas. In conversation, his rare intelligence is luminous and his gift for complex ideas and formulation knows no obstacles, only organic pauses.

He is part of any French curriculum but his ascendance over his country's youth was sharply challenged in the 1968 "May Events," the student uprisings that indirectly led to de Gaulle's downfall and were to reverberate through the national conscience for years. The summer of discontent was an outburst against an inefficient educational system and against a paternalistic regime, symbolized by a monolithic, state-controlled television network that didn't allow plurality of opinion. The revolt saw quotations from Malraux's books scrawled on college and university walls, taunting him with the Faustian pronouncements of his youth. Yet of the Gaullist cabinet members, he was the least painful to read. He called the riots "an immense lyrical illusion" and told his fellow cabinet ministers that politics were not an exercise in absolutes but in reality. "To know youth is to be part of it," he reasons. "It is not attempts at 'dialogues.' No one is obliged to accept the famous generation gap—in fact, to accept it would be madness—but neither must anyone pretend to understand too much. I must say, however, that I don't *see* the young. In music a little, yes; but not in architecture. Niemayer has talent, but he's in his sixties. The writers of my generation were in their mid-twenties when Gallimard lived from publishing 'what the young are up to.' What book by a young writer today would be assured in advance of the audience of, say, a new book by Sartre?

"In painting, what can I say? Cubism looks more and more like the last important school. Picasso said, 'I paint as I damn well please, but I'm the brother of the sculptor of the Cyclades and, by the way, of Cézanne and Manet.' During his cubist period, he was taking on the whole Louvre. Makers of contemporary post-object, conceptual, earth art, etc., with their gigantism and aggressivity, don't wrestle with Michelangelo, Titian and Cézanne on their canvases, but translate a very rare sentiment—the artist as a tracked animal, pursued and fearing being caged. At the same time, they say, 'I care so little about the idea of painting that I work with perishable materials.' You see this in America especially, where you have a way of painting that is constantly renewed and a willingness to be decorative that has all the earmarks of fashion.

"Although there is evolution in art, 'advance' in the sense we understand 'progress' in science doesn't exist. In art, you don't invent, you find out and the discovery of African art is no more an advance than the discovery of Romanesque sculpture. Progression in science is a staircase;

18

in art there is no 'up,' progress is simply elsewhere. Science has no equivalent of the presence of all earlier art nor of creativity independent of History. Titian is *after* Masaccio, but you don't view Titian's work as being later than Masaccio's in the same way you think of the internal combustion engine as being more recent than the plow."

If asked what he thinks will be the next 'elsewhere,' Malraux says it will obviously be the work of an artist who is big enough to invent new forms that are acceptable to our notions of both beauty and transcendence. Novelty is both imitation and opposition. "To understand the existence of a void is pretty easy, to know how to fill it is the mark of a genius."

The characters in Malraux's fiction know what values are, rarely what truth is. His books, even his nonfiction, are full of enemy truths squaring off. Negative forces are absent and oppressors—capitalists, Nazis, Falangists—remain impersonal if often suffocating incarnations. The conflict is not so much between inner truth and surrounding realities. He inhabits all his characters and, through them, confronts himself, writing in staccato dialogue and striking images. Revolutionary action is often politically futile since his revolutionaries gain none of their objectives and often only manage to get themselves killed. In risking his life, man can at least choose his own death and thereby escape the absurdity and an accidental and meaningless end. Someone has said Malraux's fiction isn't really novels but metaphysical reportage.

In his writings on art, the creative process is both desire to express and will to achieve. Artists are locked in combat with their own talent and their work is the triumph over the darker powers that assail them and to which they yield in their quest for perfection and ecstasy. Art is born from the lure of the elusive.

Why hasn't he written a novel in over thirty years?

"Perhaps because the novel calls for a strong narrative power and narration is today in images. The publicized and televised violence of everyday existence, hijacking and all sorts of minor events that used to be mystery for a writer, have helped to kill the novel. I mean a certain kind of novel with which we are all familiar—going from Balzac to Tolstoy. This sort of narrative received its death blow with the publication of *Madame Bovary*. Do you know what Alexandre Dumas' reaction was when he read *Bovary*? He told his son, 'If this is what literature has become, we've had it!' And right he was. Compare *Bovary* with *The Three Musketeers*.

"Subject matter exists to be transmuted, we all reach our audience in stages, remember. The narrative means of Margaret Mitchell are not inferior to Dostoyevsky's; it is in the realm of the imaginary that *Gone with the Wind* had nothing in common with *The Brothers Karamazov*. Television is a powerful means of story-telling, but it is weak in depicting intuition, fantasy, whimsy because the imaginary is not plot but a realm.

"Current theories on the novel, it seems to me, resemble the central

19

problem facing fifteenth-century painters—depth and spacial values. Flemish painters advanced cautiously whereas the Florentines pursued the three dimensions with exuberance and, like land surveyors, caught space in a net of geometry. I think that for most novelists characters are fashioned by the drama of their stories, not the drama by the characters.

"A third reason for the decline of the novel is that whereas communism has invented the mythical Bolshevik hero, there is no such thing as a mythical capitalist character."

Citizen Kane?

"Not *as* capitalist. There can be no capitalist hero since only Marxists claim that there is such an animal. No, what happened at the end of the great monarchies was The Ambitious One. This mythical character was invented as social climber in 1830 by Stendhal and Balzac and laid to rest as individualist in early Gide fiction. We now begin to see that The Ambitious One isn't to be taken too seriously. I'd say that the guy who says he is going to take on the atomic bomb single-handedly makes us laugh. The realities of our era do not pertain to the particular. I think we're beginning to realize something rather formidable, that from Nietzsche to, say, Gide, we thought values were individual. We now realize that this has been an incredible mistake. Values are not individual. Look at what has really moved the world during the last fifty years. Values are collective and the phenomenon called individualism is starting to look like what it really is, a historical myth, something nineteenth-century Western society invented like the Greeks invented Aphrodite."

He is without a shred of sentimentality and rates doubt and self-distrust as the most superficial of human feelings. Every morning, he tears up the previous day's appointments, a ritual, he says, that is accompanied by a spontaneous desertion of memory but is without regret, guilt or lassitude. He has never kept a diary. When asked why not in 1945, he said diaries are for people who like to remember. He has not written ten lines about the women in his life. Sometimes to their regret. Clara Malraux brings out volume after volume of memoirs, telling how she was part of so much of it, as indeed she was.

He can seem detached from himself, suffused only with impersonal passions, abstract apprehensions and enthusiasm once-removed. His mythomania is legendary and he has always played deliberately on the confusion of fiction and reality and even tried out his legends on new acquaintances. He has been careful never to deny being a political commissar for the Chinese communists in the mid-1920s. He has never said whether he discovered the ruins of ancient Sheba in the sands of Saudi Arabia. Sometimes events have chastefully veiled the evidence. When the Germans marched into Paris, Gaston Gallimard hastily burned whatever papers could be compromising for his authors, including a 1929 Malraux plan to liberate Trotsky from Alma-Ata, where Stalin had deported the

20

founder of the Red Army. Malraux's idea was to smuggle Trotsky out of the Soviet Union across the Himalayas.

The need for myth runs deep. It is part of Malraux's creative genius and partly responsible for the failure of his first marriage. The idol of his youth was T. E. Lawrence. He wrote a penetrating foreword to the French translation of *Seven Pillars of Wisdom,* planned a book on him but only met Lawrence of Arabia once—in a gay bar in Montparnasse.

"But mind you," he says, holding up the index finger of his right hand as an exclamation point, "the difference between Lawrence and me is that he was always sure he would fail whereas I have always believed in the success of my undertakings."

His life's adventure has been his progression from intellectual swagger to the discovery of a fraternal dignity in revolutionary movements and on to the probing on the summit of human endeavor—the creative process, which he thinks is man's only triumphant response to a seemingly absurd fate. "The nineteenth century believed it was seeing the end of wars. Nietzsche was right—and Marx wrong—in foretelling that the twentieth would be the century of national wars."

Both Nietzsche and Marx have influenced him, although on different levels. Marxism is part of the novels, not as philosophy but as part of the political equation, whereas Nietzschean ideas appear as an organic element. Malrucian man is not so much what he thinks as what he tries to discover.

"When you try to answer the question of whether human nature is infinitely changeable, you realize that science is changing the world, it is not changing us. But it's hard to grasp the infinite. We have always been better at scanning the near future. What's important is the *next* objective and there I cannot accept utter gloom. Why? Because of a certain frog's reflex—keeping the head down while disaster hits. We have always done that.

"Also, I cannot agree that unmanageable population explosion and diminishing resources will lead to nuclear blackmail by underdeveloped countries and breakdown of industrial society. To wars, yes, but to a new medieval age turned toward ritualism, no. Pre-industrial China and Japan were never particularly religious and there was Roman atheism, more pervasive than ours since everything that counted in Rome was secular.

"The difference between ours and all other civilizations is quite obviously the machine and the fact we are without precedent. Other cultures rarely knew the societies preceding them—the Renaissance knew Antiquity, yes; but Rome wasn't the inheritor of Egypt, much less of the Celts—whereas we are the sum of all others, the first planetary civilization. This is something momentous that started around 1870 when so-called cultivated humanity realized it was the inheritor of the whole planet. The next step is obviously to conceive humanity as one.

21

"Culturally, this means there are no more secrets. We don't know what hasn't been discovered, of course—ruins never unearthed, but we know everything that exists and has been." He feels most indications point toward a coming together of humanity. Worldwide materialism is one sign and another is the shift in the way we see our differences, our perception moving from inferior-superior racism toward specific differences. A third hint is the acceptance of the idea of a common explanation of human fate, even if we don't know for sure whether the next civilization will resemble ours.

In the meantime, we still live in an era of empires. "Mao used communism to reestablish Great China after the century of foreign humiliations. The bowl of rice has been a symbolic means. The United States is also an empire but it is the first country in history that has become a world power without wanting to. America has never sought political conquest. There have been episodes yes, but they don't count. America was dragged into the two world wars, didn't profit much from either conflict and has actually become the world's master by selling its products at the best price. Now, this has never happened before and the consequence is that the United States has never really had any historical design.

"I would say, naturally with a grain of salt, that America has no policy. There are five or six U.S. policies because there are several vast powers in America—powers that are generally but not only economic—which have certain designs. But if the United States has no historical will, neither does Russia. Not any longer. Nor do the Chinese. They have a national will that is very strong. They do want to accomplish the most profound revolution, but in a vacuum. When they say they want to change Tanzania, they are making propaganda.

"The lack of will is something new. The British Empire still had a historical idea of itself, but the Soviet Union and Russian communism are no longer an international fact of life. I mean, if you asked Brezhnev, 'What do you think of the basic unity of the international proletariat?' I think he'd answer like a history teacher. Lenin would have answered like a priest being questioned on his faith. Because of Stalin we tend to forget that Lenin and Trotsky were profoundly world-oriented. They believed in international revolution. Do you know what Stalin told me? He said, 'The most important thing I have to tell you is that when I was your age, we believed we would be saved by socialist revolution in Germany. And now we know that Europe will be saved by a Russian Revolution.' This said by Stalin in 1934!"

Malraux feels it is idle to speculate about the larger future because we don't know how humanity will overcome its short-term urges. "We just don't know to what degree we will manage to overcome our impulses. In certain cases I'm sure we will; in others we won't. Western man is imperfect because he is in a state of suspended animation. Science—as

22

creed not as science—is a belief in a *future* explanation. We have shaped ourselves through standardized models—saint, knight, caballero, gentleman, Bolshevik—and exemplary models belong to dreams, to fiction. Asia has always had a hunch that man's essential problem is to get hold of 'something else.'

"Do I miss public life? Not at all. To be in power is not at all what people think. In France, people are fascinated with power because they are fascinated with the *abuse* of power because Louis XIV went to bed with a flower girl. It's like the movies. Besides, I haven't been associated with power but with a man I admired, a man who because of circumstances became something absolutely unforseeable in the destiny of my country. It has been an episode in my life. There have been others.

"In any case, to change the colors of Paris, to build 'houses of culture'—you should see the one in Grenoble—doesn't give you a sense of power. There were a lot of seamen in my family and I think that in building cultural centers, I have shared the pleasure they had in building ships inside bottles. They liked them a lot and kept them a long time."

> The most significant moments of my life
> don't live with me, they haunt me and flee me alternately.

Antimémoires

2

"Almost all the writers I know love their childhood, I hate mine," is one of the first sentences in the *Antimémoires*. Malraux couldn't grow up fast enough and at forty said he didn't like his youth. "To be young is to be held back."

Georges André Malraux was born November 3, 1901, at 73 rue Damrémont, a long, prosaic street running down the less than picturesque northern slope of Montmartre. His mother was Berthe, née Lamy, a tall, pretty girl of nineteen who looked younger than her age, and his father was Fernand Georges Malraux, a strapling twenty-five-year-old with a flattering mustache and a sonorous laugh. A bit young but a handsome couple, people said. The Malrauxs had married in the little Saint Pierre-de-Montmartre church when Berthe was two months pregnant and had right away moved into the big apartment on Rue Damrémont.

Fernand Malraux was from Dunkirk, the son, grandson and great grandson of seafarers, ship outfitters and fishing fleet owners. He was going into business for himself in Paris. He was one of those men who always try to invent a better mousetrap, an inventor, a director of ephemeral companies, a believer in dizzy financial schemes, a stock market habitué and a ladies' man with few principles but a big heart. He had visited Spain once, hated it so much he swore never to leave France again and never did. He was something of a dreamer, had a gift for caricatures, knew his way with gourmet foods and the new century's ideas. His favorite aphorism was, "You must always mistrust yourself."

Berthe was the daughter of a farmer and came from the Alps. Her widowed mother, with the stately name of Adriana Romania, was of Italian descent and now lived with an unmarried daughter, Marie, in Bondy, a still semi-rural working-class suburb where they owned and managed a modest grocery.

24

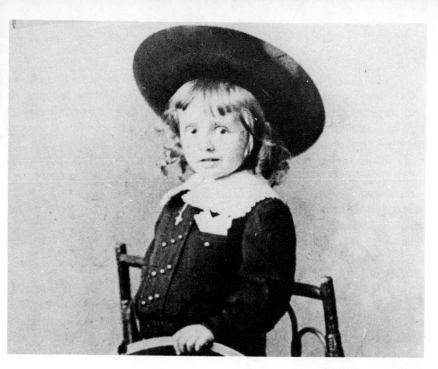

André Malraux Archives

Age four

Little André—the Georges was dropped while he was still an infant—was a serious, only child. He spent his first years quietly in the big apartment with his mother, when his father didn't sweep him off his feet during irregular if boisterous eruptions into his and his mother's life. Fernand was always elsewhere, it seemed, busy making money. Losing it, too, and recouping. The excitements of André's preschool years were playing in Parc Monceau and visiting his grandmother and aunt in Bondy, a trip that took two hours via *métro* and trolley car. The big events were taking the train all the way out to Dunkirk to visit with his father's family.

The Malrauxs were a Flemish clan that had lived between Calais and Dunkirk for centuries. The etymology of the name made it derive, perhaps via Mallaert, from Indo-European *mal-ruk* and made it mean ill-turned plow.* If Fernand was something of an eccentric, grandfather Alphonse was a character. The son of Louis Malraux, a commander of fishing fleets who died at sea, Alphonse was a master cooper, outfitter, ship's chandler proud of his master title and of his fleet bringing cod from the Banks of Newfoundland. He had married Mathilde Antoine late in life and had had three sons and two daughters, with Fernand in the middle.

* With Malraux pronounced Mal-ro, this book adopts the literate French fashion of forming adjectives from archaic *aux* noun endings: Malrucian (instead of such unpronounceable as Malrauxian or Malrauxesque). Cf. Rimbaud, *rimbaldien;* Giraudoux, *giraldien.*

25

Like his father, Alphonse apparently never learned French but spoke the Flemish dialect of the Belgian border dunes. He was a querulous and forgetful man. He forgot to insure his boats—some accounts have it that he found insurance somehow immoral—and one night lost several of his ships, including *La Zaca,* his best vessel, in a storm. This brought him close to ruin as he doled out most of his remaining wealth to the widows of his drowned men. He never completely recovered, became secretive and almost shut himself off from his children: Maurice, Lucien, Fernand-Georges, Georgine and Marie. He cursed his fate and because he was in revolt against his parish priest over some canon law trespass, could be seen on Sundays kneeling outside the church, railing against God for having brought him to despair, but determined to remain within earshot of the house of God.

André was eight years old when one winter day grandfather Alphonse got so frustrated watching a ship boy's clumsy attempts at splitting wood that he took the ax from the lad to show him. Forgetting it was double-headed, he swung the axe above his head so mightily he split his own skull. He died a few hours later at the hospital in his sixty-seventh year.

If André wasn't to remember too many facts about his grandfather but all the legends, he was to remember the big stone house in Dunkirk with its tiled walls. The house went to Alphonse's eldest son, Maurice, and stood there above the harbor and the gray Channel until it collapsed in a hail of bombs in 1940 when German air power and armor drove defeated British and French forces into the sea.

André's uncle was to become deputy mayor of Dunkirk. His wife remembered André's childhood visits. "Very early, he had a marked personality, but we were never able to get him to talk about his future. 'You'll see,' was all he would answer. When he was ten he surprised us one day. He had hurt one knee very badly and for a while we were afraid the leg might have to be amputated. Doctors and surgeons, surrounded by the family, held a hushed consultation. When the physicians were ready to leave, André, from his bed, said, 'I won't see you to the door, gentlemen.' "

Despite his disclaimers, Malraux's childhood was to ring through his fiction. Like his own father, Grabot's father in *The Royal Way* dabbled in household inventions, and André's grandfather Alphonse was to be evoked in three of his books. The *Antimémoires* was to contain savant mixes of transposed memory and acknowledged recollections. Ostensible portraits of the Alsatian Berger family were to include such paragraphs as this description of the grandfather's funeral:

As the *foie gras* succeeded the crayfish and trout and the raspberry brandy followed the Traminer wine at the funeral dinner, the reunion showed signs of developing into a festivity. Thousands of years

On vacation in Dunquerque

have not sufficed to teach men to observe death. The smell of pine and resin drifting through the open windows, and the innumerable objects made of polished wood, united them all in the memories and secrets of a common past, of childhoods spent in the shared surroundings of the family forestry business; and as they recalled my grandfather, they vied with one another in the affectionate deference which death permitted them to show unreservedly toward the rebellious old burgher whose inexplicable suicide seemed to crown his life with a secret.

A page later, the grandfather's falling out with the Church and stubborn attending mass outside the parish church was to be remembered:

Thereafter, cut off from the Church but not from Christ, he attended mass every Sunday outside the building, standing in the nettles in an angle made by the nave and the transept, following the service from memory and straining to hear through the stained-glass to catch the frail sound of the handbell announcing the Elevation. Gradually he grew deaf and, afraid of missing the bell, ended up spending twenty minutes on his knees in the summer nettles or the winter mud. His enemies said he was no longer in his right mind, but such unyielding perseverance is not readily dismissed, and for most people this figure with the short white beard and frock coat, kneeling in the mud beneath his umbrella, in the same place, at the same time and for the same purpose for so many years, seemed not so much a crackpot as a just man.

27

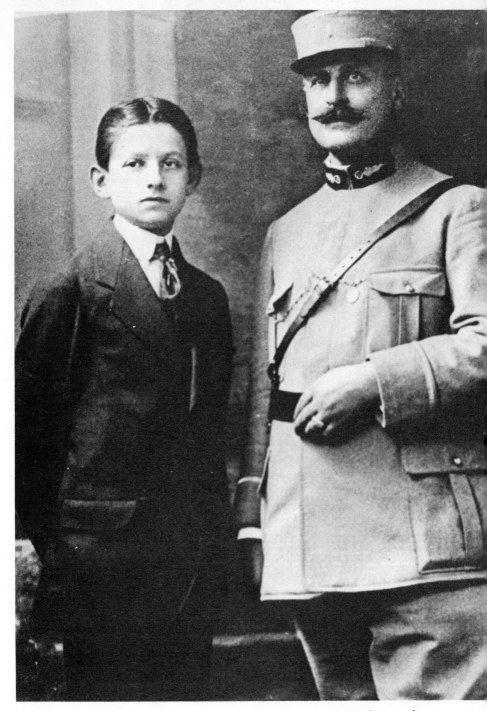

André Malraux Archives

Fils et père

By the time Alphonse felled himself, Berthe and Fernand were separated and André and his mother were living with his maternal grandmother and aunt in Bondy. If business hadn't lured Fernand from home and health, women had. His inventions, which included a necktie hanger, had naturally led him to the most amazing of new creations, the automobile. He had come up with various electrical starters and a fuel injection shield that he hadn't managed to market, but his crowning feat was a skidproof tire. Oui, monsieur, a skidproof tire, exhibited at the Concours Lépine, the new annual competition organized by Paris police chief Louis Lépine and endowed with numerous prizes and medals to encourage small manufacturers' ingenuity. Fernand's heroes were men who quickened the pulse of the century with astounding creations—Edison's incandescent bulb, Roentgen's X-ray tube—but his heart was especially with France's men of progress, Fernand de Lesseps for building the Suez Canal, Gustave Eiffel for his tower, André Citroën—another Lépine exhibitor—for his automobile gear train and Louis Blériot for being the first man to cross the channel in a flying machine. The handmaiden of progress was commerce and Fernand invested aggressively in the stock market. At one point, he seemed to have been the Paris agent for an American bank, although the name of the financial institution he represented was never revealed.

It was a heady and flamboyant era and Paris was its epicurean center, the most fabulous city with its noble architecture, its grandiose new boulevards, its smart shops, adventurous artists, celebrated fashions, elegant women and racy night life. Governments might succeed each other at a dizzy pace and the Boulanger and Dreyfus affairs make tempers flare, but the Third Republic was nevertheless politically stable and economically sound. It was optimistic and expansionist—at home democratic reforms, freedom of the press, secularized free education, and abroad new colonies. Everybody sang the ditty about Le Père Bugeaud losing his hat conquering Algeria. Colonial expansion never excited the minds of the French as it did the British, but most of North and Central Africa was nevertheless French. Indochina had been French since the 1860s, conquered by a handful of soldiers, Madagascar since 1897. In all, France now counted some three million square miles of overseas territory.

Like most middle-class Frenchmen, Fernand had his heart on the Left and his pocketbook on the Right. He was quick to spring to the defense of Jean Jaurès and his socialists and he was also a firm believer in unbridled free enterprise. Like most of his forty million countrymen, Fernand had learned to live with permanent political turmoil, but to enjoy a franc as solid as gold and an unshakable faith in progress.

Bondy was far from the excitement of the grand boulevards, in essence and significance, if not in kilometers from the Gare de l'Est railway station. Situated on the drab northeastern outskirts of the capital on the old road to Soisson and the Ourcq Canal linking the Seine and Marne

29

rivers, Bondy was a working-class county seat with an offbeat history. During the Middle Ages, Bondy Forest had been the hideout for highwaymen and cutthroats, and the old name for Rue de la Gare, where Grandma Adriana Romania and her two daughters and grandson lived above the grocery, had been Rue de Martray, in memory of the execution grounds where apprehended brigands had been quartered on the wheel. Bondy Forest was still considerable when André and his school chums roamed it, reenacting the Alexandre Dumas novels, *Ivanhoe* and other tales of swashbuckling, or when André was reading books from the municipal library filled with descriptions of rustling mystery. The woods were propitious for imaginary adventures.

There was one Dumas novel André would never forget—*Georges,* the first book he ever read. Published shortly before *The Three Musketeers* (and apparently written by Félicien Mallefille, one of Dumas' many ghostwriters), *Georges* was the story of a foundling brought up on Mauritius Island in the Indian Ocean by a Taiwanese nurse who taught him Chinese and swordsmanship. Georges Munier spent his brief, tumultuous life searching for his father, traveling through exotic lands, fighting ensnaring ladies and perfidious villains. In the end, Georges returned to his island to lead liberated slaves in an assault on plantation owners who from their hilltop barricades set fire to kegs of rum and sent the flaming barrels down on their assailants.

Was André looking for *his* father? His parents' separation and subsequent divorce didn't seem to have left indelible scars in him. He saw his jovial if volatile father almost every week. From the age of thirteen, he went to town alone, taking the suburban train to the Gare de l'Est and circulating in Paris via *métro* and bus, often seeing his father in his Left Bank apartment. Also, the vacation visits to Dunkirk, where André had over forty cousins, continued.

"I didn't rebel against my family, quite the contrary," he was to say in one of his rare adult comments on his childhood. "I greatly admired my father. He was a tank officer during World War I, which I considered very romantic."

André was in his fifth year when he began school at École de Bondy, a rather modest private institution where the principal and a teacher named Monsieur Malaval taught twenty students in two classes. The following year, a new boy joined André's class. Louis Chevasson was a short, dark kid with black eyes—Max Jacob was to call him "coffee bean"—who lived in Rue de Merlan around the corner from André. Louis was to remain a lifelong friend, join André and Clara in a Cambodian art adventure, stand trial with him in Pnompenh, shelter him from Vichy police and Gestapo during critical weeks in 1943 and much later join the Malraux Cultural Affairs ministry.

Was André's childhood really unhappy? "Not at all," Chevasson

30

told Jean Lacouture, Malraux's latest French biographer, in 1970. "To be cuddled by three women wasn't exactly a burden. His mother was a charming person and he saw his father almost every week in Paris, often with his mother. It has been suggested that his twitching is the result of bad treatment in school. Absurd. André was always afflicted with tics. As to his alleged poverty, the grocery did very well and our friend never lacked anything." [1]

He lost interest in religion at twelve. "After that I studied Catholicism in its relation to art, but I have always been responsive to what religion contains of grandeur," he was to tell *Paris-Match* editor Pierre Galante. "Admiration without participation, in short." [2] Before he was fifteen, he read Stendhal, discovered the intrigues of the will and the triumph of impulse over hesitation, admiring Julien Sorel's silent resolution in *Le Rouge et le noir* to embrace Madame de Renal before the clock struck nine. In Pierre Loti, he discovered pungent exoticism and vague sensuality.

Bondy's municipal library contained only two Shakespeare plays, *Macbeth* and *Julius Caesar,* which he read rather guardedly. His first theatrical evening—with Chevasson—was on his fourteenth birthday, a performance of Racine's tragedy *Andromaque.* For a while André wanted to be an actor. The year before, the movies had come to Bondy, beginning with a county fair tent attraction featuring the mighty four-reel version of Victor Hugo's *Les Misérables.*

He was always browsing in the library. His devotion to the municipal repository of imagination and knowledge was so constant he helped classify books and got to know the librarian well enough to allow himself to express his opinions on necessary new purchases.

Books existed not only to be read. They were sometimes difficult to get and could therefore be exchanged, bought and sold. To pay for their first movies and first illicit pack of cigarettes, André and Louis hopped into town and combed Left Bank secondhand stores and quayside stalls. Each would "do" his side of the street as they worked their way to Gilbert Jeunes on Boulevard St. Michel of Crès' on Place de l'Odéon, the two biggest Latin Quarter book marts. In the beginning, it was for fun. Later it was a way of supplementing a living.

He discovered art when he was seven. What struck him while walking through the endless classical rooms of the Louvre were Leonardo da Vinci's paintings because they had pretty skies. For years, he considered the creator of Mona Lisa as a sky specialist. One Sunday when his mother visited with a lady friend at the Place d'Iéna, André was allowed to cross the square and visit the Musée Guimet. More hangar and depot than

[1] Jean Lacouture, *André Malraux: Une Vie dans le siècle* (Paris: Seuil, 1973).
[2] Pierre Galante, *Malraux* (Paris: Presses de la Cité-*Paris-Match,* 1971), English edition trans. Haakon Chevalier (New York: Cowles, 1971).

31

museum, the Guimet was a fascinating if confusing heap of as yet unsorted Asian art and artifacts—carved Buddhas and silk umbrellas, stuffed paradise birds and rickshaws—that Émile Guimet, industrialist, archaeologist and musician, had brought back from the Orient half a century earlier. Another temple of eccentric exotica that the daydreaming André took in with awe was the Trocadero Museum across the Seine from the Eiffel Tower. Here, visitors could see a plumed helmet from the kingdom of Hawaii exhibited next to an absurd miniature of a palace in Cadiz. Here, among coral features, Montezuma's headdress was to be found.

In school, he worked hard. Despite bouts with such unusual childhood diseases as nasal and pulmonary infections that one year kept him at home a good deal, he was excellent in French and history. He was good in geography—all those exotic places—mathematics and the natural sciences but showed no notable ability for singing, sports or physics. Professeur Malaval held rather advanced views on education. Every week he laid the previous week's homework on his desk and had his students take part in the grading. In this collective evaluation of academic efforts, André often settled the finer points.

It was decided that for his *primaire supérieure* he would attend the Rue de Turbigo school in Paris and that he would commute. Even if he found Bondy at the end of every day, he couldn't wait to escape to Paris.

He was a few weeks away from the start of his final year in Bondy when the guns of August thundered. To André, Louis and the other thirteen-year-olds, it was feverish adventure come true. As President Raymond Poincaré called for the "union sacrée" of all Frenchmen when his declaration of war was read to a cheering Chamber of Deputies, daily life stood still. General mobilization meant no school. Then the war came.

The main German blow came on the front where French generals had said it couldn't happen—through Belgium. By the third week of August, the main force of the German army was sweeping over the Franco-Belgian border. Between its advancing columns and Paris there was very little to stop it. Under intense pressure, French and British forces retreated. The German advance wavered before Paris and on August 30, General Alexander von Kluck turned his army southeast, passing to the east of Paris instead of enveloping the city. The Allies rallied and fresh forces, transported to the front in six hundred Paris taxicabs, struck the flank of von Kluck's army on the Marne. The German retreat to behind the Aisne River constituted the Battle of the Marne. In mid-September, however, the Germans dug in, a French assault was checked and the front was not to move much during the next four murderous years.

Only strategic trains passed through Bondy—and returned with the first heavy casualties. André and Louis saw the taxis roll east on Meaux highway. At night the big guns were heard. On September 6 when the

First and Second French Armies and a small British force stood and fought and produced the "miracle" of the Marne, the Germans were less than thirty miles from Bondy.

Then Bondy, France and Europe settled into war. André could hold his head as high as any kid; his father had been among the first 350,000 volunteers. Fernand Malraux was a new father. The previous year he had met a Mademoiselle Godard, whom he was to marry as soon as the war was over. André's half-brother was named Roland.

Professeur Malaval celebrated the "miracle" by taking his class on a tour of the previous week's battlefield. There had been little time to bury the dead; the bodies were piled up, soaked with gasoline and burned —a sight Malaval spared his charges by ordering lunch. "At lunchtime," Malraux was to write in the *Antimémoires* forty years later, "bread was handed around to us, which we dropped, terror-stricken, because the wind covered it with a light sprinkling of ash from the dead piled up a little farther off."

André was admitted as a scholarship student at the Turbigot school for the school year 1915–16. At the end of the first term, he was at the head of his class and had made friends with Marcel Brandin and with the future musician Georges van Parys.

They just missed the horrors of the bloodiest of wars, these lanky sixteen- and seventeen-year-olds roaming a Paris without fathers, without big brothers and, increasingly, without teachers. By 1918, boys one year older than they were called up. When it was all over, France had suffered more than four million casualties, of whom nearly a million and a half had been killed in action. A third of the war dead were youths between eighteen and twenty-eight. Inevitably, this mass grave at their toes was to affect Malraux's "generation." Most of them were always to have difficulty looking the few of their elders who had survived squarely in the eyes. Many were to suffer acute guilt feelings for having been spared. Some were to seek out dangerous action to test their own mettle.

The fall of 1917 was the blackest period. Defeatism was rife in the army, in government, press and especially among workers and treason in fairly high places was spreading. Georges Clemenceau, the "Old Tiger," was brought back to power as premier to restore confidence in ultimate victory.

André wasn't particularly patriotic. If anything there was something mocking and marginal in the demeanor of this independent adolescent with his testy airs, his touchingly recherché manner of dress, his romantic look and expectant, somewhat stern gaze. Wartime gave the Turbigot school an air of improvisation. All teachers were either invalids or over sixty, supplies were makeshift, classrooms unheated and schedules juggled around at the slightest pretext. The student body was politely leftist although by no means radical. The Petrograd revolution was applauded, but the Bolshevik's separate peace with the Kaiser was resented as treason. Russia's falling out, however, was compensated by America's coming into the war. Ferdinand Foch, named Commander in Chief of the Allied armies, was considered a great man in the Rue Turbigot, but Brandin bought *Le Canard enchaîné*—he was soon to write for the new satirical weekly —and a copy of the Swiss edition of Henri Barbusse's *Le Feu* (*Under Fire*) was smuggled into the school and passed around. It was the story of a doomed platoon in the perpetual horror of the trenches and it showed that men were exploited creatures fighting a war that could in no way benefit them.

But there were other things than the war. The cinema—they all loved Charles Chaplin's tramp—and the discovery of music. On Sunday afternoons, Chevasson joined the Turbigot classmates at the Colonne concerts. And there was classical theater—Corneille's grandiloquent *Le Cid* and Molière's farcical *Médecin malgré lui*. On the subway to the Comédie-Française, André loved to impress his friends with extracurricular knowledge, showing off on such encyclopedic subjects as the usage of hats through the ages in the theater and François Villon's scabrous adventures.

Most of the Louvre was closed during the last years of the war, but Malraux returned again and again to the Guimet. "Japanese porcelain seemed to me to be the summit of refinement," he was to remember in *La Tête d'obsédienne*. "Hindu gods with arms unfurled like tentacles reminded me of the Thugs in my cartoon books. The museum was still a warehouse of Buddhas, Chinese idols, canary-colored silks on which the big butterflies of Chinese ideograms were set down. I asked the custodian what their meaning was and he invented one."

Book buying and book selling financed his increasing independence from Bondy, his grandmother, mother and aunt. With his remarkable memory and his taste for the baroque, the marginal and the quaint, he knew where to find out-of-print volumes and he knew where to sell first editions, incunabula, hard-to-find books. He did not particularly like Turbigot school, felt no affection for any of his teachers and began to slip. He had been at the top of his class the first two years—first in history and drawing, third in French and English, fourth in mathematics and geography. He was pretty average in the natural sciences, but, as Brandin was to remember, their physics teacher was terrorized by the prospect of being drafted and, to somehow cover all bets, gave his students deliriously good grades. At the end of the third year, André's average had dropped and he was eighth in his class.

He was impatient to move on and wanted to go to one of the two prestigious colleges—Henri IV or Condorcet. By the end of the 1916–17 school year, he had come to the conclusion that it was essential to enter the Lycée Condorcet. To pass the forbidding entrance exams, he decided to cram with Paulette Thouvenin, a young private teacher and daughter of

34

Axel Madsen

73, Rue Damrémont (birthplace) today

Bondy's police chief, who specialized in such "rattrapage" courses. She was a vivacious if stern teacher who had four girls and three boys cramming with her when André joined. André worked ferociously hard and Mlle. Thouvenin thought she detected in him a sense of conscious superiority. She was to remember him as a brooding boy with both a wild streak in him and a sense of reserve. However hard André crammed, he didn't make it. He would never say whether he failed the entrance exam or never actually presented himself. Ransacking its archives when he became famous, the Lycée Condorcet was never able to find a record of his attendance.

The attraction of academia snapped then and there for the young Malraux. His decision to abandon formal education was final and never given much thought later. He didn't know what he wanted but was ready to plunge forward. He was full of ambition, possessed a crafty skepticism, a flair for ostentation and a surly hauteur that people found attractive because he was so young—and looked even younger. In his mid-twenties he still looked like an adolescent. He had a restless intelligence, a prodigious memory and he loved language—trenchant apostrophe, stunning metaphor and verbal spark—and he had a gift for elliptic ideas, skittish concepts and showy principles.

He was ready to sever the cords with Bondy and the three fussing if well-meaning women. Their treat on his seventeenth birthday was a

35

theatrical evening and his choice was Aeschylus' *Oresteia* trilogy in Leconte de Lisle's translation, playing at the Châtelet Theater. A week later, he was getting off the *métro* at the Louvre station at 10:00 P.M., when someone shouted, "It's signed. The armistice!"

Valéry said to me about Gide, "I can't take seriously anyone who worries about the judgment of young people."

Felled Oaks

3

Malraux instinctively turned toward people challenging the burned-out order. During the first dizzy years of peace, this pale and intense young man striking a proud and self-protective Nietzschean pose hobnobbed with the best minds of the new era. This ardent youth without family connections, without money or diplomas, was caught up in the creative process of practically everything of importance that was written, painted or composed in Paris. And Paris, as Gertrude Stein, the mother hen of the onrushing Americans, was saying, was where the twentieth century was.

With his verbose intelligence, his flair for bookish oddities, his passion for literature and nervy taste in art, Malraux naturally gravitated toward the world of little magazines, combative publishing and the artistic avant-garde to associate with clever people—almost all older than himself —some to be world famous, others to be footnotes to a momentous decade.

First things first. Not yet eighteen, he extorted the permission from his mother and grandmother to look for an apartment in town. To his astonishment, his newly demobilized father didn't object, but in effect agreed to add to grandmother Adriana's monthly support. Fernand Malraux had returned from the war as a tank commander, physically unscathed but with deep psychic scars. He married the mother of Roland— the couple had a second son, Claude, in 1922—returned to stock market speculation, but slowly drifted into despondency, interspersed with periods of feverish and often highly lucrative activity on the market. Like millions of other veterans, he didn't like or understand the postwar era, became increasingly restive and xenophobic. To their chagrin those around him saw a marked increase in the eccentricity of his character.

André found a one-room, furnished apartment on Rue Brunel, near L'Étoile, and since he hated to count every *sou* set out to supplement the familial allocations with profits from the rare books business. In his wanderings through Paris, he noticed a new bibliophilic emporium near the Madeleine, an elegant rare books shop called La Connaissance. He ventured in and on a second visit offered his services to the owners, Marcelle and René-Louis Doyon. Doyon was a *littérateur* of the first order and was soon impressed enough by the young man's bibliophilic expertise to offer him the position of *chineur*—in Parisian argot a practice somewhere between ragpicking and secondhand dealing. The métier consisted of combing secondhand bookstores in obscure side streets for volumes that would interest the select book lovers who browsed at La Connaissance. The postwar slide of the franc was beginning and many affluent Parisians found more security in a first-edition Mallarmé than in stocks and municipal bonds. Since he would be strictly on commission and no strings were attached, André agreed.

He worked only during the morning and stayed home when it rained. He showed up at La Connaissance at 11:00 A.M. sharp with the previous day's catch—now an original edition of Cyrano de Bergerac, now eighteenth-century bawdy texts, fifteenth-century German mystics or poetry with signed woodcuts. Once money matters were disposed of, André melted enough to talk. "He had very definite literary opinions," Doyon was to write, "and he wasn't short of sarcasm." [1] Doyon thought Malraux had a vocation to be an artist of some sort, though the young man also seemed worldly and showed a developed taste for good printing and perhaps an all-round talent for publishing. Mme. Doyon found their rag-picker to be one of those men who looked awkward and ungainly at eighteen but—as she would tell Clara—who would be handsome at thirty. After a while, André gravely shook hands and disappeared until the following 11:00 A.M. rendezvous.

Malraux was no ladies' man at eighteen. He was nervously elegant but timid and his first mistresses were not literary lionesses but easy pick-ups and little demi-mondaines. His friend Georges Gabory was to remember him bragging poetically about one girl who, he said, "possessed the trifling grace of a young monkey." [2]

When Doyon decided to expand his literary activities and publish a monthly magazine, he naturally asked his young *chineur* to collaborate. When the first issue appeared in January 1920, *La Connaissance* included an article signed André Malraux, "The Origins of Cubist Poetry." The first published text by the future author of *Man's Fate* was an unctuous piece of writing that treated cubism rather severely. The first taxing sentence read:

> When Symbolism, already a tottering literary movement, dabbled in the ebbing splashes of its own final dissolution, young people who

[1] René-Louis Doyon, *Mémoire d'homme* (Paris: Connaissance, 1953).
[2] Georges Gabory, "Souvenirs sur André Malraux," in *Mélanges Malraux Miscellany,* No. II (Lexington: University of Kentucky Press, 1970).

weren't interested in publishing flabby (but prize-winning) poems or in fobbish, inaccessible carping, started to look for an artist capable of bringing forth a body of work whose new esthetics could, without plagiarism, cleanse itself.

The piece provoked an offended apostrophe in the weekly *Comoedia* by the well-known critic Jean Valmy-Baysse. What better could an aspiring *littérateur* expect than being noticed by someone bigger than himself? A month later, Malraux politely "rectified" not himself but Valmy-Baysse in a letter to *Comoedia*.[3] The Malraux byline was back in the second issue of *La Connaissance* with a critique of three books by Laurent Tailhade, an elegant if obscure contemporary poet whom André admired for showing that style in itself could be beauty. Malraux, however, wasn't so much interested in writing as in editing and publishing. His taste for *le fantastique*—that untranslatable Gallicism meaning as much the surreal and the otherworldly as spine-chilling science fiction and demonology—made him suggest to Doyon that he edit a new version of *The Martyrdom of Jesus Christ According to Anna-Catherine Emmerich,* the stigmatized Bavarian nun whose hallucinatory retracing of the Passion had made her famous throughout the nineteenth century. Clemens Brentano, the brother of Goethe's mistress Bettina, had written a book about her visions in 1837 and over the next forty years a French translation had run through twenty-six printings. Recently, several journals had recalled the existence of the "Nun from Dulum."

Doyon agreed and commissioned Malo Renault to illustrate the book. Malraux had other ideas. Why not publish excerpts of Joseph von Görres *Divine, Natural and Diabolic Mysticism?* This Prussian revolutionary and apostle of universal peace who, because of political frustrations, had turned to militant Catholicism, had written a history of Asian mythology, a biography of Swedenborg and a supposedly edifying treatise, *Die christiche Mythik,* full of divinations, black magic, devil worship and witchcraft. A French translation had gone through two editions. This time, however, Doyon said no. He couldn't see himself selling very well an abridged edition of a nearly hundred-year-old book "on the historical, legendary, physical and psychic foundations of devil mysticism." In 1960, *La Connaissance* still had unsold copies of Sister Emmerich's *La Passion de Jésus Christ.*

As a philosophical exercise Christianity interested André enough to seek out the future Nobel Prize-winner François Mauriac to argue atheism against the wealthy Catholic writer's self-centered and self-questioning faith. Sixteen years older than André, Mauriac, who was to become France's leading commentator on current affairs for nearly half a century,

---

[3] Jean Valmy-Baysse, "Il ne faut pas l'oublier," *Comoedia* (Feb., 1920), and André Malraux, "Mise au point," *Comoedia,* (Feb. 26, 1920).

remembered Malraux as "this bristling bird of prey with the magnificent eyes" vehemently advancing his argument against divine power. "At eighteen when he talked about Christ, the intractable Malraux knew what he was talking about." [4]

André was seeing many people and didn't feel he owed Doyon any allegiance. He soon met two other marginal publishers. One was Lucien Kra, a former circus hand who dreamed of matching a competitor's success in erotica. André soon found two little-known texts by the Marquis de Sade for him. Published with dadaist drawings, the little volume became a kind of under-the-counter best seller.[5] As literary director and makeup man, André was responsible for other limited editions: *Carnet intime*, a collection of droll, satirical and anticlerical poems and minitexts by Tailhade illustrated with woodcuts by Kharis; an edition of Charles Baudelaire's 1864 *Causeries*, with drawings by Constantin Guys; and *Coeurs à prendre* by his friend Gabory with drawings by Demetrios Galanis.[6]

Galanis was to widen considerably Malraux's artistic horizons and introduce him to other painters and poets. Galanis, who was forty when André met him, was born in Athens and had become a French citizen after fighting in the war. With his wife and children he lived in a small house in the Rue Cortot, where André was a frequent visitor. Malraux was sure it was only a matter of time before the disciplined painter and engraver would be famous.

André attended the reopening of the Louvre and discovered classic painting. "Watteau's *L'Indifférent* and a Rembrandt which was probably *Matthew the Evangelist* gave me the impression of discovering the classics," he was to remember fifty years later. "I knew modern painting because since the war art dealers' windows were full of modern paintings. Ancient art dealers didn't have show windows."

Florent Fels was still another adventurer in publishing, a vibrant war veteran who with his demobilization bonus had founded *Action*, a little magazine that was to bring Malraux under a healthier and more dynamic sway than the semi-clandestine publishers of exotica and erotica. The bylines in *Action* included Max Jacob, Blaise Cendrars, Jean Cocteau, Antonin Artaud, Erik Satie and the Rumanian-born father of dadaism himself, Tristan Tzara. *Action* also published the new Bolshevik authors—Maxim Gorky, Ilya Ehrenburg, Alexander Blok and Victor Serge, the Belgian-born anarchist now actively supporting Lenin's new and still-shaky Soviet regime. Even more daringly, *Action* also published the new German

[4] François Mauriac, *Mémoires politiques* (Paris: Grasset, 1967).
[5] Actually excerpts from de Sade's novels, *Les Amis du crime*, illustrated by a painter named Moras, and *Le Bordel de Venise*, illustrated with "scandalous" watercolors by G. A. Drains, appeared without Kra's publishing imprimatur.
[6] Other Éditions Kra monographs Malraux worked on included *Étoiles peintes* by Pierre Reverdy, with a frontispiece by Derain, and *Dos d'Arlequin* by Max Jacob with the author's illustrations.

40

expressionists, Franz Werfel, Johannes Becher and Claire and Ivan Goll. The magazine honored the most modern art, discussed new esthetics in every issue and reproduced works by Pablo Picasso, André Derain, Georges Braque, Raoul Dufy, Juan Gris and Suzanne Valadon's alcoholic son, Maurice Utrillo.

Max Jacob was to have a profound influence on young Malraux. Max was already a legendary personality—friend of Picasso and Guillaume Apollinaire, poet, visionary, painter, homosexual, recluse, astrologer and humorist. Born a Jew in Brittany, he had converted to Catholicism in 1909 —with Picasso acting as his godfather—after having a vision of Christ in blue and yellow while in the National Library. Jacob did much to "make" Picasso, not only sharing his bed with him (Max using it at night; Picasso during the day), but by pushing the newly arrived Spaniard toward a cubism Jacob never really liked himself but which he was the first one to understand. As a child, Max had tried to kill himself three times and no one could penetrate his various disguises of clown, martyr, saint and beggar. Like most surrealists, he believed in signs and waited for them. One of his means of earning his dinner was to read horoscopes. Just as he was becoming famous, he began to retire for long periods to a cloister in the Loire River region and after 1931 he was to live permanently at Saint Benoit-sur-Loire, subsisting by selling devout watercolors. In 1920, however, he reigned over groups of friends and one evening a week "performed" in a Montmartre café in the Rue Lamarck. At these gatherings, he would dance, mimic political celebrities, draw sketches, offer his paintings for sale and tell stories that left everyone rolling with laughter.

In Jacob, Malraux could admire not only a peerless nonconformist with a boundless creative gift, but also an artist in love with perfection, a curiously aware amateur of *le fantastique* who expressed the sharpest pain of his existence in throwaway anecdotes, "cubist" visions and surrealist texts. His most enduring writings were to be his letters and *Le Cornet à dés,* his humorous poems published in 1917. The mischievous but always gentle Jacob hated only two things—symbolism in the arts and his own life, which in one of his relatively few serious moments he called "a hell," perhaps because it was complicated by a homosexuality which he could not accept. Malraux adored Max, wrote about him in that first *La Connaisance* piece, dedicated his first book to him and allowed his admiration to outgrow his own first flush of success.

It was neither at the offices of *Action* nor at one of the Montmartre soirees, however, that André was introduced to Jacob, but at the gallery of yet another man who was to be important to him—Daniel Henry Kahnweiler. The art dealer, who together with Ambroise Vollard and Leonce Rosenberg, had discovered cubism and, like Doyon, Kra and Fels, was an occasional publisher of *éditions de luxe* illustrated by his painters, had just got back into business. A German national, he had been in Italy when the war broke out and to avoid incarceration in France as an enemy alien and service in the Kaiser's army, he had sat out the conflict in Switzerland. He had been authorized to return to France in 1920 only to discover his property confiscated. When sometime later, eight hundred pieces of Kahnweiler's art were sold on a public auction, Malraux acquired his first Derain, Picasso and Braque paintings. With his new gallery in the Rue d'Astorg and a French associate, André Simon, to protect him from any further "enemy alien" prosecution, Kahnweiler was starting from scratch again.

What did Jacob think of Malraux, whose concentrated silences had a habit of exploding into erudite eloquence and whose sexual interests were feminine despite his ephebic pallor and recherché dandyism? In a letter to Kahnweiler, Jacob made one fleeting reference to Malraux: "Also say hello to our friends, good old Satie, savant Malraux, young Radiguet, Gabory and especially the old guard: Vlaminck, Gris, etc." [7]

André also met aspiring writers and artists of his own age. Besides Gabory, whose audacious defense of the notorious woman-murderer Landru had nearly brought *Action* into trouble with police, Malraux made friends with Marcel Arland, a bespectacled bookworm who after a flirt with surrealism was to settle down as editor of Gallimard's *Nouvelle revue française*—better known under its acronym, *NRF*—and with Pascal Pia, Fernand Fleuret and René Latouche. The friendship with Latouche was to end as abruptly as the acquaintance with Raymond Radiguet. The limping Latouche suffered from fits of acute depression and killed himself. Seven years later, André was to dedicate his first novel to him. Radiguet, who had achieved success as an adolescent with wicked and clever poetry and who after his first novel, *Le Diable au corps,* was considered the most promising of the "under twenty" writers, died of typhoid fever in 1923. Pia, who became a surrealist and a newspaper editor, was a bizarre erudite, a libertine, traveler and practical joker. In 1947, Malraux was to dedicate *Saturne,* his essay on Goya, to Pia. Fleuret was a specialist in eighteenth-century bawdy texts, an authentic Paris street poet whose magnetism women found irresistible.

An evening usually began up on Montmartre—"in 1920, the savage demons of poetry still inhabited old provincial Montmartre," André was to write in 1928 in a homage to Galanis—with Chevasson coming in from Bondy and joining Malraux, Gabory, Latouche and perhaps Arland. They dropped in on a painter or poet, sometimes on Max Jacob in his Rue Gabrielle studio. Later, they would stop at La Mère Anceau, a bistro where Max loved the mutton stew. André, who as ragpicker and editor earned more than the others and often showed up in a dashing Baudelairean cape,

[7] François Garnier, *Max Jacob: Correspondance* (Paris: Éditions de Paris, 1953).

42

high collar and moleskin gloves, preferred to dine at snazzier tables, Larue's or Noel Peters, but if Jacob was along dinner was at La Mère Anceau's. It was there that André first met Utrillo. "With his heavy eyelashes rising on the forsaken void of his eyes he asked me, 'Painter or poet?', sat down and fell asleep," Malraux was to remember fifty years later.

Over dessert, Max began to draw, on paper when paper was available, otherwise on the tablecloth. He made dozens of sketches of friends and fellow-diners in an evening. The sketches of André have all disappeared—transformed, as Jean Lacouture was to ask, into french-fry wrappers or burned when the Gestapo sent Jacob to his death in the Drancy concentration camp in 1944? [8]

Sometimes they finished the night on the seamier side, at a *bal musette* behind the Bastille, at the noisy Tabarin, where one of them might pick up a girl, at one of the new jazz clubs or the raunchiest of gay bars on Place de Ravignan where Paris' most notorious "tantes" foregathered. "We were young, Malraux and I, and easily impressed by the display of real or put-on depravity," Gabory was to write.[9]

Action publisher Fels also organized dinners, where Malraux showed up dressed to the teeth. The magazine provided an atmosphere, a feel for good literature. It was passably "anarchic"—against the established order, patriotism, religion and traditional attitudes and in favor of the "psychic revolution." It was open to the new influences and championed, among the prewar forces coming into vogue, Feodor Dostoyevsky, Friedrich Nietzsche, Sigmund Freud, Henri Bergson, Luigi Pirandello, André Gide and Marcel Proust. Its young contributors were dadaist insofar as they admired the surrealist "enterprise of demolition" and in their short and usually atrociously edited pieces, spent themselves in biting sarcasm at the expense of the more ludicrous aspects of society.

Malraux's first contribution was such a hatchet job, a tart and cavalier treatment of Lautréamont, the mid-nineteenth-century poet whom the surrealist considered their mentor and predecessor.[10] Other texts followed, including a short piece of fiction in the Max Jacobean vein, "Le Pompier du jeu de massacre," and a review of *Action* house poet André Salmon's novel, *La Negresse du Sacré Coeur.*

André was busy everywhere. He was still published in *La Connaisance,* was an editor at Kra's—although he was soon to fall out with the editor's son—and, to supplement his income, continuing ragpicking and—something that really impressed his friends—dabbled in the stock market. In early 1921, Kahnweiler made him an offer that made him drop

[8] Jean Lacouture, *André Malraux,* op. cit.
[9] Georges Gabory, op. cit.
[10] André Malraux, "La Genèse des Chants de Maldoror," *Action* (April, 1920).

almost everything else—to be in charge of a series of limited editions that Kahnweiler and his associate Simon had in mind, a collection, it was understood, that might include a volume by Malraux.

Before the war, Kahnweiler had published several *éditions de luxe,* including three volumes of poetry by Max Jacob, illustrated with etchings by Picasso and André Derain. By the end of 1921, Kahnweiler and Simon would have six limited editions in the bookstores—*Ne coupez pas Mademoiselle* by Max Jacob, lithographs by Juan Gris; *Lunes en papier* by André Malraux with illustrations by Fernand Léger; *Communications* by Maurice de Vlaminck, with the author's own woodcuts; *Les Pélicans* by Raymond Radiguet, a play illustrated with etchings by Henri Laurens; *Le Piège de Méduse,* a lyrical comedy by Erik Satie with woodcuts by Georges Braque; and *Coeurs de chêne* by Pierre Reverdy, illustrated with woodcuts by (Picasso's friend) Manolo.

Les Lunes en papier—with *Le Royaume du farfelu* (1928) the only Malraux tome never translated into English—is a whimsical little tale in the cubist vein about malicious balloons, a pin cushion in the form of a cat and the Seven Deadly Sins traveling to the Kingdom of the Bizarre ("farfelu") to kill Death in an acid bath. It is a mix of Hoffman-Lewis Carroll and the scorn and gewgaw of the Max Jacob-Erik Satie-*Ballet mécanique* genre but also of Malrucian banter, nihilism and belief in the essential absurdity of life.

It opens with the moon, changing from yellow to red to green like a luminous sign and, when one of its notes falls, back to yellow again. The note falls on a lake where fountains of water shoot up and a floating cork turns into a jack-in-the-box out of which pops a bearded farmer. All this makes the moon laugh so hard that all its notes, actually its teeth, fall out. They flutter about, luminous in the night, leaving a pale trail behind them. Sitting down to the sound of tingling bells, they open up like paper flowers flung onto water. At first, the moonchildren only see unsympathetic balloons lazily lolling about. Naively, they think the balloons are busy, but once they realize the truth, they become indignant and, with their noses transformed into billiard cues, shoot the balloons onto the lake where they rebound with an elegance that makes the moonchildren jealous. Foolishly, they wish the balloons' death.

And so on, as the balloons start an agitprop play that makes a castle fall asleep, kill its inhabitants dangling from the rafters and become nine characters—the Seven Deadly Sins plus a former chemist and an exmusician made into a mandolin. They walk on their hands to show that Creation needs improvement, encounter a monster called Cable and finally electrical animals with triangular heads who lead them to the Kingdom of the Bizarre, where Death, a lady skeleton in a dinner jacket, performs a striptease to show her new rust-free rib cage. It all ends with Death being dead and the sins sitting on the castle roof wondering why they killed her.

44

Dedicated to Jacob, *The Paper Moons* carried an imposing subtitle: "A little book in which the reader may find a description of little-known combats together with an account of a voyage among certain familiar but strange objects, all being related truthfully, and graced with equally truthful woodcuts by Fernand Léger." The slim volume appeared in formidable *in folio* (12 by 19 inches) format with wide margins and large type. Léger's seven abstract woodcuts were perhaps not chosen by Malraux but by Kahnweiler. It was the second time Léger had done book illustrations (he had designed and illustrated Cendrars' *La Fin du monde* in 1919). As the father of the "modern effort" method, which aimed at creating a genuinely modern imagery adaptable to the machine age and capable of being mass-produced, Léger was just coming into his own. "He talked constantly about the visual world," said millionaire American expatriate Gerald Murphy, whose wife, Sara, studied with Léger. "He saw and remarked everything and he made you see it, too." [11] The first one hundred copies of *Les Lunes en papier* were signed by author and illustrator. Only reprinted once, in the 1945 Swiss Skira edition of Malraux's *Oeuvres complètes,* the opulent little work of whimsy was to become as rare as some of the books its author was "ragpicking" for Doyon in 1920.

The Paper Moons, which by no means was André's sole focus of attention during that tumultuous year, made only a modest stir, although his friends reviewed it. In the prestigious *NRF,* Gabory wrote, "Malraux the disemboweler of dolls, is also a vendor of little red balloons and a puppet master." [12] In a smaller but very modish magazine, Pascal Pia adroitly wrote that if Malraux was not a poet, the reason was simple oversight. "The imagination governing these pages is naive like a toy and complicated as only naiveté can be. . . . The world is only bearable because of habit, because it is imposed on us when we're too young to resist." [13] Forty-six years later, Malraux was to dismiss *Les Lunes* with regal cheek. "I wrote *Les Lunes* when I was twenty; a coffeehouse glory." [14]

By the time the little volume appeared, he was at work on *Ecrit pour une idole à trompe* (loosely, Pamphlet for a Horned Diety), a book in the same vein, and soon published a chapter in a new magazine [15] and gave two other chapters to Arland for yet another new periodical. [16] Several years later, Nino Frank, a young Italian journalist, asked for a piece for a new Roman magazine and Malraux gave him a third fragment, [17] but the book was never written.

[11] Calvin Tomkins, *Living Well Is the Best Revenge* (New York: The Viking Press, 1962).
[12] *NFR* (July, 1921).
[13] *Disque vert* (Summer, 1921).
[14] *L'Evènement* (August, 1967).
[15] *Signaux de France et de Belgique* (August, 1921).
[16] *Accords* (Oct.-Nov., 1924).
[17] *900* (Summer, 1927).

By the fall of 1921 André was in love and off to Italy, slipping into his ladylove's sleeping compartment as soon as she had waved goodbye to her mother and the Paris-Milan overnight express had pulled out from the Gare de Lyon.

> What is it that you want to understand in what you
> call the feminine psyche?
>
> *The Temptation of the West*

4

He had met Clara Goldschmidt in June, a vivacious, tiny girl a few months older than himself. She was the first girl he could *talk* to—about Hölderlin, Nietzsche and Max Jacob, about the meaning of life and the inanity of conventional ideas. When he mentioned Spain and El Greco, she answered with the Florentine Renaissance and "her" painters.

Clara was the only daughter of a wealthy family. She was born in Magdeburg in Prussia—in postwar France not exactly an endearing origin —and she was Jewish, which didn't help. She lived rather freely with her widowed mother and two brothers in chic Passy, near the Bois de Boulogne, and to busy herself worked part-time at *Action*—as a translator, to begin with. A family friend had introduced her to a friend who had introduced her to Florent Fels.

The first time she noticed André—and he her—was at a dinner organized by Fels where they and thirty others sat squeezed together around one big restaurant table. Clara was seated between André Simon's wife and her girl friend Jane, with whom Malraux talked incessantly. "He was a tall and slim adolescent, with too-big eyes," she was to write in *Apprendre à vivre,* the first volume of her memoirs.[1] After midnight, five of them continued the evening in a night club. "He danced badly, something I only realized at the end of the evening when he finally abandoned my girl friend and invited me for a tango, telling me Jane had made him understand he shouldn't show any interest in me. Was it true or was he already bending reality a bit? I assumed it was true, although nothing in me believed in feminine treachery in general, or in Jane's in particular.

[1] Four volumes have appeared under the overall title *Le Bruit de nos pas: Apprendre à vivre,* 1963; *Nos vingt ans,* 1966; *Les Combats et les jeux,* 1969; and *Voici que vient l'été,* 1973. An English translation of selections of the first two volumes, translated by Patrick O'Brian, appeared as *Memoirs* (New York: Farrar, Straus & Giroux, 1967).

. . . When he said good-night, Jane had established he was very witty, something I hadn't had the chance to discover."

They met again the following Sunday at Claire and Ivan Goll's Auteuil apartment. The Golls were Alsatian Jews who, with the Versailles Treaty, had become French, he a poet and playwright; she a translator. Both spoke German and French with equal ease and their open-house Sundays were cosmopolitan gatherings where the newest ideas from Berlin and Vienna, from expressionist cinema to Sigmund Freud, were discussed and where Marc and Bella Chagall and Alexander Archipenko told about the ferment of the new experimental Soviet art. The Chagalls had just returned from Moscow, where, at Lenin's suggestion, Chagall had decorated the Jewish Art Theater—wickedly painting his own likeness in the arms of the drama director, Abraham Efross. The "color cubists" Albert Gleizes and Robert Delaunay, whose chromatic variations on contrasted colors Apollinaire called Orphism, also show up at the Golls'. Delaunay's wife Sonia was Russian and, inspired by both cubism and the theory of complementary colors, revolutionized fashion with her dresses. Sonia was one of the first car owners to "personalize" her auto with bold color stripings.

Chagall remembered Malraux of the Goll Sundays as a youth with circles under his feverish green eyes. "I was moved by that interrogating gaze which tried to penetrate my universe," Chagall recalled of Malraux showing up at the painter's first exhibition after his return from Russia. "I recognized in Malraux the youth, the enthusiasm, a style which, unlike many others, never ossified." [2]

Goll was continually on the outlook for new talent, by inclination and because he represented a German publishing house. He and his wife were a high-voltage couple. They loved each other furiously, separated, tried to commit suicide, reconciled, separated again—all accompanied by the fracas of public quarrels. Chagall illustrated their *Poèmes d'amour.*

This Sunday, Clara and André were isolated in a deep-seated window, whispering to each other in the general din, squinting through the cigarette smoke. "The voice, a bit slangy, soon says things that are curiously condensed, things which I understand with just enough effort to feel happy, to feel that, ritualistically, I belong to the same tribe as he," she was to write. "He feels it, too. Phrases, subjects catch each other. We're twenty years old and this in 1921." [3] When she told him she would be going to Italy in August, he said he would come along. Just like that.

The next day he phoned, saying he loved her voice. During the following week they saw each other daily, explored common emotions and common tastes and dislikes. He took her to the Gustave Moreau Museum. On the Bagatelle Lake in the Bois, she showed him how to row

[2] Jean-Paul Crespelle, *Chagall,* trans. Benita Eisler (New York: Coward-McCann & Geoghegan, 1970).
[3] Clara Malraux, *Nos vingt ans,* op. cit.

and took him to his first horse race at Longchamps. They divided people they knew into "funny" and "not funny" individuals, agreed that the surrealists were beginning to take themselves too seriously. Another Sunday, they attended a "garden party organized by Fels near Versailles, found they wanted to be alone and took the train back to Paris, dragging on the boulevards for hours."

One day he told her gravely he knew only one person more intelligent than her—Max Jacob. She was someone he could talk to about everything, even death. She had lost her father when she was fourteen. "And then I'm a Jew and it is not easy for Jews to accept the idea of death because there is nothing in the Bible that really says God has promised salvation. André, too, thought constantly about death, rebelling against it. It is something that brought us enormously close together."

In reality she knew little about Judaism. She had always been treated like a prodigy in her family, had always felt more gifted than her older brothers. She had been brought up in the grander liberal tradition of settled German-Jewish wealth, spending a cuddled childhood between the big house in Passy (with a German nanny) and, until the war, summers in Magdeburg. When she told her mother about her new friend, Madame Goldschmidt was not unduly alarmed, but told her daughter that it was nice to be intelligent, because intelligent girls obviously pleased intelligent boys.

Had she ever been to a *bal musette?*

One Sunday, he took her to one of those tenderloin district dances. Clara soon found herself dancing with a gigolo, enjoying the tawdry atmosphere and the strange argot spoken by these Parisians who had nothing in common with her world in Passy-Auteuil. When the pimp vanished, she danced with André, dizzy with excitement of being in one of the lowest dives in the city. In the early hours of the morning when they left the narrow Rue Broca, several men from the *bal musette* jostled them as they swept past. It was a deliberate affront, but André and Clara paid no attention until they saw the men turn and come toward them. André pushed Clara behind him. Suddenly shots were fired at them, André whipped out a revolver and fired back. Everything happened very quickly, followed by dead silence in the now empty little street. André's left hand was bloodied and she took it into hers in their first embrace.

Up on Boulevard des Gobelins, they washed the blood at a hydrant, found a taxi and drove to Clara's house to disinfect the wound. When Madame Goldschmidt appeared in nightgown and robe, she received a simple explanation. "My friend brought me home and has come up to pick up a book." Clara's mother returned to her bedroom. "The injured hand no longer brought to mind an idea of suffering," Clara was to write. "Heavily bandaged, it hung like a parcel at the end of his arm. We were both clumsy, bewildered, happy."

They became lovers on Bastille Day, spending the evening in his garçonnière while the fireworks set the sky ablaze over L'Étoile. The next day he wasn't at their appointed rendezvous. He was seeing his father to ask permission to marry. The request was not so much a gesture of filial respect as a legal necessity. He was not yet twenty-one.

Permission refused. Because Fernand Malraux considered his son too young? Because Clara was German *and* Jewish? No one would ever say, but two years later when André was to stand trial in Pnompenh and the Goldschmidts tried to have Clara declared insane, it was Fernand who rallied to his daughter-in-law's support. Clara's planned trip to Italy was now encouraged by her mother and brothers, who hoped the holiday would put an end to her infatuation for the young parvenu. When André showed Clara his brand new passport, he grinningly told her his father had preferred to let him have a passport to travel to Italy than to get married. Madame Goldschmidt accompanied her daughter to the Gare de Lyon and saw that she was properly settled in her *wagon lit* and that she was alone. As the train pulled out, André slipped into her compartment.

It was André's first trip abroad. In Florence, they savored the emotions of a first illicit hotel check-in and were given a white-chalked room with windows on a minuscule inner court. At the Uffizi Museum, they discovered the quattrocento painters and watched Michelangelo's *David* from a trattoria while having ice cream. From the post office they sent wires to Paris announcing their engagement, carefully omitting any sender's address. She discovered he had a way of visiting a museum— storming through the rooms first and then returning to the canvases he felt worthy of his interest. "I'll buy a pair of rollerskates to follow you," she smiled. In front of Uccello's *The Battle,* he told her to watch the painting as if it contained no anecdote.

Everywhere, Clara translated. Quadrilingual (German, French, Italian and English), foreign tongues were one domain where she was his superior. His vast knowledge astonished and delighted her, as did the playfulness and sarcasm of his ideas, the sharpness of his observations. They confronted their divergent pasts one late afternoon lying in the grass near the San Miniato al Monte cemetery, their heads against the unfinished wall Michelangelo had wanted built. With the city spread at their feet and the sun reddening the spires and the rooftops, they told each other they were happy.

By way of Sienna, they traveled to Venice, where they checked into Hotel Danieli—the only hotel name Clara could remember because of George Sand novels and visits with her parents. Once the hotel bill and railway tickets to Paris were paid for, they had no more money. The Simplon Express was twelve hours late that day, making them spend the afternoon on the Lido beach eating grapes. On the Swiss border, they discovered a few Swiss francs in their possession and bought four sandwiches, which lasted them to Paris.

The Goldschmidts were at the station. Clara's Aunt Jeanne asked whether it was worth it, her mother whether she was happy, while her eldest brother Maurice told her she had dishonored the family and that he would emigrate to America. The next day, Maurice and André met formally for lunch at Fouquet's.

Fernand Malraux gave in, observing after meeting his future daughter-in-law that for a Jewish girl she dressed with taste. She rather liked him, "a dreamer who takes himself seriously, a handsome man for whom words come easily as they do for men who love women and whom women love." [4] Clara would want "something religious" to follow the compulsory civil marriage and André agreed if the "something religious" could be pantheist enough to include ceremonies in a church, a synagogue, a mosque and a pagoda. On the steps of the *mairie,* bride and groom laughingly told each other and their guests that they would get divorced in six months. When Clara's Aunt Jeanne kissed the bride she whispered, "You should have married the father."

Clara's dowry was substantial. The honeymoon took them east, to a Germany whose people, Clara felt, had been "liberated by their defeat," to Prague where they visited the old Jewish cemetery and were moved by the sight of orthodox rabbis. A few days later, André told her to be all the Jewess and all the woman she could be, a proposition she felt wasn't so much prompted by the sight of the rabbis as by a lack of ethnic self-awareness he felt in her. Just before their marriage, he had told her, "I must warn you; around forty we Frenchmen begin to resemble our fathers."

In Vienna, they toured the sights of vice, visiting working-class bordello streets. In Berlin they discovered the new expressionist cinema, so far ahead of the *Feuillade* serials and historical pageantry offered on Parisian screens that André had Clara inquire about buying the French rights to several German avant-garde movies. Everywhere, Clara translated. She had him discover Oswald Spengler, whose despairing views of mankind and of the West's inevitable decline not only echoed the German postwar mood but also André's own outlook. Malraux was to be influenced by Spengler's artistic-intuitive view of society but move away from the Spenglerian idea of civilization as organisms with a life cycle stretching from birth to inevitable death.

From Berlin, they went to Magdeburg to visit her grandfather, her uncles, aunts and innumerable cousins and in-laws. The patriarch told his granddaughter's French husband he had worked hard for "both fatherlands" since he had had grandsons killed in both German and French uni-

[4] Clara Malraux, *Nos vingt ans,* op. cit.

forms. One evening he read Heine to André, who didn't understand a word but was moved to tears.

Back in Paris—after a detour to Dunkirk to meet members of the Malraux clan—the newlyweds moved into the third floor of the Goldschmidt villa, an arrangement everybody seemed to find convenient. Clara wasn't about to settle into domesticity—she had discovered several Freudian texts she wanted to translate—and André, plunging into literary activities, found the arrangement chic, while his mother-in-law liked to have part of the huge house occupied and, no doubt, to have an eye on the young couple. Also, Clara and André had discovered they loved to travel. They would soon be off again.

But there was the army. When he received his induction papers ordering him to report in Strasbourg, they decided there could be nothing more absurd than eighteen months of playing soldier in Alsace. To their astonishment, brother-in-law Maurice offered to help. Maurice had been mobilized in Alsace and the family held considerable interests in the biggest Alsatian tannery, all of which might add up to a few influential acquaintances. Together, André, Clara and Maurice made the trip to Strasbourg. André carried with him a certificate attesting to a childhood case history of rheumatism in the joints and Maurice located a friendly physician. On the fatal day, André presented himself for his medical with the right amount of antimalaria quinine in the bloodstream to make his heart beat dangerously. He was exempt from military service.

The Paper Moons was coming out and Clara and André plunged happily into a funky, gypsylike existence. There were only three ways for him to earn a living, they agreed—avant-garde film distribution, publishing and the stock market. Why not all three? In Berlin, they had seen Robert Wiene's electrifying *Das Kabinett des Dr. Caligari,* the revelation of postwar German cinema with its startling expressionist decor and its stylized acting and makeup, Werner Krauss' sinister mad scientist, Conrad Veidt's somnambulist gliding through angular black shadows and starkly white streets and Lil Dagover's intense kohl eyes and raven hair. Since the French rights to *Caligari* were already being negotiated, André sunk a hefty sum into the rights to its new rival, *Das Haus zum Mond,* a "phantasmal drama" by expressionist stage director Karl Heinz Martin, which André simply retitled *La Maison lunaire.* With Ivan Goll's help, he also started negotiating to acquire Ernst Wendt's *Uriel Acosta,* a picture, Clara was to remember, that showed her the synagogue could be as cruel as the church.

During the winter of 1921–22, the young couple traveled a lot, but André managed to write two critical essays on art that suggested the main thesis of *The Voices of Silence* thirty years later. One text was an introduction to his friend Galanis' work, the other an essay on André Gide. "The Greek genius," Malraux wrote à propos Galanis, "is better understood by opposing one Greek statue to an Egyptian or Asian statue than by getting to know a hundred Greek statues." [5] In the *Action* article on Gide, he said art was confrontation and that while the artist underwent outside influences, he changed only by giving these influences a different range and meaning.[6]

In the early 1920s, Gide was, with Paul Claudel, the great French writer. He had given the new century its gospel by saying, "There are marvellous possibilities in every human being" and by seeking new moral and social freedom. Gide was a bisexual with a strong tendency toward homosexuality who was determined to pursue his pleasure and to make it as public as possible—he upbraided Marcel Proust for turning the men he had loved into women in his novels. The drama of Gide's life was his marriage to his cousin whose strict Calvinism could not accept his paganism and his homosexuality, but who was nevertheless the person he loved most. Besides fiction, he wrote essays, criticisms, travel and political books, drama and such unclassifiable works as *Les Nourritures ter-restres* (1897), the pagan expression of his reaction to moral disciplines, which had a profound influence on French youth in the 1920s. In *Paludes* (1895), he created a literary event, writing ironically about a writer writing a book, and in his comic 1914 novel, *Les Caves du Vatican,* concerned himself with "the gratuitous act" by which modern man freed himself—a theme that was to reverberate through Pirandello, the surrealists, Malraux, Camus, Sartre and beyond. With *La Symphonie pastorale* (1919), a love tragedy full of secret intentions written in a luminous language, his audience had widened. Malraux met Gide the first time on Boulevard St. Germain with Gide showing up munching a croissant.

Since the position of *directeur littéraire* at Kra's demanded fairly regular appearances, André had given it up for occasional publishing of erotica, an activity Clara found deliciously naughty. Since Pascal Pia was an expert in bawdy texts, he became an associate.

André was something of what has come to be called a male chauvinist, Clara discovered. One day he remarked that since the values of society were masculine, it would be amusing to imagine those of a feminine civilization. They spent the next hours compiling various hypotheses, sparring and testing each other's territory. In Italy, she had realized that what astonished him most was her ability to talk clearly about her most intimate feelings. As she would write:

> I paraded in front of him a world of children, women and men
> with whom he had never had any contact and who didn't feel life like he
> did. I explained them to him, then at other moments we climbed together
> I don't know what abstract mountain, not always with him playing the

[5] "La Peinture de Galanis," foreword to Demetrios Galanis catalogue for Galérie de la Licorne exhibit, 1922.

[6] "Aspects d'André Gide," *Action* (March-April, 1922).

leader but mostly with both of us egging each other on and developing such a taste for intellectual jousting that the playfulness of the body asserted itself and physical pleasure seemed the natural result of the pleasures of the mind. All this was as it should be, and yet I didn't appear to be totally human to him. It angered me and I began to demand a bigger slice of life—which, in love, means independence—than I would have asked for if he had acknowledged me fully.[7]

If she often felt put in an inferior position by her scintillating husband, the reverse was also true. In many ways André was dominated by his wife and some of his more exaggerated poses and gestures might have been spurred on by a situation he might often have found humiliating.

Sundays were spent at the Golls'. Ivan was busier than ever playing literary agent for the big Insel Verlag and one Sunday said he was getting the German rights to *Ulysses,* which, against all odds, Sylvia Beach and her Shakespeare & Company were publishing. If Miss Beach refused access to the writer, Ivan managed to get to the polyglot Irishman through Nino Frank, a young Italian of Swiss descent who had become a friend of the Italophilic Joyce. Frank managed to bring Goll to Joyce's apartment in the Square Robiac, where Ivan met the beautiful Madame Joyce and the daughter, Lucia, a would-be ballet dancer slowly going mad. Other Sundays were spent at the Chagalls or the Kahnweilers in suburban St. Cloud. One weekend, Clara and André visited Fernand Malraux in his house near Orléans, where André for the first time met his stepmother. The elder Malraux was in half-retirement, and with Roland intensely interested in this adult half-brother and little Claude perpetually crying, Fernand perorated on the pleasures of being French and on the lurking foreign dangers. On the way back to Paris, Clara and André agreed that the war had made Fernand Malraux into yet another narrow-minded, patriotic war veteran.

Insidious nationalism, André discovered, halted his import of avantgarde films. He had never thought of bureaucratic "visas de censure," and the commercial exploitation of *La Maison lunaire* and *Uriel Acosta* remained unauthorized. He ended up projecting the expressionist films for friends in a private screening room. The libertine book business declined when Pia was drafted, and during 1922–23 the main source of income for the smart young couple was stock exchange speculation—with Clara's dowry. André invested a very hefty sum in a Mexican mining company and saw the stock climb to feverish heights that, in inflationary francs, made them halfway millionaires. Between artistic pilgrimages abroad, they visited their bank.

One trip was to Belgium, where Antwerp's placid whores fascinated them and where, alone, André visited James Ensor in Ostend. The En-

[7] Clara Malraux, op. cit.

glish-born founder of modern Belgian painting with his visionary art, his violent tonality, grimacing masks and lusty awareness of death, was a true Malraux idol and André visited Ensor's house by the sea with reverence. The painter was courteous and showed his young Parisian admirer his stuffed monkeys on the piano and his late mother's shell shop, a surrealist beach shack where Mme. Ensor had sold seashells to turn-of-the-century tourists.

Clara and André visited Athens during a riot, gamely climbing to the Parthenon on foot because cabdrivers were on strike. On the Yugoslav border, a stationmaster delayed the train's departure to tell them his life's story and to beg them for new French books. They spent Christmas in Magdeburg and in Berlin discovered Rembrandt at the Reichmuseum and bought books about the art of the insane.

But it was at Kahnweiler's gallery in Paris that André met a German whose ideas were to set him afire. Alfred Salmony was a heavily built man with a massive face who lost all ponderousness in the presence of art, especially protohistoric Asian art, the strange forms produced by Mongolian tribes on the shores of Lake Baikal. Archaeologist and art critic attached to the Cologne art museum, Salmony was preparing a comparative art exhibit, a show that wouldn't be limited to classical masterpieces but include the diverse forms of all civilizations—a daring proposition in 1922. André was so excited he immediately invited Salmony for dinner.

Salmony, who was only a few years older than André and Clara, arrived with an enormous briefcase. After dinner, he spread hundreds of art photos on the floor. Without talking, he joggled the stills around, bringing certain photos together with others—a Thai torso with a classic Greek head, a Han dynasty head with a Romanesque bas-relief. Why did a Gandhara sculpture sometimes look as though it had come from an Athenian workshop? Why did a Wei dynasty *bodhisattva* carved in northern China in the early sixth century resemble a Romanesque statue carved six centuries later in medieval France? Clara and André were stunned. With his photographs Salmony carried André's theory of art as confrontation toward a kind of ultimate unity. In juxtaposing photographs or parts of photographs new and powerful syntheses became evident, making it seem that artists of all ages and all cultures worked in diverse ways to obtain the same ends. Maybe there was an as yet unlocked secret in art. When Salmony left, leaving behind a few of his precious photos, Clara and André talked all night, feeling there might be a new way of grasping culture.

They were taking a boat trip down the Rhine watching the vine-covered hills glide by and talking about the Rhenish culture stretching the length of the river, when by chance their eyes fell on a French newspaper in an abandoned deck chair and they learned they were ruined.

55

Cassirer, in Berlin, paid me five thousand marks for the two Buddhas Damrong gave me.

The Royal Way

5

To be ruined at twenty-two was no reason to jump out of any window. At least that was what André felt as they returned to Paris and learned the stock market had caved in and with it any claim they might have had to being well-off. His in-laws didn't quite see it his way.

The stock market collapse that saw the Malrauxs' mining stock vanish was only one of many instant recessions of the volatile French economy of the 1920s. Successive governments shied away from facing colossal costs of the war or from the fact that not only were temporary drastic and unpopular measures necessary to restore fiscal sanity but that the whole business of state was in need of fundamental overhaul. Public debt—a third of it was supposed to be recoverable through German reparations—continued to grow until the state, in effect, repudiated it by allowing the franc to fall. In 1926, when billions of short-term loans had come due and could not be paid, the franc had fallen to fifty to the dollar, finally to stabilize itself in 1928 at one fifth of its prewar value. Frenchmen became obsessed with this "Poincaré franc"—so called in honor of Premier Raymond Poincaré's attempt at recovery that year—insisting that their currency must never again be devalued. When the early 1930s Depression saw Britain devalue its pound and the United States its dollar, the French held stubbornly, and disastrously, to the 1928 franc. Paradoxically, the French economy expanded and prospered through the 1920s.

For the Malrauxs it was the end of almost two years of funky capitalism and Bohemian affluence. It wouldn't have been so bad if André had kept up the pace of the feverish period with Doyon, Kra, Fels and Kahnweiler. He still edited books—at night at home—when they weren't attending the Swedish Ballet's new "American" production with music by Cole Porter and sets by Fernand Léger and Gerald Murphy, or one of the guest performances at the Opéra of the Royal Cambodian Ballet,

56

a company whose spare grace of gestures, timbre and costumes enchanted them. Most of time, André had lived, traveled and learned—in style. In the bourgeois vocabulary there was a word for his kind—adventurer. The Goldschmidts didn't take kindly to Clara's ruin and in heated arguments with her mother and brothers—the Malrauxs now lived on Avenue Mozart in a townhouse owned by Mme. Goldschmidt—even she had to admit that the description fitted her husband. The plight was classical and usually ended with the family forgiving and discreetly subsidizing the humbled progress toward responsibility of the prodigal son or son-in-law. In André's case, however, the failure made him more audacious.

"You don't expect me to work, do you?" he asked Clara.

"Of course not," she answered, "but then?" [1]

His belief in adventure—adventure as an attitude of mind, as a slap in the face of existing values and as vindication of personal freedoms —plus his love of art and travel, combined perhaps with art dealers' gossip overheard at Kahnweiler's, made him come up with a hairbrained yet perfectly clever solution to their predicament—to go to French Indochina and "lift" a couple of Buddhist statues from little-known or forgotten temples. "We will go to little Cambodian temples, take a few statues which we will sell in America. This will allow us to live comfortably for a couple of years."

Summer, they discovered, was the wrong time of year for jungle expeditions in Southeast Asia; they would have to wait for the dry season in October. In the meantime, they worked and studied. For Fels, André wrote a foreword to a new edition of *Mademoiselle Monk,* a political text by Charles Maurras. The foreword was to be an acute embarrassment to Malraux a decade later when Maurras' *Action française* league turned fascist and the poet himself railed against Germans, Jews and romanticism as the enemies of France. Maurras, who was stone deaf most of his life, was to live to see his ideals come true with the creation of Vichy France. He was to be condemned to death, then pardoned in 1945, to live another seven years writing poetry reflecting his Mediterranean Catholicism. Malraux's foreword concentrated on Maurras' evolution from Schopenhauer-Baudelaire romanticism toward limited and disciplined classicism, saying that in so doing, Maurras did not so much contradict as construct himself. "If he would have loved to live in ancient Greece, it is because Greek philosophers were accustomed to bring their lives and their beliefs into harmony, although I see him above all as a man of the Middle Ages, ardent priest, father confessor of great men, architect of cathedrals and organizer of crusades. . . . He loves order because order represents beauty and force." [2]

[1] Clara Malraux, *Nos vingt ans* (Paris: Grasset, 1966).
[2] Charles Maurras, *Mademoiselle Monk,* followed by *Invocation à Minerve,* preface by André Malraux (Paris: Stock, 1923).

The Maurras foreword appeared almost simultaneously with the essay on Gide, a fact friends and fellow travelers were to underline a decade later when Gide and Malraux were to be the stentorian voices of a certain French Left. Later still, journalists would delight in digging up the Maurras preface as proof of crypto-Gaullism.

Clara and André decided to leave for Indochina in October and plunged enthusiastically into the preparations. They "inventoried" Khmer art at the Guimet Museum and read everything. André was famous for sniffing out rare books and at the Bibliothèque Orientale soon zeroed in on a Lieutenant Marek's 1914 account of a visit to a small temple at Banteai Srey. While Lunet de la Jonquière's three-volume *Inventaire descriptif des monuments du Cambodge* of 1911 had excellent descriptions and maps of sites along the ancient Khmer Royal Way from Dangrek to Angkor, Lieutenant Marek described the Banteai Srey temple as standing abandoned in the jungle. André also came upon an article by Henri Parmentier, chief of archaeology at L'École française d'Extrême-Orient in Hanoi, describing the remarkable beauty of the Banteai Srey ruins during a visit in 1916. André realized there were two sites of the same name, a Banteai Srey confused with the main Angkor Wat ruins and *his* Banteai Srey northeast of Angkor Thom on the right bank of the Siem Reap River. He also came upon an interesting article in the *Revue archéologique* that told how the Fogg Museum of Harvard University had come into possession of an admirable Buddhist head, and how at least eight other Khmer master-pieces somehow had found their way to the United States.

While Clara bought quinine tablets to guard against malaria, snake-bite serum and a dozen circular saws, André managed to get official backing. The officials at the Guimet he approached were amazed at his knowledge and an order was duly signed by the new Minister of Colonies, Albert Sarraut. The letter authorized Malraux to study Khmer temples and to recruit farmers and carts to transport his expedition baggage. His sole obligation was to give an account of his travels on his return.

Somewhat against Clara's will, it was decided that Louis Chevasson would join them. Clara couldn't stand the childhood friend from Bondy and called Louis "the colorless one," but she had to admit that once in the jungle with the saws, a third pair of reliable hands might be more than useful.

Their friends looked upon their upcoming adventure with a mixture of admiration and envy, even if Max Jacob wrote ironically to Kahnweiler that André would end up university professor in sinology. In his piece on Landru, Georges Gabory had written, not entirely tongue in cheek, that "the end justifies the means" and to all of them the word "adventure" had a special meaning. "The word enjoyed great prestige in literary milieux in 1920," Malraux was to tell his first biographer, Gaetan Picon, thirty years later, "a prestige it lost when the communists appended it comically to bourgeois virtues and affixed it seriously to Stalinist law and order." [3]

With Chevasson scheduled to follow three weeks later, Clara and André sailed—first-class, from Marseille October 23, 1923—arriving in Saigon twenty-nine days later after exotic landfalls at Suez, Djibouti, Colombo and Singapore and, in the Indian Ocean, a fire in one of the holds. The month-long voyage made a profound impression on the young couple.

The rigid class system aboard the S.S. *Angkor* was both metaphor and premonition of the world beyond the prow and of a society they had never known. With them in first-class traveled the top administrators and their wives, beginning or returning to a tour of duty. On the deck below were the middle-rung civil servants and the *colons* or settlers, the French middle-class merchants and craftsmen determined to carve their stake out of the colonies, and in the steerage were the Chinese merchants, Vietnamese students and other polyglot colonials. "Given his habit of speaking his mind," Walter Langlois was to write in a book on Malraux's Asian experiences, "young, brilliant, liberal and haughty André must have made quite a few enemies and very few friends during the long voyage across the Indian Ocean." [4] Although they told themselves it was bourgeois and silly, Clara and André were nevertheless impressed when one night they were invited to the captain's table.

There were the ports of call! In Port Said, little boys offered dirty postcards and their sisters on the quayside, Clara was to remember. Most fascinating was Djibouti in French Somaliland, where they plunged into the nameless streets, deserted in the noonday heat and saw famished goats which, to prevent them from suckling each other to death, had their teats encased in small sacks. The evening cool brought out the polyglot population, Somalis, Isas, Afars, Yemenites, Greeks, Armenians, Italians and Hindus. Always tourists with a taste for spicier folklore, the Malrauxs watched beautiful girls dance for them in a bordello.

The first Asian port of call was Colombo and the honey-scented island of Penang, where Clara nearly drowned in a stinking arroyo. Singapore was remembered for its Victorian monuments and the Raffles Hotel, one of the most opulent in the Orient, where Somerset Maugham had written *The Moon and Sixpence* in the Palm Court garden and candlelit dinners were served under the stars. At the bar they learned to drink Singapore Slings and in their room, a "boy" with a string around a toe pulled a huge overhead fan from behind a screen all night.

While they steamed up the Saigon River, the "Indochina French" stood leaning on the railing, telling Clara how happy they were to be home, "talking about the docile 'boys' waiting for them in their houses

[3] Gaetan Picon, *Malraux par lui-même* (Paris: Seuil, 1953).
[4] Walter Langlois, *André Malraux, L'Aventure indochinoise* (Paris: Mercure de France, 1967).

full of embroidery, chiseled silverware and jade they believed to be antique." [5]

Saigon, Clara and André decided, was a provincial French town laid out in geometric patterns. They took in picturesque Rue Catinat and learned to drink rum-soda before they were off to the administrative capital of French Indochina, Hanoi. Henri Parmentier himself was gone that week but André was received by Leonard Aurosseau, an official at the École française d'Extrême-Orient, who knew very little about Khmer art but was perspicacious enough to find the Malraux "mission" less than convincing. They sipped rum-sodas on faculty verandas for a week, improvising themselves archaeologists, but the school officials smelled the red herring and offhandedly warned them. A governor-general's regulation of 1908 declared all "discovered and undiscovered" sites in the Siem Reap, Battambang and Sisiphon provinces historical monuments and to further protect Khmer antiquities a new decree was supposed to have been enacted in Paris a few weeks earlier.

The risk only added to André's determination and sense of adventure. Besides, Professor Parmentier turned out to be a delightful old fogy who, somewhat blindly it seemed, admired the young couple's devotion to archaeology. Parmentier had no high opinion of such steamy authors of exotica as Pierre Loti, whose books André had swallowed in adolescence. Loti, said the goateed Parmentier, spoke of vultures crowding together on the branches of banana trees when everybody knew that a banana tree branch would bend too much to support a single vulture. The archaeologist spoke both authoritatively and lyrically about the Khmers, of all Asians the only people to show a true genius for architecture. More positive than the peoples of India, who avoided any precision that might hinder the flights of the imagination, Khmers took literally the idea that a temple should be an image of the cosmos and therefore invented the temple in the form of a mountain. Also, Khmer sculpture was the most exquisite in the Orient, indeed compared favorably to classical Greek art. Especially the Bayon period of the thirteenth century which saw the development of the famous Angkor "smile" that, together with the closed eyes, so beautifully expressed the total bliss the soul could achieve through Buddha.

Clara and André had seen the famous smiling Queen Jayarajadevi sculpture at the Guimet. André talked ecstatically about its beauty and told the professor about his theories of comparative art. Once when he was out of earshot, Parmentier leaned toward Clara and with a nod toward her husband, said, "So young and so wealthy. So disinterested, too."

Parmentier accompanied them back to Saigon, where they picked

[5] Clara Malraux, *Nos vingt ans.*

Musée Guimet

Khmer smile—Banyon period, Angkor Vat thirteenth century

up Chevasson arriving from Marseille. Before the trio set out for Pnompenh by train, the scholar gave them a thousand recommendations and said he would arrange for the curator of Angkor Wat to meet them and perhaps helps them get native guides and provisions.

By riverboat, Clara, André and Louis reached Siem Reap, a sun-baked sleepy harbor on the northern bank of Tonle Sap Lake which served as port for the Angkor Wat complex. Parmentier's man, a Monsieur Crémazy, was there, giving them a VIP tour of the Angkor temples and putting them in contact with various Cambodians. One was Xa, who was hired as guide, cook, translator and general factotum. He was an inveterate gambler and had been in prison for debt. By hiring Xa and paying him part of his salary in advance, André managed to offend the last Frenchman before the jungle, the local gendarme. Their final purchase was three big chests, made of camphorwood, which, Xa said, was the strongest wood there was.

In tropical helmets, Clara's Paris-designed tropical getup and strapped with bottles of drinking water they were off. Accompanied by Xa and a dozen coolies, they rode into the bush on tiny horses, with André's long legs dangling comically, Clara noticed, followed by four ox carts loaded with the camphorwood chests, their mosquito nettings, tents, stoves, saucepans, axes, lamps and Clara's pharmaceuticals. Where were they heading? They were not totally sure that the little Banteai Srey

61

temple that Parmentier had visited and written about four years earlier was still standing. Local peasants might have used the conveniently cut sandstone for other purposes or the jungle might have totally overgrown the site. According to their maps and hunches, the ruins were thirty miles, or two days' march, north of Siem Reap. In the forest, they followed a slender trail that was so narrow they had to ride in a single column. Xa rode up front, then came Clara, André with his legs dangling, Louis and, in the rear, the four bullock carts, each with two drivers wearing only loincloths. At Rohal, the last village, they made inquiries and learned that no one knew about Banteai Srey. Xa valiantly translated and questioned. Finally, an old man seemed to remember a trail that formerly led to a mount of stones a couple of miles away. Xa hired him for the following morning's final assault.

Up at dawn, the expedition followed the old man into the jungle. The forest was now very dense, the trail vanished and the heat was suffocating. The old man and some of the coolies hacked at the undergrowth with their machetes. Shortly before noon when they had almost given up, they reached a small clearing. In *La Voie royale* Malraux was to describe the sight in Claude's and Perken's discovery of their coveted ruins:

> It looked like a mason's yard invaded by the jungle. There were lengths of wall in slabs of purple sandstone, some carved and others plain, all overgrown with hanging ferns. Some bore a red patina, the aftermath of fire. Facing him were bas-reliefs of the best period, marked by Indian influence—he was close now—but very beautiful. They were grouped around an old shrine, half hidden now beneath a breastwork of fallen stone. It was a whole effort to take his eyes off them. Beyond the bas-reliefs were the remains of three towers razed to within six feet of the ground. The mutilated stumps stuck out of such an overwhelming mass of rubble that all the vegetation around them was stunted and the towers looked like candles in their sticks. An imperceptible tremor, a perpetual vibration, began to stir within the leafy depths, though there was not the faintest breeze. The great heat was beginning.
>
> A loose stone fell and sounded twice in falling, first with a muffled thud, then clearly; and Claude, in his mind's ear caught an echo of the word eer-ie . . . Something inhuman brooded over all these ruins and the voracious plants which now seemed petrified with apprehension; a presence of supernatural awe guarded with its dead hand these ancient figures holding their lonely court among the centipedes and vermin of the forest. Then Perken stepped past him, and in a flash the world of shimmering sea depths died out, like a jellyfish cast high and dry on the seashore; it lost its potency when faced by two men.
>
> "I'll get the tools," Perken said.

The sculptures were not on fallen slabs but embedded in the walls. It took two days to hack the huge blocks of sculpture from the walls. While the coolies stood timidly aside, apparently fearful of divine revenge

André and Louis Chevasson in Pnompenh

for such desecration, and Clara kept a general lookout, André and Louis worked in the sweltering heat. Their saws broke, snakes slithered over suddenly disturbed surfaces, but with the help of chisels and ropes, they managed to free seven pieces forming four blocks of bas-relief—two *devis,* or dancing goddesses, and five smaller fragments. Their fortunes depended on the *devis,* they were sure, because the smaller fragments, representing men sitting in lotus position, lacked the beauty of the feminine deities.

On the third day, the blocks, weighing about a thousand pounds, were stored in the camphorwood chests and hoisted on the bullock carts. Toward noon, they set out on the return trip, congratulating each other and estimating their blocks would make them $100,000 richer once they got it all to New York. When they reached Siem Reap, six days after they had left it, the obliging Monsieur Crémazy was nowhere in sight. Two days later—they suddenly realized it was Christmas eve—their camphorwood chests were loaded into the hold of a river steamer, labeled "chemical products" and addressed to Berthot & Charrière, forwarders in Saigon. They stood themselves, together with Xa, whose services they decided they could afford until after Pnompenh, at the railing as the steamer slipped away from the little pier.

The riverboat tied up at Pnompenh, within sight of the scarlet-roofed royal palace, in a magnificent sunset as church bells pealed.

63

Christmas in the tropics. Clara, André and Louis stayed onboard—the steamer would continue down the Mekong to Saigon—and turned in early.

Shortly before midnight, they were awakened and placed under arrest.

> If you're looking for a way to keep Indochina, I
> have nothing to suggest, because we won't keep it.
>
> *Antimémoires*

6

Released pending a trial that took six months to get underway, Clara, André and Louis first stayed in a second-class hotel. Penniless, Clara feigned a suicide, which brought them in contact with doctors, nurses and "boys." It was in the humid, pestilence-haunted wards of Pnompenh Hospital during the monsoon season of early 1924 that Malraux became conscious of realities that were to lead to his first political commitment.

A first account of the Banteai Srey episode appeared in the January 5 edition of *L'Echo du Cambodge,* the local newssheet. Three days later a longer article, headlined "Vandals and Robbers of Ruins," ran in *L'Impartial,* the big Saigon daily. This piece repeated the basic facts of the original news story, accompanied by a roused commentary by publisher Henry de Lachevrotière, who despite his sonorous name was a rather dubious upholder of colonial rectitude.

Louis Chevasson was sure their case would proceed in typical colonial fashion, that it would be slow, difficult and confused. Since he was unmarried, he suggested that he take all the blame and that Clara and André sail back to France. Once there, André would be in a position to find lawyers and exert sufficient influence to bring about his release. André refused to take the whole thing seriously, but Clara wasn't so sure they would get off too easily. "When you don't want to knuckle under, you either must be very strong or very crafty; we were neither," she was to write. "The values we questioned were easily defended. On the other hand, our defenses caved in—bank statements traced our ruin in sharply declining curves and no previous undertakings justified any sudden passion for Khmer art." [1]

---

[1] Clara Malraux, *Nos vingt ans* (Paris: Grasset, 1966).

The days dragged on. At sunset on Fridays, a military band played on the main square for Frenchmen in colonial white and Frenchwomen in mousseline prints. On Wednesdays, the hotel set up a gramophone in a large upstairs room and *colons* and their ladies from surrounding plantations came in for an evening of socializing. It was here that André first heard about David Mayrena, the legendary king of the Sedangs. The Dutchman had abandoned his rubber plantation in Sumatra for the highlands in eastern Cambodia where he had carved out a small kingdom for himself, demanding implicit obedience to his slightest command from his Moi tribesmen, somewhat like Rajah Brooks of Sarawak, an Engishman who had made himself absolute ruler in northeastern Borneo. Mayrena's innumerable concubines, his duels with local chieftains, audacious scraps with French officials, his army of elephants and bodyguard of Moi warriors were discussed in the bars of Pnompenh, Saigon and Hanoi by people who swore they had known Mayrena at the height of his glory twenty years earlier. This Kiplingesque tribal chief was to become a pathetic figure in *The Royal Way* and reappear in the *Antimémoires* as the subject of a screenplay that Baron Clappique, a fictional character in *Man's Fate,* tries to peddle to Hollywood producers.

Clara's feigned suicide plus a very real attack of dengue, or breakbone fever led to her hospitalization. The sweaty European physician and the young Cambodian doctors tolerated that her emaciated and near-destitute husband live in her hospital room with her. During the day when he was in town, checking the post office for answers to their distress letters to their families, talking strategy wiht Louis or meeting Xa, who insisted he was still their servant although they couldn't pay him, she began to translate one of Freud's texts to keep her sanity. She also made friends with two Cambodian nurses and with a very pregnant Siamese cat. After the kittens were born, the cat left them to die to join Clara on the bed. During the long rainy nights when the moaning of dying patients in other rooms kept them awake, they stayed under the mosquito netting discussing in hushed voices *all* the possibilities. One solution entertained and abandoned as too risky was for André to escape via Thailand. Every day Xa visited Clara, bringing her a flower.

For dramatic effect, Clara also began a hunger strike. Always a tiny girl—a fraction of an inch over five feet compared to André's near six feet—the combined effect of the dengue fever and her fasting soon reduced her to an alarming seventy-two pounds. The hospital apparently warned the appropriate authorities—after all, the Malrauxs were Europeans—and a preliminary hearing was granted. At the hearing, charges against Clara were dropped.

Simultaneously rescue money arrived from Fernand Malraux—there were never any letters from the Goldschmidts. They decided Clara should sail for France immediately and try to drum up support. André

André Malraux Archives

Clara and André in Saigon

was optimistic. "They've got nothing serious against us," he told her. "I'll be sailing after you before you reach Marseille."

During the evening cool she tried to walk a few paces in the hospital garden, leaning on André and listening to his reasoned talk about the necessity of understanding modern Oriental man. As long as he talked, she knew where she was. Xa brought his last flower. He had finally understood the whole story and with cruel innocence that made her bite her lips in tears he asked why she and her husband hadn't told him in the very beginning they wanted ancient stone heads. If he had known, he could have helped. He knew where to find stone heads right here in Pnompenh.

Orderlies carried her to the ambulance taking her to the riverboat. One of the Cambodian nurses would accompany her to Saigon. André walked next to the stretcher, not looking good himself, Clara noticed. Malaria attacks had given him a mustard-colored skin. They didn't know what to say to each other. When the ambulance pulled away, she looked back and saw him "under his cork helmet, in his white cloth suit and starched collar, standing with his arms dangling in the middle of the road, apart from the others, orphaned." [2]

The Cambodian nurse, who had become like a sister, helped her aboard and disappeared. André had bought Clara a first-class ticket with the rescue money from his father. She cried and smiled. She could barely expect to be invited to the captain's table this time; she had only one pair of shoes.

The food, sea breeze and fellow-passengers' solicitude brought her back among the living in a remarkable short time. She spent the first week in a deck chair—petite, frail and wrapped in blankets, trying to sum it all up in her mind. After Singapore she took short strolls on the deck, soon in the company of a one-armed man whom she was to identify in her memoirs as Charles G., an official responsible for French schools and colleges in China.

"You know my story?" she asked.

"Pious souls have taken upon themselves to inform me. I've found it all rather interesting."

"And it hasn't . . ."

"On the contrary. But if it makes you feel better, I had already decided to make your acquaintance. Yes, the moment I saw you, I thought, 'Who is this charming little waif?' "

She told Charles G. everything, except her uncertainties, underlining her husband's qualities, "his marvellous intelligence, the fervor with which he thinks, judges and sees things, the ardor with which he exults in life's joys." Her listener was a tactful man, who now and then smiled and at the end gave a sober evaluation. He made her realize that the return

[2] Clara Malraux, op. cit.

68

to France was perhaps as badly prepared as their departure for Indochina and that she ignored such crucial elements of the equation as the families' attitude, work possibilities and, despite much optimistic talk, the probable outcome of the trial. A few days later, Charles G. pointed to a slim man saying, "You know this man? You should; he's Monin, the lawyer."

Not yet thirty, Paul Monin was a courageous and influential member of the Saigon bar, a lawyer with a passion for justice—even for Annamites, as the seventeen million Vietnamese, Cambodians and Laotians were called when lumped together. Monin was neither social agitator nor radical ideologue but a liberal believer in the French Revolution and the Constitution, which, he felt, should apply to everyone living under the French flag. Like so many idealistic Frenchmen of his generation, he believed his country's overseas presence was only justified by higher ideals than one-way mercantilism. As the saying went, the British sought in colonies additional territory; the French looked for people they could make into so many African and Asian Frenchmen. The iniquities of the clammy paternalism Monin witnessed had immediately put him in the select ranks of enlightened opposition. His progressive views did not sit too well with the colonial establishment. Because he had defended Annamites in several cases, Lachevrotière's *L'Impartial* had called him a "sellout to the natives." Other stories had it that the blue-eyed lawyer had dueled with Lachevrotière, that he had helped organize a strike by Saigon dockworkers and coolies, that he had marched with them under a red banner.

When Clara got a chance to talk to Monin, he listened attentively. There was not much he could do. While they were sailing toward Marseille, the trial was supposed to get underway in Pnompenh. But, Clara told herself, she now had two friends.

Off Aden, Charles G. became her lover. "It was bound to happen," she was to write. "I accept it without remorse. Of few men do I keep such a clear memory; he knew how to be a lover without ceasing to be a friend."

From Port Said, she wired her father-in-law asking him to meet her at Marseille. The last days onboard were spent in brief-encounter introspection. "If we weren't both married," Charles G. sighed. "If we weren't what we are," she answered, "things wouldn't be what they are and *that* wouldn't change anything." Before disembarking, Monin gave her his address in Paris, saying he would expect to hear from her in a few days.

Fernand Malraux was not on the quayside, but a steward brought her a telegram from him, saying her wire had arrived too late but that she should call him in Orléans. With money Charles G. thrust into her hand in a last gesture he tried to make casual, she took the first train to Paris. Instinctively, she avoided the big house in Passy and instead stood with her suitcase in her one pair of rain-soaked shoes ringing the bell of Jeanne, a former maid of the Goldschmidts now married and running a Montmartre hotel of dubious repute.

"What a mess you've made for all of us," Jeanne exclaimed, letting her in.

"Oh, it's nothing."

"Nothing? The papers are full of stories about his conviction."

The trial had lasted two days. It had started July 16 before Judge Jodin, a colorful and far from straitlaced magistrate.* Judge Jodin had recently come from Pondicherry, the French enclave in India, with his mulatto mistress and was something of a social outcast in Pnompenh, presenting his paramour to the governor-general as his daughter. His habitual attire on the bench was a caricature of colonial dress—pith helmet, frayed tropical suit and dark glasses. André felt the presiding judge might be understanding and perhaps even view their misdeed as, if not a youthful prank, as least as nothing more than an overzealous outburst of archaeological ardor. The district attorney was maître Giordani, a quiet, outwardly gentle man. André's lawyer was maître De Percevaux while Chevasson was defended by maître Lortat-Jacob. As André sat down, he wasn't unduly pessimistic. Their star defense witness was to be none other than Henri Parmentier, chief of archaeology at L'École française d'Extrême-Orient.

As the correspondent from Saigon's *L'Impartial* noted, the two defendants were a study in contrasts. Sturdy, self-controlled Chevasson sat quiet in the dock and admitted everything while the fiery, wiry Malraux sprang up protesting his innocence. Their strategy was their first error. Chevasson gave himself the role of sole author of the alleged crime. He insisted he alone was responsible, admitting all the evidence, including the camphorwood chests, labeled "chemical products" and addressed to the Saigon forwarders. Malraux's defense was that he had never seen Chevasson until they met at Banteai Srey. Unhappily, the dossier forwarded by the Paris police—and not communicated to the defense—showed that Chevasson and Malraux had gone to the same grammar school. The Malraux dossier was not the kind that would endear a defendant to colonial magistrates. It described him as an associate of anarchists and Bolsheviks; a friend, Georges Gabory, had written a satirical defense of mass-murderer Landru that had almost led to the seizure of the magazine they both worked on. Married to a naturalized German Jew, he was the archetype of the asocial if not amoral intellectual.

The Saigon correspondent described Malraux on the bench:

> Malraux is a tall, thin, clean-shaven young man whose features are illuminated by two extremely penetrating eyes. He is very facile in his speech and defends himself with a sharpness that reveals in him

* The first name of Judge Jodin as well as those of most lawyers involved in the 1924 trial have not come down to posterity, because of the French custom of addressing judges and pleading lawyers as *maître* and making the title part of their professional names.

unquestionable qualities of energy and tenacity. In addition, he appears to possess considerable culture.[3]

The long afternoon session was given over to testimony by witnesses. The most damaging evidence was by Crémazy, recently promoted to an administrative post in Pnompenh, who told the court how the Malrauxs and Chevasson had been shadowed from the moment they stepped off the riverboat at Siem Reap. As defense witnesses, Parmentier, still fond of Malraux, told Judge Jodin that the two "amateur archaeologists" had removed the sculptured surfaces with great care and concluded his testimony with words of praise for Malraux's flair and scholarship. The old professor spoke with an authority that no one else in the courtroom possessed, but when Judge Jodin recessed until the next morning, André was frustrated and angry.

Closing arguments were heard the following morning. Prosecutor Giordani demanded a penalty so severe that others would think twice before embarking on similar plunders. Chevasson's lawyer respectfully asked the court to take into consideration the sober and blameless life of his client, but Malraux's counsel took a different tack. De Perceveaux maintained no crime had been committed at all because the Banteai Srey ruins had not been officially classified an historical monument. How could anyone be prosecuted for entering an abandoned site and making off with a few blocks of stone? And even if the site had been classified, who had the authority to carry out such classification in the protectorate of Cambodia? The governor-general, the king of Cambodia or L'École française d'Extrême-Orient, the Paris government's appointed custodian of Indochinese archaeology?

Judge Jodin refused to entertain any argument that would raise jurisdictional questions and the following Monday, July 21, handed down his sentence—André Malraux, three years prison and five years banishment from residence in Indochina; Louis Chevasson, eighteen months imprisonment. As for the sculptures, Jodin ruled they belonged to the French government.

Although for different reasons, both prosecution and defense wished to appeal the jurisdictional point that de Perceveaux had raised and both immediately petitioned for a hearing before the Correctional Appeals Court in Saigon. Pending the appeal, the two appellants were released in their own cognizance, but forbidden to leave Indochina. September 23 was set for the appeal hearing.

In Paris, Clara contacted André's mother and faced her own family. She had never met Mrs. Malraux and when they met in the Montmartre hotel lobby, they fell into each other's arms.

Penniless and so thin as to be hardly recognizable, she confronted

[3] *L'Impartial* (July 22, 1924).

her brothers and begged for their help. When she refused to even consider divorcing her "convicted felon," she was shown the door. Her mother was suffering from nervous prostration and the family doctor was of the opinion that Clara was mentally ill and should be removed to the rest home where her mother was staying. Hardly knowing what she was doing, Clara let herself be taken to the home and found herself behind a desk confronting three doctors who urged her to be "reasonable" and submit to treatment. When this argument failed, they hinted they had the power to certify her insane. She flung herself from the room and raced across the garden. One of her brothers was at the gate with the family chauffeur and triumphantly brought her back, assuring her she was mad. Fear sharpened her wits and when the doctors insisted the best thing for her was to stay at the clinic, she said she would have to notify her father-in-law. They told her to write out a telegram that would be taken to the post office, but she said that at this point her handwriting would be such as to justify internment. For the next two hours, she stood against a wall, repeating over and over again, "You have no right to keep me here" through her tears. Finally, they gave up. The brothers allowed the family chauffeur to take her back to town.

After the driver had dropped her off at Jeanne's, she realized the family now knew where she was. After a sleepless night, she sneaked out into a gray dawn and sought refuge with Simone and André Breton. After telegrams had been dispatched to Fernand Malraux and to André's *NRF* editor friend Marcel Arland and after she had conferred on the phone with Monin and Simone Breton had filled her with coffee and given her a pair of her shoes, the surrealist leader began to organize the André Malraux defense.

Moral support had already started. "L'Affaire d'Angkor" had caused a stir in the volatile Parisian press. While most news dispatches just milked the caper for its color, depicting one Georges Malraux as being apprehended hammer and chisel in hand on top of the Angkor Wat, columnists roundly condemned the audacity of the young temple robber. But three days after Clara had arrived in Marseille, *L'Eclair* had printed an open letter from René-Louis Doyon. Exasperated by the sniping attacks on his former *chineur,* Doyon wrote a reasoned plea for Malraux and pinpointed some of the more malicious inaccuracies that had appeared in such big-circulation dailies.[4] The story of the Angkor Wat robbers had even reached America. On September 21, 1924, *The New York Times* carried the following Associated Press dispatch:

> PARIS, Aug 25 (AP)—This is the story of a Paris detective who traveled half the way round the world for his quarry, and finally, in the

[4] *L'Eclair* (Aug. 9, 1924).

dense jungle of Annam, threw aside his disguise and arrested his man, who is now doing three years in jail.

An antiquary named Malraux was under the observance of the Paris police, suspected of being responsible for thefts from French museums. It was thought he had designs on collections of antiques in one of the French provinces and as a matter of routine a detective was assigned to trail Malraux and a companion, wherever he might go.

The pair went to a seaport and there took passage on a steamer for Saigon, French Indo-China, and the detective went along in the same vessel. He did not even have time to buy a change of clothing, but made friends among the crew and borrowed what he needed.

At Saigon Malraux and his friend posed as rich travelers, anxious to see the country, while the detective kept in the background. He had, however, made known his mission to the local French authorities, and when Malraux asked for guides to the remote district of Annam, the detective was among the natives assigned, but cleverly disguised.

The party scoured the region of Angkor, rich in holy relics and fine specimens of old Chinese art, and Malraux and his friend bought freely. Also they did not hesitate, conditions being favorable, to rob Annamite temples of particularly fine specimens.

The border of Siam was not far away, and the collectors, having decided to leave the country by that route, called up the native guides and dismissed them.

Then the Paris detective had his day. The humble disguise was cast aside, the French policeman stepped out and Malraux and his friend were placed under arrest.

The *Times* headlined this wire service story, "French Sleuth Trails Man to Annam Jungle, Drops His Disguise and Arrests Robber of Paris Museums and Native Temples."

Fernand Malraux hurried to Paris, hugged his daughter-in-law and came up with sensible suggestions. Paul Monin joined the strategy sessions at the Bretons, giving the political perspective of colonial Saigon. Compared with all other Frenchmen busily exploiting Indochina, Clara and André, he said, were "spotless souls."

Doyon's open letter drew response from Florent Fels and Max Jacob. The poet congratulated Doyon on setting the record straight and somewhat cautiously put himself at the disposal of the "Malraux clan." Breton was the first of the big guns to sound off with an article in *Les Nouvelles littéraires*.[5] Monin delayed his return to Saigon to be helpful and Clara got the idea of asking the most illustrious men of letters to offer themselves as guarantors of André's talent, the promises innate in his genius and the "necessity" of his continued progress. Arland did the rest.

5 André Breton, "Pour André Malraux," *Les Nouvelles littéraires* (Aug. 16, 1924).

73

At a writers' symposium held that week in Pontigny, he circulated a hastily drawn-up petition. In its September 6 issue, *Les Nouvelles littéraires* published both text and array of signatories: "We, the undersigned, touched by the condemnation which has hit André Malraux, express our confidence in the esteem with which justice usually deals with those who contribute to improve our country's intellectual patrimony. We want to act as guarantors of the intelligence and true literary value of this personality whose youth and already-accomplished work authorize the highest hopes. We vigorously deplore the loss that results from the administering of a penalty which will prevent André Malraux from accomplishing the things we have the right to expect of him." The text was signed by André Gide, François Mauriac, Pierre Mac Orlan, Jean Paulhan, André Maurois, Jacques Rivière, Edmond Jaloux, Max Jacob, François le Gris, Roger Martin du Gard, Charles du Bos, Gaston and Raymond Gallimard, Philippe Soupault, Florent Fels, Louis Aragon, Pierre de Lanux, Guy de Pourtalès, Pascal Pia, André Harlaire, Joseph Kessel, André Desson, André Breton and Marcel Arland.

Half the signatories had never met Malraux. Some, like Rivière, wanted to be sure that the Banteai Srey adventure had no mercantile motives, something Arland assured everyone of. The lineup was as brilliant as anyone could produce in 1924, running from the Gallimard publishing brothers and Catholic Mauriac to the surrealists Aragon and Breton. Clara could congratulate herself; she had opened an unsuspected reservoir of sympathy for her husband.

The appeal was coming up. Together with Simone Breton and Marcelle Doyon, Clara raised money to keep André alive in Saigon and pay for legal costs. She arranged to sell what remained of their paintings, sculptures and most of their books.

In Saigon, Chevasson's lawyer had obtained a two-week postponement, and on October 8, André and Louis faced their new judges, confident the Pnompenh conviction would be squashed. Monin had returned to Saigon, but the defendants had already retained counsel; a maître Béziat represented André and a maître Gallois was Chevasson's lawyer.

The prosecution declared the crime was premeditated and called Malraux a vainglorious liar and not at all the scholar he claimed to be. He demanded that the three-year conviction be upheld and that the defendants be deprived of their civil rights.

Malraux's lawyer stuck to the argument that the Banteai Srey ruins belonged to no one, the *res nullius* of Roman law. He cited a number of precedents that established the government's obligation to issue a decree specifically naming a monument or national treasure before it could be legally classified. Béziat finally undertook to discredit the prosecution's contention that Malraux was simply a rapacious adventurer and liar.

74

From his bulging briefcase, he pulled the letters and articles from Paris attesting to André's literary and intellectual gifts.

Since the major points had been developed by his colleague, Counsellor Gallois spoke only briefly, describing Chevasson as a sober, hard-working young man. He maintained that neither defendant deserved the label "highwayman." Moreover, he reasoned in a calculated crescendo, if these young men were to be imprisoned for taking carved stone from Banteai Srey, should not the same penalty be meted out to various governors, high commissioners and administrators who had done the same thing? "Khmer art!" he thundered. "Khmer art, everybody has the mouth full of Khmer art since these two young men's misfortunes." Instead of ordering that they be shadowed, wouldn't it have been more generous for Crémazy and other officials to simply have warned them?

The documentation and eloquence of the defense apparently had some influence on the three magistrates of the Appeals Court. On October 28, the Court reduced Malraux's punishment to one year, Chevasson's to eight months and granted both the right to petition for a suspended sentence. The verdict meant they would never serve the terms but that the convictions became part of their permanent judicial records.

Malraux immediately announced he and Chevasson would appeal because, he said, he wanted his statues. He was never to obtain a conclusive decision as the Cour de Cassation in Paris ordered a technical retrial before three different judges of the Saigon Appeals Court. In 1925, the statues were replaced in the Banteai Srey temple wall. They remained there until 1970 when Banteai Srey was destroyed in a North Vietnamese-Khmer Rouge attack on the Siem Reap stronghold of the Lon Nol government troops.

On André's twenty-third birthday, he and Chevasson sailed for Marseille aboard a freighter, arriving in Europe in the only clothes they possessed—frayed tropical suits. They were not humiliated but laughed at the judicial adventure they had experienced. At twenty-three Malraux didn't take himself or others too seriously. Yet this first Asian adventure was to lead to a cause.

"My revolutionary commitment was in reaction to colonialism," he was to say. "Until then I had never taken sides and Indochina was the touchstone to my becoming aware of—let's simplify, 'social justice.' I became involved when I realized that for the peoples of Southeast Asia only a revolutionary movement would bring them a liberal status." [6]

Clara immediately spotted her tall, emaciated husband on the gangplank, ridiculous in his tropical suit on the rainy December Marseille dock. They flew into each other's arms and before she could ask him how

[6] Gaetan Picon, *Malraux par lui-meme* (Paris: Seuil, 1953).

he was, he told her they would be returning to Saigon in a month. "The Vietnamese need a free newspaper and Monin and I will publish one," he said, offering her a package of "Indian hemp," which when smoked, he said, provoked marvelous music and colored images. "You can direct your inner show and I'll help you by reading poetry to you" [7]

When she tried the marijuana and was "outside my being," she told him about her shipboard affair. After a while she became aware of him sitting at the foot of the bed in silent tears. "Why did you do it?" he asked quietly. Then, after a long while, "If you hadn't saved my life, I would leave you."

In Paris, they met his family and most of their friends and supporters. Fernand Malraux was doing well on the stock market apparently. He agreed his son couldn't dwell on a defeat and promised that when Clara and André reached Saigon again, there would be a check for them for 50,000 francs, or a thousand 1924 dollars. "Everyone can make a mess of things once," Fernand said, making it perfectly clear that they shouldn't come to him a second time. After visiting André's mother and grandmother, they saw Pascal Pia, Marcel Arland, the Doyons. André thanked all the signatories of the manifesto and made a special trip to Benoit-sur-Loire to see Max Jacob in his monastery. "Your wife has been fabulous," Max told him.

Although he had the time to take in Chagall's new exhibition and to renew their friendship, most of André's time was taken up with preparations for the upcoming newspaper venture. He arranged with A. Fayard and Co., publishers of the recently founded *Candide* magazine, to reprint "all articles, short stories, news items, etc., in Indochina." The price was $500 per annum. From Messageries des Journaux, a subsidiary of the giant Hachette publishers, he got Asian distribution rights for a number of supplements and bargained them into reprinting a number of articles from the as yet nonexistent Saigon newspaper.

He made Chevasson the Paris correspondent and tried to enlist the political commitment of Jacob, Breton and others. Despite vocal left-wing sympathies for Abd-el-Krim and his guerrilla efforts to resist French advances in Morocco, no one was particularly interested in Malraux's conscience-raising plans for Indochina. Jacob was deep into his religious period, Breton was busy writing the Second Surrealist Manifesto and the Left in general was busy commenting on Stalin's elimination of Leon Trotsky from power, a first intimation of things being less than perfect in the Soviet Union everybody fervently believed in.

Two days before their scheduled departure, the publisher Bernard Grasset offered Malraux a three-novel contract and a $900 advance, solely on the strength of a letter recommendation from Mauriac, Grasset's star author.

[7] Pierre Galante, *Malraux,* op. cit.

76

Clara and André sailed for Saigon in January 1925. They were in third-class and spent a horrible month aboard the ship, segregated by sex—six women passengers to one cabin, six men to another. All they could think about was the journalistic enterprise lying ahead and the three books André was to write, books sure to be set in the Asia they both loved and half feared.

When they reached Saigon to begin their second Asian adventure, Paul Monin was waiting for them on the dock.

> I want comrades and not saints. No confidence in saints.
>
> *Man's Fate*

7

Paul Monin and André Malraux knew little about newspapering. Monin was a brilliant lawyer who believed the solution to colonialism was not so much a matter of ideology and class struggle as of respect for basic human rights; Malraux knew a lot about publishing, was full of ideals and could write biting editorials, but he knew little about deadlines and straight news reporting. Monin was—with a Creole grandmother—the son of a wealthy Lyons family. He had married a distant cousin and in 1919 had come to Vietnam with his wife and their newborn son, Guillaume. Mrs. Monin had remained infirm after the childbirth, had not been able to adjust to Southeast Asia's tropical climate and had been forced to return to France for a prolonged convalescence. He had stayed on and, in a very few years, had become an exceptional member of the Saigon bar. Interested in politics, he had run for the Colonial Council, lost and, in a second try in 1922, had been elected with a comfortable margin, the only progressive in this assembly of ruling notables. He had been defeated by the establishment candidate in the 1924 legislative elections and was now the rallying point of those minority forces among the colonial French who were progressive and left of center and a first uneasy bridge toward the awakening indigenous aspirations. He needed a mouthpiece and counted his meeting Clara and André among his better fortunes.

The twenty-five million Vietnamese, Laotians and Cambodians living under French rule had few rights. None of them had the right to vote, only about a thousand of them could ever hope for higher education. The French civil service had more power than the Mandarin conquerors of earlier centuries had ever had. Various taxes on crops were so high that the Annamite peasantry got to keep only a fourth of their harvests. Annamites—but not Frenchmen—could be imprisoned for debt and there was a tax on salt that was even more distressing than the similar levy in India since it applied to a population whose basic food was fish and rice.

78

Yet compared to India or even to the Dutch East Indies, conditions in the French colonies of Cochin Chine, the quasi-colony of Tonkin and the three protectorates Annam, Laos and Cambodia were tolerable. Mahatma Gandhi's entry into politics in 1921 had been marked by the jailings of 20,000 Indians for civil disobedience and sedition, and during one month of 1922, British authorites had imprisoned another 10,000 for political offenses; Gandhi's march to the sea to protest the British salt monopoly, which landed 60,000 Indians in jail, was still a few years away. In the Dutch East Indies, Indonesians who had helped Dutchman Hendricus Sneevlier create the Indies Social-Democratic Union were sentenced to hard labor for life and Sneevlier deported back to Holland.

But to the Vietnamese, Laotians, Cambodians and their French rulers, events in colonial India, Dutch Indonesia, Portuguese Macao or Japanese Korea were minor sideshows compared to the convulsions taking place in China. The huge country to the north had long since lost its coherence. It was a semifeudal country in perpetual civil war being modernized from without by competing expansionist powers—Great Britain and Japan and, to a lesser degree, the United States and the new Soviet Union. Rival warlords with private armies controlled entire provinces and fought each other with a barbarity that hadn't changed since the Middle Ages. The warlords, sometimes manipulated by one or another foreign interest, sometimes operating as simple bandits, shifted their alliances continually while the Nationalist government, the Kuomintang, tried to impose its will on the four hundred million Chinese, of whom barely five million lived in cities.

The leader of the Kuomintang—the "people's party" formed by intellectuals who had studied abroad and somehow representing everything that belonged to the twentieth century in China—was the aging Sun Yat-sen, a converted Christian educated in the United States. Sun had become provisional president of a newly declared Republic of China after the 1911 overthrow of the effete Manchu dynasty. Without control of the army he had soon found himself powerless and driven from Peking by shifting combinations of warlords backed by foreign powers. In 1920, however, he had managed to set up an opposition government in Canton, in the south. His aim, and that of the Kuomintang, was to forge an army strong enough to march northward against Peking and finally create a unified Chinese Republic.

Cholon, Saigon's huge Chinese community with its own pipeline to events up north, was abuzz with rumors. In October 1924, a workers' demonstration in Canton had turned into a bloodbath when a volunteer corps sponsored by Cantonese merchants had slaughtered the workers, only to be routed in turn by a "workers' army," organized by the Kuomintang. As Monin and Malraux outlined the scope of the political action of their soon-to-be-born newspaper, Sun Yat-sen died of cancer.

Sun had been at the lowest ebb of his national leadership in 1922. Frustrated by his inability to attract either Western or Japanese aid and out of sorts with his Canton warlord host, he had withdrawn to Shanghai. There, he had sought help from the Comintern—the term for the Third International founded in Petrograd in 1919 at the instigation of Leon Trotsky at an international conference chaired by Lenin himself. The Comintern provided militant communists all over the world with a central organization and, as an intended part of Soviet foreign policy, fomented and supported revolution wherever appropriate.

The Soviet commissar serving with the Kuomintang was a revolutionary Malraux was soon to hear about through the Cholon grapevine—Mikhail Borodin, who before the Russian Revolution had been a schoolteacher in Chicago and who one day was to beg André to intercede on his behalf with Stalin. Born Mikhail Grusenberg in 1884 in Vitebsk, the same village as Chagall, Borodin had joined the Jewish Social Democratic Bund in his teens, switched to the Bolshevik Party in 1903 and three years later had been arrested and exiled for revolutionary activities. He had emigrated to the United States and after a term at the University of Indiana at Valparaiso, had set up a school for immigrants in Chicago. When Lenin's Bolsheviks overthrew the czar, he had returned to Russia and become an agent in Mexico, Scandinavia and England, spending six months in prison for inciting a riot in Glasgow before being deported.

In 1923, Lenin had made Borodin the Soviet commissar to China. His job was to direct the Chinese revolutionary activities in accordance with orthodox Marxist lines, that is, toward helping the "bourgeois" revolution of the Kuomintang and Chiang Kai-shek. The small Communist Party of China accepted the Soviet view that there was as yet no basis for installing socialism in China because the proletariat was very small and no Marxist revolution could possibly be based on a peasant uprising. Since Borodin was acting on the orders of the Executive Committee of the Communist Party of the USSR, he was not to be held responsible for the disastrous outcome of this policy when Chiang massacred his communist allies in Shanghai in 1927.

Monin installed Clara and André at Saigon's Continental Hotel in the heart of the European district, close to his law office and to the office space they rented in the Rue Taberd for *L'Indochine,* as they decided to call their daily newspaper. If all went according to plans, the first issue would appear in June 1925.

In the meantime, Monin took Malraux on a trip through rural Vietnam to introduce him to the physical dimension of the colonial reality and, together with Clara, began to put a staff together.

The trip to the country first took Monin and Malraux to Phan-Thiet, a fishing town northeast of Saigon famous for its "nuoc-mam," the national fish spice sauce. At Phan-Thiet, where fifteen years earlier Ho

80

Chi Minh had taught school, they met a friend of Monin who ran a garage. Their arrival coincided with an outbreak of pestilence and they hurried on to the Dalat highlands where they ran into coolies fleeing rubber plantation "recruiters" and saw one emaciated man die on a straw mat. Vietnamese rubber plantation laborers were contracted for three years, encouraged to run up debt in company stores and kept on subsistence salaries. When recruiters came to outlying villages, able-bodied men fled into the jungle.

In Cambodia, things were worse. Villagers were taxed according to a census that no longer corresponded to reality. As in Gogol's Russia, dead souls were counted for live to increase the tax yield.

Back in Saigon, Sun Yat-sen's death gave Clara and André a firsthand insight into colonial justice. A Chinese merchant named Huyn Vikanh was jailed—authorities said "kept under surveillance"—for having collected money among the Cholon Chinese for the Kuomintang on the occasion of the Chinese leader's death. It took all of lawyer Monin's considerable persuasive powers to transform Huyn's incarceration into a deportation to his homeland.

If the *L'Indochine* staff was limited it was dedicated. Dejean de la Batie, the son of a French diplomat and a Vietnamese mother, was the managing editor. He had been recruited from *L'Echo Annamite,* a small paper owned by Vietnam's only authentic political figure, Nguyen Phan Long, and had a ready answer for anyone accusing him of leaving the Vietnamese for the Europeans: "Being neither fish nor fowl, I have the appreciable advantage of being both at the same time, although my natural inclination is toward the underdog." [1] Another Eurasian, Louis Minh, who owned a sizeable printing plant and had civil service printing contracts, was commissioned to print *L'Indochine.* Others were Phan van Truonh, and two young intellectuals, Hinh and Vinh. Vinh was a gentle young man, dominated by his mother, subtle and courageous, while Hinh, the son of a mandarin from Hue, was touchy and fervid, a ticking bomb ready to go off any moment. Vinh became close to Clara and one day introduced her to his secret fiancée, a tiny girl even more timid than he. Every night he dreaded returning to his mother who knew nothing of his political activities or of his clandestine liaison. He was to become Malraux's model for Hong in *The Conquerors* and, to a large extent, for Ch'en in *Man's Fate.* Somewhat later, the little staff was to be joined by Nguyen Pho, a native of Hanoi whom everybody was later to suspect of being a police informer.

The first issue would appear in early June, it was decided. At the hotel at night, André pasted and repasted the dummy of the first issue.

Before publication, it was decided to send polyglot Clara to Singapore to line up collaboration with one of the vastly superior English-

---

[1] Clara Malraux, *Les Combats et les jeux* (Paris: Grasset, 1969).

language newspapers of the Crown Colony and to send the eloquent André to Hanoi to seek the blessings or at least the tacit neutrality of the governor-general.

Clara was shadowed by an undercover agent during her three-day stay in Singapore. She saw the editor-in-chief of *The Straits Times,* who grinningly admitted he had no high regard for the French press in Saigon and agreed to an exchange of news stories. André's mission was more delicate. Press laws demanded prior government approval for Chinese or Quoc-ngu-language newsprint. French-language newspapers, while theoretically free, were subject to intimidating bureaucracy.

Since relatively few Annamites read French, what Monin and Malraux really wanted was the right to publish part of their newspaper in Quoc-ngu. Interim governor-general P.I. Monguillot refused to see Malraux. His secretary claimed that native-language newspapers already gave the administration enough headaches and refused permission to print in Quoc-ngu. André returned to Saigon convinced of the government's as yet vague but nevertheless very real hostility.

They all wanted everything to be just right and the first issue was set and reset during a heat wave that made tropical Saigon nearly unbearable. One noisy ceiling fan gave the front office the impression of a clammy breeze—it also made all paper not weighted down sail through the air. The composing room where they did their own proofreading was a sweltering oven without a fan.

After still more delays, *L'Indochine*—"a daily newspaper dedicated to Franco-Annamite rapprochement"—appeared, undated, June 17, and all 5,000 copies were distributed free, Clara unloading armfuls of the eight-page newssheet herself in the Rue Catinat. The leading article was a Paris-datelined interview with Paul Painlevé, the brilliant Sorbonne mathematician but rather ineffectual politician who had been premier for two months during the darkest days of 1917 and who since April was again the head of a French government. Painlevé had granted the interview to Jean Bouchor three weeks before his ascension to power, but what he had to say was of interest to anyone in Indochina. The soon-to-be-premier said that the Indochinese people "should have an advisory voice in the affairs of the colony," that since education was the best means of assimilation, Annamites should have access to all levels of French schooling and that both the "French and indigenous press should be free." *L'Indochine* was off to a commanding start.

The next day, *L'Indochine* contained a defiant attack on Maurice Cognacq, the interim governor of Cochin Chine, written by Malraux, and on July 8, Malraux scornfully attacked Henry de Lachevrotière, the publisher of *L'Impartial.*

A land scandal was the first controversy the new daily plunged into. On July 27, the government would auction off 21,000 acres in Camau, the southernmost region of Vietnam and the richest agricultural area of the whole of Indochina. *L'Impartial* and *Le Courrier saigonnais* had given ample space to Cognacq's inspection tour of Camau, stressing how the governor had made sure illiterate peasants would not be exploited by French settlers or plantation syndicates.

On July 23, Cognacq visited Saigon and on the eve of his arrival, Malraux ran a page one editorial denouncing the upcoming Camau "auction" as the third scandal the governor, together with Lachevrotière, was allegedly involved in, the two others being a monopoly in the Port of Saigon and an alleged real estate swindle in Khan Hoa. In the present case, Malraux wrote, "not one French paper in Saigon apart from this journal printed the collective petition from the dispossessed Camau proprietors."

L'Indochine's intervention proved salutary to the public coffers, insofar as the exposure nearly tripled the price of the 21,000 acres. Cognacq and a syndicate of investors had expected to buy the land for 100,000 piastres ($200,000), but the final going price was 280,000 piastres.

The small office in the Rue Taberd was a center of happy, conspiratorial effervescence. Clara and Vinh had their desks in the back, she writing a fashion and beauty-hints column and translating explosive items from *The Straits Times;* he interviewing often frightened Annamites. A few Europeans also showed up, often with stories that were unverifiable— Saigon's mayor Rouelle, who had won against a government candidate in the 1925 elections, a drugstore owner from the provinces. When Monin and André weren't off to Louis Minh's printing shop with copy and proofs, they wrote editorials and polemics and read them out loud. If hard news was never their forte, mordant polemics with *L'Impartial* and the other establishment sheets was. When *L'Impartial* tried to discredit Monin by reprinting the Chinese original of a *China News* dispatch concerning Monin as proof that the lawyer had become "a paid adviser" to the Kuomintang, Malraux wrote an open letter to Lachevrotière on the front page of *L'Indochine,* accusing the publisher of falsifying the translation. "We request anyone who is curious about your recklessness to look up in the public library the third and fourth ideographs below the dot, on the left, in the Sino-French dictionary. If they don't mean 'law, legislation' I will give the cost of 1,800 secret subscriptions to *L'Impartial* to the distinguished sinologist who will give me their meaning." Even Clara managed to provoke *L'Impartial.* When she found and translated a dispatch telling how Koreans had poisoned their own wells to protest against Japanese oppression, the Lachevrotière paper accused *L'Indochine* of inciting the Vietnamese to follow suit.

The days were never long enough. The next day's paper was written and edited during the day, printed at Louis Minh's at night and hit the street in the early afternoon. Between 5:00 P.M. and the sudden tropical nightfall everybody relaxed. Often Monin and André went up on the roof terrace for a half-hour's swordplay. Both were passably good with épées and fencing was about the only sport André was ever to practice. To egg them on, Trinh, Minh and Clara occasionally made bets on who would win.

Sometimes Clara was off visiting with friends and smoking opium—the first time she vomited in the rickshaw taking her back to the Rue Taberd. Her friends included an import-export businessman and his wife and an older widow, Yvonne, a former socialist agitator, who taught her how she could abort herself.

In the evening, they met again in Monin's law office, at the paper or in restaurants, usually to discuss political action with Vietnamese. Clara was always the only woman.

At the end of June, André received good news from home. On the 15th, the Cour de Cassation had squashed his and Louis Chevasson's conviction of the previous October. The victory was far from complete, however, because the decision was on a narrow jurisdictional question of infringement of court gag rules during the October 9 session. The high court did not pronounce itself on the guilt or innocence of the defendants but referred the case back to the Saigon Appellate Court for retrial before new justices. In its June 29 issue, *L'Indochine* carried the story, stretching the truth a bit when it said the conviction had been overruled "because coded police evidence of a confidential and political nature had been withheld from the defense."

L'Indochine was the only Saigon daily to carry up-to-date news from China and to follow the rapidly deteriorating situation of the confrontation of Great Britain and the Kuomintang government. On June 18, the Kuomintang ordered all Chinese crews on British ships to walk off their jobs. Two days later, *L'Indochine* made space for a last-minute bulletin "from our special correspondent," saying "All British ships stopped. Yesterday at two o'clock a general strike was declared by the crews of all the British vessels." On June 23, *L'Indochine* reported that Chinese drafts were no longer accepted in English banks and that the Kuomintang government had ordered Chinese ships to sail directly to Canton. Two days later it ran a story about street fighting in Canton and on June 26 said Canton was under a state of siege, that Europeans were sending women and children to Hong Kong and were fortifying themselves at the foreign concession of Shameen.

In the columns of *L'Indochine,* the Hong Kong-Canton events were seen as proof that Asians could muster physical forces to challenge a great European power and, perhaps more important, that a native government could command great moral strength. This moral force, the newspaper opined, was the consequence of the principle that people had the

84

right to self-determination and of "the dispersal of certain republican ideals that France had always propagated."

Such views both frightened and angered Cognacq, Monguillot, Lachevrotière and the rest of the establishment figures, who were convinced Chiang Kai-shek and the Kuomintang had engineered the disturbances in Hong Kong and Canton to further international communism. Monin and his staff countered with informative interviews and editorials that, indirectly, proved the colonial rulers were right in fearing a spread of the Hong Kong-Canton fever. Sun Fo, the son of Sun Yat-sen, was interviewed and stressed that in order to achieve its goal—China's freedom—the Kuomintang party had accepted anyone willing to help, including communists. Another Kuomintang leader, Dr. You Wenchew, went further and attacked oppressive measures adopted by Governor Cognacq, especially restrictions on news from China, as prejudicial to the future of the French colonies.

When Lachevrotière had translated the *China News* ideogram for "legal counsel" as "paid adviser," he had only been technically wrong. The burning China issue sucked Monin—and Malraux—deeper and deeper into open opposition, not only in the columns of their defiant little paper but also in direct political action.

While de la Batie and Clara managed to talk Hinh out of attempting to assassinate Cognacq during an upcoming public ceremony, Monin and Malraux attended secret meetings in Cholon. The Chinese community had been an early financial backer of *L'Indochine* and Monin and the Malrauxs had become members of the local Kuomintang party in a noisy ceremony in a sweltering restaurant. The Cholon Kuomintang leaders were Dong Thuan and Dang Dai. The latter was a cultivated and eloquent teacher who had been to Europe and with whom André spent long hours. Through the Cholon pipeline, Monin learned that French arms had shown up in the hands of marauding warlords in southern China. In a signed editorial the next day, he quoted Kuomintang foreign affairs minister Wu Chao-tu as protesting these sales to the French consul in Hong Kong, adding that the essential motivation for European presence in China was greed, that the huge country had become little more than "an immense battlefield where the appetites of all the great powers confront one another."

L'Indochine began to interest police, something Clara couldn't help find flattering. There had been various indications—their postman had told them their mail was being scrutinized at the post office and several subscribers had come by the office to say officials had asked them why they supported "a Bolshevik paper." Clara and André had the distinct impression they were being followed. To be sure, they one day split and quickly ducked into opposite side streets. Sure enough at the intersection a man stood looking confused.

Had police infiltrated them? One morning, de la Batie, Hinh and Vinh came to Clara and told her they had spent several nights tailing Nguyen Pho. Every night he had eaten in luxury restaurants where a dinner cost more than any one of them earned in a week and they had discovered that he had moved into his own house. When Pho came into the office, they all avoided his eyes. A few days later when Clara was spending the late afternoon siesta alone stretched in a wicker chair on the roof, a shadow slid toward her and stopped. It was Pho saying he had to talk to her, "the first white woman who had treated me like a friend."

"Clara, you have no right to doubt me. I give you my word of honor that I have nothing to do with police. Hinh, Vinh and Dejean are wrong in suspecting me. They have proof of my loyalty. I wouldn't betray my friends for money."

Why shouldn't I believe him? I believe so easily what people tell me? But why shouldn't I believe the others? They had solid arguments.

"Clara."

I felt his voice insisted too much.

"Pho, I don't want to judge. You should talk to them."

"It's you I want to convince, Clara. I can't live with the idea that you despise me."

"Why do the others believe . . ."

"I don't know. They often speak out of tune, sometimes in places where they'd be better off keeping their mouths shut. We're being watched, you know that." [2]

They let Pho stay. One day twenty years later, Pho rang the doorbell of Clara's Paris apartment. He was barely seated before he told her that the people they had worked with in Saigon back in 1925 had been men without character. "You were wrong in having confidence in them. They accused me of being a police informer; then, after you left, they made me managing director."

The Hong Kong-Canton events held the front page attention, but sometimes *L'Indochine* had to admit it had no news from China. An item in the July 17 issue noted that although all communications with Hong Kong had been cut, it had obtained telegraphic information in "roundabout ways" and the next day it presented a series of bulletins on the effects of the work stoppage by nearly 500,000 men; the population of the Crown Colony was reduced by one third, most of the newspapers were shut down, the English had to do all household chores themselves and many firms were closed due to lack of native help. "The strikers have obtained their results by taking measures against the members of the families of those who refuse to go out on strike."

In the June 30 issue, Than van Truong summed up *L'Indochine*'s position by saying that the events in China were a lesson for the future,

[2] Clara Malraux, op. cit.

86

not a threat of an immediate communist revolt. "Let us hope that the governments of Europe and the United States will draw from the present events the lesson necsesary to modify their attitude toward Asia and eventually arrive at a sincere and lasting reconciliation of two races which, although they are so different in color, nevertheless represent the most advanced elements of mankind." Perhaps even more prophetically an anonymous Annamite contributor warned that exasperated Vietnamese, unable to wait for the fulfillment of French promises, might move, not toward communism, but toward the communists. "And the communists, here as in many other countries in Asia, might be welcome, because of their promises to respect the rights of the oppressed, as saviors."

What did editor Malraux write? In the August 14 issue, he published "Selection of Energies," "the first of a series of articles in which we will examine our colonization, its virtues and defects, and the hopes it has given birth to. These articles will also suggest certain methods of conciliation."

Taking a long view of colonialism and French presence in Asia, Malraux wondered whether the colonial system could accommodate the inevitable demands for reforms and whether France wasn't really backing the wrong side. Since young Annamites were deprived of any possibility of education in France, they might rise in revolt. The crime was not that the French were colonizers, but that Frenchmen failed to recognize their logical allies—the young Annamites who possessed the great energies and among whom were students so determined to acquire an education that they stowed away on ships to China, England and America, preparing themselves for the time when Indochina would be free.

The article ended with concrete proposals—that Cognacq either recognize the Annamites' right to travel or create a special commission in Hanoi to examine individual requests, a commission responsible to the public for its decisions. "This would allow us to show that we know better than to raise against us one of the purest, most beautiful and perfect clusters of energy any great colonial power can hope to direct."

The continuation of Malraux's series was never to appear because with the August 14 issue, L'Indochine suspended publication. By that date, the colonial administration had had enough and choked off the little newssheet by simply pressuring Louis Minh to stop printing it.

It had taken the colonial powers two months to silence the feisty little paper which had dared to castigate the Cognacq administration, to expose the collusion if not the corruption of its officers, to urge Annamites to demand reforms and to go so far as to espouse and publicize the Kuomintang revolutionary cause. Indirectly, the pressure had started to build in July when Lachevrotière's L'Impartial began a smear campaign, accusing Monin and Malraux of being "Bolsheviks," a campaign that increased in stridency with the growing unrest in China. On July 17, L'Impartial had unearthed the Huyn Vi-kanh affair, pointing to Monin's defense of the Chinese merchant as proof that the lawyer was a communist committed "to drive France from the Far East by bringing about the union of the Chinese people and the people of Indochina."

Monin and Co. had almost won—by default. The new Leftist government in Paris appointed Alexandre Varenne, a socialist member of the National Assembly, the next governor-general of Indochina; in its July 31 issue, *L'Indochine* had hailed the appointment of "this friend of liberty" as a harbinger of "numerous and productive reforms." But Cognacq had pulled a fast one. On August 14, Minh came to the Rue Taberd offices to tell Monin and Malraux that he could no longer print their paper. He had been told in no uncertain terms that if he continued to accept work from the "Bolsheviks," he might suffer a drop in government printing jobs and a typographers strike in his plant. Monin immediately tried to find another printer but all other shops in Saigon, it seemed, had gotten the word.

Monin and his team refused to lie down. Since the Rue Taberd offices included a printing press, all they needed was type. They had no illusions about finding printing material locally and an editorial bull session decided Clara and André should go to Hong Kong to buy and bring back type so *L'Indochine* could be launched again, preferably before the end of Cognacq's governorship.

On the bridge of the ship taking them across the China Sea, André nonchalantly told Clara he had been told by an officer that the captain had just radioed ahead to warn British authorities that he had on board his ship "the reddest Bolshevik in all Annam." To feel better, Clara and André threw overboard the daybook pages containing a few Hong Kong names and addresses. But the Crown Colony was paralyzed by a general strike by all Chinese and messages to colonial authorities had a way of falling on strange ears. When the ship docked, the Malrauxs were the only passengers whose suitcases were carried ashore by coolie baggage handlers, a telling gesture by a people in insurrection toward those it knew to be on its side.

Their luck held. The next day they learned that the local Jesuits, who published a modest paper, were modernizing their printing shop and selling their old type. Clara and André got the address and in the noonday heat began scaling the Peak until coolies caught up with them and mutely forced them into rickshaws for the remainder of the climb. The view was magnificent, the strike-silenced harbor below, Kowloon and the Chinese mainland behind them. The Jesuits received them cordially. A part of the type would only be available in a week, but the rest was at their disposal immediately. The transaction was accomplished in no time and the fathers even promised to have the type delivered to their Saigon-bound vessel and to forward the remaining cases a week later.

Clara and André had imagined all sorts of difficulties, long searches and uncanny complicities. Instead they found themselves tourists until their return to Saigon. According to Clara, they spent one exquisite evening as the guests of a British tiger hunter they had met on the ship and made an excursion to Portuguese Macao to take in the sites of vice, playing fantong, watching teen-age prostitutes wait for clients with their families and peering into opium dens. "This false vacation lasted four or five days," she was to write. "We knew manifestations protesting crushing treaties were taking place in Canton, Peking and Hankow. We took part in this action through our newspaper, which must have had some importance since authorities had tried to suppress it. But we would be returning to Saigon with the means of its rebirth." [3]

On the dock, the Malrauxs distractedly signed papers and watched the quayside crane lift their boxes of type into the hold of their Saigon-bound ship. On the dockside in Saigon, they saw the type being unloaded and confiscated, on the pretext that certain papers had been filled out incorrectly at the port of embarkation. But a week later the smaller consignment the Jesuit fathers had forwarded themselves arrived and cleared customs with ecclesiastic punctuality. It was with this second batch of type that the paper was to be resurrected.

[3] Clara Malraux, op. cit.

> I see in Europe a carefully ordered barbarity,
> where the idea of civilization and the idea of order are
> daily confused.
>
> *The Temptation of the West*

8

Nearly three months separated the folding of *L'Indochine* and the birth, a day after André's twenty-third birthday, of its successor and those three months were to be the most mysterious period of Malraux's life. If he was in China, if he met Borodin and Mao Tse-tung, if he became one of the Committee of Twelve, if he took part in the Canton insurrection, if he helped patch up differences between the Kuomintang and the Chinese communists and as reward was named Commissioner of Propaganda for the Twantung and Kwangsi provinces, it would all have had to happen between the August 14 suspension of publication of *L'Indochine* and the November 4 launching of *L'Indochine enchaînée* (Indochina in Chains).

A legend was to grow of Malraux as a people's commissar of Mao's ragged armies, hero of the 1925 Canton uprising, if not the 1927 Shanghai insurrection. Over the years, Malraux was to learn to answer inquisitive questions with half-confidences, heavy silences and sometimes bafflingly accurate details, all adding to the legendary persona of the magnified *homme engagé* thrust into the crucible of dangerous and significant events.

Malraux was never above adding to the colorful apocrypha himself. In a 1933 letter to Edmund Wilson thanking the American critic for his review of *The Conquerors,* he was to write: "I went to Asia at the age of twenty-three in charge of an archaeological mission. I abandoned archaeology, organized the Jeune Annam movement then became Kuomintang commissar in Indochina and later in Canton." [1] Malraux was not to coincide with the legend until the mid-1930s when, ironically, he had begun to outgrow the need for it. Yet for half a century rather than setting the record straight he was to stand accused by Leftist leaders of the worst kind of opportunism. In 1937, for example, Leon Trotsky was to com-

---

[1] Edmund Wilson, *Shores of Light: A Literary Chronicle of the Twenties and Thirties* (New York: Farrar, Straus and Young, Inc., 1952).

90

plain that Malraux had worked for the "Comintern-Kuomintang alliance and as such had been one of those responsible for the strangling of the Chinese revolution." [2]

The only piece of objective testimony to the China Connection was by writer-diplomat Paul Morand, a prolific author. Morand described how he had arrived in Hong Kong on his way to a new posting in Bangkok in August 1925, "exactly at the same time as Malraux arrived from Canton, coming from Saigon." Upon arriving in Bangkok, Morand fell gravely ill and in November was taken to Saigon and hospitalized, one day to receive the visit of Malraux. "I saw him come in looking like a ghost," Morand was to write, "pale, thin, looking like a hunted man, he was infinitely sicker than the patients around me." [3]

Clara and André were in Hong Kong buying type from the missionaries. Did they push on the extra eighty miles to Canton? Clara was to say no. Did André meet Borodin, whom he was to describe so vividly in *Les Conquérants*? Clara was to say no. Monin and Dang Dai in Cholon knew Borodin and could have described the Soviet commissar in sufficient detail for André to assemble the rich portrait. Did André go to Canton alone from Saigon? Clara was to say they never had the money for the three-thousand-mile round-trip railway ticket. But what is deducted from Malraux's documentary knowledge of China must be added to his gift as a writer. Between 1928 and 1932, he was to complete four novels, all set in Asia and three of them saluted for their quasi-journalistic authenticity. Two of them were set in a China in revolt and both were hailed for brilliantly conveying the fever, progress and horror of revolution. One of them was a masterpiece, hailed as perhaps the first book to reveal the true nature of the century's politics in action and for its eyewitness feel for a convulsed China. If *The Temptation of the West,* with its Spenglerian title, was a "remote" exchange of views between a young Chinese intellectual in Europe and a young European visiting Asia, and *The Royal Way* was about an archaeologist and an adventurer in the jungles of Cambodia, *Les Conquérants* and *La Condition humaine* were retellings of the 1925 Canton events and the Chiang Kai-shek forces' slaughter of Shanghai's communists in 1927. The events in Canton did not take place the way Malraux described them, but *The Conquerors* was to contain powerful images—street scenes from Shameen, feverish meetings, children running after demonstrators with crimson flags. What also made *Man's Fate* a modern classic was its evocative images of a city under siege, of the enemy's armored train whistling in the night, of a terrorized terrorist hurling himself with his bomb against the wrong official car. André was not in Canton in 1925 nor in Shanghai two years later. He and Clara were to make a visit during an around-the-world trip in 1931—his only visit to China until his

2 Leon Trotsky, *Une littérature de fossoyers.*
3 Paul Morand, *Papiers d'identité* (Paris: Grasset, 1931).

91

ministerial mission in 1965. In the fall of November 1925, he was a very engagé journalist in Saigon anxious to get his paper off the ground again.

When *L'Indochine enchaînée* began publishing November 4, it was more fly sheet than newspaper, reduced in size and in frequency but defiantly printed on the old press under Monin's veranda and determined to attack the government until it drew blood. Reduced to half the size of *L'Indochine,* it was a biweekly, appearing on Wednesdays and Saturdays. According to a front page editorial in the first issue it was a temporary newspaper "awaiting the day, certainly far distant, when the government will agree to return the type that belongs to us." Above the list of contents was a wood-block caricature of Maurice Cognacq looking like a stuck pig.

The missionaries' type had no accents and the first issue looked characteristically un-French. One evening, while Monin and Malraux were out, Clara received a strange visit of five Vietnamese men clad in black kai-ao robes.

> Their hands were busy under their long robes and finally came up with a tiny bundle. Before handing it to me, they bowed deeply as you do to a person you respect—the *lai* salute they had refused to execute when facing government employees. Very quickly their skilfull hands—they were typographers used to handling minute masses—untied the corners of their offering—type stolen at work, a hundred characters with *accents graves, aigus* or circumflexes. . . . I would have wanted to express our gratitude, our desire to work on their behalf, but I was alone and I didn't know any Vietnamese. So I got up and, with closed hands like a Chinese *quaninh,* I bowed deeply.

There was something provisional about *L'Indochine enchaînée,* something touching and slightly out of touch also. Political positions were hardening to the left and to the right of the little paper and its directors, Malraux and Monin.

Dejean de la Batie was the first defection, leaving them to return to *La Cloche fêlée,* the satirical journal Monin and Malraux had lured him away from six months earlier. Imperceptibly, public opinion among educated Annamites was beginning to leave behind the reforms Monin and Malraux stood for—André's galvanizing of Indochinese "energies"—in favor of as yet vague national aspirations.

In their editorials, Monin and Malraux believed that Indochina had reached a turning point but that it was not yet too late to reform the colonial government, although time was running out. When it came to concrete proposals they suggested social reforms. André wrote a long piece about infant mortality, saying the government could easily reduce the appallingly high death rate by a concerted propaganda effort. He said leaflets could be distributed demonstrating how women should look after their

92

newborn babies and that if the leaflets were expressed in pictures so much the better.

Monin and Malraux put all their hopes in the new governor-general. They published eloquent "open letters" to Alexandre Varenne, Monin predicting that the arrival of the socialist governor "will mark the inevitable hour of chastisement." On November 19, the day after his arrival in Saigon, they wrote that "for this country, governor Cognacq had done as much harm as a war," and pleaded with Varenne not to be blinded by the brilliance of his reception, that tragedy lurked behind that comedy of errors.

Varenne's first day in Saigon was sweet music to liberal ears. He had appeared in a plain dark suit instead of the governor-general's uniform and had refused to take part in ceremonies "paid for by Annamite taxpayers." But from there on it seemed to be all compromises and sellouts to the vested interests of the colonial establishment. He, or his secretary, refused to meet Monin and Malraux and it was first with sadness, then in anger, they heard his official speeches stressing that his first order of business was social reform "not Annamite reforms" and that in regard to alleged abuses of power in the past, it was best to forget. Before the end of November, *L'Indochine enchaînée* sarcastically wrote: "yesterday a socialist, today a conservative . . . yet another conversion under the sign of the piastre."

Before Varenne, himself a former journalist, left for his official residency in Hanoi, the liberals tried to at least make him *promise* reforms. Nguyen Phan Long invited him to a meeting at City Hall and politely formulated several Annamite demands, including the immediate lifting of press censorship. Varenne's answer made the assembled progressives' blood freeze in their veins. He predicted that if the freedom of the press was granted immediately and if, as a result Annamites would, through extravagant expressions of their ideas, provoke troubles throughout the country, the resulting reactionary backlash would be of such proportions to sweep away all progress already accomplished.

Varenne's short administration, as it were, was to be less negative than his first ten days would have one believe. Actually expelled from the Socialist Party for having accepted the Indochina post, he was essentially an honest man who did what he could. By the time he resigned in September 1926, he had abolished imprisonment for debt for Annamites, a tremendous relief for the millions of peasants crushed under taxes and debt loads at usury interest rates. He had increased Annamite representation in local councils, made University of Hanoi degrees acceptable in France, reinforced real estate legislation and created a short-lived cooperative bank. Clara and André were to run into Varenne in 1933 during an Arctic cruise. He was anxious to be introduced and, Clara was to write, "for a moment I was silly enough to feel that to meet Varenne and his wife somehow compromised us and to get upset when a photo was taken of the four of us against the backdrop of an iceberg. That was childish, and I was the first to admit it."

In early December there was an attempt on Monin's life. One night, the lawyer woke up to see the mosquito netting around his bed drawn aside and the shadow of a Vietnamese lean toward him with an open razor. Monin careened off the other side and so surprised the would-be assassin that the man ran to the balcony, jumped into the garden and disappeared into the night. The scene was to become the opening of *Man's Fate*.

Monin told everybody the next morning—Clara knew only André's Gilette safety razor and for a while couldn't figure out how a razor could be a murder weapon—and all agreed the would-be assassin must have been paid by police to arrange a murder that would look like a suicide.

The Malrauxs spent a depressing Christmas. They were broke, sick and tired; Clara barely over an abortion performed by her friend Yvonne—it was not the moment to have a child—André, as Paul Morand had noted from his hospital bed, looking pale and emaciated. And their relations with Monin were deteriorating. Mrs. Monin and her young son joined the lawyer following a lengthy convalescence. The birth of her child had left her physically diminished, a severe attack of phlebitis practically reduced her to a wheelchair and her presence in the big home, now turned into a printing plant, put between the two couples a distance that the imminent failure of the newspaper couldn't help but exacerbate. As Clara was to put it:

> We could hardly hide it from ourselves anymore, the printing-boat was about to sink and, without panicking, those onboard began, not so much to consider fleeing, as to think about new possibilities. Monin moved closer to the Kuomintang. André remembered the Bernard Grasset contract. He wrote a letter to the publisher, mentioning a book in the works and, sometime in November told me: "Now, the only solution left is to write." Defeat performs curious transmutations on people, all of us seemed to be our own caricature. I saw myself, now madwoman now crybaby, unable to keep up with my own self-esteem, still less with my own ideals. Him? How many hours did I spend trying to understand him without hurting my idea of him, without hurting myself.
>
> We were already thinking about leaving. Monin was thinking about Canton; we about our return, although we didn't have the means.[4]

The fare of their passage back to France was found—a not entirely disinterested gift from the Cholon community leaders. Dang Dai, the Kuomintang intellectual who was to be the model for one of the characters in the book André was about to write, and Dong Thuan arranged for a col-

---

[4] Clara Malraux, *Les Combats et les jeux* (Paris: Grasset, 1969).

94

lection among Cholon merchants to pay for the Malrauxs' passage to Marseille in return for André's lobbying in Paris in favor of suppressing gambling in Saigon and legalizing it in a casino, to be built, it was hoped, in the Cholon district. To Dai and Thuan the events in China justified this. Up north millions of Asians were discovering both nationalism and social revolution and the demands on the Cholon community for funds increased constantly. Since both Cholon's Chinese and Vietnamese natives were inveterate gamblers and illegal gambling was a fact of life in Saigon, why not legalize it? In a column in his newspaper Monin had said that the new governor was, in principle, for legalized, controlled gambling, "preferring to see the kitty go to charities than into police pockets." For the Cholon Kuomintang leaders part of the kitty was to help underwrite revolution in China.

One last cause was to unite the talents and ardor of the two directors of *L'Indochine enchaînée* and briefly dispatch André to Pnompenh as a court reporter—the Bardez Affair, so named after a commissioner in charge of collecting taxes in a section of rural Cambodia who had been murdered by rebellious villagers. In the face of passive resistance in the village of Krang-Leou, Bardez and his two Cambodian guards had taken one of the villagers hostage, a measure that had had the desired effect of making the village pay up. Once the tax had been collected, however, Bardez had refused to free the hostage. This had provoked the normally placid Cambodian peasants to such fury that they had seized Bardez and his two underlings and beaten them to death. Troops had been sent to Krang-Leou and some three hundred men rounded up. At random, seventeen men were chosen to stand trial.

What had provoked Monin—and Malraux—was the administrative decision to appoint a civil servant to hear the case instead of bringing the arrested villagers before a regular court. André went to Pnompenh for the "trial," convinced in advance the Bardez Affair contained all the elements of an odious fiscal regime and a judicial system "based on informing." What he saw he found appalling. The prime witness for the defense was Bardez's driver, but he had been killed a week earlier while "resisting arrest." The villagers' attorney, a maître Gallet, was served poisoned herb tea one morning, collapsed but recovered sufficiently to appear. The "judge" was openly biased, civil servants intervened constantly in the proceedings and the defense was barely allowed to speak, although Gallet managed to shout, "the crime of Krang-Leou is a crime all Cambodia has committed because it is the result of general discontent."

At the end, one of the villagers was sentenced to death, four were given life imprisonment and seven others were given infinite hard-labor terms. Five were acquitted.

Sarcastically, Malraux concluded:

We cannot repeat it often enough, our penal system must be

95

changed before it can be put into effect in the colonies. I would like to see, for example, a legislative code based on the following principles: 1) any accused will have his head cut off; 2) he will then be defended by a lawyer; 3) the lawyer will have his head cut off; 4) and so on.

The next time Malraux was to see the Cambodian capital was on his return from his historic meeting with Chairman Mao Tse-tung.

Two days before New Year's, 1926, Clara and André sailed for Marseille. Monin, who had welcomed them on the same dock a year earlier, did not accompany them to the ship, but their two Chinese friends, Dong Thuan and Dang Dai, were there, handing Clara a box of *lichees,* a fruit from southern China. Prophetically, the figures on the box were a pair of dancing girls dressed in red.

There were always to be two Asias for Malraux—a real and a mythical one. The passion for Asia, and for vanished cultures, reflected his fascination for the light strange civilizations threw on his own, "that quality of the unusual and the arbitrary which is so revealing." What he brought back with him was a large and fully lived experience. Although limited to Indochina, this experience was nevertheless the core of a confrontation between Eastern and Western ways. What he had witnessed up close were the antagonists in the struggle for this enormous continent emerging from centuries of torpor and Western cultural aggression. The images he was to set down in *Les Conquérants* and *La Condition humaine* were those of a giant China convulsed in revolt; what he had lived was an angry, suffering Indochina biding its time. What he brought back with him were habits, odors, friendships and tensions.

Under the management of Nguyen Pho, the suspected police informer, *L'Indochine enchaînée* struggled on for a few more issues before it quietly folded in February 1926. The demise was marked in Henry de Lachevrotière's *L'Impartial* by accusations that Monin and Malraux had pocketed years of advance subscriptions. Shortly after the Malrauxs' departure, Monin went "underground" and, via the Cholon pipeline, to Canton. The lawyer was now totally radicalized, convinced that real power, the power to change things, was only to be found in such revolutionary movements as the Kuomintang. Nothing was known of his activities in China. He was to resurface in Saigon in 1927 to die destitute of malaria at the end of the year, leaving behind a gravely sick widow and young child. Guillaume Monin was to become a journalist. Lachevrotière was to be killed in 1950, by a bomb thrown into his car by Vietcong commandos while on his way to the Saigon tennis club.

The passage back to France was in second-class, and to escape the shipboard mediocrity André began to write. The beginnings of *La Tentation de l'Occident* were letters to Marcel Arland, now a full-time editor at the prestigious *Nouvelle revue française,* or *NRF,* letters about the Asian vision of the world—André and Dang Dai had talked and talked about Oriental man's point of view—about the recent Pnompenh trial and its three hundred Khmer peasants in the grips of colonial might, about Nguyen Pho and Hinh and about possible European attitudes toward Asia. The result was the first book for Bernard Grasset, a book attempting to come to grips with the two cultures through an exchange of letters between fictitious Eastern and Western intellectuals, a cultivated Frenchman and a Chinese scholar.

The Frenchman is called A.D., perhaps an abbreviation for André, a twenty-five-year-old on his way to Asia who, in his first letter, is full of dreams about a mythical Asia—palaces and temples, pagodas and intriguing women peering from behind curtains. The Chinese scholar is twenty-three-year-old Ling traveling in Europe. Most of the eighteen letters are written by Ling, the first dated Marseille and all the others from Paris. A.D.'s first note is written aboard a ship taking him to Asia and the subsequent letters are from Canton, Shanghai and Tientsin. The slim book is more metaphysical essays than novel, diary or travelogue, a rather melancholy and austere mix of naive provocations and haughty pessimism, a study in comparative psychology with a rare respect for Confucian ideas. What the confrontation of East and West suggests to Malraux is not the superiority of one or the other, but the arbitrariness of *each*.

A.D.'s discovery of Asia is lyrically cinematic. Snow falls over China and the islands, and the vision of falling snow "fades" into the white funeral gown of a princess with a red jewel between her lips, frozen cicadas falling off trees and magicians burning beautifully smelling wood. Every spring covers Mongolia with Tartarian roses, white flowers with crimson hearts, as caravans of tall camels cross the steppes carrying loads of round bundles that open like pomegranates when the caravans halt. The scene changes to old men in a sunlit courtyard making magical gestures as they describe the buildings they have known in Turkestan and Tibet. The elders, in turn, give way to European adventurers who have married Mongol women and become generals in the Manchurian armies, fierce and despotic men. These adventurers fade into the portrait of a cunning and all-powerful emperor stretching his thin, transparent hand over all the Chinas—China at work, China full of opium and full of dreams—a blind man sitting huddled in the Forbidden City. He is followed by still older shadows of Tang emperors, the din of their courts where all the world's religions and superstitions clashed. This is followed by images of warriors waving weapons adorned with horse tails, of generals who have died in their tents after sixty victories and of a frosty night falling on ancient triumphs.

In his answer, Ling says that Europe evokes few beautiful ghosts. In Paris, he is an attentive tourist, reading much and visiting museums— "the artist is not the person who creates, but the one who knows how to feel"—monuments and churches.

Ling discovers that Europeans have single-track minds, all con-

97

centrated on goals and accomplishments, whereas Chinese people try to conceive life as a whole, as a series of possibilities. In Rome, he tries to understand the great past, goes on to Athens before returning to Paris, where he wonders whether the core of Western existence isn't absurd. He is intrigued by men's obsession with feminine conquest. "What is it that you want to possess in what you call the woman's soul?" He feels Westerners try to impose mental rules and values on their passions and after analyzing Asia's traditional concept of the woman, says it is vain for a man to try to discover in himself what it is that makes him love.

When young Chinese read your books they are first astonished by the conceit that you understand women. Quite beside the fact that I consider such efforts contemptible, it is evidently something doomed in advance. Man and woman belong to different species. What would you think of an author writing about the feelings of birds? That he's giving you a deformed view of his own feelings. This is what we think of a writer talking about women's sentiments. Yet, it is through this effort to understand that European woman's strength has come. It seems that you have taken her hand and put it on your shoulder. Woman interests you because she takes possession of you although it is you who make the effort that makes this possible. Insofar as you want to understand her, you identify with her.

A.D. answers that all erotic play is in being at the same time *the other,* to experience one's own feelings and to image the sensations of one's partner. Ling writes back that the difference between Western man and Asian man is perhaps in the way they dream, the Chinese becoming a sage through dreaming. "He doesn't imagine himself conquering cities, glory or power but reaching perfect understanding of everything." Later, Ling writes, "Our universe is not submitted, like yours, to the law of cause and effect, or rather, this law, which we admit, is without force since it doesn't admit what it cannot justify. For us, an unaccountable act is only the effect of an unknown cause because it happens in a life we ignore."

From Canton, A.D. sums up his two years in Asia by writing that his Western notion of Man has changed, that he can no longer conceive an individual independently of his or her *intensity.* In Shanghai, he meets a pessimistic Confucian sage, who tells him Asia's tragedy is that its mind is being emptied. In Europe, Ling realizes that Christian morality is linked to deep impulses within the Christian individual and that Confucian morality is a social ethics, "responsible for both the virtues and defaults of my race." In the book's last letter, A.D. writes despairingly about Europe from Tientsin—Peking's port city, where in 1858 a treaty was signed opening China to European interests—saying the basic conflict of the Western world is insoluble since it is between man and what he does. Europe, he says, is a vast cemetery where only dead conquerors lie, their melancholy deepening as it wraps itself around their illustrious names.

La Tentation de l'Occident, which was not to be translated into English until 1961, touched on a theme that was always to preoccupy Malraux—the individual versus society. It was a dilemma that, in *La Tentation,* he felt Asia had solved better than the West. In relation to a French existentialism yet to be born, *La Tentation*'s central statement on the absurdity of Western civilization was to be of historic importance. The slim volume, published by Bernard Grasset a few months after Malraux's return to France, presaged faults and qualities in its author's future writing, his intensity expressed in intellectuality rather than feeling and his virtuoso lyricism, but also his penetrating views and, as one of the book's early admirers said, his robust pessimism.

What will be the fate of this violent generation, so marvelously armed against itself?

D'Une jeunesse européenne

9

He could not look you in the eyes. His eyes were following in every direction an invisible bee. His shoulders contracted as if a dagger was tickling him in the back. His cigarette-burned fingers trembled, tried to free themselves. The moment someone approached, the haggard face seemed to grow more anxious. A punished child, a youthful rebel who as yet had embraced only death—this was Malraux back from Asia.

So wrote Jean Prévost, a contemporary of Malraux who was to be killed in the World War II resistance movement after a short literary career.[1] There were other portraits. Maurice Sachs, Cocteau's friend and secretary who lived a strange, indebted life, and was to become the only Jew in French letters to collaborate with the Nazis, wrote that to meet Malraux was to be impressed.

> There are several writers that people in the know are beginning to talk about—Julien Green, Georges Bernanos, André Malraux. I've met Malraux and he produces the most vivid impression. In his gaze there is something of an adventurer, something melancholy and at the same time resolute; the handsome profile of an Italian Renaissance man, yet a very French appearance. He talks very fast, very well, seems to know everything, fascinates you and leaves you with the impression you've met the century's most intelligent man.[2]

The France Clara and André returned to in the spring of 1926 was quite different from the country they had left to go art hunting in Cambodia three years earlier. The postwar euphoria was giving way to apprehension and confusion. Politically, France was torn and weakened by waltzing governments succeeding each other in chaotic fashion, none last-

[1] Jean Prévost, *Les Caractères*, text written in 1926 (Paris: Albin Michel, 1946).

[2] Maurice Sachs, *Au temps du boeuf sur le toit* (Paris: NRC, 1939).

ing long enough, even if it had the capability, to come to grips with the country's problems.

The core of France's difficulties was its economy, and its corollary —the fiscal system. Since the end of the war, successive governments had shied away from facing the fact that unpopular measures were necessary to restore fiscal sanity. Since 1918, huge Ministry of Finance deficits had been hidden from the country—through the imposition of a second "extraordinary" budget never submitted to parliamentary scrutiny and constantly running three times the "ordinary" budget.

During the fourteen months following Edouard Herriot's resignation after a non-confidence vote in the Senate in April 1925, there were six successive governments. Some were overthrown by the confused and fickle Chamber of Deputies, others resigned in order to reshuffle their ministers and maintain a precarious National Assembly majority for a few more weeks. Paul Painlevé, the brilliant mathematician and mediocre politician who had given *L'Indochine* an exclusive interview for its maiden issue, lasted seven months. His administration was defeated by a three-vote majority in the Chamber when he proposed to get the state out of hock with a one percent capital gains tax. He was followed by the tenth Aristide Briand administration.

In mid-July 1926, when billions of short-term treasury loans had come due and the coffers of state were empty, the franc fell to fifty to the dollar and a mob formed outside the Chamber of Deputies, blaming the elected officials for the latest crisis. Some of the rioters crossed the Seine to the Place de la Concorde and stoned buses with American tourists, held responsible for plotting the franc's fall—and cursed, together with the Left Bank American literati set, for living it up in Paris on overvalued dollars. To avoid public panic, the Left caved in to demands for a political truce and a call for a third return of the man it hated most—Raymond Poincaré.

"We never see you except in times of trouble!" a communist deputy shouted when Poincaré presented his cabinet to the National Assembly. It was meant as an insult, but contained a large measure of truth.

The climate of 1926 was summed up in this "restoration." Poincaré represented moral, monetary and colonial order. A conservative with integrity, he was an ardent patriot. His government was seen by the Right as a victory for law and order—in May, the last Moroccan leader made his submission ending the "pacification" of North Africa, and after the Poincaré investiture the value of the franc rose immediately. On the far Right, Charles Maurras' *Action française* made progress, especially in university and intellectual circles, repeating again and again that the Germans, the Jews and the communists were the enemies of France. A splinter group headed by Georges Vallois cast nostalgic glances across the Alps at Benito Mussolini's now four-year-old regime and created a French fascist party.

At the opposite end of the spectrum, the Communist Party, led by

101

the adventurous steelworker Jacques Doriot, tried to regain its losses—its membership had fallen from 130,000 to 55,000 since 1923 and most disillusioned Leftists had joined the Socialist Party. French communists were too individualistic to accept completely the diktats of the Third International in Moscow. Following Lenin's death in January 1924, Trotsky had demanded heavy purges in the French party and dispatched hatchetmen to Paris to enforce the party line. What Doriot's communists lacked in numbers they made up for in ingenuity and militancy. A remarkable feat in 1926 was their drawing the surrealists and a good hunk of the rest of the intelligentsia into their ranks. On March 1, *La Révolution surréaliste* anounced that "vast areas of agreement exist in the communists' and our aspirations" and less than a year later, Louis Aragon, André Breton and Paul Eluard became party members.

Slightly to the right of the *Parti communiste français,* the socialists were fighting an uphill battle to retain the allegiance of the working class, beset by a sense of oppression and helplessness. The collapse of a general strike in 1920 had almost destroyed the trade-union movement. Ruthlessly put down by the government with troops, police and strikebreakers, the work stoppage had ended with hundreds of labor leaders in jail, the *Confédération générale du travail* (CGT) outlawed and thousands of workers jobless. "For the next sixteen years, ninety percent of the French workers remained unorganized," William L. Shirer was to write in *The Collapse of the Third Republic.*

> They sank into a deep apathy, convinced that there was no hope for them—from the unions, from a hostile government, from a rural-dominated Parliament that had no comprehension of a city's laborer's lot, or from the employers, who, encouraged by the collapse of the strike, were now determined to eliminate the unions completely, deal with their employees on an individual basis and on their own terms, and even to sabotage the eight-hour day, which Parliament had voted in 1919, and the mild social-insurance legislation which the two chambers were threatening to enact, and finally at the end of the 1920s did.[3]

By temperament and affinity Malraux might have been expected to join the now flourishing surrealist movement. Instead, he was drawn toward the more elitist milieu surrounding his publisher Bernard Grasset and, in less than two years, to gravitate to the inner circle of Gallimard, the most important French publishing house. Although he remained a friend of the painter Philippe Soupault, the writer Robert Desnos and the dissident Marxist theoretician (and André Gide relative) Pierre Naville, he always disliked the surrealists for their noisy clannishness and personally loathed Breton's authoritarian leadership.

[3] William L. Shirer, *The Collapse of the Third Republic: An Inquiry to the Fall of France in 1940* (New York: Simon & Schuster, 1969).

Clara and André had found a smart new apartment at 122 boulevard Murat not far from Mrs. Goldschmidt's stately mansion. They couldn't afford it and lived in dire poverty, both hard at work, he finishing *La Tentation de l'Occident* and writing magazine pieces before plunging into *Les Conquérants,* she translating. Grasset published her translation of *Tagesbuch eines Mädchen,* an Austrian book by an anonymous authoress and a little later Gallimard accepted her Sigmund Freud translation.* She also translated several texts by Christian Grabbe, a nineteenth-century playwright rediscovered by the Berlin expressionists.

The estrangement between Clara and her family remained total. Her younger brother had married and become a father and Clara sometimes caught a glimpse of her mother taking her grandchild to the Bois in a new perambulator. André's family, on the other hand, moved closer. Grandma Adriana Romania had sold the grocery in Bondy and together with her daughters took an apartment a few blocks from Clara and André, who fell into the habit of having lunch there every day until Clara's wifely pride and her low tolerance level for feminine cackle, quarrels and insidious meddling made her put a stop to it. The three ladies' chitchat and hovering interference apparently didn't disturb André as long as he was fed because when Clara said she would henceforth make their own lunch, he thought she was being silly. André's father also moved in on them. Fernand Malraux had suddenly found his second wife—and mother of his two adolescent sons—incompatible. While waiting for a divorce to go through, he had moved back to Paris from Orléans and now invited himself for dinner every Wednesday.

Clara was not happy. She had not gone through what she had gone through in Southeast Asia to be hemmed into the role of exemplary daughter-in-law, attentive to what neighbors might say and implicitly answerable for her comings and goings. She also resented a couple of remarks by André. He had vetoed her suggestion that she take a job by saying, "Why exhibit our poverty?" and had thrown icy water on her budding literary ambitions by saying, "Better be my wife than a second-string writer." It hurt, although she realized it was not necessarily an incorrect assessment of her writing abilities. She hated her own semifailures, reared up, provoked him and resented that the price she had to pay for living with him seemed to be her own erasure.

A long illness healed things. Rheumatic arthritis struck André and nearly paralyzed him. For three months he stayed in bed in their furnitureless apartment, too weak even to reach the toilet without her help. The medical bills wiped them out financially, but the long months together reminded them of Pnompenh when dengue fever had felled her and he had slept in her hospital room. Again, they lived on each other and on hope.

* Freud's 1908 *Über infantile sexual theories* (On the Sexual Theories of Children).

Before *La Tentation,* dedicated to Clara, came out in August, André had published "Les Lettres d'un Chinois," an extraordinarily dense article revealing a synthesis of the Chinese mind when confronting Western reality.[4] In an accompanying piece called "D'une jeunesse européenne," he took his own generation to task, saying it was afraid of confronting its own negative attitudes. "On A European Youth" was prophetic of the gathering storm of the 1930s and in its prescient feel for a youth waiting for a cause.

> We must now have the guts to look inside ourselves so as to dis-cover Europe's mystery. At the core of a civilization, whose strength has always been a gross individualism, a new power is dawning. Who dares to say where it will take us? Our era, so full of ghostly echoes, won't admit its nihilistic, destructive and essentially negative beliefs. . . . What will be the fate of this violent generation so marvelously armed against itself? [5]

Although it reflected the mood of 1926—the yearning for both order and escape, *La Tentation de l'Occident* was only politely received. For its author, it nevertheless opened the pages of the best magazines and the doors of the most important literary circles, where, inevitably, Malraux was "someone back from China." One was the *salon* of Daniel Halévy. This foremost French Nietzsche scholar—he liked to tell people that it was in his Italian summer house that "dear Friedrich" had met Lou Andréa Salomé, the only woman Nietzsche had loved—had created Grasset's *Cahiers verts* collection, publishing short works by what he considered forgotten authors and by very young writers. Once a week, this truculent personage with his beard and perennial corduroy jacket played host in his apartment overlooking the Seine and the Pont Neuf to a mixed crew of intellectuals and fellow travelers. It was at Halévy's that Malraux met many of the writers who were to become his friends and that many others discovered his formidable verbosity. Perhaps inevitably, when Halévy reviewed *La Tentation,* he wrote that it was by a young author "who had just spent three years in China."

Another privileged meeting ground was the Pontigny encounters, the annual summer symposia organized by the philosopher Paul Desjardins in a former Cistercian cloister near Auxerre, in Yonne *département,* a hundred miles southeast of Paris, and attended by numerous French and European intellectuals. It was at the 1924 Pontigny symposium that Marcel Arland had collected signatures for the Malraux trial defense.

Arland was now editor at NRF and the encounters were dominated by Gallimard's star authors—Gide, Paul Valéry and Jean Paulhan. Desjardins invited Malraux to the 1927 encounters after being impressed with

4 *NRF* (April, 1926).
5 *Écrits* (March, 1927).

104

André's grasp of the French Revolution during a meeting in Paris. Also of Malraux's and Arland's generation at Pontigny was André Chamson, a writer-journalist who had also been published in Halévy's *Cahiers verts*. Chamson was an ardent art lover and Malraux and he were soon deep into esthetics and ethics. Although Pontigny was a "serious," all-masculine affair with a penetrating odor of Thomist Catholicism and a whiff of pederasty, André brought Clara along, the only woman taking part in that year's encounter.

The people Clara and André invited to their spartan but supermodern apartment were slightly less illustrious but no less lofty or eccentric. Guests sat on snakeskins or shared Arabian hassocks—Clara innocently insisting the furniture had not yet arrived from Saigon. The Malrauxs showed off what was one of Paris' first automatic garbage chutes and André never forgot to mention that the indirect lighting was "from Jansen's." The cuisine Clara whipped up—meatloaf with curry was one repeated specialty —often left people with mixed emotions, but André forewarned their guests before they sat down, Oriental-style, on floor mats, that there were restaurants for those requiring gourmet cooking. Madeleine and Leo Lagrange, both lawyers and both active in the Socialist Party, were new friends who ate on the floor at Boulevard Murat as were Alexieff, a Russian refugee painter who could not understand how Frenchmen could be poor, and Louis and Simone Martin-Chauffier, a literary couple they met at Pontigny.

The Italian-Swiss journalist Nino Frank, who was a friend of Ivan and Claire Goll, had introduced Goll to James Joyce and knew *everyone* in the arts, was a perspicacious observer who came to dinner. He had first met the Malrauxs at the Golls and in his *Mémoire brisée* was to leave a vivid sketch of them:

> Ivan with his Rhine-country smile and, behind the glasses, his heartiness. Claire with her triangular face and blonde locks, is stretched out on a couch, very much Berlin poetess, saying playful things which Clara, one finger slightly raised, tries to answer in frisky and affected phrases. Around them an air of feminine impudence. But the interest is elsewhere, in the young man Ivan introduces me to and with whom one starts to talk easily—kind of tight, guarded. His gestures are adroit and open, contradicted by the face which is still adolescent, by the long hair and a hint of a little sad and vaguely begging smile.[6]

More exotic friends than Nino Frank were the wealthy Orientalist Maurice Magre and his mistress Suzanne Paris. Magre lived a clockwork Jekyll-and-Hyde existence while smoking his eight pipes of opium a day. He was a model husband until two o'clock in the afternoon, when for the next twelve hours he left home for the studio loft of Suzanne. After sunset,

[6] Nino Frank, *Mémoire brisée* (Paris: Calmann-Lévy, 1967).

this Oriental erudite and this failed actress withdrew into a world of dreams and hallucinations, propelled by his inexhaustible knowledge of classical travel *récits* and Asian history. The Malrauxs often joined them for dinner, invariably at the same Place des Ternes restaurant. Later, they all climbed to the studio loft. While Maurice, Suzanne and Clara stretched out with their opium pipes, André told fascinating tales, stimulating Maurice to tell others. If André told of Timur Lang, the Samarkand king who ravaged Iran, Baghdad and Delhi before dying on a march against China, Maurice told about Genghis Khan's body being returned to the capital of his steppe empire by his sons in a litter with drawn curtains so his soldiers wouldn't know he was dead, this following his defeat at the frozen Yangtse River, where Toongun horsemen had hacked his Mongol bowmen to pieces because they didn't know how to stand on ice.

Maurice and Suzanne were later to travel to India to attend an ashram and to return both edified and bemused by Buddhism. The Malrauxs were to remain friends until Maurice's premature death.

Charles Edgar du Perron—called Eddy du Perron—was an important new acquaintance who soon became a friend and to whom *Man's Fate* was to be dedicated. A Dutchman born in Indonesia of Creole-Dutch-Javanese parentage, Eddy was a writer whose breezy irony and studied detachment covered a despairing pessimism and a feeling that he was more spectator than actor in his own life drama. The son of wealthy colonialists, he had come to Paris to live and to write. He had a special admiration for Stendhal, whom he physically resembled, and shared with André a love for Asia. Their pessimism was different, however, Malraux seeing in action, even political action, a goal beyond despair while du Perron refused to betray his own pain. "For me," he wrote, "there is no place in society." His one classical book, little known outside Holland, was to be *Het Land van herkomst* (The Country of Origin) (1935), an autobiographical novel of his life in Paris alternating with vivid memories of his Javanese childhood. "There are few books as good on the East Indies," Martin Seymour-Smith was to write; "and few books recapture the mind of a child so exactly." [7] André was to appear in *The Country of Origin* under the name Hervelé and in his *Antimémoires* Malraux was to remember du Perron on a flight over Indonesia from Hong Kong:

> Over there is an island called Balé-Kambang, which Eddy du Perron gave me when I dedicated *La Condition humaine* to him. He died when the Germans entered Holland. He thought all politics meaningless, and history too, I believe. He was my best friend.

Two years older than André, Eddy was a little man with big brown eyes who looked much younger than he was and whose childhood and

[7] Martin Seymour-Smith, *Funk & Wagnalls Guide to Modern Literature* (New York: Funk & Wagnalls, 1973).

youth in the East Indies made him see European affairs with bemused bewilderment. With people, Clara thought, he showed an honest naiveté while insisting he could ferret out the best in everybody. Eddy introduced the Malrauxs to the writings of Eduard Douwes Dekker, another Dutch-Indonesian who had used the pseudonym Multitatuli—meaning "I have suffered much"—and whose *Max Havalaar* novel-pamphlet in 1860 had been the first cry of indignation over the colonial treatment of Javanese and as such had led to concrete improvements. A doctor in Java, Multitatuli had been a haughty "man of action," an atheist and a romantic who had attacked the mediocrity, unctuousness and conventional religiosity of his time with both scorn and touching and somber tales of Javanese beauty.

The Malrauxs saw Eddy almost daily during the spring of 1927 when Chiang Kai-shek disarmed procommunist trade unions in Shanghai and neither the Comintern nor the Chinese Communist Party dared take action. During the past year Chiang had made rapid progress in bringing China under Kuomintang authority and was now strong enough to turn on his communist allies. The Shanghai massacre began at dawn on April 12.

The events were hotly debated. André was sure the slaughter of the communists would force the Soviet Union to reverse its policy of support of the Kuomintang and to tell the Chinese Party to stop trying to collaborate with the Nationalists. But that again brought up the old Marxist dogma that communist revolution could only be based on a proletariat since a peasantry was not a revolutionary class. As he was to say a year later, "the question is not to define the revolution, but to make it happen." André was beginning to write *The Conquerors*.

One day, Clara ran into her mother in the street. After a moment's confusion, they embraced. Everything seemed simple. Mrs. Goldschmidt took her daughter home to the big house Clara had known since she was born. For New Year's, Mrs. Goldschmidt sent Clara 5,000 francs, which she had the force to return "precisely because I could use it." After another cold interlude, mother and daughter made a lasting if uneasy peace.

Malraux was involved in art and developed a fleeting passion for the movies. His long stay in Asia had not only familiarized him with Khmer sculpture, but also with Indian and Chinese art and he was especially fascinated by recent discoveries in Afghanistan of a "bridge" between early Christian and early Buddhist sculpture and their common Greco-Roman past. If Apollo had become Christ in the West, he had become Prince Siddhartha in the East. Christianity was dominated by the tragic image of an execution, Buddhism by the tranquil picture of meditation. Buddha's eyelids were lowered, the drawing of his face was tightened and movement disappeared from sculpture. In Tashkurghan, samples of a hybrid Greco-Buddhist art form—sculptures of Buddha still with open eyes—had been discovered. With du Perron, Malraux discussed art, and Eddy was to remember André saying that the artist caught in the act of creating

107

was more fascinating than the finished painting. To Marcel Arland, André confided that he would one day want to write about art.

Sergei Eisenstein's *Battleship Potemkin,* the triumph of the new Soviet cinema, electrified Malraux, as it did other French intellectuals who in the mid-1920s were discovering the cinema. Eisenstein's retelling of the doomed 1905 Odessa uprising against czarist oppression and the mutiny aboard the battleship was epic filmmaking. The building up of a rhythmic structure in the cutting or "montage," the use of pictorial symbols as "themes," the emphasis on the masses rather than the individual protagonist, the episodic development of the narrative made *Potemkin* at once exuberantly youthful and enormously creative. Eisenstein had conceived his film as a series of images assembled in a completely new, revolutionary manner and the result was a very powerful and exciting film.

Les Conquérants was assembled like a film. To tell his story of the 1925 Canton uprising, Malraux had his own memories of Indochina, stretching from the Pnompenh trial to the revolutionary politics of the Cholon Kuomintang, to journalistic run-ins with poiice and colonial authorities and what he remembered of the week in Hong Kong with Clara during the general strike in August 1925. His indirect sources were press clippings of the events in Canton and Paul Monin's eyewitness reports after his year in the Kwantung province capital. The novel was written in fragments with the "gray parts," as Malraux called the connective passages, added later. It had three parts. In "Outward Bound," Malraux established the background—Hong Kong paralyzed by general strike—so that, after showing Borodin's and Garin's tactical struggle, he found focus on the personal tragedy of the lonely and probably dying Garin in the final part, entitled "The Man." More generally, Malraux contrived to subordinate the revolutionary situation to Garin's personal revolt by placing it in the perspective of the European impact on the events—Chinese revolutionaries are outnumbered in the book by Russian, French, German and Italian adventurers or insurgency technocrats in charge of the revolution together with Chen-Dai, the Gandhi-like Kuomintang leader "whose entire life is a moral protest."

Malraux wrote *Les Conquérants* in the present tense, in a tersely notational style, advancing cinematically from one scene to the next by means of a suspended shot or a fadeout. His use of headlines and radio flashes—reminiscent of John Dos Passos' collage of newsreel headlines, phrases from popular songs and "camera eye" points-of-view when the author himself enters the field—added to the dramatic immediacy, staccato and sweep of phyiscal action in a fluid and uncertain revolutionary situation.

In the first draft, Garin was called Starin, a name evidently derived from Stavrogin, the willful revolutionary who lost faith in revolution and hanged himself with a rope smeared with soap in the last pages of Dosto-

108

yevsky's *The Possessed*. Since his teens, Malraux had counted Dostoyevsky among his favorite authors; he and Arland had long discussions about the "apostle of fraternal love" and the *NRF* frequently published commentaries on Dostoyevsky. Now, Malraux carefully studied the 1871 novel where the crime is committed by an impassioned and prejudiced society and where the revolutionaries' struggle for absolute freedom is situated outside time. Like the brilliant and cruel nobleman Stavrogin, the complex, impatient and commanding Garin has a certain aristocratic contempt for the masses and for society. "The possibility of reforming society is a question that doesn't interest me," he says. "I don't love mankind. I don't even love the poor, the people, those for whom I am going to fight." The irony of *The Conquerors* is that it is this alienated hero, who knows he is dying of malaria and dysentery, who is engaged in promoting social upheaval.

Garin is more metaphysical rebel than revolutionary, someone who finds justification in being a man of action, but also someone who *opts* for his own alienation. "To direct, to determine, to constrain—that is life," he says. This statement by a man in love with power for its own sake is justified insofar as his propaganda work for the Kuomintang and the Comintern has convinced hundreds of thousands that their lives and their individual identities are important. In them he creates a dream of victory, a hope for the future when they will live in dignity—another Malrucian key word. "What binds me to the Kuomintang, is above all a need for a common victory," Garin says. His "intensity" needs continuity and projection. Ten years later, Malraux was to write that men united by both action and hope accede to a realm which they cannot reach alone.

Garin is opposed by two other revolutionary "types"—Borodin, the Bolshevik technocrat, and Hong, the terrorist. In a chapter omitted from the novel but later published in the surrealist magazine *Bifur*, Malraux lets Garin discuss Borodin, calling the Russian "a businessman, hard-working, brave, audacious on occasion, but very simple, his chief characteristic being the intensity with which he is obsessed by action. . . . Nearly all the Bolsheviks have the cult of the technician, but if they are also Jews they usually feel that this is not enough; they also have an intense curiosity about moral forces." [8] Malraux also has Borodin reflect on Garin, saying "What is annoying about Garin is that you never know when you wake up whether he has committed suicide during the night."

Hong, who says, "There are only two races—the poor and the others," and hates idealists because they claim they can introduce order into things, was based on the wiry, touchy Hinh, who had worked on *L'Indochine* and had proposed to assassinate Governor-General Maurice Cognacq on a Saigon street. In Borodin's eyes, the terrorist is expendable, but in Hong's eyes the Comintern is not radical enough, a charge Leon

[8] *"Les Conquérants,* fragment inédit," *Bifur* (Dec. 31, 1929).

Trotsky was to echo when he reviewed *Les Conquérants* from his Turkish exile two years after its publication. Twice a week Hong has men assassinated whom the Comintern wants to protect. "Every murder," says Garin about Hong, "increases his self-confidence." Hong is perhaps the only character in any Malraux novel who has no doubts.

Malraux underscores the absurd horror of terrorism when Garin is taken to identify the bodies of Klein, the German-born Comintern executioner, and three Chinese revolutionaries. Their already stiff bodies have been stood against the wall of a workshed. The first-person eyewitness account is that of a never clearly identified Central Committee envoy visiting the Comintern cadres:

> As I turn around, I see the body of Klein—I recognize it immediately because of its height—a large spot in the middle of the face, the mouth has been slit larger by a razor. My muscles contract again, so much so that I hold my arms tightly against my body and I, too, have to lean against the wall. I look away from the open wounds, the great black splotches of clotted blood, the eyes turned inward. All the bodies are alike. They have been tortured. One of the flies, buzzing around, lands on my forehead and I can't raise my arm to brush it away.
>
> "We must close his eyes," says Garin almost in a whisper, moving toward Klein's body.
>
> His voice arouses me and with an awkward, quick gesture I chase the fly away. With two fingers stretched apart like scissors, Garin makes a movement to touch Klein's white eyeballs.
>
> His hand falls away.
>
> "I think they've cut off the eyelids."

This passage comes toward the end of the book, when Garin no longer possesses the strength to guide the revolution effectively and simply wonders whether there is any merit in revolutionary bloodshed.

Les Conquérants was an immediate success. Arland was one of the first friends to read the manuscript and immediately serialized it in six *NRF* issues between March and July. Grasset brought out the published volume in September. By mid-fall, the book was, as du Perron noted, "the book of the year and the success of the season." *Les Conquérants* was mentioned for the Prix Femina—after the Prix Goncourt, the most prestigious literary prize—but failed to win, because, as *L'Oeuvre* noted, the brilliant scenes of horror and murder frightened the social orthodoxy and the sense of patriotism of the jury members. With the exception of Marc Bernard in *Cahiers du Sud,* all reviewers were favorable, André Billy in *L'Oeuvre* going so far as to recommend it for the Prix Goncourt and Georges Duveau writing in *La Révue européenne* that "it is already commonplace to consider André Malraux as one of the very first writers of his time."

Banned in the Soviet Union and Mussolini's Italy, *Les Conquérants* was an instant dud in English. Winifred Stephens Whale's translation, published by Cape at Aldous Huxley's suggestion, sold very poorly in Great Britain despite a favorable review in *The New Statesman*. This first English-language critique of a Malraux book called him "as discriminating as a good novelist, but the material he has chosen is, incidentally, so vivid and so exciting as to constitute in itself a 'document' of some importance. We are not told whether the French book, of which the present volume is a translation, appeared under the disguise of fiction or history. We have heard *Les Conquérants* referred to as a novel. Obviously, the author's own experience plays a very large part in the story, if story it is. At all events, this narrative of a few months spent at the headquarters of the Kuomintang in Canton is unfolded almost as plainly and baldly as an official report. There is little expense in detail, in the picturesque; but such trimmings as M. Malraux allows himself are relevant and impressive. Their cumulative effect is oddly terrifying." [9] When Harcourt and Brace brought out an American edition of Whale's translation, sales were not much better than in Britain (eight hundred copies sold).

In an afterword written twenty years later for Grasset's post-World War II reissue, Malraux was to say that if *Les Conquérants* "has managed to remain afloat, it is not because it describes this or that episode of the Chinese Revolution, but because it has shown a type of hero in whom were united ability to act, culture and lucidity—values linked indirectly to the criteria of the time."

In a larger perspective, *The Conquerors* could be said to have probed the malaise of the late 1920s, formulating a moral distress and foreshadowing possible new attitudes. In 1972, Cecil Jenkins would write that in *Les Conquérants* Malraux was "through the influences bearing upon his work—Nietzsche, Dostoyevsky, Spengler—helping to crystallize the 'new' or 'alternative' European intellectual tradition now moving to the fore as a result of this malaise and to which one may broadly apply the term existentialist. His work not only strikingly parallels that of Heidegger, but clearly anticipates certain features of Sartre and Camus." [10]

As if to baffle critics busy analyzing *Les Conquérants,* Malraux brought out *Le Royaume du farfelu,* a short poetic meditation in the *Lunes en papier* vein, this time a fairy tale told against a background of Oriental splendor, all magic, luxury and strange things happening with the appearance of inevitability. *Le Royaume du farfelu,* never translated into English, was published by Gallimard in November 1928 in a sumptuous limited edition. The kingdom of the bizarre of the title is the former city of Isfahan in western Iran, a near-mythical place Malraux had already written about in a short story he ran in *L'Indochine* and reworked for the literary magazine *Commerce.* In the first version, Isfahan is a city in ruins, defending itself in silence against Cossack invaders who never set eyes on the de-

[9] *The New Statesman* (Oct. 26, 1929).
[10] Cecil Jenkins, *André Malraux* (Boston: Twayne Publishers, 1972).

fenders. The most memorable passage concerns centuries-old angelfish in sacred pools, which the invaders catch and cook because they are starving. In the end the Cossacks give up their siege.

Le Royaume du farfelu begins with the nameless hero arriving at the marketplace of a strange land. Phoenix sellers offer birds rising from the ashes. Dragons offered at the market are so beautiful that anyone watching them overcomes sufferings and sorrows. The dragon seller says his animals may also be used as barometers, for when the crests on their backs are vertical rain is forecast. The cloth vendors have shops with fabrics in all colors of the rainbow, vendors of orange-colored eggs and tattooed ducks also sell paper horses and priests stir cauldrons where little copper gods are being brewed.

The hero meets the fate reserved for all strangers; he is thrown in jail, where he dreams of his own city with its harbor filled with ships, "where the squirrels and the shrew mice played in the rigging." When the stranger is taken before the ruling prince, one minister reports that Babylon is no more, another that in the furthest forests of the kingdom are only the white bones of dragons gleaming with black insects. The stranger is ordered into the army where he will serve his time as historian of the prince's wars and he is given as an assistant an old man who knows how to cast spells. The old man has tossed the dust-laden roses of Tartary into the blood of mermaids and has cut the throats of Persian guards defending the royal palace of Isfahan.

The old man is prophesizing disaster for the prince's new war against Isfahan. The people of Isfahan have blocked the gates of the walled city and covered them with dirt so that the gates are indistinguishable from the walls and in addition they have built thousands of low walls within the city, forming a maze in which the invaders will lose themselves. The invaders' camp is plagued by scorpions. Fear takes possession of the army, which knows it is trapped. It nevertheless advances into the Kingdom of the Bizarre, the former city of Isfahan, now a nightmare. Victory is no longer possible, the invaders are merely waiting for the day of their defeat since they are cut off from behind by a second enemy army. One night, the narrator slips out and wanders through the silence of the labyrinthine city. An officer takes him to a row of statues by quiet pools. The statues turn out to be men who begin to fish for the angelfish. The narrator survives it all and ends up on the shores of the Black Sea a seller of seashells, like James Ensor's mother.

Le Royaume du farfelu has tended to divide critics and scholars, many viewing it as a somewhat embarrassing regression after *The Conquerors,* a few seeing it as one of Malraux's most satisfying works. In 1973, Jean Lacouture, Malraux's most political biographer, would see in *Le Royaume* a reminder that "the conquest of hope is made on both viscid and

112

arid grounds, peopled with ridiculous puppets and grinning shadows." [11] Ten years earlier, André Vandegans devoted a hundred and fifty pages to an analysis of *Le Royaume* and found the slim volume to be Malraux's most poetic work of fiction, the full flower of a free-form creativity only germinating in the 1921 *Lunes en papier.*[12] Robert Payne, Malraux's first British biographer, would compare *Le Royaume* with Samuel Coleridge's *Kubla Khan:* "Malraux's Isfahan is as imaginary as Xanadu, and where Coleridge describes a fleeting glimpse of Paradise, Malraux, haunted by death, describes a fleeting glimpse of death's kingdom with all its defenses, its panoply and its monuments." [13]

[11] Jean Lacouture, *André Malraux,* op. cit.
[12] André Vandegans, *La Jeunesse littéraire d'André Malraux* (Paris: Pauvert, 1964).
[13] Robert Payne, *Portrait of André Malraux* (Englewood Cliffs: Prentice-Hall, 1970).

113

His face was only a few inches from hers, but he felt as if the blind desire linking his body with this woman's were someone else's.

The Royal Way

10

The third volume of the three-book contract André had signed with Bernard Grasset on the eve of the second Vietnam sojourn was to be *La Voie royale*. He delivered the manuscript in early 1930, his last book not to be published by Gallimard.

Le Royaume du farfelu started a lasting association with the publishing house founded by Gaston and Raymond Gallimard, both of whom had signed the 1925 petition in favor of the convicted Pnompenh statue-snatcher. Malraux had already written for Gallimard's *Nouvelle revue française* (better known by its initials, *NRF*) and had been a friend of its editor, Marcel Arland, since 1920. He now became a friend of Bernard Groethuysen, one of the more influential editors at Gallimard's, and was himself offered the job of "artistic director."

The position was vague but over the years it brought the Malrauxs financial stability and the means of what they wanted most—to travel. When they weren't off to Iran or Pamir or on a round-the-world trip, he worked rather freely as an editor, occupying a tiny office under the rafters that he called Dr. Caligari's cabinet. Through Malraux, Louis Chevasson also found a position at Gallimard's.

Malraux knew his way around books and over the next seven years picked ideas for books, selected manuscripts, edited them and saw them through printing and even promotion. He edited a Life and Works of Leonardo da Vinci in which he included comments on the Renaissance painter by Goethe, Stendhal and Henry James and wrote his own essay on the little-known last years of Goya plus a small biography of Vermeer. An editor with only an elementary grasp of English, he was responsible for introducing D. H. Lawrence, William Faulkner and Dashiell Hammett to French readers, writing his most famous forewords to the Lawrence and Faulkner translations. *"Sanctuary* is the intrusion of Greek tragedy into the detective story," Janet Flanner quoted him as saying in one of her fortnightly Letters from Paris in *The New Yorker*.[1] By far his most important creation at Gallimard—and lasting indirect contribution to French letters—was the *Tableaux de la littérature française* series, in which thirty-five modern authors wrote on the preceding centuries' leading figures, Malraux contributing an important essay on the erotic author Choderlos Laclos himself.

Groethuysen—everybody called him Groot—was a disinterested Marxist with the fervor of a St. Augustine and the first of many *heimatslose*, refugees and eventually stateless persons to be dredged up in Paris during the stormy 1930s from the four corners of Europe. The son of a Dutch physician who had gone mad and a Russian mother, Groot had become a francophile at twenty, a friend of André Gide and, at Gallimard's foreign department, the man who introduced Franz Kafka, German philosophy and modern Russian writing to France. A totally verbal person, he talked about ideas as others talked about food, lived with Alix Guillain, a journalist at the Communist daily, *L'Humanité*, with such freedom that he never imposed his friends on her; nor she hers on him. He introduced Malraux to Master Eckardt, the thirteenth-century German speculative mystic and persuaded Gide to join the Communist Party.

Groot spent hours rewriting translations charitably handed out to refugees from fascism and never managed to finish his life's work, a history of the bourgeoisie. "He had read everything, continued to read everything in the same way as he listened to people, by wedging himself into the author's thinking," Clara was to write of him. "He was practically never wrong. . . . Alix's strong point was her conviction: she believed in the perfection of the USSR as the first Christians believed in God reincarnate. A little less perhaps because in a confused fear of disappointment, she never made a pilgrimage to her place of miracle." [2] Groot and Alix came for dinner at the Malrauxs' every Wednesday. In 1972, Malraux was to call the chubby editor-philosopher, who died in 1946, the one "of all the men I have known who most surely incarnated the idea of the intellectual genius. He attached no importance to what he wrote and was the only oral genius I have known. I've known lots of talkative people, but not this kind of verbal person." [3]

The success of *Les Conquérants* brought an end to the shoestring existence, transforming his marginal reputation into recognizable renown, but it also altered his and Clara's life. She had always felt his fabulations and "mythomania," as she called it, a part of his talent and indeed a part of his psyche. He had always "rectified" experience to fit an intense per-

[1] Janet Flanner, *Paris Was Yesterday, 1925–1939*, ed. Irving Drutman (New York: The Viking Press, 1972).
[2] Clara Malraux, *Voici que vient l'été* (Paris: Grasset, 1973).
[3] Jean Lacouture, *André Malraux*, op. cit.

sonal vision, but now he was not only billed by others as a participant in the Canton uprising, he began to fictionalize their joint Asian past. In some of his accounts, the Cambodian art caper became politicized, with her German background raising murky suspicions; in others she no longer existed. As the retelling of the jungle trip to Banteai Srey grew in color and daring, it seemed increasingly incongruous that a tiny and apparently fragile girl like Clara could possibly have taken part in the expedition. In some accounts of the Saigon newspaper venture, her contributions were transferred to Vietnamese collaborators, in others her intercession on his behalf with Paris intellectuals became an Annamite effort.

Clara was more puzzled than angry. André not only insisted on his right to transform personal experiences, otherwise too limiting and redundant, into stories, he seemed to believe that rearranged in this fashion, events appeared more plausible. For a long time, reality seemed only valid if transformed. *Les Conquérants* takes place in a China he had never seen, *Le Royaume du farfelu* speaks of an Iran he had not yet seen. Myth had always seemed a means of self-defense to him and myths were neither truths nor lies, but means of investing lives with meaning. To "invent," to re-create and transpose was to transform experience into consciousness and it was perhaps as essential to him as adventure in faraway places seemed a means of self-discovery.

Clara looked on, "fascinated," she was to say, as fiction became truer than reality. She read *Les Conquérants* wondering how much more she would be diminished in the future.

> Given the strength with which non-existing things sprang into life for him, it is no wonder that my presence was often a burden. It limited him. I will leave it to others to decide whether this limitation was beneficent or harmful to his work. In any case, the taste for myth was an integral part of his creative power and I was certainly wrong, when seeing him satisfying this need in the daily life, I tried to nag him into remaining within certain bounds of credibility. At the time, he was—and was not yet, André Malraux—his legend, which he tried out on others and which sometimes brought ironic smiles on peoples' faces that hurt me. When the legend denied me totally, I could die. I didn't yet understand that the legend was a necessity to his genius. I sometimes saw hints of this, but I wouldn't, and couldn't accept it.[4]

Imperceptibly, untruth entered their marriage and modified its intensity. In taking a couple of holiday lovers, she stayed within their agreed social contract, but when she created scenes because he reciprocated, she overstepped their covenant. But it was not time for introspection or for Clara to reclaim a part of her existence, and they both plunged

---

[4] Clara Malraux, op. cit.

116

forward into their first trip abroad since 1926. This time: the Soviet Union and the real Isfahan.

They sailed from Marseille aboard a freighter, the only passengers onboard, and after calls at Italian and Greek ports, made landfall in Batum, the port city on the Black Sea coast of Soviet Georgia. The first evening was spent in a dim and crowded tavern, where a dwarf in a top hat led a raw-voiced chorus of smelly men in an elegiac sing-along. The whole thing, Clara and André told each other, was more Dostoyevsky's Eternal Russia than the new USSR they had expected to see.

After a train ride across the Caucasus Mountains and a stopover in Tiflis, which looked like a plundered Nice, they reached the oil city of Baku on the Caspian Sea. Their plan was to cross to the Iranian city of Pahlavi, but the Intourist official who found them a sleazy hotel said they weren't supposed to be traveling around southern Russia by themselves. After a few days, however, they were granted an exit visa and on a tiny steamer crossed the iridescent green Caspian Sea, lunching on the deck with the German ambassador to Teheran.

Persia captivated them. So much so that they returned again in 1930 and again the following year. After Pahlavi and Recht, famous for its twenty kinds of melons, and with the assistance of the French consul in Pahlavi, they reached Isfahan, total Thousand and One Nights enchantment, yet completely without relation to the city of André's fiction. They stayed at the only Western hotel. The palace of Shah Abbas was immaculately beautiful and the *maidan,* the great dusty square surrounded by glowing mosques, was scarcely changed since the city had been the capital of a great empire. Clara—and her husband with her—was adopted by the local Jewish community. André went on a metaphysical binge and sat under flowering pomegranate trees in miniature gardens talking with Sufi masters and Islamic sages. Before leaving, they lured the driver of an aging taxi to take them up to the mountain grave of the greatest of Persia's rulers, Darius.

On the way to France, André began writing his new novel, which he had already decided would be a meditation on Asia and on death and somehow include the story of David Mayrena, the legendary plantation owner who had carved a small kingdom for himself in the Cambodian uplands. The title was easy; the novel would be called *La Voie royale* after the ancient Khmer Royal Road that stretched northwest from Angkor across the Dangrek Mountains into Thailand.

During the writing, death became an obsession. When Groot and Alix came for dinner, metaphysics invaded everything as they took turns expressing their after-death beliefs. Clara felt haunted by her childhood *idée fixe*—how could anyone accept life if there was no prime mover, no "orchestra conductor?" Alix, on the strength of her Marxist faith, thought

117

she could accept the total void. One evening, Groethuysen picked up an African diety carving from the bookcase and said, "Suppose that after death we wake up facing *him*?" After quick smiles, André tried. "And what if it would be before the Christians' god?" After a long silence, Groot said that if he would wake up facing the Christians' diety, he'd say, "Lord, I didn't think it could all be that dumb." Once the book was finished, they decided to eliminate death from their dinner conversations.

Sex also held Malraux's attention in *The Royal Way* and Julien Green was to remember a literary luncheon where André perorated brilliantly on the subject. The gathering included, besides Green and Malraux, André Gide, Emmanuel Berl, Jacques Schiffrin and Robert de Saint Jean. The essence of Malraux's thesis was that eroticism could only exist in countries with a high notion of sin. A little later when Malraux asked Gide to define for them what a Christian was, Gide tried to evade the question, but Malraux insisted, saying it was a question Gide had touched upon in his recent essay on Montaigne. "Touched upon," Gide answered, "I touch upon everything." [5] Another evening the conversation turned to literature and Gide was to write in his *Journals* that "despite Berl's and Malraux's extraordinary eloquence, I tried to take part in the conversation, but I had a hard time keeping up with them and understanding their thinking." [6]

Gide and Malraux were becoming friends, Gide already the tolerant and luminous elder statesman of French letters—the Nobel Prize was not to come until 1947—and Malraux a new assertive influence. Since the clever *Les Faux monnayeurs* (*The Counterfeiters*) in 1926—Gide's only novel according to his own criteria (the others he called *récits*)—he had traveled extensively in Black Africa and, in the recently published *Voyage au Congo* and *Retour au Tchad,* had denounced the excesses of colonial rule.

Esthetically, the two Andrés were far apart, Gide admiring artistic perfection, Malraux creation "in the making," but they shared a high regard for Dostoyevsky, Nietzsche and Baudelaire—of Gide's writing, Malraux was a fervent admirer of the early, self-mocking *Paludes.* At Gallimard's they were a strong influence. It was for Malraux's *Tableaux de la littérature française* that Gide had written the Montaigne essay. Gide's *Journals* of the 1929–33 era was to be full of references to publishing ideas and literary work accomplished with Malraux. During these years, they exchanged views liberally and constantly. When Malraux wanted to create a Gallimard edition for new writers, he wanted Gide to have veto power, but Gide said that he would prefer to have the right to impose flunked candidates. In 1933, they were to become comrades-in-

[5] Julien Green, *Journal* (Paris: Plon, 1972).
[6] André Gide, *Journals: 1889–1949* (Paris: Gallimard, 1949).

arms against fascism and go to Berlin together to plead with the new regime for the liberation of German communist leaders.

Published in October 1930 following serialization in *La Revue de Paris* magazine, *The Royal Way* is both meditation on death and heroic retelling of the Banteai Srey expedition. Unlike *Les Conquérants* with its scores of characters, *La Voie royale* is basically only about two men, Perken and Vannec. The middle-aged Perken is Mayrena, as is, in caricature, Grabot, who doesn't appear until the middle of the book. Young Vannec is largely a self-portrait. Perken, half Dane, half German, is the *heimatslose* European in Asia, an adventurer who in the past has acted as a semiofficial maverick agent in the interior for the Thai government. He is obsessed with death although he feels that real death is not the stopping of the heartbeat but moral and physical decay, the collapse of a person's will and sense of metaphysical absurdity. For fifteen years, he has been maneuvering to take over a whole tract of the mountainous interior, draw together a score of tribes into one private state, await the inevitable battle with the Thai government and surrounding countries—this to enshrine himself in History. In the Jungle, Perken and Vannec eventually come upon Grabot, not the king of the Moi tribes but their prisoner, someone they have blinded and harnessed to a treadmill.

Claude Vannec is a trained archaeologist who can think of only one way of making a fortune—to uncover Khmer statues, get them out of Cambodia and sell them to the highest bidder. On a early page, he outlines his views on art, telling the director of the French Institute in Saigon that time does not exist in art, that what interests him is art's secret life, fashioned by the deaths of men, "in one word: every work of art tends to become myth."

Perken and Vannec meet on a ship sailing toward Asia—the book opens with a taut discussion about eroticism in which Perken says it is not essential for a man to know the women he is making love to. With the exception of two pages in *Man's Fate, The Royal Way* contains the only sex scene in Malraux's oeuvre, a languid, compelling end of chapter where Perken, with a wounded and infected knee he knows will kill him, has smoked opium to deaden the pain in order to take a woman a last time, a native girl with a face of Asiatic impassivity and a sleek, hairless body.

> In a slow, persistent rhythm they rose and fell, a rhythm that, though unchanged, was ever gaining in intensity, until the whole room seemed pervaded by their movement. Like a spent wave they sank, and slowly rose again, the muscles growing taut, the pools of shadow deepening around them. When, helped by her, he put his arm around her, he knew her fear of him was passing. She let one hip take her weight, so as slightly to change position. For an instant a ray of yellow-golden light,

119

as a whiplash, flickered across her back, vanished between her legs. The soft warmth of her body flooded his senses. Suddenly, she bit her lip; a little willful gesture that showed her inability to subdue the heaving of her breasts. He scanned her face and bluish eyelids as though they were a mask. His face was only a few inches from hers, but he felt as if the blind desire linking his body with this woman's were someone else's . . .

Perken agrees to team up with the art-hunting Vannec because he needs money for machine guns and because he would like to eliminate Grabot, who had vanished mysteriously in the bush. Deep in the rain forest, Perken and Vannec suddenly see armed warriors, naked men with thick lips and spears glittering in the sun. After finding the Khmer temple ruins and hacking away two enchanting stone *devis,* which Vannec thinks will fetch a half-million francs if brought out intact, they deliberately strike out into unknown territory. Everything goes wrong; they are deserted by their guides, sometimes they catch glimpses of the half-savage tribesmen, but a jungle trail takes them to a Moi village, where they discover Grabot, so mutilated he appears to have no human qualities. He has been blinded, his matted hair falls around his face and he has been yoked by leather thongs to a treadmill spending his days crawling around the airless hut in interminable circles, and living only for the day when an impossible revenge will be granted him.

Perken and Vannec free Grabot from the treadmill, but make no attempt to escape the village. They seize the hut belonging to the chief but find it empty. The tribesmen are invisible, but their presence is felt and at dusk comes the confrontation. Perken marches out of the hut to face the warriors and their aged chieftain to parley for his life, advancing across the compound by the will to defy torture and the fascination of torture itself. The only hope lies in his relentless will, but he steps on a poisoned war dart. When he falls, he half expects the Mois to hurl their spears at him. Bleeding and in pain, he gets up and continues the march and, through subterfuge manages to gain freedom for himself and Vannec. They make their way to the first Thai township where an opium-addicted English doctor tells Perken that he will die of his wound. Temporarily abandoning his art treasures and exalting his act of loyalty as something that sets him apart from the great mass of men—Vannec offers to accompany Perken to Savan, "his" village or kingdom. As they set out in a losing race against the advancing railroad and the military columns that will not only free Grabot but pacify the whole region, Perken fights to wrest a grandiose moral victory from his "monstrous defeat" by living out his own death, by attempting to turn this imposed death into a free act.

The ending of *La Voie royale* contains Malraux's first grandiose pages, Perken lying in a crowded hut, with "his" natives watching him silently, and he watching himself die, fascinated by his own disintegration and the pain of knowing that all those around him will see another sunrise.

120

The mosquitos torment him, but he has no strength to brush them away. He realizes he is still alive because he suffers and tells himself that if he begins to remember things, it is because he is dying.

La Voie royale was a success although its welcome didn't match the electrifying reception accorded *Les Conquérants*. Critics were favorable, with John Charpentier writing in *Mercure de France* that Malraux was sure to receive the 1930 Prix Goncourt. In *L'Action française,* Pierre-Eugéne Drieu La Rochelle, an anguished writer who had become a friend in 1927, wrote a lengthy homage, analyzing Malraux's three books set in Asia, calling *La Tentation de l'Occident* "a youthful essay, revealing a brilliant and highly endowed young man," *Les Conquérants* "the first product of the union of idea and action" and *La Voie royale* a novel showing further progression. "Like most Frenchmen, Malraux can't invent; his imagination takes off from facts. One has the feeling he cannot really escape what he has known. The events in his books have a rough-hewn characteristic which shows a direct transfer of reality to plot. But through a brief and fast series of events, Malraux makes his intellectual temperament stand out. One single line of events and, under it, a single character, a hero. This hero isn't Malraux, it's the mythical representation of his ego, more sublime and more concrete than himself."

While drifting toward opposing political camps, Malraux and Drieu La Rochelle were to remain friends until the latter's suicide in 1945.

The publication of *La Voie royale* again brought to the surface the Banteai Srey incident, the Pnompenh trial and appeal. When *Candide*'s star critic André Rousseaux interviewed him, André admitted that the story of Vannec was autobiographical, while insisting on the attenuating circumstances of his case—the nonclassification of archaeological sites in Cambodia and the fact that no court had actually ruled on that issue. Rousseaux came away baffled. Instead of the fascinating anarchist he had expected to interview, he had listened to endless pleas from someone obsessed with "burgeois order." "I cut the interview short and ran away. I had expected for a moment to skirt pure anarchy and despite myself I admired his lucid and gloomy despair, the horrible and sublime beauty. I must admit that pure anarchy doesn't exist, except in Mr. Malraux's books." [7]

La Voie royale appeared in October. On December 20, Fernand Malraux took his own life. André's father had suffered a massive stroke a year earlier and, fearing he might be permanently paralyzed, preferred to commit suicide. There was also talk that he was ruined, but Clara and André weren't so sure that in a macabre imitation of Perken he hadn't been tempted by "the adventure of death." He was fifty-four.

The suicide had not been totally unexpected. Six weeks earlier,

[7] *Candide* (Nov. 13, 1930).

the elderly woman cleaning his apartment had come to see Clara and André to tell them in a panicky voice about his father's plans. To change Fernand Malraux's mind, they had invented a whole story, that his youngest son, Claude, was suffering a contagious disease and that Roland, the elder of the two sons Fernand had with his second wife, would have to come and stay with him. The stratagem had seemed to work. The presence of the adolescent son had in fact cheered him but after a while he had become dejected again. A few days after Roland's return to his mother for Christmas, Fernand had opened the gas valves. When the devout cleaning woman found him the next morning, his face was serene and his hand was on a book on Buddhist concepts of the afterlife. The burial brought Clara and André to Dunkirk, where this twice-divorced man who had killed himself was nevertheless given a Catholic ceremony and on a cold, blustery January day was interred in the parish cemetery by the sea. André had never met so many Malrauxs.

The probate revealed what everybody had suspected—there was no fortune. No money even for the education of the teen-aged boys. Claude wanted to study agriculture and Clara and André put him through school. Roland felt no urgent vocation but since he had a gift for languages and was restless, they sent him to learn German in Magdeburg where he could stay with Clara's uncle and family. A few years later, he became a militant communist and spent several years in the Soviet Union.

In the April issue of *NRF,* Trotsky reviewed *Les Conquérants,* inviting its author to answer his criticism in the same pages. It had taken the better part of two years for the book to reach Trotsky on the Turkish island of Prinkipo near Istanbul, where the Kemal Ataturk government allowed "the enemy of the people," as Leon Davidovich was now called in the USSR and the Comintern, to spend a quiet exile with his wife Natalya.

The former Commissar for Foreign Affairs had always been a passionate reader of French—preferring Anatole France to Marcel Proust —and had just been visited by Pierre Naville, the Marxist theoretician relative of Gide and friend of Malraux who encouraged Trotsky's decision to ask the French government to allow him to live in France where he felt he could be closer to current events. Trotsky had just written *The Permanent Revolution* and started a *Life of Lenin.* He was obviously intrigued by the story of the 1925 Canton events and Russia's role in that phase of the Chinese Revolution, a role which, after Lenin's death, had provoked a clash between Trotsky and Joseph Stalin.

Calling *Les Conquérants* a "fictionalized chronicle," Trotsky praised the book's style and its daring, but his review was also an indictment—of Stalin and the Comintern for having promoted the unholy alliance with Chiang Kai-shek and of Malraux for not drawing obvious conclusions. "The author's truly profound sympathy for insurrectionist China is unquestionable, but it is corrupted by excesses of individualism and of esthetic caprice." Trotsky noted that the book "lacks a natural affinity between the author, in spite of all he knows and understands, and his heroine, the Revolution." What is missing, Trotsky suggests, was precisely the knowledge of *how* to fight a revolution.

The book's political lesson, Trotsky said, sprang from the events, in spite of the author. The tragedy of Canton was the caliber of men chosen by Moscow and the Comintern, "the little bureaucracy of foreigners" (Borodin, Garin, Klein, etc.) who aligned themselves with the right wing of the Kuomintang *against* the people, represented by Hong. It was all the fault of Borodin—and behind him of Stalin and the Comintern, that Hong resorted to senseless acts of terrorism. When Hong demanded exemplary punishment of the most notorious bourgeois leaders, all Borodin would answer was, "You can't touch those who pay. . . . To make a revolution is to pay its army," a quote Trotsky hammered home as the root of evil which eventually led to the Shanghai massacre of China's communists by Chiang Kai-shek. After saying that "a good dose of Marxism might have saved the author from fatal mistakes," Trotsky concluded:

> The book is called *Les Conquérants*. In the author's mind this double-edged title, in which revolution is also tarted up to mean imperialism, refers to Russian Bolsheviks, or, rather, to some of them. Conquerors? The Chinese masses rose in order to accomplish a revolutionary insurrection, with the October Revolution as their example and Bolshevism as their banner. But the "Conquerors" conquered nothing. On the contrary, they handed everything to the enemy. If the Russian Revolution inspired the Chinese Revolution, the second-generation Russians managed to fumble revolt in China. Malraux doesn't draw these conclusions and doesn't seem to have thought them out, but they are nevertheless there, standing out against the background of his remarkable book.[8]

Malraux's answer was not so much a young author's expression of gratitude toward a man who, when it came to Marxist revolutions, spoke with authority, but the riposte of a writer feeling the truth of creative emotions, and, when it came to actual "game plans," of a fellow-strategist. When Trotsky wrote that *Les Conquérants* was important *in spite* of its author, Malraux remarked that Trotsky showed a profound ignorance of artistic creation, because:

> Revolutions don't happen all by themselves, nor do novels. This book isn't a "fictionalized chronicle" of the Chinese Revolution because it deals first of all with the relations between people and a collective undertaking, making only the documented events answerable to Trotsky's arguments. He finds that Garin makes mistakes, but Stalin finds that he, Trotsky, makes mistakes. When we read in [Trotsky's] *My Life* the ago-

8 "La Révolution étranglée," *NRF* (April 1, 1931).

123

nizing story of his fall, we forget he is a Marxist and maybe he even forgets it himself.[9],

Borodin, Malraux added, was after all a Marxist and in 1925–26 the Chinese Communist Party realized it had no other options. The Comintern also "had no choice." Malraux's argument was that in order to give the Chinese proletariat the class consciousness it needed to gain power, it was necessary first to eliminate the consciousness of the so-called secret societies, which grouped all politically aware Chinese and of which the Kuomintang was by far the strongest. In merging with the Kuomintang, the Communist Party moved from being yet another freemason clique to being one of the doctrines of the most powerful of societies.

Trotsky could not drop *Les Conquérants* on this note of rebuke and proposed a rebuttal. The *NRF* never published the answer, but it eventually appeared in the dissident communist magazine *La Lutte des classes.* "I must correct myself after having read Malraux's piece," Trotsky wrote somewhat peevishly. "In my article I suggested that a good dose of Marxism would be useful for Garin. Now, I no longer think so." When the Edouard Herriot government authorized Trotsky to take up residence in France in 1933, Malraux was to be one of the first to ask to see him—a request Trotsky granted, according to Naville, because the advent of Adolf Hitler made him feel all progressives should close ranks.

During the summer of 1931, Clara and André returned to Iran and continued east—around the world. From Iran they crossed into Afghanistan by way of the already Sovietized Tashkent and Termez where turbanned caravaneers from Samarkand squatted in the shade of spiny trees beside a Russian airfield. The Malrauxs' maiden flight took them across the Pamirs to Kabul, still almost a forbidden city. Afghanistan was in the midst of a civil war, with one usurper just boiled in oil. If the *divas* of Banteai Srey had eluded André, he managed to buy Greco-Buddhist sculptures from a recent Afridis excavation near Peshawar. With Clara and various native helpers, he got the stone carving across the Khyber Pass, down the Himalayas to Rawalpindi and, with oxen pulling an engine-less Model T Ford part of the way, to Lahore and on to Bombay, where Clara's English got the Bodhisattvas through British customs and on board a freighter sailing for France.

India captivated them. "There is something at once bewitching and bewitched in Indian thought which has to do with the feeling it gives us of climbing a sacred mountain whose summit constantly recedes," André was to write in the *Antimémoires.* They felt India was the most religious and most affectionate country, with superstition swarming like mayflies around Buddhist temples. They found Benares a melancholy garden and its crowds silent. They studied erotic temple sculpture and in

[9] "Réponse à Léon Trotsky," *NRF* (April 1, 1931).

124

the Hanuman temple saw monkeys pursuing mysterious errands around a sacrificial stone and heard the story of Buddha's promise to the monkeys that if they behaved well, one morning they would become humans. Buddha's promise explained why a great wail of monkeys could be heard every dawn. Every evening, the monkeys hoped and every morning they wept.

At dawn, André was up and went to the Ganges. Under the monsoon clouds, brahmans dipped in the water while on the shores funeral pyres flickered dimly in the fog, but no monkeys wailed. From Burma, Clara and André went to Hong Kong and, finally, China—a Canton not at all like the Canton of *Les Conquérants,* Hangchow, Shanghai— *Man's Fate* was already germinating in him and he took notes. After Peking and the Great Wall, they boarded a train that traveled north for days, suddenly into colder weather and Mongol faces. On a platform one day, they saw twenty young men in Western dress, shouting ecstatically and jumping up and down. Someone managed to translate into pidgin English that war with Japan had just broken out and that the young draftees were dancing for joy.

After Korea and Japan, North America—"discovered backwards" —Vancouver, Seattle, San Francisco and a train ride across a United States deep into its Depression. Nothing really surprised them, André was to remember forty years later, because they were avid moviegoers and Hollywood and newsreels had made the American Way familiar to them. In New York their money ran out and they spent two very poor weeks while awaiting a telegraphed money order from Gaston Gallimard.

The revelation for André was the Metropolitan Museum. While Clara discovered speakeasies, he stalked through Far East and primitive art rooms on the second floor and found medieval European art on the main floor. What struck him was that in America the European Middle Ages was treated like an outlandish period, whereas Chinese statues faced Greco-Roman sculpture. This both confirmed his theory that an Etruscan vase can rub shoulders with a Picasso terra-cotta and astonished him as a daring sweeping away of Greco-Roman tradition and classicism as the only linear yardstick. It also set him thinking about barbaric arts. Perhaps they were not regressive at all, but new and high stylizations in their own right.

When Gallimard's money order reached the Western Union office, where they had become twice-a-day visitors, they bought fresh clothes and had themselves invited to several parties. They would be back, they were sure. On the ship back to France, Marshal Henri-Philippe Pétain was at the head of the captain's table.

Malraux was thirty years old.

The France he and Clara returned to was fast polarizing and the Malrauxs were barely inside the door of their new Left Bank apartment in the Rue du Bac before they, too, were swept up in political radicalization. While they had been in America, the Depression had finally hit, although it was never to be as bad as in Germany, Britain and the United States. Following the crash of the Kreditanstalt bank in Vienna, the financial panic in Germany and, above all, the abandonment by Great Britain on September 23, 1931, of the gold standard and the forty percent devaluation of the pound sterling, the "Poincaré prosperity" screeched to a halt and unemployment doubled. The slump was the worst economic and financial crisis France had experienced in a hundred years and it was aggravated by the failure of the fumbling National Assembly to take sensible measures. As a result, popular rancor and resentment wasn't so much directed against the party in office as in the United States and Britain, but, as in Germany, against the republican regime itself. In Berlin, the discontent brought Hitler to power at the beginning of 1933; in Paris it spawned an explosion of right-wing "leagues," whose objective was the overthrow of the Third Republic in favor of strong one-man rule or, in the case of Charles Maurras' Action française, restoration of monarchy. Other leagues included such semifascist student bodies as Jeunesses Patriotes and Solidarité Française, the latter financed by the wealthy perfumer François Coty and with members wearing blue shirts, black berets and jackboots. The most reactionary, far-right group was Le Francisme, which drew its inspiration from Hitler and Mussolini and worked openly for an outright fascist regime although it never caught on with more than a few thousand youths. The largest of the leagues was the paramilitary Croix du Feu, originally a nonpolitical association of decorated war veterans, now taken over by François de La Rocque, an energetic, retired lieutenant colonel. La Rocque was able to mobilize street demonstrators on an hour's notice and on November 26 showed his strength by leading his Croix du Feu members, assisted by storm troopers from Action Française and Jeunesses Patriotes, into the great hall of the Trocadéro, where thousands were attending the final gala of the International Disarmament Congress and breaking it up. Although some of the most distinguished men in Europe were on the platform, including former premier Painlevé, Lord Robert Cecil, Salvador de Madariaga—Spain's King Alfonso XIII had abdicated in April and the Spanish Republic instituted—they were swept away by La Rocque and his rowdies while other assault groups cleared out the audience and even police sent to protect them. Since the proceedings were being broadcast, all of France heard it. Overnight La Rocque was a household name. In the spring of 1932 the successive conservative administrations had been so thoroughly discredited by their disastrous policy of severe deflation and economic retrenchment that the electorate voted the Left back into power. At the same time, Malraux, Romain Rolland, André Breton, Louis Aragon, André Gide and Paul Nizan founded *L'Association des artistes et écrivains révolutionnaires*. The time of intellectual aloofness was over.

126

The blatant anti-Semitism of the leagues hurt Clara personally. In general, things were not going well for her family. Because of her younger brother's reckless investments in Indochinese companies and because of the final devaluation of the Poincaré franc, Madame Goldschmidt was practically ruined. The Magdeburg uncles together with Madame Goldschmidt's eldest son managed to hide the extent of the ruin from her by sending money from Germany, but her youngest son continued to skid into disastrous financial adventures—and his mother to secretly support his wife and children. In 1933, the revenues from the German investments stopped and Madame Goldschmidt was told the truth. She sold the mansion in Passy and moved into an six-room flat on the ground floor of Clara's and André's apartment building in the Rue du Bac. Soon, mother and daughter were to see Action française and Croix de Feu demonstrators march in closed ranks down Boulevard St. Germain toward the National Assembly. On André's side, the fall of 1932 marked the death of his grandmother and, a few months later, his mother, felled by an embolism.

To counteract or at least neutralize the influence of the right-leaning *Candide* and *Gringoire*, Emmanuel Berl, financed by Gaston Gallimard, launched a new weekly, *Marianne*. Ten years older than Malraux, Berl was of an old French-Jewish intellectual family—a distant relative of Marcel Proust and Henri Bergson—who had been a friend of Clara and André since 1928. As Gide noted, Berl possessed an intellect as bright and sharp as André's, even if he was more polemicist than writer, the author of only two books, both on the decline of the bourgeoisie. Berl was an elitist revolutionary because he was convinced the sclerosis of the bourgeois classes was permanent and irreversible and that only a *tabula rasa* sweep could save Europe. He had written ecstatically about *Les Conquérants* and called Garin the "new man." He understood André perfectly, Clara felt, when he wrote that "for Malraux what makes a revolutionary tick is not faith (always oversimplified), nor information (always sketchy), nor discipline (always out of date), but a certain availability and courage."

Paul Morand and Antoine de Saint-Exupéry (the latter's *Vol de nuit* had just inaugurated the aviation novel craze) were early contributors to *Marianne* and Berl counted on André to write for the magazine also. As it turned out, the Malraux byline was to appear only five times in five years in *Marianne,* although always above important articles on Indochina, Trotsky and fascism among others. André was nevertheless a frequent visitor to the magazine offices, initially for mental jousting with its publisher-editor, later because of one of Berl's collaborators—Josette Clotis, a pale and slender young writer who apparently was unaware of the effect her vivacious beauty had on everyone she met.

During the summer and fall of 1932, however, André had little time for magazine writing or flirting with pretty young writers. He was at work on the novel which, within a year, was to make him world famous.

127

"Don't you think it's stupidly characteristic of the human race that a man who has only one life can lose it for an ideal?"

"It's very rare for a man to be able to endure— how shall I say— his condition, his fate."

Man's Fate

11

Malraux wrote the copy for the first advertisement for *La Condition humaine* himself and the few lines in the June 1933 issue of *NRF* are perhaps the best summing up of the intentions behind his most famous novel.

No one can endure his own solitude. Whether it is through love, fantasy, gambling, power, revolt, heroism, comradeship, opium, contemplation or sex, it is against this fundamental angst that consciously or not, the characters of this novel—communists, fascists, terrorists, adventurers, police chiefs, junkies, artists and the women with whom they are involved —are defending themselves, engaged as they are to the point of torture and suicide in the Chinese Revolution, upon which for some years the destiny of the Asian world and perhaps the West depended.

La Condition humaine—which became *Man's Fate* * in English— immediately entered the French language as a stock expression in political parlance. Until the 1950s, legend had it that Malraux took it from Pascal's famous reflection in the *Pensées:* "Let us imagine a number of men in chains and all condemned to death. Every day some of them have their throats cut while the others look on. Those who remain see their true condition in the fate of their fellows and look at one another in sorrow and without hope, awaiting their turn. This is the image of the condition of man." "La Condition humaine" appears also in one of Montaigne's essays, and in one of Madame de Maintenon's letters to her father-confessor there is the actual phrase: "There is a horrible void in all human conditions." In 1954, when *La Condition humaine* was presented as a stage play, Malraux was to tell interviewers that his title could be taken as a

* A British edition, translated by A. Macdonald, appeared in 1948 under the title *Man's Estate.*

souvenir of the writings and ideas of all three—Pascal, Montaigne and the most influential woman in Louis XIV's life.

La Condition humaine is the story of men waiting to have their throats cut, the story of a handful of people caught in the intrigues, anguish and above all the violence of a revolutionary situation. Like the earlier novels, the plot advances through action to apparent success to failure, with its tragic heroes beginning with a major purpose, undergoing conflicts and arriving at the perception of truth. As in Les Conquérants the cast is a motley of expatriate revolutionaries, multinationals and a few sharply drawn Chinese. As is not the case in the earlier novels, people here have families—wives, husbands, sons and in-laws.

The scene is Shanghai on the eve of the showdown between Chiang Kai-shek and the communists—still nominally allies—in March 1927. The Kuomintang coalition is winning over warlords and reactionaries and holds Canton and Hankow (now Wuhan) halfway to Peking. In Hankow, Borodin has set up the Comintern capital to balance an earlier anticommunist coup by Chiang and of necessity the hard-pressed communists cooperate with Chiang's Nationalists. Between Hankow and final triumph in Peking lies the huge, industrialized port city of Shanghai with its large concentration of foreign influence. In the struggle for China, Shanghai is more than major port and modern center of commerce. To both factions of the Kuomintang coalition—the Nationalist majority and the smaller urban communist forces—the question of who takes Shanghai will largely determine who will ultimately rule the huge country. When La Condition humaine opens, Chiang's Nationalist armies are approaching and the communists inside Shanghai are cut off from Hankow. Kyoshi Gisors and Katov, two of the communist leaders, crazily take things in their own hands and succeed. They stage an insurrection, capture the city and divert an arms shipment. By distributing the weapons, they turn a general strike into a revolution. But from the beginning, foreign business and diplomatic interest—alarmed precisely by the success of the initial uprising—negotiate with Chiang and the Nationalist armies to squash the rebellion. As the city falls to Chiang, a deal is made and one portion of the action ends with the communists receiving orders from the Kuomintang coalition and their leaders to surrender to the Nationalists, an act they know will mean their own extermination.

Kyo Gisors is half French, half Japanese; Katov is a Russian. Kyo and his wife May, a young German doctor who has turned communist out of hatred of suffering and oppression, are the revolutionary couple, "a partnership consented, conquered, chosen." They fight for "human dignity," which to them translates simply into absence of humiliation. "No dignity, no real life is possible for anyone working twelve hours a day without knowing why," says Kyo. Old Gisors is Kyo's opium-addicted French father, a widowed one-time professor of sociology at Peking Uni-

129

versity who has organized revolutionary cadres but avoids action himself. When Kyo is captured, Old Gisors makes hopeless attempts to have him set free and after his son's death is plunged into a grief he at first refuses to drown in opium. At the end, however, he flees to Japan and into opium, refusing to join his daughter-in-law in Moscow to prepare for another day at the barricades.

Ch'en Ta'erh is a young terrorist who in the opening pages hesitates for an existentialist moment before plunging his knife into a sleeping man it is his duty to kill. Later, this missionary-educated former gunrunner seduced into joining the revolution by a recruiter playing on his illusion of heroism, draws away from the others, defies both discipline and doctrine and insists on assassinating Chiang by turning himself into a walking bomb and hurling himself in front of the general's speeding automobile. He throws himself in front of the wrong car and dies trying to give terrorism a meaning. His gratuitous, "personalized" terrorism not only blurs the frontier between the revolutionaries and their opponents, it makes him die in political and actual loneliness as someone who has parted with the revolution. It is his attempt at Chiang's life that triggers the repression.

The counterrevolutionary forces are represented by König, Chiang's police chief in Shanghai, whose memory of humiliation in the hands of Bolsheviks during the Russian Revolution makes him torture others in order to prove to himself that men in torment have no dignity. If no one can stand torture, then dignity is simply being the torturer instead of the victim. Ferral is the straightforward and intelligent French entrepreneur who negotiates with the encircling Nationalists on behalf of Western commercial interests. He is rapacious, sensual and is lost in his dreams of loans, bank rates, concessions and the international money market. His mistress is the wealthy Valérie—a freer and more sophisticated version of the "new woman" than May. When she abandons him for another man, he goes to a pet shop, buys every bird in the place together with a kangaroo, takes them to her hotel and, in her absence, sets them free in her room. By allowing himself an act of revenge, he is almost human, but next he picks up a Chinese whore for the pleasure of humiliating her.

Other foreigners include the shopkeeper Hemmelrich, a would-be revolutionary saddled with a wretched wife and incurably sick child constantly in pain. Cruel irony frees him to join the insurrection. During his absence from his shop, his wife and child are killed in a grenade attack. The Baron de Clappique is an inordinately complex character, a fallen aristocrat and former antiques dealer in Peking, now a rootless, surrealist figure who provides relief from metaphysics with tall stories and silly exploits. He wears a black patch over one eye and a perpetual evening jacket. He becomes involved with the revolutionaries because he runs out of money and can be of some help to them. A sometime police informer,

130

he knows a good deal about the forthcoming Nationalist attack and tells about it in the Black Cat Café where he is usually to be found after dark.

When Clappique learns from the Nationalist police of the planned repression, he immediately tells Kyo, who asks him to go back for more information. They agree to meet at the Black Cat. With time to spare before the rendezvous, Clappique goes to a gambling saloon and the information he has, vital to Kyo, is forgotten.

As Clappique loses his last money—and with it his means of leaving Shanghai—at the roulette table, he seems to understand everything, feeling his life suspended to the whim of the absurd ball spinning over the numbered slots. In the end, he destroys his identity papers, disguises himself in a sailor's uniform and, once aboard a departing ship, plunges back into mythomania and alcohol, saying men don't exist because "a costume is all it takes to make you escape yourself."

If Ferral's and Valérie's lovemaking is an erotic contest of will that she loses by melting into her own orgasm and Clappique discovers his intercourse with a whore in a hotel is being watched by voyeurs in an adjoining room—a scene cut from the book but published in Marianne [1]— Kyo is deeply in love with his wife. May, he feels, has freed him from his loneliness and his bitterness. On the morning of the insurrection, she tells him she has just been to bed with another man, an old friend. This is within the rules of their marriage and, besides, they may all be dead tomorrow. Although he knows that for May sex has not meant emotional surrender, he also knows "the fundamental mysogyny of almost all men."

> The essential, what caused pain in him, was that he was suddenly separated from her, not by hatred—although there was hatred in him, not by jealousy (or was jealousy precisely this?), but by a feeling that has no name, as destructive as time or death: he could not find her again. He opened his eyes. Who was she, this familiar athletic body, this face with its averted profile, elongated eye that started at the temple and sank between the forehead with the hair brushed aside and the cheekbone? Who was she? Someone who had just slept with someone else? But was she not also the one who tolerated his weaknesses, his afflictions, his outbursts of irritation, the one who had helped nurse wounded comrades and held wakes with him over dead friends? The sweetness of her voice still hung in the air. No one can command himself to forget. Yet this body was suddenly suffused with the poignant mystery of a familiar person suddenly transformed, the mystery of a mute, a blind or a crazy person. And she was a woman. Not a different kind of man; someone different.

Not until after the collapse of the revolt does Kyo regain this intense relationship with her, when they walk together in dense fog in "no

[1] *Marianne* (Dec. 1933).

man's land" streets, just before they are attacked by Nationalist militiamen and Kyo is arrested.

As the noose tightens around the city—an armored train, never really seen but heard whistling in the night, is the most chilling realization of the approaching Nationalist armies' might—Kyo manages to slip through and go to Hankow to talk Borodin and the Comintern high command into rescuing the insurrectionists in Shanghai. He doesn't get to see Borodin, but is received by Vologin, a graying Comintern secretary, organizer of the first insurrection in Finland in 1917. All that Vologin can give Kyo is a long lesson in revolutionary realpolitik, a lesson that is interrupted by the arrival of Ch'en. Vologin does not normally see terrorists because he considers them to be "narrow, arrogant and lacking in political sense," but he has Ch'en shown in when Kyo tells him Ch'en wants to murder Chiang Kai-shek. Vologin refuses to sanction the assassination, saying Chiang may make anticommunist decrees but won't murder them all because his son is in Moscow. Also, "we must not consider assassination—after all, as the chief path to political truth." Separately, Kyo and Ch'en make their way back to Shanghai.

The revolutionaries all die. Ch'en finishes himself off with a bullet in the mouth, unaware that he has thrown himself under the wrong car. Captured Kyo swallows his cyanide pellet knowing they have lost, but that he has given his life a meaning. His last thoughts go to May, not to the revolution, because it is she, not political action, who has liberated him from himself.

The worst fate is reserved for Katov, the "apparachik" Comintern organization man, who is the last one caught in the repression dragnet. When he is thrown into a school hall where two hundred wounded prisoners wait to be taken out and shot, he is put with Kyo in a space reserved for those who are to be thrown alive into the boiler of a locomotive—their deaths signaled back to those in the school hall by the shriek of the locomotive whistle. But Katov has three cyanide pellets with him to commit instant suicide. At night when the condemned and wounded men lie in rows on the floor and Kyo swallows his cyanide, Katov gives his pellets—one of them rolls away in the darkness—to Suan and another frightened Chinese comrade next to him. When they silently commit suicide, he feels deserted.

> In a clatter of rifles striking against one another six soldiers were approaching the condemned men. All the prisoners were awake now. The new railway lantern showed only long, vague forms—tombs in the earth already turned over—and a few reflections in the eyes. Katov managed to raise himself. The one who commanded the squad took Kyo's arm, felt its stiffness, immediately seized Suan's; that one also was stiff. A muffled rumor was spreading, from the first row of prisoners to the last. The chief of the squad lifted the foot of one of the men, then of the

132

other; they fell back, stiff. He called the officer, who went through the same motions. Among the prisoners, the hum was growing. The officer looked at Katov.

"Dead?"

Why answer?

"Isolate the six nearest prisoners!"

"Useless," answer Katov. "I gave them the cyanide."

"And you?" he finally asked.

"There was only enough for two," answered Katov with deep joy. "I'm going to get a rifle-butt in my face," he thought to himself. The murmur of the prisoners had become almost a clamor.

"Come on, let's go," was all the officer said.

Katov didn't forget that he had been condemned to death before, that he had seen the machine guns leveled at him, had heard them fire . . . "As soon as I'm outside, I'm going to try to strangle one of them, to hold my hands tightened to his throat long enough so they will be forced to kill me. They will burn me, but dead." At that very moment one of the soldiers seized him by the waist, while another brought his hands behind his back and tied them. "The little fellows were lucky," he said to himself. "Well! let's suppose I died in a fire." He began to walk. Silence fell, despite the moans. The lantern threw Katov's shadow, now very black, across the great windows framing the night; he walked heavily, with uneven steps, hindered by his wounds; when the swinging of his body brought him closer to the lantern, the silhouette of his head vanished into the ceiling. The whole darkness of the vast hall was alive, and followed him with its eyes, step by step. The silence had become so great that the ground resounded each time his foot fell heavily upon it; all the heads, with a slight movement, followed the rhythm of his walk, with love, with dread, with resignation. All kept their heads raised; the door was being closed.

A sound of deep breathing, the same as that of sleep, began to rise from the ground; breathing through their noses, their jaws clenched with anguish, motionless now, all those who were not dead yet were waiting for the whistle.

The only survivors are those who realize the vanity of action, Old Gisors, Clappique and Ferral. Old Gisors is—beyond political utopia— the ultimate hope. Even if victory is denied them, he says, men who struggle for a good future find new values. He used to urge his students to join the communists—not because Marxism is a superior doctrine but because it is a will. "You must be Marxists not in order to be right but in order to conquer without betraying yourselves," he used to tell them. In one of his detached analyses, he says a civilization becomes transformed when its most oppressed element becomes a value. Like Garin in *Les Conquérants,* Old Gisors is the archetypal fellow traveler, a quasi-Marxist in the face of triumphant fascism, yet too lucid not to realize that a revolution obeys obscure inner laws of fate. When in the last chapter, May

133

comes to Kobe, Japan, where he lives with his opium and his memories on a hill overlooking the bay and the harbor, he says he will not join her in Moscow. Since Kyo's death, he says, he has discovered music, which alone can speak of death.

He took her hand.

"You know the phrase: 'It takes nine months to make a man, and a single day to kill him.' We both know this. May, it doesn't take nine months, it takes sixty years to make a man, sixty years of sacrifice, of wanting to do things.† And when a man is complete, when there is nothing left in him of childhood, of adolescence, when he is really a man, he is good for nothing but to die."

She looked at him, stunned. He was looking at the clouds.

"I loved Kyo as few men love their children, you know." He was still holding her hands. "Listen, one must love the living and not the dead."

"I am not going to Moscow to love."

He looked out over the magnificent bay, drenched in sunlight. She had withdrawn her hand. "On the road to vengeance, little May, one finds life . . ."

"That's no reason for seeking it."

Malraux wrote *La Condition humaine* during the fall of 1932, when Clara became pregnant. He wrote a large part of the novel, which he called "a reportage," at Eddy du Perron's suburban house in the pretty Vallée de Chevreuse south of Paris. To tell the complicated events leading up to the massacre of the Shanghai communists, Malraux relied on notes taken the previous year in China during his and Clara's round-the-world trip, on newspaper clippings and on talks with Georges Manue, a journalist friend who had covered the 1927 events from Shanghai and Nanking and had even interviewed Chiang Kai-shek.

A persistent legend was to grow that for Kyo Malraux had been inspired by Chou En-lai.‡ The future Premier of the People's Republic had studied at the Sorbonne in Paris and, once back in China in 1923, had become the political head of the Whampoa Military Academy in Canton—an institution that in *Les Conquérants* Garin had founded. When Chiang attacked the communists who had set up soviets in the Yangtse Valley in 1927, Chou had fought the Kuomintang forces, but during the Shanghai events in March, his role had been relatively obscure. A more likely original for the portrait of the novel's dominating character was Kyo Momatsu, a young Japanese journalist who had been in Paris in 1922 and was a friend of Ho Chi Minh. Momatsu was to translate *La*

---

† Curiously, in Haakon M. Chevalier's *Man's Fate* translation, Malraux's sixty years come out "fifty years."

‡ As late as 1972, Cecil Jenkins will call "Chou En-lai the historical counterpart of Kyo," in *André Malraux.*

134

Condition humaine into Japanese and die covering the Vietnam War in 1970.

Old Gisors was part Gide, part Groethuysen and Ferral was inspired by André Berthelot, a French banker in China during the 1920s and, as president of the French Chamber of Commerce, the actual go-between in Western business interests' negotiations with the Nationalists. Clappique, of whom Malraux was so fond he used him again in the *Antimémoires* more than thirty years later, was partially inspired by René Guetta, a journalist at *Marianne*. Ch'en was the second reincarnation of Hinh, this time a more fleshed-out character than Hong in *Les Conquérants*.

Malraux turned in the manuscript at the end of 1932. Gaston Gallimard was deeply impressed by the novel—Gide wasn't on first reading—and also found the title striking (he was a great believer in titles). André wanted Gallimard to push for a Goncourt prize, but the publisher felt the powerful action, the exotic locale and sometimes disconcerting lyricism might go over the heads of the Goncourt jury members.

La Condition humaine was serialized in six issues of *NRF* from January through June 1933, and was in the bookstores by September. The triumph was immediate, lasting and worldwide. *Man's Fate* was an instant classic. In *Izvestia,* Ilya Ehrenburg prefaced his review from Paris by reporting how the book was already in its twenty-fifth printing in France. "It is not a book on the revolution, it is not an epic but an intimate journal, an X-ray of the author himself fragmented into several characters," Ehrenburg wrote. "For Malraux, the individual's willpower begins where it ordinarily ends—after illusion and beliefs have been abandoned." In America, Edmund Wilson wrote in *The New Republic,* "I don't know of any modern book which dramatizes so successfully such varied national and social types. Beside it, even E. M. Forster's admirable *A Passage to India* appears a little provincial; you even—what rarely happens nowadays to the reader of a French novel—forget that the author is French." If this wasn't enough to coax an American publisher into bringing out a translation, Leon Trotsky got off a letter to Simon and Schuster saying "only a great superhuman purpose for which man is ready to pay with his life gives meaning to personal existence. This is the final import of the novel which is free from philosophical didacticism and remains from beginning to end a true work of art." [2] The first edition of *Man's Fate,* translated by the University of California, Berkeley professor Haakon M. Chevalier, appeared in 1934 published by Harrison Smith and Robert Haas, Inc. Haas was a wealthy native of San Francisco who spoke perfect French and who in 1935 was to merge with Bennett Cerf and Donald Klopfer's Random House. Eleven years older than Malraux, Haas,

[2] Isaac Deutscher, *Trotsky,* Vol. III, *The Prophet Outcast: 1929–1940* (London: Oxford University Press, 1963).

who was William Faulkner's editor, met André during a trip to Paris in 1935.

La Condition humaine naturally interested communists and Russians. The beaten Chinese communists were now on the eve of their famous Long March. After squashing the Shanghai communists in 1927, Chiang Kai-shek had turned against Chu Teh, commanding the communist elements of the Fourth Army, cut these forces to pieces and forced whatever survivors were left to fall back on the mountains at Chingkang-shan, where Chu Teh had been joined by another beaten leader, Mao Tse-tung. During the next years, Chu and Mao had set out to convert the peasants, to abolish rent, dispossess landlords, redistribute land, suppress moneylenders who were the bane of the Chinese peasantry, and establish rural communism. They had carefully avoided positional warfare with the Nationalists and retreated from urban centers. Although this policy was successful, it had been branded as heretical by the Comintern and the Central Committee of the Chinese Communist Party. Since orthodox Marxism insisted that communist revolution could be based only on a proletariat, Mao's peasant-based communism had been anathematized, even if by 1930 Maoist soviets were governing rural areas of Hunan, Kiangsi, Hupeh and Kuantang, rapidly winning respect for their austere integrity and, incidentally, patriotism, since the Kuomintang with its standing armies, almost ignored the stepped-up Japanese encroachment on Chinese territory and sovereignty.

La Condition humaine had one enthusiastic Russian reader—Joseph Stalin. The novel was not too flattering for the Comintern nor for Stalin's China policy, at least as it had been practiced in 1927, but to the Russian leader, Malraux was one of two good Frenchmen—the other being Pierre Laval. The socialist politician who had formed a right-of-center cabinet in 1931 and had been premier for almost a year, visited the Soviet Union in 1933 and returned to France saying "Stalin felt a real liking for two Frenchmen—Malraux and myself." Accounts were to vary on what Stalin told André the following year in the dead of night at Maxim Gorky's summer dacha, but there was no doubt that Malraux was both hero and valuable ally to Moscow. He was a founding member of the Association of Revolutionary Writers and Artists and La Condition humaine appeared as Adolf Hitler had become Germany's new chancellor, blaming Germany's communists for the Reichstag fire that allowed him to seize power. Solidarity on the Left was now a matter of course and with Man's Fate, Malraux was beginning to look like one of Europe's leading antifascist writers. Orthodox Marxists did not consider him one of them, but practiced a policy of a very outstretched hand. The invitations and the wooing were soon to come, but for the moment André was more interested in what was happening in Germany than in visiting Moscow. German communists escaping to France called at the Malrauxs' apartment at 44 rue du Bac—

The twentieth printing, after Goncourt prize, of *Man's Fate*

Gustav Regler and Manes Sperber among others, or were sent there by André Gide and Bernard Groethuysen (the first thing Sperber was to remember André asking him was to explain why fascist regimes didn't produce great art).

In December, *La Condition humaine* and its thirty-two-year-old author received the Prix Goncourt, following a unanimous vote by the literary jury. The prize, the jury said, not only crowned *Man's Fate* but the "whole of the three Asiatic novels—*The Conquerors* and *The Royal Way* together with this novel." In New York, Haas rushed Stuart Gilbert's translation of *La Voie royale* into print.

Malraux loved the prize and the glory—and Clara with him. Not everything was perfect between them, but they were the proud parents of a little girl. The birth of Florence—Clara had been moved when André had suggested they name their daughter after the Renaissance city where they had first been happy—had brought them closer again.

137

He caressed the child's head and felt the chin seeking his hand. He hardly knew the traits of the little face, what he knew by heart was its expressions because the child hadn't really existed for him until that first smile.

Days of Wrath

12

Nineteen thirty-three had been a heady year. Florence had been born March 28—"so fully expected by me and accepted by André," Clara was to write—as the Magdeburg Goldschmidts were forced to abandon their business, and Clara's nineteen-year-old cousin Erwin arrived with his teen-aged "Aryan" fiancée. In June, André had met Louise de Vilmorin and a few months later, Clara had taken off for Palestine to spend a week with a mad twenty-year-old Sabra called Soussia, a sun-tanned student from Haifa who had said he couldn't live without her. It had all been quite civilized. Everybody except Soussia played the game by the rules. It had been understood that upon Clara's return Louise would leave for America. André had gone to Marseille to meet the returning Clara. The gesture had touched her and, she was to write, "after a vacation from each other, the joy of seeing each other again was very real." [1]

If Clara had hated Josette Clotis, calling her "a half-crazed provincial arriving in Paris with a list of star intellectuals she wanted to bed down," she accepted the aristocratic Louise. Josette Clotis, who signed her letters and sometimes her articles Jo Clo, was from the hills above Nice, wholly Mediterranean although she looked Scandinavian with her pale complexion, auburn hair, gray eyes and high cheekbones. The daughter of a small-town mayor, she was as tall as André, had gone to boarding school and had one passion—literature. At eighteen, she had written *Le Temps mort,* a sensitive novel, which, André said, evoked wild fruits with an acidulated aftertaste. Gallimard had published her novel in 1932 and she now wrote a weekly column called "Under the Lamp" for Emmanuel Berl in *Marianne.* She loved expensive clothes and all shades of blue. In her room she had blue curtains hung like fish nets. "That way I see the sea," she said, "but not any sea, mine. The Mediterranean." She had seen

[1] Clara Malraux. *Voici que vient l'été* (Paris: Grasset, 1973).

138

Clara with Florence

Greta Garbo in *Anna Karenina* three times and said she wanted two children, a son to be named Guillaume—after Apollinaire; and a daughter, to be called Corinne—after Madame de Stael's superior woman heroine. André dazzled her. The fame, the pitch at which he lived, his tales of adventure and what she later called "his combination of intelligence, egotism and sometimes hypersenitive susceptibility," totally captivated her. In her, André found girlish timidity, delicate physical perfection and youthful exuberance and he called her his "source vive"—his living fount.

Clara hated her and tried to foist her off on Roland, now a handsome nineteen-year-old.

> She leaned over my girl's crib and said, "I want to have a baby like that, too." I advised her to see my brother-in-law; she preferred to stick to her own idea, which, as with so many obsessions, finished by happening.[2]

André was introduced to Louise de Vilmorin by Gaston Gallimard at a garden party. "You are made not only to understand each other, but to like each other," the publisher said in introducing them. A year younger than Malraux but matching his verbal gift, she was as aristocratically romantic as her name. The Vilmorin-Andrieux family had been landscape gardeners for kings, nurserymen who, in the Tuileries and Versailles gar-

[2] Clara Malraux, op. cit.

dens, had grown Marie Antoinette's beloved roses. "I was born among baccarat roses, next to an enormous poppy flower that frightened me," Louise said. The chic and dithyrambic Louise de Vilmorin, who was an intimate friend of Coco Chanel and Jean Cocteau and had *her* table at Maxim's, was actually Mrs. Henry Leigh Hunt, the wife of a Wall Street banker who had married her when he was twenty-two. Hunt had been a friend of the family, a wealthy man with a physique of a film star who had come home from Wall Street every evening with a white orchid which Louise, dressing for dinner, would pin on as a corsage. Louise made perpetual back-and-forth trips between Paris and New York, now separating now reconciling with her Henry. After she had borne him three daughters, they divorced in 1935.

Louise now lived with her four "dear brothers"—her elder sister, Marie-Pierre, became Mapie de Toulouse-Lautrec, an admiral's wife and a cooking expert—in the Verrières-le-Buisson family chateau on the southern outskirts of Paris. When she wasn't attending mundane occasions in town, she was painting bad cubist canvases. André, who, as Georges Braque said, "smells good painting with both his nostrils," told her that her paintings were atrocious, but he was in awe of her gift for conversation. "Write," he advised her. "Write as it comes to you but at the same time watch that intoxicated butterfly exuberance that comes over you whenever you're talking. Writing is a solitary and controlled art. You have to mistrust words . . ."

"In other words, you're telling me to shut up."

That, she was to remember, was their only tiff.

André thought she was born to write. "She speaks without preparation or precaution, with a kind of chastened delirium, radiant and colorful, which makes one think of the great lady companions of queens," he was to say. "This young society woman was unquestionably born to tell love stories, adventures of stolen jewels, treasures rifled from stagecoaches." [3] In a foreword to a collection of her poems, he wrote: "the key to Louise de Vilmorin wasn't so much her episodic mundanities (I've seen fewer royal highnesses at Verrières than protégés), nor her famous graciousness but in an impulsive and whimsical fantasy." [4]

She wrote *Grace de Sainte Unefois,* a slim novel about amorous emancipation, submitting pieces of chapters to André. The manuscript was unanimously accepted by the Gallimard reading committee and was published in May 1934. "This is my bouquet of lilies of the valley," she wrote in her dedication to André. "I have picked all these sprigs in my Verrières meadow for you, naughty sir, who will see me weep if the book's fate is catastrophe. If it is successful, gentle prince, all the stars of heaven will follow you in procession and I will lead the dance of love."

[3] Pierre Galante, *Malraux,* op. cit.
[4] Louise de Vilmorin, *Poèmes* (Paris: Gallimard, 1970).

The book was a success. In the *NRF*, Cocteau praised it as the work "of someone who knows nothing except how to write." Other critics lauded the easy and pure style and the ironic, elegant touch. Louise de Vilmorin was an overnight sensation. André warned her: "Literature is a vanity fair where you must defend your own parading foot by foot." Three of her later novels—*Le Lit à colonnes* ran through nineteen editions— were made into movies. The most famous was the sparkling society comedy *The Earrings of Madame de* . . . , directed by Max Ophuls from a Cocteau screenplay and starring Danielle Darrieux, Charles Boyer and Vittorio de Sica.

Parisian gossip quickly picked up on the liaison. The lovers didn't hide but flirted outrageously across tables whether they were at Maxim's or at Marius', the parliamentarians' Left Bank restaurant, and as an in-joke Coco Chanel had Louise model a bridal gown in her new collection. When they met, even Clara was impressed, saying she was jealous of so much graceful lightness. But a deal was a deal. When André met Clara at Marseille on her return from Haifa, Louise had gone to America. Circumstances—André might say fate—were to reunite Louise and him much later in life.

For the hot-selling and politically aware author of *Man's Fate* there were other things to do besides charming a willowy twenty-two-year-old and basking in upper-class femininity. Colonel François de la Rocque's "leaguers" were marching in Paris and in Berlin a new Nationalist-Socialist chancellor was establishing a racial dictatorship—every new batch of left-wing refugees from Berlin and Cologne confirmed rumors of mass arrests of communists, if not yet of Jews. In February and March the Bulgarian-born Comintern executive Georgi Dimitrov and Ernest Thälmann, the secretary-general of the German Communist Party, had been arrested and charged with burning the Reichstag. In September, Dimitrov and three codefendants were to go on trial in Leipzig, with Hermann Göring advance-billed as the government star witness. Thälmann was simply kept in prison without trial.

In Paris, Malraux and André Gide lent their names to a protest movement. They headed a quickly formed *Comité de défense Thälmann,* and when the Leipzig trial was announced, were the first to back "counter-trials," to be held in Paris and London. These propaganda countertrials were the idea of Willy Münzenberg, the short, square, former shoe factory worker who held together the German exile movements in Paris, Brussels and Amsterdam and who three years before the Communist International made it official policy advocated a "wide front" against fascism. More activist than theoretician, Willy was the head of a worldwide and powerful body, the International Workers' Aid, known in Party slang as "the Münzenberg Trust." The IWA was run from Moscow as an autonomous body and not subject to the control of local parties, giving it a great measure of independence and, according to the Hungarian-born Arthur Koestler, who joined the exiled Germans in Paris, allowing imaginative propaganda to flow into newspapers, periodicals, films and stage productions. The Münzenberg Trust was active everywhere, setting up canteens in famine-stricken southern Russia, helping strikers in British and German general strikes. It had connections from Meshrabpom-Film in Moscow to the New York magaine *P.M.*

Koestler first met Malraux when the Münzenberg Trust set up a fascist study center, Institut pour l'Etude du Fascisme, and Koestler and others were sent out to canvass support and money. "I went to see him at his office at Gallimard's, his publishers, and we talked while walking up and down in the pretty garden at the back of the Gallimard building," Koestler was to write. "As a fervent admirer of Malraux's, I was overwhelmed by the occasion, but went on bravely about the great prospects for the *Institut,* and its even greater need for donations. Malraux listened in silence, occasionally uttering one of his characteristic awe-inspiring nervous sniffs, which sound like the cry of a wounded jungle beast and are followed by a slap of his palm against his nose. At first this was rather startling, but one soon got accustomed to it. When I had had my say, Malraux stopped, advanced toward me threateningly, until I had my back against the garden wall and said: *'Oui, oui, mon cher, mais que pensez-vous de l'apocalypse?'* [5] 'Yes, yes, my friend, but what do you think of the apocalypse?' With that he gave me five hundred francs, and wished me good luck."

In July, Malraux met the sixty-year-old Leon Trotsky for two days at the exiled leader's villa at Royan, near Bordeaux. The Herriot administration had granted Trotsky permission to live in France on the condition he did not reside in the greater Paris area and refrained from all political activities. To live in Royan, overlooking the Gironde estuary, was not as difficult as refraining from taking part in current events, and despite failing health, Trotsky undauntedly continued his work as an anti-Stalinist pamphleteer. During his two months at Royan, he received no fewer than fifty callers, among them, apart from French Trotskyists, several members of the British Independent Labour party, German communists and Paul-Henri Spaak, future secretary-general of the North Atlantic Treaty Organization (NATO), at this time leader of Belgium's Socialist Youth and an ardent Trotsky disciple, and Carlo Rosselli, the eminent Italian antifascist. Most visitors called in connection with a conference of parties and groups interested in the idea of a new International to be held in Paris in August. Trotsky was active in the preparations, writing "theses" and resolutions and taking a close interest in the details of organization. He hoped to win over many of those who stood outside

[5] Arthur Koestler, *The Invisible Writing: An Autobiography* (New York: Macmillan, 1970).

the established International, but only three of fourteen small parties, the German Socialist Workers Party and two Dutch groups, joined the Trotskyists in working for a Fourth International. All others were frightened off by the fierceness of Trotsky's opposition to both reform and Stalin; even the three who joined did so with reservations and instead of forming an International merely organized a preliminary body. Trotsky, however, was pleased with this start.

Clara was to have accompanied André to Royan, but little Florence contracted bronchitis and to her regret Clara had to stay in Paris.

André and Leon Davidovich talked for the better part of two days about the future of Europe, conflict in the Far East which eventually would see Japan and the United States at war with each other, about Stalin, whom Trotsky always called "the Other," about Thälmann's arrest, Soviet cinema—to his astonishment, André learned that Trotsky had never seen Eisenstein's *Potemkin*—art and death. Nine months later, when under pressure from an unholy alliance of the Kremlin and a hysterical right-wing press, the newly formed center-left coalition government of Gaston Doumergue had expelled Trotsky (whose next exile had become Norway), Malraux published a stirring report of the two days spent with the founder of the Red Army.

What was totally absent from his voice, Malraux noted, was the desire to please and the insistence which in so many people betrayed their need to convince others in order to convince themselves.

What almost all great men have in common, regardless of the awkwardness with which some of them express themselves, in this intensity, this mysterious mental concentration which seems to stem from what they believe, but overwhelms their dogma and which comes from the habit of considering thought as something to conquer not something to discuss. In the realm of the mind, this man has created his own world and taken up residence in it. I remember the way he told me about Boris Pasternak:

"Almost all young Russians follow him right now, but I have no great taste for him. I'm not a great admirer of the art of technicians, art for specialists."

"To me," I answered, "art is first of all the highest and most intense expression of an experience that counts."

"I think that this kind of art will be born again all over Europe. In Russia, revolutionary writing has not yet come up with a great work of fiction."

"But isn't the true expression of communism to be found in film rather than literature? There is a cinema before and after *Potemkin*, before and after V. I. Pudovkin's *Mother*."

"Lenin thought communism expressed itself artistically through film. In regards to *Potemkin* and *Mother*, lots of people like you have told me about these pictures, but I must tell you that I've never seen

143

them. When they first came out, I was on the front. Later, other movies were showing and when they were re-released, I was in exile." [6]

Art and communism led to questions of the individual and communism, a central theme in *La Condition humaine,* which Trotsky had hailed as the revelation of a great and original talent. Now, he maintained that Russia's communist millions building a new tomorrow with a new five-year plan were to be likened to Christians living for eternal life with little regard for the individual.

The next day, they talked history and geopolitics. Trotsky became impassioned when discussing the future of Russia, saying that even under "the Other," the Soviet Union would fight expansionist Japan to the hilt. He prophesized that to protect its interests, the United States would take over China, a move that inevitably would lead to a U.S.-Japanese confrontation in the Pacific. When Malraux talked about death, Leon Davidovich cut him off, saying, "I believe death is first of all the consequence of an odd phasing out of body and mind. If the two wore down at the same time, it would be simple to die. There wouldn't be any resistance." Later, Malraux told other details of his two-day meeting. When asked why he failed in his bid for power in Russia after Lenin's death, Trotsky answered, "Because I was expecting too much." When they were talking about Chiang Kai-shek's son, who, as a student in Moscow in 1927, had publicly repudiated his father and said he was ashamed to be his son, Trotsky commented, "People have the children they deserve."

After intermittent lobbying by Gallimard, the Goncourt prize was awarded December 1, while Clara was still in Palestine. The prize was worth about $200 in the devalued currency of the time, but it immediately boosted the book's already enormous popularity and escalated foreign sales (*La Condition humaine* was eventually translated into thirty-five languages) and André and Clara celebrated New Year's together with the certitude that they were financially independent.

They had little time to think about themselves in early 1934 as both were increasingly involved in politics and in events on the other side of the Rhine.

If the "countertrials" organized in Paris and London had not impressed the new regime in Berlin to the point of freeing Thälmann and Dimitrov, the Leipzig tribunal trying Dimitrov and his three codefendants had found him not guilty. Since the Comité de défense Thälmann had collected thousands of signatures and the Nazis seemed to hesitate on what to do with the two communist leaders, it was hurriedly decided that Malraux and Gide should go to Berlin to present the signatures and an accompanying petition to Hitler. They left for the German capital January 4.

[6] *Marianne,* April 25, 1934.

144

The mission had a good chance of succeeding, they told themselves. If anybody had been foolhardy, it was the Nazis, engineering the Reichstag fire and accusing one of their staunchest enemies of committing it in an open court, where he benefitted from both quasi-legal jurisprudence and international publicity and where, to their humiliation, he was actually acquitted. Dimitrov was now being held at the Moabit prison in Berlin.

If Reichkanzler Hitler never deigned to meet the two French intellectuals, his Minister for Propaganda and Information did receive them. "What you are seeking is justice," Joseph Goebbels told them, "what we're interested in something else—German justice." The minister would not promise anything. Before leaving Berlin, Gide spent an evening at a sleazy gay cabaret and Malraux an evening trying to look up Oswald Spengler and another day trying to see his in-laws. Spengler, whose historical philosophy the Nazis were making part of their propaganda, was no longer around (he was to die the following year) and the Magdeburg Goldschmidts had no desire to come to Berlin but sent their regards.

It was hard to say whether the propaganda countertrials and the international petitions had anything to do with it, but at the end of February, Dimitrov was released, supposedly at Hitler's direct orders.

Shorty after Malraux and Gide's return, Clara went to Germany on a mission. A member of numerous committees, perpetual translator at meetings and, behind the scenes, helpful intermediary for new streams of socialists, communists and/or Jewish refugees making it to Paris, Clara worked with the communists because she found they knew how to be effective. When a lawyer and a Protestant minister asked her to accompany them to Wuppertal where twenty union leaders were to go on trial, she accepted. When they got to the industrial Rhineland city, the lawyer, the preacher and the famous author's wife were barred from the courthouse —it had been decided that the trial could be held *in camera*. Outside, Clara mingled with the defendants' wives, all working-class women sullenly watching their men being rushed in. Ten minutes later, the three French nationals were being told to follow a plainclothes detective to the police station. Clara spoke German too well not to raise suspicion, but to the question "When did you leave Germany?" she could answer, "I was born in France." After verification with the French consulate in Cologne, where the trio was expected for dinner, they were released and even granted an interview with the presiding judge. With Clara translating, the French lawyer and the judge had a surreal discussion about new German jurisprudence which, the judge said, made an act a misdemeanor even if it had been committed before a law making it an offense had been passed. The twenty defendants were on trial for having belonged to a union before 1933, when it was legal to belong to one. At the consular dinner in Cologne, a young attaché talked discreetly about torture in German prisons.

After a visit to Berlin to deliver a petition full of sonorous names

145

to the Justizministerium and a walk down cleaned-up boulevards emptied of the young men hanging out, of gigolos and the loitering unemployed Clara used to see, they returned to Paris, breathing easier as the train pulled across the Rhine Bridge from Kiel to Strasbourg.

Alix and Groot came to dinner with Liuba and Ilya Ehrenburg, Gustav Regler and Manes Sperber and everybody stayed half the night. Regler, "handsome as Siegfried," was a multilingual novelist and poet with a wry humor who had been a boy soldier in 1918 and was to become political commissar to the International Brigades in Spain—and as such Ernest Hemingway's favorite communist. Sperber was a Marxist who had come under the influence of Alfred Adler, a precise writer with a devotion to books and art who worshipped André and did much to keep his anti-fascist ardor at a boiling point. Together with Münzenberg, Sperber had created the Center for Fascist Studies for which Koestler was busy canvassing support. The expulsion of Trotsky in February by the Doumergue administration and the continued riots in Paris streets of Croix de Feu and Action française right-wingers were indications "it could happen here." Colonel de La Rocque had just muffed his chance in the February 6 riots on the Place de la Concorde. Sixteen rioters had been killed and police and guards had lost one killed and 1,664 injured, but who was to say the leaguers, this time 40,000 strong, couldn't succeed a next time in crossing the Concorde Bridge and invade the Chamber of Deputies. The Place de la Concorde confrontation had started with hysterical news stories in conservative newspapers claiming the government had secretly brought tank squadrons and regiments of black Senegalese troops into the capital with orders to "mow down" demonstrators, rumors that had baited *L'Humanité* into calling on communist war veterans to join the Croix de Feu veterans. As Münzenberg and the other Germans said, it was exactly what had happened during the last months of the Weimar Republic, when German communists, willing to do anything to topple the "bourgeois" government, had joined Nazi unions in carrying out a public transportation strike. Now on the Place de la Concorde, French communists had been at the side of royalists and fascists pelting police blocking their way to the Chamber of Deputies.

There was a novel in all this no doubt, but when friends—and Gaston Gallimard—asked what would be the follow-up novel to *La Condition humaine,* André said "a story about oil." He had been impressed by Baku, the Soviet oil refinery town on the Caspian Sea, Clara and he had visited on their trip to Iran, but he had no clear plot line in mind. The "story about oil" translated more as a fascinating exotic setting for Persian legends than a need to tell about budding Soviet industrialism in old Azerbaijan and Uzbek lands. His talent needed a sweeping background where Destiny and its darker ambiguities could be played out in poetic loneli-nesses, suffering, defeat and death. Political trials in Germany and right-

146

Josette Clotis

wing riots on the Place de la Concorde somehow couldn't inspire him as a writer although as engagé intellectual and, very soon, as speaker at vast rallies, quotidian events could give his proverbial eloquence a new accent of ringing vehemence and rousing temerity. What he also needed was an adventure that Clara could not be part of, a danger not shared by her.

The marriage was on the skids, despite the presence of now one-year-old Florence, or Flo, as her mother called her. André resented Clara's political radicalism, made fun of her comrades, and he continued to see Josette. Clara's mother was now nearly totally destitute and practically living off her son-in-law's charity. The Rue du Bac apartment was beginning to feel cramped, with Florence and her live-in nurse sharing one room and André's writing taking another room. They could afford to move, but didn't.

After one quarrel, Clara left home. Nothing steadied her nerves better than train rides and after zigzagging through western France for one night, she snapped to in Bordeaux and called home. "How stupid I am," she told herself. "I love him and no doubt he loves me. It is difficult to love and we deserve each other. Let him leave on his trip if that's really what he wants." [7]

The trip was a stunt perhaps inspired by T. E. Lawrence, whose

---

[7] Clara Malraux, op. cit.

147

Seven Pillars of Wisdom Malraux had Gallimard publish in French—an aerial archaeological expedition to the supposed ruins of the Queen of Sheba's capital in Saudi Arabia. "These legendary lands have always beguiled the eccentric," André was to write in his *Antimémoires* in describing the 1934 publicity stunt. The expedition was undertaken with a friend, Edouard Corniglion-Molinier, a superb flyer and film producer two years older than André, and a mechanic named Maillard and was bankrolled by Paris' biggest afternoon newspaper. The trio took off from Orly airfield February 22 in a brand new Gnome & Rhone Fernam 190 plane loaned to them by Paul-Louis Weiller, the director of the Gnome factory and Corniglion-Molinier's friend and former Air Force commander.

If any legend was of sufficient magic to spellbind Malraux it was the story of the Queen of Sheba and the mad efforts through the centuries to find the mysterious desert capital of this seductress who tossed flowers at Solomon's beard and whose blinding beauty had only one flaw, a slight limp. If the Bible only mentions her chastely—in Kings I and Chronicles II—the Koran, which calls her Balkis, gives other tantalizing details of her visit to Jerusalem to test Solomon's wisdom. The Bible tells of her coming with a great train of camels bearing spices, gold and precious stones and of her learning everything she wanted from the King of Israel and of him sending her and her people back to her lands after blessing her and giving her "whatsoever she asked." The Koran tells how Solomon receives her in his throne room entirely paved with glass. Imagining the room to be in water, she lifts her robes enabling Solomon to see her legs. Ethiopian history tell the story more boldly. When, after six months in Jerusalem, Balkis expresses her wish to return to her capital of Ma'rib, Solomon cannot conceal his despair at not having been able to initiate her to his bed. To honor her departure he offers a sumptuous dinner at which he sees to it that she is served only highly spiced dishes. Before retiring, the queen, guessing Solomon's intentions, makes him promise not to make any attempt upon her virtue. "I so promise," says Solomon, "on condition that you take nothing that is in my dwelling." She accepts and goes to bed. During the night, the spiced food so tortures her that she gets up to take a cup of water. Solomon is waiting for this moment and after drinking of his water, she gives herself to him. The son, born after her return to Ma'rib, is the founder of the ruling line of Ethiopian emperors and the forefather who allows young Emperor Haile Selassie to call himself the King of Judea. Christian commentators later suggested more edifying reason for Sheba's game leg, which had inspired Flaubert to write *La Tentation de St. Antoine,* a book Malraux had read, fascinated, as a teen-ager. Here, a radiant Queen of Sheba offers herself and her kingdom to tempt the saint—"we shall sleep together on swan's down softer than clouds, we shall pour wines kept cold in the hollow of fruits, we shall gaze at the sun through emeralds . . . ah, how you will lose your-

148

self in my tresses, caress my breasts, marvel at my body and be scorched by my eyes, between my arms, in a whirlwind." As the holy man is about to succumb to the temptations of the flesh, her pet monkey lifts her skirt and reveals her goat's hoof. It didn't bother Flaubert or his 1870s readers that eight hundred years separated the near-mythical eighth-century B.C. Yemenite kingdom of Sheba and the Egyptian saint, Anthony (251–350).[8]

Even more fascinating were the historical efforts to find Sheba and its fabled capital. As before the expedition to Banteai Srey, André poured over records at the Société de Géographie library. The Roman geographer Strabo told of Aetius Gallus' march into Yemen and about his legions, cursed by Shebaean stargazers, wandering for months before dying, mad, in the desert. For centuries, according to Persian scholars, Arabs would come across the legionnaires' skeletons still in their bronze armor, their skeletal fingers holding up helmets filled with seashells. Two medieval Persian scholars located the ancient kingdom in southwestern Yemen and in the 1880s two Frenchmen and an Austrian, disguised as Arabs, made daring excursions into the savage region, following the Kharid River. Most interesting was scholar-explorer Jean Charcot's retelling of the adventures of Joseph Arnaud, a pharmacist and grocer who in 1843 had accompanied a Turkish mission to San'a and had written, "On leaving Ma'rib, I visited the ruins of ancient Sheba, where there was nothing to be seen except mounds of earth." Disguised as a Turkish candle seller and leading a hermaphroditic donkey, Arnaud traveled through Yemen, exhibiting his donkey, which could copulate with him/herself, to the Bedouins as an eighth wonder of the world. The glare of the desert sand brought Arnaud close to blindness. When he was recognized as a heathen in Al Hudaydah, he managed nevertheless to flee, with his ass, to Jidda, the Red Sea coastal city where the French consul took him into his protection. The consul was an amateur archaeologist and asked Arnaud to draw up a plan of Ma'rib. Since Arnaud was too blind to make a drawing on paper, he was led down to the beach and with a stick drew an outline of the city and the temple of the sun in the wet sand. The consul copied these sand drawings in his notebook, while the Arabs, fascinated by the appearance of a blind man scribbling on the sand, spoke of him kindly, thinking he was mad. Then the sea came in and washed the drawing away. "It was as though everything that concerned Sheba, when re-created, summoned the elements that hurled it back into eternity," Malraux commented in one of the articles he wrote in *L'Intransigeant*.[9]
London, 1904.

Arnaud recovered his sight, went to Paris with his donkey, which

[8] Gustave Flaubert, *The Temptation of St. Anthony, or A Revelation of the Soul* was printed privately for subscribers by M. Walter Dunne, New York and London, 1904.

[9] The big-circulation afternoon paper published Malraux's heavily illustrated account in daily installments, between May 3 and 13, 1934.

149

he presented to the Jardin des Plantes zoo, and went on a second expedition to Yemen. The hermaphroditic donkey died of starvation in the zoo while Arnaud ended his life in dire poverty in Algiers. "I would have liked to have known you, Arnaud," Malraux wrote in the *L'Intransigeant* account. "I would like to have seen your zouave beard, your solemn air, your candles, your casual heroism, your simple and charming genius for adventure. Perhaps, unwittingly, I went to Sheba in search for your ghost. Or perhaps it was in search of the ghost of your donkey, which I would also have liked, and who no doubt died between the polar bear and the penguin, seeing neither of them, stupefied by the Paradise assuredly promised to donkeys by Allah, but unable to understand, absolutely unable to understand, why it was being kept a prisoner."

Malraux's original idea had been to search for Ma'rib, disguised Arnaud-Lawrence of Arabia style, as an Arab, but after hearing his stuttering attempts at speaking Persian, Corniglion-Molinier had persuaded him to take to the air. "I was able later, and on many occasions to verify the exaggerated idea Malraux has of his knowledge of the Persian language and history," Corniglion-Molinier was to recall. "Every time he tried to use the language, the Arab porter or the erudite old man to whom he was speaking would register utter surprise and show that he understood nothing of what he was saying. I said, 'Why add to the list of scholars or romantic adventurers killed in such expeditions without reaching their objective, when there is a much greater likelihood of finding the city, if it exists, by flying over it?' "

At Orly, Malraux, Corniglion-Molinier and Maillard were given a spectacular send-off by *L'Intransigeant* reporters and in the Fernam 190, modified for added fuel capacity, they roared into the night. They reached Cairo via Rome and Tripoli (where they were especially impressed by Italian airmen and Italian airbases). In Cairo, Hassan Anis Pasha, himself a Queen of Sheba fan and controller of Egyptian aviation, provided them with excellent British maps of the Arabian Peninsula, maps which showed important landmarks in different places from French air force maps. In Cairo, Malraux visited the Mariette Museum and for one evening fascinated a group of young intellectuals by talking about Stalin and Trotsky. Telegraphic demands to Aden proved fruitless. The Royal Air Force considered the whole southern part of Saudi Arabia a strategic area and refused to approve the Queen of Sheba hunters' flight plan.

In a temperature of 104 F. in the shade, the trio landed at Djibouti in French Somaliland across the Red Sea from Aden. On each of Malraux's Asian voyages, Djibouti had been a port of call so Somaliland was nothing new. Through the air force radio, Captain Jean Esparre, commander of the French Somali coast squadron, had heard about the expedition and he and his men were out on their landing strip to welcome the first civilian plane from France to land there. At night, Esparre's Arab cook served shrimps and enormous crabs prepared with curry and served with Algerian wine, the only wine, the captain said, that could stand the heat. After dinner, they talked about the mission and Malraux asked about the Royal Air Force across the Gulf of Aden. Esparre said the British were making mysterious bombing missions, apparently to lambaste dissident Bedouin tribes on the fringe of the coastal Hadhramaut region, although from this side of the Gulf it was not really clear what the RAF was up to. The British were intensely suspicious of any foreign planes equipped with a trap door for photography. Any such plane landing on British-controlled soil was ransacked for film. Exposed film was automatically developed and either seized or returned intentionally "fogged" to its owners.

Esparre and his lieutenant Paul Gambert put their guests up as comfortably as possible while they prepared for the final assault—the ten-hour nonstop flight Djibouti-Ma'rib-Djibouti, a fifteen-hundred-mile round trip if the Ma'rib ruins were where they were supposed to be. Since they had to avoid British installations and bases, their flight would take off from south of the fortified oil island of Perim, and skirt the Hadhramaut region before heading inland toward their *terra incognita*. Landing en-route could mean death. If thirst wouldn't be the end, marauding Bedouin tribes might. To give themselves a fighting chance, they bought Arab robes and headgear.

They took off at dawn, a lyrical dawn in Malraux's *L'Intransigeant* account, full of Muslim odors of burned grass, pepper and camels. After crossing the Gulf, skirting Perim and staying in the coastal cloud layer in order not to be spotted, they headed inland and after four hours spotted the Yemenite capital of San'a, buried in a valley in the Hodeida mountains, and as such an important landmark before the "geological solitude," as André called the desert in his newspaper account. Their last landmark would be the Kharid, the largest river in the region.

They couldn't find the Kharid, but were sure they were right over it. The river appeared on all maps, but all they saw was a string of villages. After a while they realized the river was subterranean, that the trees and villages forming a thin line of vegetation and human presence followed the underground stream. With little over five hours' fuel left, they finally winged into the desert at six thousand feet and with perfect, twenty-mile visibility.

> At last, to our right, we begin to make out a vast, almost white spot, a stretch of colossal lumps in the middle of the sand. Is it a geological accident? An error? We tell ourselves we must wait, get closer, but already deep within us we have recognized towers, and we know this is it.

Suspensefully, *L'Intransigeant* cut the narrative here to continue the story in the next day's edition.

We get closer and closer; we watch it grow as eagerly as a starving man eats. The shaken mind must choose in a jumble of dreams. If we follow both the Bible and legend, if this is the city of the queen, it is contemporary with Solomon's. Is this enormous monument, which looks like a tower of Notre-Dame with terraces tumbling down to the petrified skeleton of a river the place about which the Envoy says in the Koran, "I saw there a woman governing men on a magnificent throne; she and her people worship the sun?" The queen to whom Solomon sent the one among his seals that can only be deciphered by the dead?

They descended and with Corniglion-Molinier banking the plane at forty-five degrees, Malraux and Maillard snapped photos of what they imagined to be an abandoned oasis. They saw monuments outside a vast horseshoe wall on the tower side and another mass of stones, isolated columns and nomads' tents. On dark spots flashes appeared. They were being fired upon by men with old rifles.

In true "Perils of Pauline" style, they headed back watching the sinking fuel indicator and scanning the horizon for the Red Sea shore. They crossed the shark-infested water fearing they would have to ditch but crawled over the palm treetops to a landing strip at Obock in northeastern Somaliland, which Captain Esparre had told them about. They were met by the region's only white man, an irrepressible sergeant from Marseille, who, while his Somali soldiers refueled their plane, forced them to down glasses of Pernod and put a live gazelle aboard their plane as a gift before allowing them to take off.

After radioing triumphant dispatches to *L'Intransigeant* announcing they had discovered the mythical capital of Sheba, they flew to Addis Ababa, landing on the racetrack while a polo match was in progress. Instead of taxis, horse-drawn sulkies crisscrossed the streets of the Ethiopian capital. Some women wore traditional dresses, veiled apparitions under tall headdresses and draped in robes that left one shoulder nude. The men wore white pants that fit the calves so tightly that, according to legend, they were never removed. The French ambassador had them introduced to the emperor, the 225th monarch of the world's oldest dynasty and descendent of that one night's union of the Queen of Sheba and Solomon, with kingly hyperbole. Corniglion-Molinier was introduced as one of the greatest pilots of modern times, Maillard as the engineer-in-chief of the expedition and Malraux as someone who had received awards from all the world's academies. Haile Selassie said he was not surprised they had found the ruins; he always knew of the existence of the city of his illustrious ancestress. Before flying on, André bought several strange canvases, with iridescent colors, from an Ethiopian painter.

They flew back along the North African coast. Taking off from Tunis despite a less than promising weather forecast, they ran into a hailstorm over the Aurès mountains. Malraux was several times to describe

152

what were the ten most harrowing minutes he had ever experienced. With the hailstones hammering on the metal frame and threatening to break the cockpit windshield and actually damaging the rudder, they were being tossed like a shuttlecock in the eye of the storm, losing altitude and expecting to hit any of the jagged peaks or slam into the mountainside. When the altimeter fell to twelve hundred feet, André watched Corniglion-Molinier and saw a strange transformation on his face—he looked like a child. They came out of the thunder clap over a valley and managed to land in Annaba (then Bone), in eastern Algeria. As they were being driven into town and life slowly flooded back into him, the car passed a glover's shop advertised with a shingle in the form of a huge red hand. The image was always to stay with André.

As they crossed the Mediterranean and flew toward Marseille with a refueling stop in Barcelona, Clara and André Gide decided to meet them in Lyons. The reunion was joyous and the next day, all five made the last hop to Orly and landed in dangerous fog.

The seven front-page articles in *L'Intransigeant,* published with aerial photographs under the overall title "Discovery of the Mysterious Capital of the Queen of Sheba," caused a certain stir. But various scholars soon wrote letters to the editors, wondering whether the aerial explorers hadn't mistaken the Ma'rib ruins with Temma. In America, *The New York Times* and *Herald Tribune* published long articles on the discovery with maps of Yemen. The *Times* interviewed Dr. Richard Gottheil, professor of Semitic languages at Columbia, who expressed guarded skepticism, as did most other specialists consulted by the press. William Albright, Gottheil's confrere at the Johns Hopkins University, was certain Ma'rib was Queen Balkis' capital but since many archaeologists who had visited Ma'rib had already returned with full reports, the claim to have "discovered" her capital was not serious. "Malraux is not known as an archaeologist," he declared firmly.

Had they discovered the capital of Sheba? It was not until 1951 that real excavations began, headed by Wendell Phillips, which cleared the Temple of Balkis from the sand, unearthing statues of stone and bronze. Following outright threats to the lives of the archaeologists and blatant xenophobic reaction by the San'a government, the diggings came to an end in 1952. During the 1960s and early 1970s, civil war—which saw Yemen split into rival Arab and People's Democratic republics—prevented further archaeological research. Late in life, Malraux was to dismiss the 1934 expedition as a lark, which didn't prevent him from making the Queen of Sheba, Arnaud, his hermaphroditic donkey and the ruins in the sand always eluding explorers part of an evocative chapter of the *Antimémoires.*

What fascinates French intellectuals in communism
is energy at the service of social justice; what separates
them from the communists is the means of this energy.

Antimémoires

13

The interlude over the desert was just that, an interlude. Once back in Paris, André was swallowed up in politics and, by midsummer, 1934, he and Clara were in Moscow. The aftermath of the Place de la Corcorde riots had been a further polarization of public opinion. The narrow defeat of the leaguers emboldened the Right and led to a rapid growth of the Croix de Feu organization. It was no longer primarily a right-wing war veterans' group but a popular mass movement, drawing into its ranks those who favored order, honesty, nationalism and patriotism. On the Left, the events led to serious talk of a *Front populaire,* and to the surprise of almost everyone, including the socialists, the communists reversed their previous stand and took the lead in the creation of this broad left-of-center coalition.

The signal had come from Moscow, and on Bastille Day, 1934, the communist leaders held a crucial meeting with Socialist leader Léon Blum. Two weeks later, they signed a pact calling for joint action against fascism, for the disarming and suppression of patriotic leagues, for parliamentary reapportionment and an end to government deflationary decree laws. The agreement put an end to thirteen years of fratricidal conflict between the two labor parties and paved the way for the Popular Front. By October, the Front was enlarged to include the Radical-Socialists, the largest party in the Chamber of Deputies, who, despite their name, were the traditional representatives of the *petite bourgeoisie.*

The about-face in communist policy in pushing for an alliance with the socialists and the liberal middle class was dictated by Stalin, who apparently was becoming alarmed by Nazi Germany. A year later, he was to tell French Foreign Minister Pierre Laval in Moscow that he "understood and fully approved the policy of national defense being followed by France in order to maintain its armed strength at the level re-

154

quired by its security," a statement that completely surprised French Communist Party chief Maurice Thorez who only months earlier had thundered in the Chamber of Deputies, "We are against national defense. We are supporters of Lenin, of revolutionary defeatism," and had appealed to the socialists not to vote for military credits. Stalin's reversal left Léon Blum and the liberals astonished—and a little troubled. In the Chamber, the socialists had constantly opposed French big defense expenditures, despite Hitler's rearming on the other side of the Rhine.

Clara and André were frequent visitors with Liuba and Ilya Ehrenburg in their Rue Caumartin apartment. Ilya Ehrenburg was creatively a minor talent but he was a good journalist and at this time was *Izvestia's* roving correspondent in the West. At the Ehrenburgs', André was one night introduced to Constantin Fedin, the first Soviet novelist to try to understand the Revolution from a psychological point of view. Fedin talked with great sincerity about the writer's lot in the Soviet Union. The 1920s had been very free, but in 1932 things had changed. The Central Committee of the Communist Party had disbanded all proletarian literary organizations, replacing them with a single Union of Soviet Writers. The step had been designed to put an end to factional squabbles but it circumscribed the writers' scope by imposing on them the obligation to deal with "socialist realities." Socialist Realism—the expression was ascribed to Stalin himself—was fundamentally a reaction against certain trends in literature. Its positive aspects included attempts to improve language and style and to upgrade a literature becoming increasingly barren because of party-line themes and treatments. It said that the boy-loves-tractor genre, novels, plays and films about the production processes and collective farms should give way to works focusing on human beings, on ordinary citizens and their personal lives. The reactionary aspect of the Socialist Realism "reform" was that it was against what was sweepingly described as "bourgeois formalism," a phrase meaning all experiments with form and technique.

The Union of Soviet Writers—the very act of adhering, though formally a voluntary one, was too closely bound up with material and other advantages to be anything but compulsory—was about to hold its first congress. The way Ehrenburg and Fedin explained it, the congress would be of utmost importance. Its organizers, they said, wanted the congress to be an "open" one. In short, would André accept an invitation to become a delegate, to be one of the "big name" foreigners whose presence would make the convention, well, more open than the 1930 Khrakov meeting where a group of "proletarian authors" had tried to exclude all writer-delegates who hadn't agreed with them, a coup organized by Andrei Zhdanov, a close associate of Stalin. Zhdanov, Fedin said with a grave but significant gesture, would if not chair, at least stage-manage the upcoming congress.

155

The other members of the French delegation would be Louis Aragon, Paul Nizan (already in Moscow) and Vladimir Pozner, all orthodox members of the French Communist Party, plus the elder playwright Jean-Richard Bloch, a soon-to-be party member. Forty formidable Western authors of Leftist persuasion had been invited. Thomas Mann was to lead the big delegation of exiled Germans, Theodore Dreiser might come from the United States and sympathy messages had already been received from Bernard Shaw and Upton Sinclair.

Malraux said yes. He was interested in visiting Moscow, not only to attend the congress, but also to meet the officials of Mezrabpomfilm which was to make a screen version of *La Condition humaine* and to make a sidetrip to Azerbaijan SSR to do research for his "story about oil."

After a short visit to London, Clara and André sailed for Leningrad from Southampton together with the Ehrenburgs aboard the S.S. *Dzershinsky*. Clara was to remember the passage through the Kiel Canal from the North Sea to the Baltic, with German workers silently presenting the closed fist salute to the ship with the hammer and sickle on the funnel.

The August 17 to 31 All-Soviet Writers' Congress was an impressive affair, held in the Great Hall of Columns draped with immense banner pictures of Shakespeare, Lenin, Molière, Heine, Gorky, Stalin, Gogol and Cervantes. "I am as nervous as a young girl before her first dance," Ehrenburg told the foreign authors. Kolkhoze farmers brought immense baskets of fruits while school "pioneers" blew trumpets and subway construction workers and twenty-five thousand other Muscovites mingled with the writers. Uzbek farmers offered Maxim Gorky, who chaired the congress, a bathrobe. Everywhere, Clara noted, an amiable crowd, which laughed easily and showed quick gestures of courtesy. At night when the delegates returned to the National Hotel, the Red Square was filled with stretched-out drunks, sleeping off their vodka, under the benevolent eye of the police.

The absence of Stalin from the congress and the numerous banquets were discussed at length. Up to the last minute it was hoped the Father of the People would appear. Aragon announced very early that Stalin would offer directives for the centuries to come.

The directives came in Zhdanov's opening keynote address. "Our literature is permeated with enthusiasm and heroism and it is optimistic because it is a literature of the rising class—the proletarian class," Zhdanov said, repeating Stalin's phrase that Soviet writers were "the engineers of the soul." Ignoring Marx and Engels' general reluctance to dogmatize about literature, Zhdanov outlined Socialist Realism as a theory that made it imperative for Socialist Realist writers to infect readers with class ideology and to fabricate a hortatory art designed to support the goals of the state. He was followed by Gorky, who presented himself as a social philosopher and materialistic atheist, contemptuous of all philosophies except Marxist-

156

Leninism. Plato, Kant and Bergson were to be dumped, together with detective stories, invented by capitalists to prevent the growth of class consciousness. Apparently forgetting the subject matter of his own novels, the elder statesman of Russian letters finished by denouncing bourgeois literature for being full of murderers, swindlers and thieves. Malraux endured this sitting next to Gustav Regler and a full-bosomed interpreter from *Pravda*, who tried her best to translate Gorky's address for them. When toward the end Gorky's reading of his forty-page address Gustav was muttering to himself, André asked the interpreter what he was saying. "I think he's groaning," she smiled bravely. "He has good reason to," André sighed.

Malraux was the only noncommunist among the major foreign delegates (Thomas Mann had sent his son, Klaus, in his stead and Dreiser never came) and his address was expected with some apprehension. He had been generously introduced to the Soviet public in articles and interviews in *Pravda* and *Literaturnaya Gazeta,* but in the new socialist realist perspective, *Man's Fate* with its emphasis on individuality could no longer be considered exactly orthodox. *Les Conquérants* had never been published in Russia and *La Condition humaine* also belabored the theme of the relative futility of revolutionary action. Individualism and literary innovation were the real issues of the congress with the "Zhdanovists" campaigning against modernists who were in search of new forms. Their main targets were James Joyce's *Ulysses* and the works of Marcel Proust and John Dos Passos. During his triumphant trip to Hollywood, where he was to have directed a screen version of Dreiser's *An American Tragedy* for Paramount Pictures,* Sergei Eisenstein had met Joyce and become so interested in Joyce's methods of creating imagery, he had had Ehrenburg approach the author's Italian friend Nino Frank with a proposal to make a film out of *Ulysses.* Together with the playwright Vsevolod Vishnevsky, Eisenstein had boldly taken up the cudgels on behalf of Joyce, calling *Ulysses* a "perfectly outspoken portrayal of men in the capitalist era" and calling its author a writer who had "revealed the amazing secrets of the life and mentality of the people of the dying era" and given rise to new literary current in France, England, the United States and other countries. Describing Joyce as "a monstrously powerful realist," Vishnevsky accused the Zhdanovists of failing to understand the objective value of Joyce, however "decadent" and "nihilistic" he may indeed seem to be from a social point of view.[1] Vishnevsky also defended Dos Passos and mentioned a questionnaire circulated by *Literaturnaya Gazeta* showing the American author to be the most widely read among Soviet writers.

---

* Actually directed by Josef von Sternberg in 1931.
[1] Quoted by Gleb Struve, *Russian Literature under Lenin and Stalin: 1917–1953* (Norman: University of Oklahoma Press, 1971).

The counterattack came in a speech by Karl Radek, a savage, intelligent Comintern official and journalist who spoke seven languages, walked among the guests like a ghost from the past and at one banquet shouted that Malraux was perhaps the greatest sinner of them all. Revealing his cultural illiteracy, Radek accused *Ulysses,* set in 1904, of omitting the 1916 Irish uprising. As for Proust, even the meanest of Dostoyevsky's characters were towers of suffering compared to Proust's "drawing room heroes." Dos Passos was "a great revolutionary artist," Radek admitted, but his formalistic innovations, which some Soviet writers admired so much, were where he erred. "He inserts newspaper clippings in order to paste together the background which he is incapable of portraying." Radek finished by opposing Socialist Realism to all bourgeois attempts at finding new forms. "I wish to say to Soviet and foreign writers, 'Our road lies not through Joyce but along the highway of Socialist Realism.'"

Radek's verdict on Joyce, Proust and Dos Passos was accepted by Soviet writers in silence. Even Vishnevsky failed to rise in defense of Joyce, preferring instead to rebuke his friend Yuri Olesha, whose expressionist 1928 novel *Envy* had been a completely fresh approach to the conflict between the old and new Russia, telling the stories of a "new man" and his anachronistic and reactionary brother with equal sympathy. The French delegates preceding Malraux on the podium didn't say much about Socialist Realism. Aragon talked glowingly about nineteenth-century French artists, Rimbaud and Zola, Cézanne and Courbet, while the elder Bloch proclaimed "The individual—yes; individualism, no!" The Danish writer Martin Andersen-Nexö asked Soviet writers not only to write about days of struggle and work, "but also for those hours of quiet when a man is alone with himself." Most speakers, however, adroitly praised Socialist Realism while at the same time reserving for themselves small portions of individual freedom. Of the Russians, only Olesha defended his right to speak about human emotions divorced from a political context, while Nikolai Bukharin, once a close friend of Lenin and still editor-in-chief of *Izvestia,* showed he didn't understand the purpose of the conference by delivering an earnest defense of the young poet Boris Pasternak.

When Malraux asked Gorky what he thought of Radek's pronouncement on Joyce, Gorky answered—in a translation by the Odessa poet Isaac Babel—that he had found Joyce's work "disgusting" but had not heard Radek's speech. Malraux said *he* had found Joyce a milestone in the liberation of the expression of human feelings. Gorky turned the conversation to the emigré writer Ivan Bunin who had won the 1933 Nobel prize, but when André switched to Nietzsche, Gorky warned that in the name of socialist humanism he was obliged to say there was absolutely no positive value to be found in Nietzsche. Babel had to use all his linguistic diplomacy to soften Malraux's answer—Nietzsche was one

158

With Gorky, Moscow, 1934

of the most important and most fecund authors, precisely from a socialist-humanistic standpoint.

When they went on to Dostoyevsky, and Gorky proclaimed a rather low opinion of the author of *Crime and Punishment* because Dostoyevsky was a preacher and a "theologian," André lifted his characteristic finger, "Attention, there are two Dostoyevskys, the Dostoyevsky who asks what the world is and gives out-dated answers and the Dostoyevsky who asks 'What is life and what is man to man?' The Dostoyevsky who in the name of the lonely individual asks this question and tries to find an answer is a progressive thinker." Gorky brought Tolstoy into the argument, saying the answers were simpler than Dostoyevsky imagined. "The simplest and most important question is 'What have I done?' "

"The fundamental adventure for a writer is his own astonishment in the face of life," André said. "Do you agree with me that behind every artist you find the question, 'What is life, what does it mean?' "

According to Babel, Gorky and Malraux had more or less the same opinion.

Clara liked Babel. He was not much taller than she was and he was rumored to have seven mistresses, each with a different apartment. He was Jewish in a marvelous way, she felt. "He could as easily have been brigand as Talmudic scholar." Meanwhile, André discovered that the

159

ssians had published their own version of *Man's Fate,* a montage of his novel with large hunks dutifully translated from his original but with other sections edited and with inserts expressing the Soviet point of view of the Chinese Revolution.

What would be the subject of his address? his hosts wondered. The poet Vassily Kumbach asked Regler whether André Malraux would remain loyal to the Revolution. Gustav answered that instead of talking about loyalty and disloyalty, the Party should be grateful for sympathizers of André's stature who were worth a dozen Aragons. "Does the lion in the zoo worry about the wild cats in the next cage?" the German asked, to which the poet answered, "What happens if they're in the same cage?" "André will never be in the same cage."

Eyes were peeled on the rostrum and ears on the simultaneous translation when the slim, thirty-two-year-old Frenchman with his nervous tics walked to the speaker's stand. "If writers are the engineers of the soul," Malraux warned after a generous praise of the host country, "don't forget the engineer's highest function is to *invent.*" His speech was entitled "Art is a Conquest."

> Art is not an act of submission but a conquest. A conquest of what? Nearly always of the unconscious and quite often of logic. Your classic writers give a richer and more complex picture of the inner life than the Soviet novelists, and so it sometimes happens that a reader will feel that Tolstoy is more real to them than many of the novelists attending this congress. If you reject psychology, then you arrive at the most absurd kind of individualism. Everyone tries to think out his own personal life, whether he wishes to do so or not. If you eliminate psychology it simply means that people who have seen deepest [into man] keep their discoveries to themselves. The works you admire the most, those of Maxim Gorky, have never stopped showing the psychological and poetic insight I demand here.[2]

It became Radek's task to answer this daring speech. "Malraux is a brilliant writer, recognized by our enemies," said Lenin's old comrade-in-arms. "I believe the fear our comrade Malraux expresses for a budding Shakespeare being strangled by the care we bestow on literature proves Malraux's lack of confidence in those who will bring up the child in our socialist daycare center. Let this Shakespeare be born—and I'm sure he will—and we will know how to bring him up!" Radek was followed by a certain Comrade Nikulin, who said the ending of *La Condition humaine* was the saving grace of Malraux. "I must mention a sentence by Comrade Malraux which has provoked various commentaries: 'Those who believe political passion to be above the love of truth should abstain

---

[2] An abbreviated French translation by Helene Reshetar of the 1934 stenographer's verbatim of Malraux's address and of Radek's and Nikulin's interventions were published in *La Revue des lettres modernes* (Nov., 1972).

160

from reading my book; it's not written for them.' Does that mean that Malraux is indifferent to the present state of affairs in China? Is it possible that he only bows to the dead, without thinking about the living? What is pessimism without hope?"

Malraux jumped to the platform and asked for the floor to answer Radek and Nikulin. Ehrenburg tried to smooth things out, feeling André's nervous tics had upset Radek, but Malraux stepped to the speaker's stand. "If I believed politics to be less important than literature," he said, "I wouldn't be in charge, with André Gide, of French efforts to free Comrade Dimitrov, I wouldn't have traveled to Berlin on behalf of the Comintern defense of Dimitrov and I wouldn't be here!"

His short rebuttal was applauded.

At a later banquet attended by Foreign Minister Vyacheslav Molotov, Bukharin, Zhdanov and hundreds of others, Radek marched drunk among the guests in a strange penitent mood, denouncing all those who rejected Socialist Realism. He tore open his shirt to show he still had a heart and began to talk about the failure of the Russian Revolution. "We are still far from our objective," he said in a high-pitched voice. "We thought the child had come of age, and we have invited the whole world to admire it. But it is self-knowledge, not admiration, that we need. The Revolution is no safari, no source of easy thrills. Heroism has no worth in itself. Executions must be evaluated, not made mysteries of. We are still all petit bourgeois!"

When Radek ran into Malraux, he began to upbraid him. "Why does Malraux ask the young communists what they think about death? Why does he adopt this negative attitude in a century in which the individual has at last been given the chance to fulfill himself in community with others?" Radek asked people around them. "Comrade Malraux, too, is a petit bourgeois!"

Other receptions had their surreal moments. At one of them the intense Leonid Leonov, whose famous *The Thief* was set in a Moscow underworld in the middle of the New Economic Plan (NEP), suddenly burst into a Dostoyevskian delirium of self-immolation, accusing himself of being a "Soviet barbarian." André insisted on proposing a toast "to the great absentee, Leon Davidovich Trotsky."

André and Clara spent their best moments away from the congress, first with Eisenstein, who wanted to make the film version of *La Condition humaine*. The maker of *Potemkin* was fast becoming a "non-person"—the Malrauxs couldn't know it and he himself had only a presentiment of it—and he often came to the Hotel National to work with André on the screenplay. When the weather was good, they sat on park benches "talking out" scenes for the script. Eisenstein wanted the movie to end with an exalted moment of triumph instead of the novel's hope-for-another-day scene in Kobe with May asking Old Gisors to come with her to Moscow.

161

"He wanted to finish with the imminent takeover of Shanghai by revolutionary armies and with Katov walking toward the locomotive and his death," Malraux was to remember. "Because of his wounds, Katov would limp and with each halting step, Eisenstein would fill a diagonal part of the screen with approaching communist armies. He made the whole scene in an accelerating montage of the limping Katov and the approaching liberation until Katov's back filled the screen and, on the soundtrack, the locomotive whistle was being drowned out by machine guns attacking Chiang Kai-shek."

Vsevolod Meyerhold wanted to adapt *Man's Fate* to the stage, but the famed director of the Moscow Revolutionary Theater didn't entertain Malraux on park benches but took him around to little-known side streets of Moscow and showed him Dostoyevsky's adolescent home. An old woman caretaker let Meyerhold and Malraux handle a Bible covered with annotations and the word *nyet* scribbled in many places.

Religion was always just under the surface. A young statistician Clara became friendly with said she had a six-year-old daughter taken care of by an old woman during the week. "This woman takes good care of her, it's not that, but all day she tells the kid that her father and I will go to hell unless she prays for us." Visits to Moscow's museums became painful for Clara and André when their interpreter translated the signs under the paintings: Auguste Renoir, Bourgeois painter whose works reflect late nineteenth-century social conflict. At question-and-answer sessions during a near-compulsory tour of a local factory, André told audiences what they expected to hear about dignity of work and the new rapport among socialist workers, but he also asked questions that brought reproachful gazes. What do you expect from life? What do you think of death? Clara remembered him asking:

> The women were more courageous than working women in France, they accepted to play his game. The meaning of our lives? To make socialism triumph. That was clear. But what do they think of death? "We will be happy to die for socialism," was the general answer.
>
> "Have you noticed," André asked me, "that they never imagine to die, only to be killed?" It was true.[3]

When Ehrenburg took them for a walk in the Kataygorod district, Clara distinctly smelled opium emanating from a house. It didn't exactly astonish her since Babel had told her the frontier police watching the long border had other things to look after besides opium smugglers. The sweet smell turned the conversation toward other illicit fragrances and Ehrenburg told them the greatest poet was someone it was perhaps best not to talk about. They insisted and learned her name was Anna Akhmatova, a thrice-married poetess who was not afraid of writing bluntly about women's pas-

[3] Clara Malraux, *Voici que vient l'été*, op. cit.

162

sions, a lucid and laconic woman whom Zhdanov had called "half nun, half harlot" and threatened to have expelled from the Writers' Union. Her name brought up Osip Mandelstam, a poet whose work had developed from classicism to a near-surrealist, even cubist style. Mandelstam was hopelessly out of tune with the era. As they walked on, Ehrenburg told them that Pasternak was allowed to do only Shakespearean translations and that Boris Pilnyak, who was of mixed Volga-German and Jewish descent and whose *The Naked Year* had been the first Russian novel wholly about the Revolution, had been sent to a labor camp in the East. Pilnyak's sin, it appeared, was *Mahogany,* a 1929 novel full of eccentric townspeople who made it clear the author believed all rulers, czarist or Marxist, were the same.

Toward the end of the congress, André was invited to Gorky's summer *dacha* together with Bloch, Aragon, Andersen-Nexö and a German who had escaped from a Nazi internment camp dressed in Tyrolean lederhosen. His name was Willi Bredel and André listened with great interest to his story of captivity and escape. Late at night when some of them had dropped out and the remaining guests were at the *zakusky,* they heard a car pull up and after a while the steps of men in heavy boots. André's description of this nocturnal meeting with "the master of one seventh of humanity" was to be passably zesty:

> Everybody stopped talking. It was Stalin looking like a benevolent police captain. He asked me what was happening of interest in Paris. "A new Laurel and Hardy movie," I said, showing him a crazy game of finger crossing that Stan Laurel had made famous, and everybody tried to imitate when they got out of the cinema. Stalin sat down between his body guards. While eating the *zakusky,* I had the impression I had lost my passport. I didn't feel it in my breast pocket. Unpleasant feeling in Moscow, huh? So I lean down to look on the floor. And what do I see under the table? Stalin, Molotov and the rest of them trying to twist their fingers like Stan Laurel.[5]

When Clara met Stalin at the parapet of the Kremlin roof during a Red Square parade, she found him sexy. She had all the time to study him because the parade of men and women in uniforms, folkloric costumes and sports garb below lasted three hours. "I saw him most of the time from profile, a profile not without nobility and a hint of the Orient. His black eyes were bright, the gaze firm, the mouth sensual, the fingers plump, the body not very tall but not little either. . . .When we got back to the hotel, André asked me what I had thought of my neighbor up on the roof. Candidly, I said, 'I wouldn't mind spending a moment in bed with him,' an answer which exposed me to a few difficulties."

The Malrauxs' nearness, if nothing else, to Stalin spread among

---

4 Jean Lacouture, *André Malraux,* op. cit.

163

the delegates and at one of the closing receptions André was approached by a shrunken man in too-big clothes. It was Mikhail Borodin, the former *éminence grise* of the Chinese revolution and main character in *Les Conquérants*. The disastrous outcome of the Soviet Union's China policy had not had an unduly harsh effect on Borodin. After his return from China following the Shanghai massacre, he had become People's Commissar for Labor. Recently, however, he had been demoted, but he was now the editor of the *Moscow Daily News*. It was long ago since he had taught school in Chicago but he had never forgotten his English and to be the editor of Russia's English-language newspaper was not bad. Not really, but. Borodin had their glasses filled and led Malraux to the side. "Since you are on such good terms with the authorities," Borodin said in a low voice, "perhaps you will be able to put in the right word to help me get an apartment with central heating." What struck Andé was the way History destroyed its own idols.

With Gorky, Malraux discussed the publication of a vast encyclopedia to be edited by a galaxy of scholars, and published in Russian, English, French and Spanish. Gorky was enthusiastic but nothing came of it.

Nothing came of anything—of Eisenstein's film of *La Condition humaine* or of the stage version, for which the eager Meyerhold had said Sergei Prokofiev would compose the music. Inveterate travelers, Clara and André didn't return to France at the end of the Writers' Union Congress but stayed another four months in the Soviet Union, traveling east as far as Novosibirsk in south-central Siberia, and returning for another long stay in Moscow before heading home. They couldn't know it, but during their months in the Soviet Union one epoch came to a close and a new, frightening era, which would sweep away most of the people they had met at the congress, was beginning.

Two months before the opening of the congress, Stalin's close associate Sergei Kirov had been murdered in Leningrad—a crime History would eventually say that Stalin had, if not inspired, at least seized upon as a pretext for an all-out assault on all political rivals, opponents and critics. The fates of the intellectuals the Malrauxs had met during the hot August congress were to be varied. If Zhdanov rode out the whole Stalin era and after World War II become the Stalinist who shaped cultural policy, Radek was already a condemned man, shot after a 1937 show trial, a year after Gorky died under mysterious circumstances. Joyce's defender Vishnevsky lived to alter history so as to give Stalin a heroic role in a syncophantic *The Unforgettable 1919,* while Olesha disappeared into the camps in the late 1930s suddenly to reappear, "rehabilitated," in 1956 and live until 1960. Borodin's relative obscurity as the *Moscow Daily News* editor enabled him to escape the purges of the 1930s, but in 1949 he was arrested in one of Stalin's anti-Semitic drives and died in a Siberian labor camp two years later.

164

Babel took Clara for a last long walk along the Moskva. The autumn had colored the trees along the river and Babel told her he had everything from mistresses to money plus coddling friendships with Gorky and Stalin, with whom he sometimes spent long evenings before an open chimney fire in the Kremlin. The benefits of these flattering friendships, he said, were that he was a writer who couldn't write, an exceptional situation for a member of the Writers' Union.

Three hours later, Clara was on a train to Paris. André followed a week later. On November 23, a "Moscow Report" meeting was organized at the Paris Mutualité Hall. André Gide and L'Humanité editor-in-chief Paul Vaillant-Couturier were on the dais. Malraux spoke without notes and said the things expected of a fellow traveler of his stature. When it came to the relations between Marxism and Soviet literature, he had to say a few things that might have slightly grieved his communist audience. "To pretend that art can express a doctrine means dealing in non-reality," he said. "Between art and doctrine are living human beings."

What had struck him in the USSR was the deep fraternity of the Russian people, not Stalinist conformity. What the times demanded were such fraternal bonds, not division or scorn, but a unity of all progressive voices.

To write propaganda would never be in the Malraux style, but if there was a book that came close to it, a novel written less spontaneously than the others, it was Le Temps du mépris, a novel dedicated "to our German comrades." This long short story of Kassner, a German communist organizer, his internment by the Nazis and his almost miraculous escape, which in English became Days of Wrath, contained none of the ideological conflict of The Conquerors or Man's Fate. Although the theme was still the individual struggling with his destiny in the face of suffering and death, the new novel was a story of revolt and escape, not an anguished vision of revolt and defeat.

Shelving "the story about oil," Malraux wrote Le Temp du mépris during the winter 1934–35. For the main plot, he used the story of Willi Bredel, the communist organizer he had met at Gorky's the night of Stalin's unexpected appearance, but also the strange tale of the Boris Savinkov, a Socialist revolutionary leader whom the czarist police had arrested knowing that in him they had caught the linchpin in the whole anti-czarist terrorist movement. When his name had been shouted out, another prisoner had stepped forward, deliberately sacrificing himself to save the leader. The irony of Savinkov's life was that he had been arrested by the NKVD secret police in 1924 when he tried illegally to reenter the Soviet Union.

Malraux also used the memories of various friends and members of the big German refugee colony—Gustav Regler, his friend Manes Sperber and pieces of anonymous adventures retold by members of the astonishing Münzenberg Trust. For the "feel" of Nazi Germany, Malraux relied on his own Berlin visit with Gide on behalf of the Free Thälmann Committee.

Like Borodin in *The Conquerors* and Katov in *Man's Fate,* Kassner is a party technocrat, an organizer of the German communist underground. He is arrested when he deliberately walks into a police trap to save his comrades. He is questioned, tortured and put in isolation in an almost pitch-black cell. Losing his sense of time and fearing creeping madness, he tries to retain his sanity by replaying Beethoven symphonies in his mind and by thinking of his wife Anna and their child, both in safety in Czechoslovakia. The music and personal life fail him as he yields to nightmarish fantasies and a sense of defeat made overwhelming by his realization that in the carefully stripped cell he has no way even of committing suicide. He tries to file his thumb fingernails razor sharp on the cell wall to perhaps use them to open his veins, but realizes that protein deficiency makes his fingernails soft.

What saves him is a comradely message tapped through the wall from a neighboring cell. The message is repeated and repeated and painstakingly he decodes the alphabet used for the tapping, often brutally interrupted by unseen guards. This triumph gives him courage and makes him prepare a long, imaginary speech on the theme of fraternity within the revolution.

He is suddenly released because, he learns, another prisoner, probably dead from torture by now, has declared himself to be Kassner. In the street, he realizes he is about to go mad because his imprisonment has actually only lasted nine days. A party contact risks his life to smuggle Kassner out of Germany, flying him through a harrowing hailstorm across the Sudeten mountains to Czechoslovakia. In Prague, Kassner is reunited with Anna and their child, after looking for her at a huge party rally. They both know he must slip back into Germany again to continue the struggle.

Le Temps du mépris came out in the summer of 1935, two months after Hitler had tested the mettle of the Versailles victors by tearing to shreds the military restrictions of the Treaty and drafting half a million men into a new German conscript army. Ten years later when the young journalist Roger Stéphane interviewed Malraux on the Alsace front and told him communists tended to prefer *Le Temps du mépris* to his other novels, Malraux characteristically replied, "Naturally. It's a dud." To which Stéphane said that communists had found Malraux's other novels "confusionists." The answer was, "Truth is always confusing." [5] In 1935, the communists liked it. If the *L'Humanité* reviewer reproached Malraux for his choice of subject, Aragon wrote in *Commune* that the communist in the new book had quite another dimension of truth than the earlier heroes, while in Russia a certain V. L. Omitrevsky wrote that with *Le*

[5] Roger Stéphane, *Fin d'une jeunesse* (Paris: Table Monde, 1954).

Temps Malraux had "found his truth in communism." [6] A few months later, a twenty-three-year-old student in French North Africa adapted, unauthorized, the novel into a play that he and a small theatrical group of students and workers staged in a wooden café in the port of Algiers. His name was Albert Camus.

Whatever the merits of *Le Temps du mépris,* which Robert Haas brought out in Haakon Chevalier's translation at Random House in early 1936, it was the first noteworthy French report on Nazi police repression.

[6] J. P. A. Bernard, *Le PCF et la Question littéraire* (Grenoble: Presses universitaires, 1972).

> I won't even go into the irony, the insult and the
> slander which must give the Ethiopians a nice desire to
> plant signs reading, "Shoot without spitting!"
>
> *Crapouillot*

14

During the early summer of 1935, when Mussolini openly prepared to invade Ethiopia—and in so doing furnished an explanation for the Royal Air Force alert in Saudi Arabia during the Queen of Sheba overflight—the Malrauxs rented a house near Pouilly-sur-Loire, the famed white wine town in central France. Nino Frank, who had known the Malrauxs since their return from Indochina, visited with them and little Florence. Clara had bought a secondhand, four-cylinder Rosengart and when it was decided to go for crayfish in Pouilly the evening before André was to go to Paris on business, Frank came along. "She drove in her own inimitable way, to the tune of her companion's sardonic remarks," Frank was to write. The little car couldn't quite make the uphill slopes of the sinuous landscape and at one long hill they all had to get out in the rain and push. "As usual, Malraux was patient and ceremonious toward Clara, but with an indefinable added irritation, heightened by the insistence of Clara queenly behind her wheel, that he was somehow responsible for the Rosengart's death throes."

The observant Italian, who in 1926 had found Clara exasperating, soon realized that as a couple, she and André were only a shadow of their former selves. "His manners have become more cutting; he is more self-confident and his verbal thrusts are accompanied by ellipses and figures of speech in which the affirmative is expressed by the negation of its opposite, a whole verbal spark which fascinates. In contrast, Clara is falling behind."

After André's departure the next morning, Clara allowed herself unsolicited confidences. Her husband, she told Frank, was becoming increasingly nervous, tense and unbearable; at his night table he kept a huge supply of sugar lumps which, practically without waking up, he consumed during the night—a kilo every other day, she specified, and, like a tracked

Roger Viollet Archives

Clara, circa 1935

animal, he had to face a door or some other exit when he was working. "Today," Frank was to write thirty years later, "it is easy to understand what was then concealed—the progressive dissolution of an affection whose parts had up to then been in harmony, one of the partner's trying to go further and only he drawing near to any 'after.' " [1]

The political horizon grew darker during the rainy summer. The ruling conservatives again believed Bolsheviks were about to take over France. Communist gains in municipal elections in May, combined with announced intentions of a large left-of-center coalition for the national elections due in the spring of 1936, spread panic among conservatives. They now echoed Hitler's propaganda that the defense agreement Pierre Laval had negotiated with Stalin was a step toward war and demanded an understanding with Germany and a freehand for Italy to undertake its Abyssinian conquest.

Malraux cut short the wet Pouilly vacation to be in the center of efforts to organize an antifascist conference, a kind of Parisian answer to the previous summer's Moscow conclave. When in June, the International Writers' Congress convened in the muggy old Mutualité Hall, it brought together an extraordinary cohort of European intellectuals, ranging from Romain Rolland and Aldous Huxley to Bertolt Brecht and E. M. Forster.

[1] Nino Frank, *Mémoire brisée,* op. cit.

169

The Spanish novelist Ramón Sender and Paul Nizan, just back from Moscow, would talk about humanism, André Chamson and Tristan Tzara would speak about nationalism and culture, Heinrich Mann and Gustav Regler about creation and dignity, while the theme "Defense of culture" would call Alexis Tolstoy, André Gide, Alfred Döblin and Malraux to the speaker's stand. Greetings were sent from Ernest Hemingway, Theodore Dreiser and James Joyce. Although Huxley came away thinking the conference was nothing more than a public meeting organized by the French Communist Party, such "opposites" as the skeptical E. M. Forster were followed at the speaker's stand by the fiery Aragon and *L'Humanité* editor-in-chief Paul Vaillant-Couturier sat next to the liberal critic Julien Benda, while backstage the Romanian religious author Gala Galaction drank to the health of the Danish poetess Karin Michaelis and Kafka's friend Max Brod discussed the draft resolution with the Red Army political department's Alexander Shcherbakov.

Malraux and Ilya Ehrenburg got the Soviet ambassador to fire off telegrams to Stalin demanding that Boris Pasternak and Isaac Babel, the two writers the French proletariat loved the most, be sent to Paris. The way Pasternak told what happened next deserves a Malraux retelling:

> The next morning, the phone rings at Pasternak's. His girl friend answers. Who? The Kremlin. Livid with fear, she turns toward him, hiding under the blankets. Dumbfounded, he listens, "Stalin orders you immediately to go and buy a set of Western clothes, tonight to take the train to Paris, where day after tomorrow you will deliver a speech on Soviet culture!" Rather than getting up, Pasternak prefers to plunge into a feverish slumber, filled with dreams of secret police and labor camps. Then he goes to the Gum department store and arrives in Paris in an unbelievable rabbi's dress and a kind of Mao cap which won't exactly allow him to walk unnoticed on the boulevards. Luckily, we're about the same size.

On the Mutualité stage, Pasternak declaimed a poem, which Malraux read in translation. It said that politics were a waste of time and that instead of discussing politics, they should all go to the country and gather flowers.

History has not recorded how Babel was told to get himself to Paris, but once he was there he shuffled onto the platform unable to take the conference seriously, told Jewish stories, laughed at his own jokes, captivated everyone by his modesty and gentleness, and was wildly applauded.

But the conference had not been called for the pathetic clowning of Soviet authors. In fact, Soviet justice suddenly became an issue when on the second day, Trotskyites in the audience brought up the "Victor Serge affair," obliging the more lucid delegates not only to denounce fascism in Germany and Italy but to come to grips with the arbitrariness of the

170

Gisèle Freund; Magnum

Paris Writers' Conference, 1935

Soviet system. André Breton and the populist Henri Poulaille brought up the question of Soviet repression in general and, in particular, the continued imprisonment in Russia of the Belgian-born anarchist, pamphleteer, agitator and "revisionist Marxist" Victor Serge. Malraux and Gide chaired the meeting that evening and after some discussion gave the floor to Serge defender Madeleine Paz. *L'Humanité*'s Paul Vaillant-Couturier and Louis Aragon tried to intervene, but the lawyer and editor of *Contre le Courant* was allowed to speak. She told the audience that in their fight against fascism, they should not forget the crimes committed against socialists in the "fatherland of socialism." Demanding the right to answer on behalf of the Russian delegation, Mikhail Koltzov assured the audience that Serge "had been deeply involved in the Kirova plot"—conveniently forgetting that the murder of Kirov had taken place two years *after* the Belgian's arrest.

On a personal level, the Victor Serge affair was the beginning of the split between Malraux and Trotsky. A few months before the publication of *Le Temps du mépris,* André had refused to intervene on behalf of Serge, a refusal that Trotsky resented. Although his fascination for Trotsky's historical dimension remained intact, Malraux's sense of political efficiency made him realize that Leon Davidovich was a romantic and increasingly anachronistic symbol. Trotsky had not been able to rally anti-Stalinist communists, and his Fourth International, although strong on intellectuals, was weak on contacts with the working class. In 1936, when the Norwegian government deported him and Natalya, on an oil tanker, to their last—Mexican—exile and the retreating forces of Republican Spain desperately needed Soviet aid to offset Italian and German military support of General Francisco Franco's insurgents, Malraux totally abandoned Trotsky's cause and called him "an obsessed crank." In 1971, however, Malraux was again to pay tribute to "the wandering Jew of the revolution."

> Trotsky had a verbal eloquence that Lenin didn't possess. Trotsky always maintained that, whatever we have accomplished, the main problem is still not solved. That was the theory of the permanent revolution, while Lenin was a practitioner of the staircase theory, each step was a victory. There was something of a squirrel collecting nuts in Lenin, whereas Trotsky, when he had reached three new steps said, *"Now* we're facing the fundamental problem of the revolution." The word prophet fits him very well.[2]

The air of the Mutualité was never completely cleared of the Victor Serge affair and it was a tense, hollow-eyed and chain-smoking Malraux, shaken with more nervous tics than ever, who strode to the speaker's stand to pronounce the closing address. His speech was called "The Work of Art" and contained the themes of his life work, not only the current "revolution-

[2] *Magazine littéraire* (July, 1971).

ary" preoccupations but also his philosophical inquiry into the nature of art, which were to be his major topics twenty years later.

His voice was raw and nervous and remembered by many who attended the conference. After retracing the difficulties encountered in even getting the conference under way, he launched into the subject.

> By the anger it has provoked, we know our conference exists. We have permitted some people who have been gagged to speak and we have allowed a joint responsibility to exist. It is in the nature of fascism to be nationalistic; it is our nature to be of the world. Our goal is to defend culture, but this conference has shown that a work of creation is nothing when love recedes from it, that a work of art needs us, needs our wants and desires because a heritage is not something that is transmitted, it is something that is conquered. Every work is created to satisfy a need that is passionate enough to give birth. When the need recedes from it as blood from a body, a mysterious metamorphosis begins. The work of art enters into the shade and only a new generation's needs and passions can summon it back again. Until we bring our passion to it, it remains like a great statue with sightless eyes confronted by a long procession of blind men. But the need that draws one of the blind men to the statue will also open both his and the eyes of the statue.
>
> If we go back a hundred years, we find that works of art we now regard as indispensable were ignored. Go back two hundred years and we realize that the nervous, radiant smile of Gothic sculpture is synonymous with a grimace. A work of art is an object, but it is also an encounter with time. I am aware that we have made the discovery of history. Works that went unloved to the attic may find themselves unloved in a museum, which is not exactly a happier fate. Every work of art is dead when there is no love.
>
> Nevertheless, there is a meaning to this movement. Arts, ideas, peoples, all humanity's old dreams, if we need them to live they need us to live again.[3]

Three months after the conference, Mussolini invaded Ethiopia and proclaimed the foundation of a new Roman empire. The aggression demanded sanctions from the League of Nations, but the French and British governments hoped to draw Italy into an effective anti-German front and Mussolini was convinced that France and Britain, who during the previous century had carved up most of Africa among themselves, could hardly object to his civilizing missions against savage Abyssinians. Laval, who had become Premier in June and now stalled on the ratification of the defense agreement that, as foreign minister, he had negotiated in Moscow with Stalin, tried both to give Italy a free hand and to placate League of Nations demands for sanctions. When an October 10 fifty nations agreed that Italy had indeed resorted to war, France yielded to British pressures and voted with the majority. But Laval immediately set to work to emas-

[3] The speech was reprinted, verbatim, in *Commune* (Sept., 1935).

ulate the sanctions to the point that they were harmless to Italy's war effort. To show where their hearts and stomachs were, wealthy Frenchmen started to eat spaghetti and drink Chianti in Italian restaurants and sixty-four intellectuals, spearheaded by Henri Massis and Thierry Maulnier, denounced the "powers of disorder and anarchy" defending "savages" against the civilizing mission of Italy.

On November 4, Malraux gave the Left's answer at a Rally for the Defense of Ethiopia. His speech was a scathing attack on *all* colonialism. Defenders of colonialism, he said, pointed to the benefits colonialism bestowed on conquered people. In their view, to civilize meant to Europeanize. But the countries that were Europeanizing the fastest, he said, were those who were independent. Muslim women in Morocco, Tunisia and India were still veiled; Persian woman almost no longer and Turkish women not at all; Mandarin rule no longer existed in China or in Japan, but it existed in Indochina. There were hospitals in independent Siam, but in neighboring French Cambodia people were too poor for hospitals. If French Indochina was compared to independent Thailand, French Morocco with independent Turkey, the "benefits" of colonialism soon became obvious. Modern colonialism was invented when the West had discovered it was more practical to conquer people's things than their minds.

> No civilization—white, black or yellow—began with warriors. It started when lawmakers or priests began to civilize the warriors, when facts could yield to arguments. All civilization implies a respect for others. It is precisely when Ethiopia seeks specialists that she is sent cannons. If Ethiopia wins this war, she will be no more or no less Europeanized than if she loses. To kill tens of thousands is of course one way of getting them into hospitals, but it is not necessarily the best way. What a paradise colonies would be if the West were to build hospitals for those it has killed and gardens for those it has deported! [4]

A month later, he addressed a rally in the Wagram Hall marking the second anniversary of Georgi Dimitrov's acquittal, denouncing the scandals of Nazism and its treatment of "our German comrades." A few months later, he was in London speaking before the International Writers' Association for the Defense of Culture. He stressed that the intellectual wishing to retain the cultural values of liberal democratic society had not so much to opt for communism as opt *against* fascism. Besides, Marxism and democracy were not irreconciliable insofar as both were universal and dialectic whereas fascist ethics were specific and incapable of change. Marxism and democracy mobilized man's energies against his fate, fascism mobilized man against another man. "It has always struck me that fascist art is incapable of depicting anything but the combat of man against man,"

[4] The speech was edited and reprinted in *Crapouillot* (June, 1936).

174

he told the meeting. He was followed by H. G. Wells, who predicted the use of atomic weapons in a future war.

In May, 1936, Malraux was in Madrid, invited by Left-leaning Catholic author José Bergamín, who had attended the Paris and London assizes and offered Madrid as the host city for the projected 1937 conference. "What the word culture expressed is the idea of transforming destiny into consciousness," Malraux told the Ateneo Hall audience. "A revolution only gives us the possibility of our *dignity;* to transform the possibility into reality is up to each individual."

He became fond of saying that what was important was to choose one's enemies. The choosing was reciprocal, as evidenced by the virulence of militant right-wing attacks on Malraux. In 1943, for example, Lucien Rebatet was to draw a portrait of Malraux of these Front populaire years. Remembering the "mascarade" of the prewar left-of-center coalition and its rallies, Rebatet wrote that Malraux was always there, "with his face of a sex maniac devoured by tics, a kind of second-string Bolshevik gentleman-author * whose writings were practically unreadable yet were admired in bourgeois circles and even among impressionable young conservatives, thanks to an inflamed vocabulary and an obtuse way of retelling Chinese news items shredded into a thick broth of adjectives." [5]

Like many others, Malraux felt acutely the weakness of the democracies in the face of the rising fascism. The Abyssinian war and the collapse of the League of Nations over it were painful examples. Despite all the Laval administration had done to water down the League sanctions against Italy, Mussolini was so resentful at France for failing to back his aggression that in December he denounced Franco-Italian accords signed ten months earlier, including a secret military agreement.

At the beginning of May 1936, Emperor Haile Selassie fled Ethiopia and the Italians entered Addis Ababa. For all practical purposes, the League of Nations died that spring. Fifty-two nations had combined to resist aggression and all they accomplished was that Haile Selassie lost all of his country instead of only half and the League further offended Italy by allowing the emperor a hearing at the Assembly, and then expelled him for taking the invitation seriously. Isolationist United States had never joined the League, Japan and Germany had already left with Italy soon following suit and France, which for two decades had based much of its foreign policy on the international body, felt resentful. Conservatives and Catholics who in the name of "Latin civilization" were

---

* In French, "espèce de sous-Barrès bolcheviste," in reference to Maurice Barrès (1862–1923), the nationalist, anti-Semitic writer and self-styled educator of his generation for whom literature was a substitute for action and who was always a gentleman charming his opponents.
[5] Lucien Rebatet, *Les Décombres* (Paris: Denoel, 1943).

ready to condone Mussolini's aggression, blamed Great Britain for the fiasco of the League and for driving Italy into the arms of a restless and aggressive Germany. During the Abyssinian crisis the Laval government had asked London for definite guarantees that England would come to France's aid if Hitler moved into the demilitarized Rhineland or tried to attack France. The British had refused and on March 7, Hitler reoccupied the Rhineland. His excuse was the much-delayed French ratification of the Franco-Soviet pact, negotiated by Laval and Stalin.

On April 26, France went to the polls in heavy rain and returned— with a record eighty-five percent of registered voters casting their ballots— a Leftist coalition. The advent of the Front populaire was welcomed by the masses as a thrilling victory promising long-overdue social and economic reforms, and by a dismayed Right as bringing France to the brink of red revolution. The head of the coalition government was socialist Léon Blum, a man prey to self-doubts, self-criticism and given to airing his soul-searching in public. Blum and his party had spent their entire lives in the opposition. Now, just turned sixty-four and without any cabinet experience, the Socialist leader formed a government and the experiment of the Popular Front was launched.

But the great event of the summer of 1936—and one Malraux was soon to be deeply involved in—happened in none of the predictable "hot spots," but in Spain, where on July 18 a full-scale military rebellion took place. As in France, Spanish general elections had given power to a *Frente popular,* a coalition of radicals, socialists and communists. Its program was more anticlerical and democratic than socialist, but it was enough to provoke monarchists, fascists, the Church and the army. Plans for a coup had been worked out as early as 1934 and had received the vague blessings of Mussolini. The right-wing rebels, under general Francisco Franco, expected quick victory and most others expected it for them. Instead, the republic rallied the workers of Madrid; beat off the military conspirators—of the armed forces' two hundred generals, one hundred and eighty-five joined the rebellion—and asserted its hold over most of the country.

Malraux had been in Madrid in May. When he and Clara landed at Madrid's Barajas airfield in a private plane piloted by Edouard Corniglion-Molinier four days after the coup and rolled into the capital full of rumors and conflicting military communiqués, Spain was rapidly sliding into civil war.

So they came in long columns from all countries,
all those who knew poverty well enough to die fighting it,
and some had guns and those who had no guns used
their hands, and one after another they came to lie down
on the earth of Spain.

Man's Hope

15

With the Spanish Civil War, Malraux's legend came true. In this
conflict, he was to incarnate Garin, Gisors, Katov, Kyo and Kassner, to
flesh out his *homme d'action* and, by energetic and intelligent intervention,
try to influence the course of revolutionary events. In this war, in which
he was not to be a journalistic camp follower but to command an international air squadron, he was also to write his best novel. *L'Espoir*—
which to echo with *Man's Fate* became *Man's Hope* in English—was
also the best book about this war, which was the culmination of one
hundred and fifty years of passionate quarrels in Spain but was seen as
the conflict in which the great issue of the age was at stake.

Malraux's intervention was immediate and decisive. Within a few
days of his and Clara's landing in Madrid, he was back in Paris negotiating
the purchase of planes and other war matériel on behalf of the besieged
Republican government, meeting personally with Premier Léon Blum to
try and persuade the Front populaire leader to back, at least underhandedly,
the Frente popular on the other side of the Pyrenees.

The Spanish Civil War was instantly the dominating topic of international affairs and, in France and Great Britain, the theme of passionate
domestic controversy. The great issue of democracy versus fascism seemed
to be at stake in the elected Republican government's attempt to fight
back an armed forces' coup, started in Spanish Morocco July 17 and
rapidly spreading. When the Malrauxs landed in Madrid, true war rather
than rebellion and resistance to it, was in progress. The government held
the extreme northwest corner of Spain and about the southern half of the
country. Madrid and Barcelona were on the Republican, or government
side, but lightning coups had made Seville and Cordoba fall into the hands
of the Falangists, or Nationalists, as the rebels called themselves.

The first days were murderous. With communications difficult,

177

nonexistent or confusing, each town found itself on its own, acting out its own drama in a vacuum. It was the first radio war, with the rebel Radio Seville broadcasting resounding claims of victories and Radio Madrid trying to reassure both a bewildered and fast-polarizing civil population and incredulous foreign governments. The geographical differences within Spain were a prime factor in the social disintegration as the great cloud of violence spread. Regional feelings and age-old separatism resurfaced. As sovereign power ceased to exist, individuals acted without constraint. Within a month nearly a hundred thousand people perished arbitrarily and without trial as both sides evoked martial law and legitimacy. Bishops were torn to pieces and churches profaned. Educated Christians spent their evenings murdering illiterate peasants. The majority of these crimes were the work, on both sides, of men convinced that what they were doing was not only right, but noble, and the slaughter caused such hatreds that, when some order was eventually established, it was geared only to the rationalization of these early events of the civil war. The Madrid Council of Lawyers reported that in the first weeks of the war, 9,000 workers were killed in Seville, 2,000 in Saragossa, 5,000 in Granada, 7,000 in all Navarre, with historians eventually agreeing on 40,000 as the number of Nationalist executions during the whole war. International attempts to stop the atrocities were of no avail. Chief conspirator General Emilio Mola reacted to a French Red Cross suggestion of exchange of political prisoners by saying, "How can you expect us to exchange a caballero for a Red dog? You have arrived too late, those dogs have already destroyed the most glorious spiritual values of our country." [1] The majority of the executioners were men who considered that they had a duty to extricate the heresies of liberalism, socialism, communism and anarchism that were destroying their own beautiful and timeless Spain.

On the Republican side, revolution swept through all towns and cities where the Nationalists' uprising had been defeated. Committees were formed, nominally proportionate to the parties of the Popular Front, together with the anarchists, but in fact reflecting the real political strengths on the local level. The first step, common to all Republican Spain, was the proscription of right-wing parties, requisition of hotels, rightist newspapers, factories and the houses of the rich. Roads were guarded by patrols of militiamen and various subcommittees were set up to deal with daily life. "Republican Spain," as historian Hugh Thomas was to write, "constituted less a single state than an agglomeration of separate republics. The regional confusion was as it had been in the 1870s or in the Napoleonic Wars though greatly increased by class and religious passion."

[1] Hugh Thomas, *The Spanish Civil War* (New York: Harper and Row, 1963).

178

The military timetable of the Nationalists had been to win within five days and in inaugurating the nominal *junta* leadership in Burgos, Mola shouted from a balcony in the main square, "Spaniards! Citizens of Burgos! The Government which was the wretched bastard of liberal and socialist concubinage is dead, killed by our valiant army. Spain, the true Spain, has laid the dragon low and now it lies, writhing on its belly and biting the dust. I am now going to take up my position at the head of the troops and it will not be long before two banners—the sacred emblem of the Cross, and our own glorious flag—are waving together in Madrid."

Mola ruled northern Spain while Franco controlled Morocco and the Canaries. On the mainland, Franco remained for a long time something of a myth. He was spoken of constantly, but no one seemed to know where he was. The third leader of the junta was General Gonzalo Queipo de Llano, who ruled Nationalist Andalusia and in nightly broadcasts threatened to kill the families of Republican soldiers and boasted of the terrible sexual powers of the legionnaires and the *regulares*. In Seville, Queipo's dashing portrait was plastered on walls and soon photographs of Franco appeared. Falange posters were enormous, covering entire facades of buildings. "The Falange calls you, now or never." There was no middle ground. Patrols of Falangists prowled the streets, stopping suspicious persons, demanding papers and shouting *¡Arriba España!* (Arise, Spain!). Notices everywhere called on citizens to abstain from talking politics and there was a silence in Nationalist-held cities which strongly contrasted with babel-like conditions in Republican territories The Falange, whose numbers swelled with its successes, acted more as a political police than a political party and Willy Messerschmidt, the German aircraft manufacturer who traveled in Nationalist Spain in August, reported that the Falange appeared to have no real aims or ideas and to be composed mostly of "young people for whom it is good sport to play with firearms and round up communists and socialists." As the war progressed, the Nationalists showed increasing religious fervor; mass attendance became compulsory for rank-and-file Falangists and propagandists represented the ideal Falangist as half monk and half warrior. The ideal feminine Falangist was a combination of Saint Theresa and Isabel the Catholic. Archbishops, bishops, canons and priests daily implored the protection of the Virgin for the Nationalist troops, begging her to arrange for their swift entry into Madrid.

On July 18, President of the Republic Manuel Azaña had accepted the resignation of Santiago Casares Quiroga as prime minister and in the hope of rallying the middle class had appointed in his stead his liberal friend José Giral, a professor of chemistry by profession. Bypassing the Spanish ambassador in Paris whose loyalty he was not sure of, Giral

179

Eve of war. Prime Minister Manuel Azaña (right) riding through the streets of Madrid.

sent a telegram directly to Prime Minister Blum of France. "Are surprised by a dangerous military coup," the wire read. "Beg of you to help us immediately with arms and airplanes. Fraternally yours Giral."

Since the insurgents *were* the armed forces—the small Spanish Navy remained loyal to the government—the Republic's most urgent need was the means of fighting for its survival.

In Paris, Blum immediately summoned his closest advisers, including his foreign secretary Yvon Delbos and his war minister, Edouard Daladier, who all agreed it was in the national interest to send the Spanish Republic whatever arms could be spared. Giral asked for twenty Potez bombers, eight light machine guns, eight Schneider cannons, 350,000 machine gun rounds, 4 million cartridges and 20,000 bombs. Because Croix de Feu and Action française leaguers were already demonstrating in sympathy with the Falangist rebels, it was decided to keep the arms shipment a secret for the time being. However, a military attaché at the Spanish embassy who was a fanatical supporter of the Falange, immediately leaked the itemized list to the right-wing press which exploded it in banner headlines on July 23, the day Blum, accompanied by Delbos, flew to London for consultation with the British government.

The Conservative government in London was more than alarmed at the idea, fearing that if France shipped arms to the Republic, Mus-

180

solini and Hitler might aid Franco and the Falangists and the result might be the European war England dreaded. In the hall of Claridge's, foreign secretary Anthony Eden asked Blum, "Are you going to send arms to the Spanish Republic?" "Yes," Blum answered. "It is your affair," Eden replied, "but I ask you one thing. Be prudent."

If Blum was not particularly surprised by the initial British reaction, he was totally taken aback by the storm that broke out on his return to Paris. Delbos was the first to waver and on July 25 Blum began to cave in to the mounting opposition of the Radical-Socialist partner in his coalition. By an afternoon cabinet meeting the first of three meetings over a fortnight dealing with Spain and eventually leading to the so-called Nonintervention Agreement, Blum had given in. At the end of the cabinet meeting it was announced that "in view of possible international complications," the French government would "suspend the shipment of arms to the Republic of Spain." Malraux's first intervention as he landed in Paris a few days behind Blum was to become the buyer of arms and airplanes.

During the week in Spain, André had quickly sized up the situation in military terms, and quickly realized that the mortal weakness of the Republican forces was that it had no planes. Half the planes of the air squadrons that had remained loyal had been on Moroccan air bases on July 17. On the 19th, they had been recalled to Madrid and to refuel had landed in Seville without knowing the city was already in Queipo de Llano's hands. Queipo had seized the planes and had the pilots shot.

From the first hours inside Spain, André had seen evidence of demoralizing confusion. On their way down in the Lockheed Orion belonging to the French Air Ministry—in aviation circles Corniglion-Molinier had all the right connections—André had had his flyboy friend make low-altitude reconnaissance swoops. Nothing had moved on the roads and trains were immobilized on railway stations. Judging from factory smokestacks, industry had shut down and the only smoke billowing from town centers had come from burning churches. The only activity they had seen was around military camps, where men, busy around machinery and trucks, had dashed for cover as soon as they heard the plane.

When they had landed in Madrid, workers in makeshift militia uniforms had surrounded the Lockheed for a tense five minutes until a car had pulled up and José Bergamín and a government representative had greeted them. On the way into town, they had seen both the same militia patrolling streets and building sandbag barricades. Clara had found the sight moving, "streets full of armed militiamen and militiawomen, all dressed in the same work clothes, all equal in an admirable equality, men and women, adolescents and adults. Streets where only government-req-

181

uisitioned cars moved and were checked at each big intersection. Swelling above it all, radio loudspeakers shrieking day and night." [2]

Like Bergamín, Clara believed it was a moving but lost cause and that her and her husband's gesture could only be symbolic. Not André. He cruised the streets, attended meetings of the Unión General de los Trabajadores (UGT), the socialist trade union congress, giving the raised fist *¡Salud!* which had replaced the *Adiós* greeting in Republican Spain and soon became as famous as the *¡No pasarán!* (They shall not pass!) slogan. With Corniglion-Molinier, he had flown to Barcelona. Here, he had met the anarchist leader Buenaventura Durriti and his revolutionary armies bursting westward to battle Falangists holding Saragossa. This metalworker, who was to become Negus in *L'Espoir* and also appear in various disguises in the novels Ernest Hemingway, George Orwell, Gustav Regler, Arthur Koestler and Upton Sinclair would write, was a man of violence to whom the first flush of revolutionary success had brought enormous self-confidence. His column had set out with such excitement that they were two hours away from Barcelona before discovering they had forgotten ammunition. As Malraux and Corniglion-Molinier had returned to the airfield to fly back to Madrid, they had seen a gesticulating Durriti arguing with the airport commander about passage to Madrid. Graciously, they had given the anarchist a lift.

In Paris, Malraux had to act fast. While the Blum administration was willing to close its eyes to quick private arms transactions for Spain, it worked publicly in favor of a Nonintervention Pact, by which France, England, Germany, Italy and the Soviet Union would agree not to send arms to the belligerent factions in Spain. While Germany's initial reaction was similar to Britain's and Berlin actually discouraged early requests from Franco for airpower, Mussolini intervened more brazenly—60,000 Italian soldiers were eventually to fight in Spain—by immediately sending aid, especially Savoia 81 transport planes. The conquest of Abyssinia had left the Duce anxious to display his personality in some new way—his dealings with Hitler were still exploratory and undefined. The western Mediterranean could be this new field and, as Italian diplomats repeated endlessly, Italy was not prepared to see the establishment of a communist state in Spain.

As Blum set August 8 as the tentative date for the signing of a Nonintervention Pact—the thrust of French diplomacy was that speed was of the essence and that once the Great Powers had decided not to ship arms, the civil war would quickly burn itself out—Malraux had to get whatever planes he could buy across the French-Spanish border before the deadline. One of his brothers-in-law knew people at the Potez aircraft manufacturers and together with President Azaña's special envoy managed

[2] Clara Malraux, *Les Combats et les jeux,* op. cit.

to close a deal with Air Minister Pierre Cot for twenty-two Potez 540 bombers, followed by the purchase of a dozen Bloch 200s. Some of the Potez 540s were already in Toulouse. After the August 8 arms embargo, André managed to get a few more planes, "bought at the flea market," out of France. Throughout 1936 Malraux would fly back to Paris for meetings with manufacturers and Air Ministry officials, pleading for more planes and from his apartment in the Rue du Bac, make long-distance calls all over Europe. In October, the Air France manager at Barcelona saw a whole squadron of new planes fly in from France commanded by Malraux, "lean, gaunt and eyes flashing." Malraux had a chat with him and an hour later a quarter-million gallons of aviation fuel were "transferred" to Republican registry.

On August 8, two days after Italian fighters had supplied cover for merchant ships ferrying Franco and three thousand men and equipment of his Army of Africa from Morocco to southern Spain, the first planes of Malraux's air force landed at Madrid's Barajas field. The Republican government was more than grateful, made André a "coronel" and gave him the right to form and command a wing of foreign mercenary fliers. The unit was immediately baptized the ₊España Squadron.

What could this chain-smoking elitist who didn't even know how to fly a plane accomplish? A lot. His fame as a writer, his far-flung contacts with influential people, the respect the Republican leaders showed him was to give him an ascendency and an influence that would always impress his little army of pilots and mechanics. Colonel Malraux fought for his squadron, protected it from the Republican government and from the soon-to-arrive communist cadres. Because the unit owed its existence to André, it was virtually a private air force with its own chain of command, its own resources, and its own political program. Above all what impressed his men was André's personal courage. He flew sixty-five missions as a gunner-bombardier himself.

The España Squadron airmen were paid fifty thousand pesetas a month. They were Frenchmen, Germans, Americans, Italians, Russians and one Algerian. Malraux's chief lieutenant was Julien Segnaire, a hawk-like French air force reserve officer who had first met André at one of the Defense for Thälmann rallies and who would later write the commentary to Malraux's Vermeer book.

Although their marriage was for all practical purposes ended, Clara was sometimes with André in Madrid, sometimes in Paris. One day in September when André Gide had just returned from Moscow and caused consternation in leftist ranks by denouncing Soviet mentality as being more stultifying than the climate in Hitler's Germany, he visited the Malrauxs in their Rue du Bac apartment. André had just arrived from Madrid and was soaking in a bath while three-year-old Florence was tearing petals off a dahlia to make a "salad," as Gide noted in his diary. Clara was brooding. She had proclaimed complete sexual freedom in Madrid and André had announced that the marriage was over.

The España Squadron had not much time to train. Franco's Army of Africa was assembled in Seville and began marching north to drive a wedge clear through Spain, cut off the whole Portuguese frontier from the Republicans and join forces with the Army of the North, then turn east and advance toward Madrid along the Tagus river. The Army of Africa was directed by Franco with Colonel Blanco Yague, the bespectacled commander of the Foreign Legion, the actual commander in the field.

Yague's motorized force advanced two hundred miles in one week and on August 10 reached Merida, where the Republican militia gave Yague his first real contest of the war. The battle was fought over the Guadiana river. The Republicans were driven back, counter-attacked with reinforcements from Madrid, and a flank of Yague's army turned instead on Badajoz on the Portuguese border. The Battle of Badajoz, fought hand-to-hand in the Plaza de la República in the shadow of the cathedral, was ferocious. Once masters of the town, the legionnaires killed anyone with arms and rounded up unarmed militiamen and mowed them down in the bullring. Executions continued for days.

On August 23—two weeks after its creation—Malraux's little air force was throw against Yague's new eastward advance toward Madrid. After taking Navalmoral de la Mara, the hot, dry valley of the Tagus stretched out in front of Yague forces without any serious natural obstacles. Madrid's reinforced Estramadura army met the advancing Yague forces. One of Yague's columns, commanded by Major Carlos Asensio, a veteran of Moroccan warfare, was nearing Medellin—a village famous for being the birthplace of Hernán Cortés, the conqueror of Mexico— when Malraux's air force appeared in the cloudless late afternoon sun.

The attack did not stop the Army of Africa. The militia on the ground was no match for the legionnaires and Moroccans who outmaneuvered them, forcing them to retreat from their position or risk being cut off. Nine thousand Republican troops, including two thousand anarchists who refused their commander's orders in battle and launched senseless sidetracks, fell back into the parched Tagus valley.

On August 28, Asensio's column joined the rest of Yague's army at Navalmoral and the move east along the north shore of the Tagus resumed. Resistance was rare. The Government did not want to risk losing all its men in one engagement and retreated all the time. Some of the troops refused to dig trenches because they considered this cowardly. On September 2, the Army of Africa reached the outskirts of Talavera de la Reina, the last town of importance before Madrid.

During these months, Malraux and his men lived at the Hotel Florida on Madrid's Gran Via. In the restaurant a far-out crowd of Malraux's airmen, journalists and camp followers of war and revolution met

184

at all hours and discussed everything openly despite the strict military secrecy imposed by the government. In one end of the restaurant was a huge blackboard and sometimes Malraux and Segnaire could be seen drawing up the next day's flight plans. Once a blond volunteer was suspected of being a Nazi infiltrator and it became Clara's job to grill him in German—and recommend his dismissal.

Everybody, it seemed, was at the Florida or was soon to show up. If the timid George Orwell was to reach besieged Madrid only in December and Ernest Hemingway and John Dos Passos in early 1937, Ilya Ehrenburg and Mikhail Koltsov were the *Izvestia* and *Pravda* correspondents—Ehrenburg making frequent trips to the northern front, both on journalistic assignments to interview the fiery Durriti in the trenches or on missions for Soviet ambassador Marcel Rosenberg. The *New York Times* correspondent was Herbert L. Matthews, who was to write glowing lines about the commander of the España Squadron: "My favorite Frenchman was André Malraux, a true idealist and a brave man—they were pretty well all brave, for that matter. Malraux headed a group of French aviators who nearly all got themselves killed at the beginning of the war flying the crates the Government picked up second-hand, anywhere it could." [3] In his *Spanish Diary*, Koltsov depicted Malraux several times. Under August 18, he wrote: "Seeing a lot of people at the airport, especially military men. André walks back and forth—tired, emaciated, irritable. He hasn't slept for several nights; he is constantly called from one place to another. The commanding of the squadron is done standing up, in hasty conversation." Georges Soria, *L'Humanité*'s correspondent, was to fashion the most vivid portrait.

> Wound up like a rubberband, a lock of hair over one eye, a half-burned out cigarette stub between the lips, full of tics and dressed kind of sloppy chic, his daily conversation was a bouquet of images and brilliant interjections which literally fascinated the people surrounding him. He used this verbal power with a tyranny that was easily forgiven. In the roving little international circle of writers who had rushed in to show their solidarity with the Spanish people, André Malraux held the very first spot. Everybody admired him for confronting the dangers of an aerial warfare for which he was not prepared. His legend grew as the battle for Madrid enflamed the minds. . . . Malraux speaks very bad English and German, neither Spanish, Italian nor Russian. How was he constantly at the center of attention with the most prestigious personalities hanging on to him? He expressed himself in a French full of grand syntactic complications and in a vocabulary never thinned by any desire to be understood by those around him. For Frenchmen it was a treat, for the others . . . I remember a conversation between Malraux and Hemingway during which Ernie stared at his glass and resigned himself to

[3] Herbert L. Matthews, *The Yoke and the Arrows* (New York: Braziller, 1957).

185

wait until Malraux had finished his gasping improvisations before putting in a word. The two men had respect for each other, but didn't like each other. Ernie rather sought out simple and silent types and hated to hold forth and theorize on politics and literature.[4]

The Malraux-Hemingway meeting Soria referred to was still a year away. In July 1936, Hemingway was in Wyoming and still of two minds about going to Spain.

Whatever the day's mission, Malraux appeared fresh-shaven for evening cocktails at the Florida bar, retelling crazy dogfight details and discussing the military and political situation. In the fast slide to the Left of the Republican forces, the España Squadron was in the orbit of orthodox communists and as such was opposed to the Trotskyite *Partido obrero de Unificación marxista* (POUM). The POUM was particularly strong in Barcelona and many foreigners, including George Orwell, joined this party in the romantic belief that it embodied a magnificent utopian ideal.

In August, Clara had an affair with one of André's airmen and further irritated her husband by fraternizing with POUM followers. Following a stormy argument, Clara went back to Paris, where in early September André made one of his periodic visits, soaking in the bathtub the day André Gide came calling.

If Franco's Army of Africa overran Talavera and on September 3 was no more than eighty miles from Madrid, Mola's Army of the North captured San Sebastián and Irún, cutting off the Basques from the border. In Asturias, the Republicans held on to many towns—at Gijón where the water supplies ran out, the defenders were nightly treated to Queipo de Llano smacking his lips on Radio Seville, actually turning several of the beseiged men half mad.

In Toledo, seventy miles south of Madrid, Nationalists held the near-impregnable Alcázar fortress and every attempt to storm it was rebuffed. The well-trained and protected Falangists inside the old fortress possessed all the ammunition they needed. They were entirely cut off from the outside world, had no electricity and had no knowledge of the state of the war, but held parades in the courtyard and a fiesta in honor of the Assumption in the cellars with flamenco dancing. Insults and boasts were exchanged through megaphones. On August 17, a Nationalist plane dropped messages of encouragement from Franco and Mola and news of Yague's advance.

Malraux was several times in Toledo, realizing how disorganized the Republicans were and trying to intervene in the civilian authorities' squabble over the protection of El Greco's paintings in the city's churches and museum. His planes made several frustrating raids on the Alcázar,

[4] Jean Lacouture, *André Malraux*, op. cit.

186

sometimes stopped from bombing by hostages put on the fortress roof by the defenders, sometimes by such war ruses as white flags planted in the inner courtyard. In *L'Espoir,* Toledo was to represent the "lyrical illusion" of mass frustration.

The proximity of the Nationalists was brought home to Madrid's population on August 27 when German Junker 52 bombers dropped explosives on the War Ministry. These bombings were History's first big-city air raids.

On September 4, President Azaña accepted Giral's resignation as Premier. The obvious choice of replacement was Francisco Largo Caballero, nicknamed "Spain's Lenin" but actually a socialist whom the Falangists had tried to assassinate. Largo Caballero, however, refused to take office unless the Popular Front agreed to let the Communist Party join— he invited the anarchists to join, but they refused. No communist party had ever been part of a Western cabinet and for fear of being compromised, the Party central committee opposed the move. Moscow, however, ordered them to join and Largo Caballero formed his coalition government.

The first task of this "Government of Victory," as it called itself, was to avoid immediate defeat. Five days after it had been formed, a newly equipped Nationalist force of Franco's flank hurtled north and made contact with the southernmost units of Mola's Army of the North. This junction cut off a large portion of Republican territory to the west and encircled Madrid to the west. Franco's major propaganda victory was the taking of Toledo, accomplished at high cost and with the usual bloodbath. The Alcázar was relieved on September 27 and in Burgos three days later Franco was named Head of State in Nationalist Spain—his real coup d'état, as Thomas was to write. The new slogan was "One State, One Country, One Chief" and Franco was now called Caudillo—a bad translation of *Führer.*

Political changes also occurred on the Republican side. The anarchists, the POUM and other factions, including Basque separatists, joined Largo Caballero's government—leaving the fiery Durriti, who held a part of the northern front against Mola, as the only anarchist leader refusing to join the coalition.

On October 7, the Nationalist offensive against Madrid began, with Yague's planes flying over the city demanding the evacuation of the civil population. The situation was getting desperate. In an attempt to achieve discipline, Largo Caballero ended the sporty freedom of the militiamen, making them dependent on a central staff, but at the same time he refused to mobilize Madrid's large building trade to dig trenches. To maintain the militiamen's faith and to diminish their suspicion of regular army commanders, Sovet-style political commissars were established throughout the armies. It was a major victory for the communists, who had already showed themselves to be the most effective Republican propagandists.

On October 10, everything changed. Massive Soviet aid began. Three days earlier, the Soviet government, which in August had refused to export arms, denounced "the military assistance to the rebels by certain countries" and declared itself free of the Nonintervention Pact. The Republic had tried everywhere to get supplies. The supply from French and other sources was as small and unreliable as that from the Spanish war industry itself and Largo Caballero appealed to Washington for permission to buy U.S. arms, intimating that collapse of the Republic would cause the fall of the French Popular Front and therefore foreshorten the fall of democracy. The U.S. Secretary of State Cordell Hull turned the request down, saying that while America had no law against aid to Spain, it had a policy of "moral aloofness." [5]

For months, Italy and Germany had openly violated the Nonintervention Pact they had themselves finally signed. While Hitler's aid was limited to arms, Mussolini sent whole military formations. Soviet aid—and Stalin's okay to Comintern plans to form "international brigades"—was to enable the Republic to keep going for more than two years.

The eleventh-hour rescue from the Soviet Union was celebrated at the Florida bar with the uncorking of the last Moët champagne. The little air squadron was hard pressed. Colonel Malraux's Paris connections proved frustratingly unreliable. Pierre Cot's promises of allowing more planes to slip out of France were never fulfilled and the Blum government even refused to allow new American aircraft, bought by the Spanish Republic, to leave France. Hidalgo de Cisneros, Malraux's superior in the now tightened command, saw the U.S. planes sit on an airfield in Toulouse and wept.

As Franco's forces massed toward Madrid from the south, Mola announced that by October 23 he would be sipping coffee on Madrid's Gran Via and on the Republican side Largo Caballero fell from power for refusing Stalinist requests for disbanding the Trotskyite POUM. The España Squadron was moved to Albacete, a hundred and fifty miles southeast of Madrid.

Albacete, a dusty town famous for its rum and its cutlery, was the staging area of the new International Brigades. Here, the polyglot volunteers were divided into companies, according to language. Most were Frenchmen and Germans, but a total of forty-three nationalities were presented in the Brigades, firmly managed by the Comintern and behind that organization, by Moscow. Overall command was vested in a *troika* of communists while the military command was in the hands of André Marty, an arrogant and paranoic Frenchman who, in Hemingway's *For Whom the Bell Tolls,* was given the fictional name "Comrade Massart." Obsessed with an imaginary fear of fascist spies, the blue-eyed Marty, who had

    [5] "The Foreign Relations of the United States," State Department Papers, Vol. 2, 1936 (Washington, 1952–54).

188

Stalin's confidence, suppressed all political disagreement and cracked down so hard on dissent that he caused a lowering of morale and, as the war progressed, an increase in desertions. The English poet and volunteer Stephen Spender tried to escape and was almost shot.

In this Tower of Babel, Malraux and his fliers were the odd men out. The España Squadron was not under Marty's command and instead of being billeted in the hastily set up camps, André and his men stayed at the Regina Hotel. Dressed in a Spanish air force uniform and with a cigarette dangling in the corner of the mouth, Colonel Malraux showed up at the eccentric welcoming addresses Marty staged every afternoon in Albacete's bullring. While Marty told the newcomers that discipline was everything and that ill-prepared volunteers were nothing more than criminals, André strolled down the ranks, discreetly enquiring if anybody knew how to fly an airplane or repair one. When in early November three Frenchmen acknowledged they were aviation mechanics, Malraux waited for them outside the bullring, brought them to the Regina bar and calmly enlisted them in his outfit.

Friends and acquaintances were showing up. Gustav Regler turned up as political commissar for the 12th Brigade, a job Louis Aragon envied him. The surrealist leader and Elsa Triolet toured Spain, appearing on the platform of a van purchased and equipped by the Revolutionary Writers' Association.

The squadron flew sorties all along the southern front as well as support missions to Alicante, the Costa Blanca port a hundred miles away where Russian arms shipments and many volunteers were arriving. By the end of November, when Madrid's ill-armed urban masses backed by Russian arms and the International Brigades resisted the Nationalists' all-out attempt at taking the capital, the España Squadron moved to Alcalá de Henares, Cervantes' birthplace twenty miles northeast of Madrid.

The Battle of Madrid opened on November 8 and the main battle-ground was the University City at the northern outskirts, the one area where Mola's Nationalist army, consisting mainly of Moroccans and legionnaires supported by Germans and Italians, managed to maintain a foothold. Here they had broken through after an uncharacteristic retreat by Durruti's anarchists who had rushed down from the Barcelona front. The battle scene was eerie, with Nationalists and Loyalists grappling in hand-to-hand fighting as they struggled to gain control of floors and even rooms in faculty libraries, laboratories and lecture halls. But the furthest Mola got to sipping coffee on the Gran Via was the Institute of Hygiene and Cancer. His army's advance was prevented by the continued defense of the Hall of Philosophy and Letters. On November 21, while the battle was still raging, Durruti was killed, apparently by one of his own men, an "uncontrollable," who resented the new anarchist policy of flat-out support of the government.

189

In early December, Malraux's air force was moved to near Valencia, now the Republican seat of government. When Ilya Ehrenburg met Malraux, he found the España Squadron commander totally preoccupied by war. "I have known him when he was fascinated by the Far East, by Dostoyevsky and Faulkner, then by a fraternal feeling toward workers and revolution," Ehrenburg was to remember. "In Valencia, he only talked about bombing fascists and when I talked about literature, he frowned and stopped talking." [6]

Malraux told Ehrenburg that he was hopeful he could acquire twelve new French bombers and in early December he popped up in Geneva to huddle with French foreign secretary Yvon Delbos. The España Squadron had lost half its airmen and half its planes and rumors circulated that the unit would be incorporated into the new, largely Russian-trained "international" air force. Hidalgo de Cisneros, it was said, had thought of disbanding the Squadron because of the loss of so many planes in accidents. The decision was postponed, however, because of fear of adverse reaction in France.

On Christmas Eve, Malraux received orders to attack the Teruel to Saragossa road a hundred miles northeast of Valencia and to seek out and destroy a suspected Nationalist airfield. To help locate the field, he was given a local farmer who had once seen the camouflaged landing strip. Malraux hoped the man, who had never seen a plane up close, could recognize geographical features from the air. Bad weather caused a postponement but on the 26th two Potez 540 bombers revved up their engines at the España Squadron airfield outside Valencia. The plane André climbed aboard never made it into the air. At the end of the earth runway, it nosed over and skidded crazily into a hedge. Everybody walked away safely, André pretty smashed up but without actual bone fractures. The plane was a total loss.

The other Potez, piloted by the Algerian Belaidi, copiloted by Camille Taillefer and with daredevil machine gunner Raymond Maréchal and the Teruel farmer aboard, accomplished its mission and bombed the camouflaged Franco airstrip. On its return flight, it was attacked by Heinkel fighters and shot down over the Sierra.

The next day, the España Squadron headquarters learned that Belaidi had managed to crash land between Mora de Rubielos and Linares, some forty miles east of Teruel. Although no one knew whether the area was in fascist or loyalist hands, Malraux immediately organized a rescue mission. With some of his men, he drove toward Mora de Rubielos. When they reached Linares, they were greeted by crowds of silent sympathizers. After arranging for hospital facilities, André climbed up the steep, jagged mountain on muleback, escorted by the villagers. Peasants were already

[6] Ilya Ehrenburg, *Memoirs: 1921–41,* trans. Tatania Shebunina (Cleveland: World Publishers, 1960).

190

bringing down the wounded and the body of Belaidi on whose coffin the Potez machine gun had been laid. The Descent to Linares with the villagers forming a chain of fraternal hope was to be one of the major themes of *Man's Hope* and some of the most beautiful pages of his writing.

Next, the España Squadron was moved to a new hot spot, the Córdoba front, where on February 8, Málaga fell. This Nationalist victory, greatly facilitated by the presence of eight mechanized Italian Black Shirt battalions, was not so much the result of extraordinary bravado as of the Franco forces' growing superiority. Their sea blockade on the Mediterranean and the closing of a large stretch of the French border increasingly made resupplying the Republican armies difficult. But all in all, the Republic seemed to hold its own. Madrid was safe and the Teruel victory was followed by the rout of thirty thousand Italian Black Shirts at Guadalajara (where Gustav Regler had loudspeakers installed on the front and had Italians of the Garibaldi Brigade urge their countrymen on the fascist side to defect).

To protect Republican soldiers and refugees fleeing from Málaga—four thousand Republican sympathizers left behind were being shot—the Valencia high command asked Malraux to throw everything he had against the Italian conscripts, not only against their fast and excellent new Fiat fighters in the air but also the tanks and half-tracks catching up with the refugees and Republican army stragglers on the road to Almería and continuing a gruesome massacre. The España Squadron did its best, managing two sorties a day with makeshift repairs carried out at night. It protected the exodus from Málaga as best it could and bombed Cádiz where the Italian troops disembarked. The casualties piled high. The new Fiat fighters were faster and better armed than the battle-scarred Potez 540s and Bloch 200s.

It was the España Squadron's last stand. At the end of February, whatever was left of Malraux's gallant little air force was merged with the "internationals." But it was not the end of Malraux's efforts on behalf of Republican Spain. There were still the speaking tour of America, the writers' congress, *Man's Hope* and the movie he was to make from the book.

191

The Revolution is busy solving *its* problems, not
ours.

Man's Hope

16

André arrived in New York on February 24, 1937, together with
Josette Clotis, who, after the final parting with Clara, was henceforth to
be his companion. In dockside interviews, he spoke soberly about the
chances of a Republican victory. The war would be won, he felt, not on
the battlefields, but in the hearts of the common people. The armies and the
air force would not decide the issues; the future belonged to the people. To
a New York *World-Telegram* reporter, he said Franco had made too many
promises to both peasants and landowners and that the next harvest would
be crucial. "He cannot keep faith with both. When the time comes for
the harvest, the peasants will ask for land and implements, all the things
he has promised. He will be unable to keep the promises. The peasants may
not burn the crops, but they certainly will not continue to support Franco.
The end will come." [1]

On behalf of the Spanish Medical Bureau's fund-raising campaign—
Gustav Regler was touring Latin America—Malraux plunged into a whirlwind of speaking engagements. Although the Roosevelt administration tried
to maintain a "moral embargo" and actually had Congress pass two resolutions banning arms shipments when a Jersey City firm received a State
Department license to ship $2.7 million worth of aircraft engines to
the Republican government, American liberals were fervently behind the
Loyalist fight against fascism. The Lincoln Battalion, commanded by the
black Texan Oliver Law, had been in Spain for six months and nearly
three thousand American volunteers were presently fighting in the Brigades.

No one granted Malraux an interview in Washington, but the audiences he addressed in New York and Philadelphia and at university rallies
at Harvard, Cambridge and Princeton before flying to the West Coast were

---

[1] Robert Payne, *Portrait of André Malraux,* op. cit.

192

more than sympathetic. Although the simultaneous translation, sentence by sentence, made everything feel dragged out, he managed to raise his audiences to a pitch of excitement. Alfred Kazin was a very young literary critic who together with a radicalized girl working for *Time* named Harriet attended the Meeting for Spain at New York's Mecca Temple.

That night at Mecca Temple, Malraux had told the great story, soon to appear in *L'Espoir* and in the film he made of the novel: one of the planes of his volunteer squadron had been brought down among mountain villages behind Loyalist lines. There were no roads down the mountain, only mule paths. Single file, the entire populace followed the stretcher bearers as they brought the wounded aviators down the mountain. At each of the villages through which they passed, the people were waiting, each village when the wounded had passed, was emptied of its inhabitants. When those wounded in the face were carried past, the women and children began to cry. And, said Malraux, "when I raised my eyes, the file of peasants extended now from the heights of the mountain to its base; it was the grandest image of fraternity I have even encountered." Malraux also told the story of how, on the first day of 1937, toys sent to the Spanish children from all over the world had been heaped up in the center of the great bullring in Madrid. Just as the children went to collect them, a squadron of Junkers bombarded the city; they did not come near the ring. But when the raid was over, and the children went back to pick up their toys, none of them, not even the little boys, would touch the toy airplanes, which were left in a heap of their own. When Malraux spoke of the mountain side, Harriet was literally uplifted from her seat under the storm of his sentences. Although he had to stop every few sentences for the interpreter to catch up, and would draw in his breath like a swimmer, he spoke with such fire that his body itself seemed to be speaking the most glorious French.[2]

There were many more stories and Malraux told them well, with a savage edge in his voice, usually brief, graphic and terrible stories. "Once some tenants were searching the ruins of a bombed-out house for their possessions," he said. "There was a line of them, similar to a line passing buckets at a fire. They passed shattered objects along the line until they reached their owners. A man picked up a baby and handed it along the line. It finally reached its mother. In the age-old gesture of motherhood she took the dead child and held it to her breast, and the head fell off." Inevitably, he was asked to talk about his experiences in building up the Republican air force. "We had many freaks," he told a meeting one evening. "The first freaks were the tragic kind—men who had not flown since the World War but claimed they were good fliers. Some were given good planes, but they broke them up immediately, killing themselves. We had an American who pestered the war offices for days trying to put across an

[2] Alfred Kazin, *Starting out in the Thirties* (Boston: Little, Brown & Co., 1962).

idea he had for a trotting bomb; he said his bomb would trot into enemy territory and then explode."

Louis Fischer and *The Nation* organized his biggest engagement, a New York rally. "What is the gift of fascism?" he thundered. "The ecstasy of what makes us different from one another, the irreducible and constant differences such as race and nationality. By its nature fascism is static and exclusive. Democracy and communism have different opinions on a proletarian dictatorship, not on fundamental values. We want to preserve and recreate not unmovable and particularist values, and on a world scale— not German or Nordic man, not a Roman or Italian man, simply man." Everywhere, he granted interviews. Asked why he had risked his life in Spain when he could have lived a life of ease as one of France's famous novelists, he answered, "Because I do not like myself." When a writer asked him why he regarded fighting as more important than writing, he said, "Because death is a greater triumph."

Some questions were sticky, especially from Leftists irritated by the Communist Party's meddling in literature, uneasy at its political gyrations and shaken by the Moscow trials. Among writers and critics such as Edmund Wilson, Sidney Hook, Dwight Macdonald, Philip Rahv and Mary McCarthy Trotskyism was becoming something of a vogue and Malraux was often asked how he could close his eyes to Stalin's purges. "Trotsky is a great moral force in the world, but Stalin has lent dignity to mankind," André remarked at a dinner given by *The Nation*. "Just as the Inquisition didn't detract from the fundamental dignity of Christianity, so the Moscow trials didn't retract from the fundamental dignity of communism." Such answers pleased neither main-line communists nor Trotskyites and from his Mexican exile Leon Davidovich himself jumped into the fray by attacking Malraux as a crypto-fascist.

When Trotsky wrote to *The New York Times* to denounce Malraux, André snapped back, "Mr. Trotsky is so obsessed with whatever concerns his personal fate that if a man who has just come from seven months of active fighting in Spain makes the statement that help for Republican Spain comes before everything else, such a statement must necessarily hide something." The attacks continued after *L'Espoir* appeared, with Trotsky accusing Malraux of "falsehoods" in his descriptions of Spanish scenes and of being "all the more repulsive because he sought to give it an artistic form." In a letter to the Trotskyizing *Partisan Review,* Leon Davidovich wrote that Malraux's behavior was "typical of a whole category, almost of a generation of writers; so many of them tell lies from alleged 'friendship' for the October Revolution, as if the revolution needed lies." [3]

Through Robert Haas, his Random House editor, André met for the first time Ernest Hemingway, who was finally on his way to Paris and

[3] Isaac Deutscher, *The Prophet Outcast: 1929–1940* (London: Oxford University Press, 1963).

194

Arriving in Los Angeles, 1937

Spain. Together with Joris Ivens, the Dutch documentary filmmaker who had been interested in filming *Man's Fate* in Moscow in 1934, Hemingway planned a documentary designed to acquaint American sympathizers with the plight of the Spanish people. John Dos Passos was engaged in fund raising for the film and together with Hemingway and Archibald MacLeish was forming a company to help with the funding and eventually with the distribution of the completed film. Hemingway and Dos Passos disagreed on matters of emphasis. Dos Passos wanted the film to stress the predicament of the common people in the midst of civil war while Ernest was far more interested in the military aspect. Malraux rattled off all the important contacts Hemingway would need in Valencia and wished him good luck.

From New York, Josette and André flew to Los Angeles, where they were put up at the Hollywood-Roosevelt Hotel as guests of Donald Odgen Stewart. If Haas had been their guiding hand in New York, Haakon Chevalier became their factotum and interpreter on the West Coast. A French teacher at Berkeley, Chevalier had spent his formative years in France and had published a book on Anatole France and tried his hand at a novel. He had translated *La Condition humaine* and friends described him as a man who "knew French poetry, French wines and intelligent people." Chevalier had broad connections with activists on the Left and was delighted to accompany Josette and André through the whirlwind of Los Angeles and Bay Area engagements.

195

All Hollywood wanted to meet Malraux and following a major address to an overflowing rally, André and Josette were asked to countless receptions, cocktail parties, dinners. Money for the Spanish Medical Bureau poured in. Reuben Mamoulian, Miriam Hopkins, Dorothy Parker, William Saroyan, Clifford Odets, and many other actors, screenwriters, playwrights and directors heard Malraux speak. Inevitably, he was invited to a studio and visited Ernst Lubitsch as he was shooting *Angel* with Marlene Dietrich and Herbert Marshall at Paramount. La Dietrich was wearing a near transparent nightgown and during the break talked with Malraux. "During this scene," according to Chevalier, "all the studio personnel were avidly watching, not Marlene Dietrich, but 'the young Frenchman who had been fighting in Spain.' " [4]

Malraux had landed in Los Angeles clutching *The Maltese Falcon,* which he had read in English during the flight and the first thing he asked Chevalier was to meet Dashiell Hammett. When they met, Hammett was not prepared for Malraux's enthusiasm and compliments on his writing which, André said, Hemingway had copied. Hammett had more than inspired Hemingway. Hammett's ladyfriend Lillian Hellman asked about Spain. At the suggestion of MacLeish, she was soon to join Joris Ivens and Hemingway in the making of their documentary. When André returned to Paris, he convinced Gaston Gallimard to bring out Hammett's entire oeuvre in French.

After Hollywood, it was on to San Francisco and Berkeley. On the day of his arrival, he spoke at a large luncheon at the Sir Francis Drake Hotel, chaired by Chevalier and with violinist Yehudi Menuhin and French essayist Julien Benda as guests of honor. The following Sunday morning Chevalier organized a faculty breakfast at Berkeley where for a change Malraux didn't speak on Spain but on art. To Chevalier's disappointment, his colleague J. Robert Oppenheimer couldn't make it. The physics professor was a new acquaintance and Chevalier would have liked to have been able to introduce him to Malraux. The Depression and Nazism had awakened Oppenheimer's social conscience and he was a joiner and a doer to such an extent that he was later to tell the head of the U.S. wartime atomic project that he had "probably belonged to every communist-fronted organization on the West Coast." Fifteen years later, Un-American Activities committees were to establish Malraux's fund-raising tour for Republican Spain and the missed Sunday morning rendezvous the point of departure of Leftist attempts to worm into the physicist's good graces.

Before returning to France from New York, Josette and André made a swing through eastern Canada, addressing meetings in Toronto and Montreal. After the Montreal rally, an old worker came forward and

[4] Haakon M. Chevalier, *Oppenheimer: The Story of a Friendship* (New York: Braziller, 1965).

put his gold watch in André's hand. Why? "I have nothing more precious to give our Spanish comrades," the old man answered.

In Spain, Malraux had been taking notes for a book and for nearly two months now he had told anecdotes ˎand real-life dramas about the conflict. The goodwill—and ignorance—about the civil war, he had encountered in the U.S. and Canada, had impressed him. The only books he had seen about Spain had been by Marxists, and Americans, among others, didn't read communist authors. What he would write would be a factual novel that could perhaps give the motives of the Republican side and the climate of the war. Even if such a book couldn't possibly influence events, it might weigh in favor of justice and an outcome still in question. Translating these sentiments into a title was easy enough, he felt. Just one word summed it all up—*espoir* (hope).

It would have to be a quick book. By the time he was back in Paris in April—and the most notorious atrocity of the war, the bombing of Guernica, took place—the first hundred pages of the new book had been written. The pages included many of the stories he had told audiences in America and the much-quoted line that victory would not be on the side of the just, but of the most efficient. By May, Haas had a chapter translated and appearing in *Collier's* under the title "This Is War." As André finished the book, Léon Blum's Popular Front collapsed, unable to overcome its own divisions and to stand up to a determined opposition of industry and finance and the fierce enmity of France's upper and middle classes. On July 1, André delivered the final manuscript to Gallimard and went to Spain.

Malraux flew to Valencia to remit the proceeds of the fund-raising tour and to attend the Second International Writers' Convention. With the exception of the Basque provinces, nothing had changed much during the five months André had been in America and written *L'Espoir*. As the Nationalists had realized that a major offensive against Madrid would be too costly, Franco had boosted fascist morale by mopping up isolated Loyalist enclaves in the North. With this decision began the "Basque Tragedy," leading to the German bombing of Guernica April 26 by Heinkels and Junkers of the Condor Legion. For three and a half hours, the small town had been bombed and machine-gunned. Foreign journalists visited the town that night and the *Daily Express* correspondent had cabled London, "I walked through the still burning town. Hundreds of bodies had been found in the debris. Most were charred beyond recognition. At least two hundred others were riddled with machine gun bullets as they fled to the hills." [5] Eyewitness evidence had been important because the Nationalists accused the Basques of inventing the atrocity as propaganda. The horror of Guernica reached a worldwide audience through

[5] Noel Mons, *Daily Express* (April 27, 1937).

197

Picasso's painting *Guernica,* which was to be exhibited by the Republican government at the World's Fair in Paris in 1938. During the writing of *L'Espoir* Malraux had met Picasso in his studio and it had been decided that some of the preparatory sketches for the painting would illustrate the book.

The Writers' Convention, which started July 4 in Valencia and moved to Madrid and Barcelona before ending up in Paris (Ehrenburg called it "the moving circus"), was ostensibly the follow-up to the Paris and London assizes of 1935 and 1936. José Bergamín had promised Madrid as the host city for the 1937 conference and President Manuel Azaña, himself a former writer, and the new Juan Negrín government, which had replaced the Largo Caballero cabinet in May, were anxious to hold the event, which drew a bevy of important authors from all over the world to Republican Spain. In reality, the conference was a Soviet diversionary tactic to dampen the international scandal provoked by the assassination of POUM leader Andrés Nin and to read André Gide out of the progressive Church. Bergamín, who was not even a communist but a Left-leaning Catholic, lent himself to all this.

Since the beginning of the Soviet intervention, the Kremlin had in effect waged a civil war within the Spanish Civil War, culminating with the torture and death of Nin in the hands of NKVD agents and the purging of the Trotskyite party in Catalonia. Many Spanish leaders were disgusted with this whole affair and Largo Caballero had fallen from power because he had refused to join in the suppression of the POUM and several able generals associated with him had been eliminated. Before Nin's mutilated body had been found, a widespread campaign in Spain and abroad had asked, "Where is Nin?" The main aim of Ehrenburg, Alexis Tolstoy and the Soviet delegation to the Writers' Convention was to try to save Stalin's respectability, but for many communists, like Arthur Koestler, the Nin affair caused their final disillusionment with Russia—their "god had failed" when put to a test. Stalin's top man in Spain, Vladimir Antonov-Ovseenko, who had commanded the Red Guard which stormed the Winter Palace in St. Petersburg in 1917, was eventually recalled to Russia to disappear in Stalin's 1940's purges.

In his book, *Retour de l'URSS,* Gide had described his disappointments with Russia, where, as the pontiff of Leftist French intellectuals, he had been invited with honors. He had found Soviet vegetables mediocre, the beer passable, housing bad and discovered that without competition, state production made for inferior goods. Everywhere he had found a stultifying conformity, an intellectual apathy alternating with a superiority complex plus a complete ignorance of the rest of the world. He had found the hopeful spirit of the people wonderful and moving and admitted that because of the emotions that communism aroused, the truth about Russia

198

was usually told with hate and the lies with love. In speaking of the loss of the original communist doctrine, he had wondered whether the passage from mystique to day-to-day politics always resulted in degradation.

For *Retour de l'URSS* Gide was now called another "Hitlero-fascist." "This book is in itself insignificant, but the fact that it appears at the very moment when fascist guns are trained on Madrid gives it a tragic meaning," said Bergamín. "Gide's book is not a critique, it is a calumny!" [6] When the delegates weren't being driven around Valencia, Madrid or Barcelona in government-requisitioned Rolls-Royces, they listened to Ehrenburg and Alexis Tolstoy (a distant relative of Leo Tolstoy) out-maneuver Hemingway, dadaist Tristan Tzara and other speakers. The conference had other incongruities. As on many occasions of this kind, the national anthems of the different nations were played so that Stephen Spender, who had nearly been shot trying to escape the International Brigades the year before, found himself giving the clenched first salute while the band trumpeted "God Save the King."

To Spender, the outstanding figure of the Congress was Malraux. "In 1937 he had an air of battered youth, with face jutting pallidly over his intently crouching body as he looked at his audience," Spender was to write a decade later. "He wore a tweed suit into whose trouser pockets he thrust his hands. The Congress was dominated by his nervous sniff and tic. One day at Madrid, Hemingway, wistfully looking in Malraux's direction, said, 'I wonder what Malraux did to get that tic? It must have been at well over ten thousand feet.'

"My French at this time was far from good, but in the course of several days of listening to Malraux's conversation and watching, I formed certain impressions. The purpose of his life of adventure mingled with artistic creation was to write out a personal legend and an environment of activity. His politics were those of a liberal individualist but as a result of his immense self-confidence he had a certain impatience with the ineffectiveness of others. Malraux told me that he had always insisted on liberal justice in the Malraux Squadron of the Republican Air Force, and he had refused to allow the communists to interfere with him. *Il faut agir* was for him the secret of his novels as well as his politics. He renounced a static background and wrote out of a life of travel, movement, war, politics." [7]

Malraux was nearly killed when the car in which he and Ehrenburg were traveling to Madrid hit an ammunitions truck. The Madrid meeting that evening was told about the mishap and when André appeared on stage with Gustav Regler, he was greeted by thunderous applause. Even if, as

[6] Mikhail Koltzov, *Diario de la guerra de España* (Paris: Ruedo Iberico, 1963).

[7] Stephen Spender, *World Within World: The Autobiography of Stephen Spender* (New York: Harcourt, Brace, 1951).

Spender said, Malraux was the dominating figure at the conference he never brought up the murder of Nin and he sat silently through the denunciation of Gide.

His answer came in *L'Espoir*. The big, powerful book with its high concentration of ideas and high-fidelity emotional ring was written when victory was still possible. It was written from the perspective which the Loyalist victory at Guadalajara and the formation of the Negrín government implied—that a victory over Franco and fascism was only meaningful insofar as it brought with it social reform and insofar as the all-out war effort was undertaken on a broad enough front to include progressive bourgeois forces, something which implied abandoning partisan factionalism, respect for private property and discipline on the battlefield. Finally, it implied an unconditional alliance with the Soviet Union, the only great power willing to back the Republic with more than pious rhetoric.

L'Espoir appeared in November—without Picasso's *Guernica* illustrations because Picasso had sent all the sketches to the Museum of Modern Art in New York. The book made an immediate and commanding impression in France and had a great pro-Republican influence in intellectual circles in many countries. The Loyalist position had never been set forth so convincingly and the Republican government was delighted. As Azaña said to Max Aub, "Ah those Frenchmen! Only they can create a philosophizing Guardia Civil officer."

L'Espoir was first of all Malraux's triumph over himself, the triumph of objective truth and reality over fantasy and myth. Contrary to the earlier novels, this book was not dominated by night scenes. Here a sense of daylight and openness, a sense of pure joy of being alive in the sunshine prevailed. Not that the horrors of war were absent. Here was war up close. Here, Malraux had one of his characters say that if torture appeared so often in war it was also because torture seemed the only response to betrayal and cruelty.

Influenced by Tolstoy's *War and Peace,* film narrative techniques and journalistic writing, *L'Espoir* is the story of the first nine months of the war, as far as the España Squadron's intervention on the Teruel front in early January 1937. *L'Espoir* is a broad canvas and all attempts at concentrating the novel on a single protagonist is abandoned for the epic sweep with many men engaged in the complex conflict between the ideal and the possible, between what the individual can "be" and what the individual can and must "do," between *être* and *faire*. As the anarchist leader Hernandez, the idealistic captain at the siege of Toledo's Alcázar tells an intelligence chief:

> The communists want *to do* things. You and the anarchists, for different reasons, want *to be* things. Thats the drama of all revolutions like this one. The myths we live by are contradictory—pacifism and the need to protect ourselves, organizations and Christian fables, effectiveness

200

and justice and so on. We've got to put order in our myths, turn our apocalyptic vision into an army, or die. It's as simple as that.

The three leading characters are Magnin the pilot, Hernandez and Manuel the card-carrying communist. But there are many others—Scali, the Italian art historian who has become a bombardier, Ximenes the devout traditionalist Spaniard, Garcia the anthropologist turned intelligence chief, Gardet the machine gunner, the organization men—Vergas, Pradas, Golovkin—and the anarchists, Puig and Negus. Magnin is Malraux himself, although there are also parts of the author in Garcia. A lot of Shade is *New York Times* correspondent Herbert Matthews, parts of Scali are Koltzov, Guernico is José Bergamín, while Attignies is España Squadron second-in-command Julien Segnaire. Several secondary characters are connected with the arts. Lopez is a sculptor, Alvear, the father of one of the pilots, is a former professor of art history and Scali is the author of monographs on Masaccio and Piero della Francesca. When Alvear and Scali meet, Alvear wonders whether the benefits of revolution will be greater than the losses entailed by the new order, adding:

> I like people for what they are, not for their ideas. I want true loyalty among friends, not the sort of loyalty that hangs on political opinion. I want a man to feel responsible to himself—and that you know Monsieur Scali, whatever people may say, is the hardest thing of all—to be responsible to oneself, not to any cause, not even to the cause of the oppressed.

In retrospect, Alvear had come to represent the European liberal intellectual of the interwar years—Thomas Mann, Roger Martin du Gard, the man of culture who until Hitler marched into Poland remained convinced that revolution could only spring from a profound skepticism and that nothing is more revolutionary than a constant revision of one's own principles and, indeed, of all human behavior. For Scali, what threatens the revolution is not the future but a present getting out of control.

People talk a lot in *L'Espoir,* but as in Malraux's earlier novels there are passages of abstract horror conveyed with astonishing power— the fascist execution of prisoners outside Toledo, with a prisoner instinctively backing away from the ditch his body is supposed to fall into.

The psychology of torture is analyzed when Scali interrogates a captured aviator. The Nationalist pilot refuses to believe that Republican fliers have, when captured, had their eyes put out before being executed, just as Scali himself had refused, even when faced with photographic evidence, to believe that anarchists on his side have committed atrocities. Violence, however, no longer seems to fascinate Malraux. The characters who will not allow ends to justify the means are presented more favorably than those who want above all to win.

Critical reception in November 1937 was predictable. Right-wing hostility to the book was very real. André Rosseaux, who in 1930 had interviewed Malraux and had been disappointed in finding the author of *La Voie royale* a less than full-blown anarchist, now accused him of being a total anarchist while at the same time scolding him for writing only communist propaganda. According to *L'Action française, L'Espoir* added up to the opposite of its intent—a denunciation of Marxist mythology as it was applied in Spain. On the Left, Louis Aragon called the novel Malraux's defense of his ideas, while *L'Humanité* expressed the party line by lauding the author for underlining the necessity for discipline and for describing war with lucidity.

L'Espoir was to grow in hindsight. Ten years after its publication, Henry de Montherlant took up the defense against those accusing Malraux of being a mere journalist: "You often think of Tolstoy. The pages on the executions are the height of the art of writing. In Malraux intelligence and action are reconciled, a rare feat." [8] Writing in the early 1950s, Arthur Koestler, who was himself in Spain during the Civil War (and became a prisoner of the Nationalists in Málaga), could compare *L'Espoir* to *For Whom the Bell Tolls,* saying the art of Malraux is so different from Hemingway's "that it can almost be said to occupy two opposite poles within the novelist's range. Their outlook is similar insofar as they both regard physical courage and a life of adventure as supreme values. But these same values are expressed in contrasting attitudes and idioms. Courage, in Hemingway's world, has an embarrassingly exhibitionist, adolescent, dumb-hero quality. Courage in Malraux's world is lucid and intelligent bravado, with a discursive Gallic flourish.[9] In 1968, Denis Boak was to write that *L'Espoir* was not only "one of the best factual books on the Spanish Civil War, comparable in its descriptions to Orwell's *Homage to Catalonia* or Koestler's *Spanish Testament,* it is much more profound, with its insights into what can be called the metaphysical meaning of events, their ultimate significance as part of the general human condition." [10] In 1973, José Bergamín, exiled in Paris, would say *L'Espoir* was not so much "an inspired reportage, as Camus said, but a kind of black-and-white X-ray plate, like Picasso's *Guernica,* of Spain's plunge into the abyss of 1936. Malraux's novel is both testimony and indictment which are more topical today than thirty years ago." [11]

Malraux was not in Paris when *L'Espoir* hit the bookstalls. With Josette, he was shuffling between besieged Madrid and Barcelona, engaged in a desperate attempt at creativity to shake up world opinion in general and American opinion in particular to the realities of bleeding Spain. The project was a movie, to be based in part on *L'Espoir*. It had its origin in

[8] Henry de Montherlant, *Carnets* (Paris: Table Ronde, 1947).
[9] Arthur Koestler, *The Invisible Writing,* op. cit.
[10] Denis Boak, *André Malraux* (London: Oxford University Press, 1968).
[11] Guy Suarès, *Malraux, La voix de l'occident* (Paris: Stock, 1974).

Hollywood and in the disappointing reception Americans had given *The Spanish Earth,* the austere documentary Joris Ivens had filmed, Archibald MacLeish and John Dos Passos had helped finance and for which Lillian Hellman and Hemingway had written the narration and Virgil Thomson the music. While Josette and André had toured the Hollywood cocktail circuit and Paramount studios, the idea of a "real movie," a feature with individualized characters played by professional actors and a plot line, had been discussed. Always preoccupied with effectiveness, André had listened to literate Hollywood saying that only such a film would make sense, meaning that it could be booked into thousands of theaters and produce the shock effect American opinion needed. The idea of doing a picture or two on the Spanish Civil War had not escaped corporate Hollywood and in 1937 at least two such films were being considered—making the Negrín government send former surrealist filmmaker Luis Buñuel to California "on a diplomatic mission" to supervise, as technical adviser, *Cargo of Innocence,* which Metro-Goldwyn-Mayer had in development (and never made because of the turn of events in 1938). The idea of a film had again been discussed during the Writers' Congress in Valencia in July and Negrín had expressed more than passing interest. He and his foreign minister, Julio Alvarez del Vayo, assured Malraux of financial assistance if and when such a project could get off the ground.

Autumn brought a big lull in the war with the apparent stability of both Spains seeming to preserve the stalemate. With armies of about half a million men each, the two Spains had forced an order in their respective zones that hadn't existed before 1936. Nationalist Spain was a military state, although, according to German estimates, forty percent of the population was considered unreliable. On the Loyalist side, a degree of unity had been achieved. On October 31, Negrín announced the transfer of the central government to Barcelona, a move that henceforth made Madrid play a diminishing part in events. The jagged front ran north-to-south from the central Pyrenees and the French border to Teruel, and west in an immense arc around Madrid and south to the Mediterranean east of Málaga. The fascists held western two-thirds of Spain and the Republicans the eastern third of the country.

On the diplomatic front, the initiative seemed to be on the Loyalist side. While Franco was quarreling with Germany, the Negrín administration's continued political moderation allowed a new rapprochement with the wobbly French government that had followed the collapse of Léon Blum's Front populaire and even with Great Britain. British Foreign Secretary Anthony Eden even came up with a laborious plan for the withdrawal of "substantial portions" of foreign volunteers from Spain and the day after this plan was approved by the Nonintervention Subcommittee, even Hitler said that "from a German point of view, a 100 percent Franco victory is not desirable." On November 20, Franco accepted the British "volunteer plan" with reservations and ten days later the Republic also accepted, though for different reasons. President Azaña believed the acceptance meant the suspension of hostilities.

Instead the war flamed up again in December, with the Republic launching an attack against the old Aragonian archbishop's seat of Teruel —to prevent the Nationalists from pushing to the Mediterranean coast and cut Loyalist Spain in two. The Battle of Teruel, fought in the worst Spanish winter in memory, saw a hundred and ten thousand Republicans attack the hilltop city. Teruel was defended by some ten thousand Franco troops, helped by the wintry onslaught which turned the sloping approaches into sheets of ice. By New Year's Day, 1938, the center of the town had been reduced to ruins and a week later, the Nationalist commander gave up. It was against these developments and the subsequent increased political and economic strength of the Republic (strength even noted in Berlin) that Malraux got the government's okay to make a film about the war.

If Malraux had never directed a film, he was an enlightened *cinephile*. Not only had he tried to import German expressionist films in 1922 and written novels that acknowledged borrowing narrative devices from the movies, he had sat on park benches in Moscow "talking" *Man's Fate* into script form with Sergei Eisenstein and in Hollywood watched Ernst Lubitsch shout "Roll 'em" and "Cut!" And there was the *Spanish Earth* precedent. If Joris Ivens, with the collaboration of Hemingway and Lillian Hellman, had been able to make a documentary, why couldn't the author of an already significant factual novel transpose his written fiction to the screen, especially since much of what he would put in front of the camera would be events he had personally experienced?

While insisting the film should not be regarded as an adaptation of *L'Espoir,* Malraux wrote a script structured around the España Squadron's bombing of a camouflaged fascist airstrip east of Teruel, ending with the crash landing of one of the bombers in the mountain above Linares. As in the book—and in reality, the film would end on the note of human solidarity—the peasants carrying the wounded crew members and the dead pilot's coffin down from the crash site. Since the purpose of the film was to show other aspects of the war, new episodes were invented —a behind-the-enemy-lines uprising of workers and farmers in support of an approaching Republican offensive, guerrilleros fighting Franco's armored units and, in general, sequences showing the Loyalist army in combat. To stress the fact that the film would not be an adaptation of *L'Espoir,* it was immediately baptized *Sierra de Teruel.*

A country two years into civil war was not the easiest location for feature filmmaking. It was tempting to make the picture in France. Malraux's command of Spanish was rudimentary although by now he understood the language. Why not shoot all interiors in a French studio and limit filming in war-torn Spain to actual action footage? Tentative casting began with Pierre Larquay, who had just finished the clever *Ces Dames aux chapeaux verts,* opposite Alice Tissot, chosen for Magnin's part, and Erich von Stroheim set to play the downed German pilot, Schreiner. In the end, money decided the film's nationality. The hard-pressed Loyalist government had no foreign reserves for film production and while it was understood that raw film stock and laboratory work would, by necessity, be French, *all* filming would have to be done in Spain. The "up front" budget was 100,000 francs and 750,000 pesetas (about $75,000 in 1938 money).

The screenplay was elaborated in hotel rooms in Barcelona and in Perpignan, the first city on the French side of the Pyrenees in Loyalist hands a hundred and fifty miles north of Barcelona, where liaison was set up. The first men hired were Max Aub and Denis Marion. Aub, whom Malraux had met during the Writers' Congress, was a Spanish playwright who spoke perfect French and Marion was a bespectacled young Belgian who was later to write a book about the film adventure.[12] Starting with the script Aub and Marion were the jacks-of-all-trades throughout the making of the picture. Marion transposed André's written ideas for scenes and sequences into screenplay form which Aub translated into Spanish. Louis Page, a solid cameraman who had already shot films for Zoltan Korda and G. W. Pabst, was signed on as cinematographer and his wife as script girl.

With Malraux retaining final veto power, Aub was also casting director. José Sempere, a Barcelona vaudeville actor, was chosen to play the squadron commander (to soothe Spanish susceptibilities, Magnin became Pena on the screen) and José Lado, who critics were to believe was a nonprofessional, was cast as the peasant who climbs aboard the bomber to indicate the enemy airfield. Pedro Codina was cast as Schreiner, Andrés Mejuto as Muñoz and Julio Pena as Attignies.

Difficulties never let up. The war was slowly creeping toward Barcelona and the suburban Monjuich Studio where *Sierra de Teruel* started rolling August 1. The Taking of Teruel had been a short-lived victory for the Republicans. In February, General Juan de Yague's Falangist troops had retaken the city with a vengeance and since then had never stopped advancing. In April what Loyalist Spain feared most had happened—advance units of Yague's troops, accompanied by Italian Black Shirts, reached the Mediterranean at the mouth of the Ebro River, effectively cutting the Republic in two. But the day after the filming started, Republican artillery managed to contain Yague's armies on the Ebro. The slow and relentless Battle of the Ebro—the Republic's real last stand, was to last a murderous six weeks.

The Republic lost command of the air in early August and Bar-

[12] Denis Marion, *André Malraux,* Collection Cinéma d'aujourd'hui, (Paris: Seghers, 1970).

celona was bombed daily—and nightly, mostly by Italian planes taking off from Mallorca island. At each air raid, the Barcelona command cut the city's already dwindling electric power, instantly interrupting all filming at the Monjuich stages. In September, power was rationed by rolling blackouts. Fresh negatives didn't arrive from Paris for weeks and André didn't see his "rushes" for seven weeks. On September 28, the gasoline shortage forced the government to ban all nonessential travel and transport. The most essential props were nearly impossible to obtain. The government had no planes to spare and it took Aub and his assistants three months to get a "live" Potez bomber for a couple of hours of exterior shooting. Aerial shots of the mountain crash site were made from a different aircraft but before the filming had started, the studio carpentry department had created a handsome plywood interior of a Potez cockpit mounted on rollers for perfect make-believe pitch, yaw and roll movements. Six tanks required for the dramatic appearance at the end of one sequence were never obtained and the sequence never shot, but the Army put two thousand new recruits at the disposal of the filmmakers to play extras in the Descent to Linares scene. This climax, which Malraux wanted to be a lyrical note of tragic beauty capable of lifting the film above melodrama, could no longer be filmed in Teruel, now in fascist hands, and was staged at the Sierra de Monserrat northwest of Barcelona.

The war moved forever closer. By October only twenty-eight of the thirty-nine sequences planned had been filmed. Among the casualties was a scene at a military hospital of a mother kissing her airman son's nearly shot-off face until his cries of pain stop, remembered thirty-five years later in *Lazare*. Conscientiously, Marion calculated they had filmed six hundred setups in August, but that the September total was seventy-three. All incidents were not tragic. In an air raid bombs fell so close to the studio one night when no one was there that cast and crew the next morning found the sets stained with color—bomb fragments had fallen into paint pots and splashed the decors.

The summer was unbearably hot and with Josette at his side, a forever busy André directed in a tennis outfit. For a night scene around a camp fire, the movie projectors lit up the Monjuich hill above the blacked-out city. Fortunately it was a night no bombers came in from Mallorca. In mid-August, André and Josette attended a gloomy dinner in honor of Theodore Dreiser at the Majestic Hotel where everybody sat around in candlelight because the power was out again. President Azaña and Premier Negrín had invited the elder statesman of American letters to Barcelona in the hope that he would intercede with President Roosevelt and try and get food to Spain and Dreiser had been duly appalled. The hotel had been damaged by a bomb, the elevators didn't work, there was no sugar, butter or milk and some citizens were reduced to eating weeds. The international press corps had been hauled up from the front

206

and *New York Times'* Herbert Matthews, *Pravda*'s indomitable Señorita Boleslavskaya, veteran U.S. free-lancer Louis Fischer, the London *Times'* Henry Buckley and exiled German playwright Ernst Toller, who had spent five years in prison for being the chairman of the Bavarian Soviet Republican Party, all dutifully ate pale soup, bread cobs and squid. There was a plentiful supply of the hotel's best wines and Dreiser was soon drunk enough to announce that the civil war was all the fault of Catholics and Free Masons and that he hoped to God America would have sense enough to stay out of it. Boleslavskaya translated Dreiser's words for André who finally couldn't take Dreiser's rantings any longer and interrupted to say the war was in no way due to any of the causes advanced by the author of *Sister Carrie*. If the war had happened, it was because people had abandoned the hope of directing their own affairs and felt that war was the only possible way of removing the dictators from power. In this they were wrong, of course, because the war could only reinforce the power of the dictators, leaving the people worse off than before. Boleslavskaya translated into English, with Dreiser finally saying to Malraux, "He's a Frenchman and a Catholic. I wouldn't expect him to think otherwise." Matthews, who listened with appalled politeness, occasionally interrupted to suggest they change the subject, but the gloomy evening was not over until after Dreiser had made advances to Josette, insisting that she sit next to him and becoming ill-tempered when she refused. After three days in Barcelona, Dreiser was off to London.

The war closed in. In November, after the last Republican strongholds on the far bank of the Ebro had fallen to Yague and the International Brigades had suffered up to seventy-five percent casualties, Matthews, Buckley and Hemingway pulled out. Together with *Life* photographer Bob Capa, the trio had paid their way across the Ebro with cigarettes and nearly drowned when their rowboat was carried by the current toward the jagged ruins of a bridge. Boleslavskaya gave a wake in her Majestic suite, where Hemingway told André and Josette about the collapsing front. Both authors were drinking Scotch and at one point, Hemingway accused Malraux of having pulled out of the war in order to write huge "masterpisses" like *L'Espoir*. On November 15, when André saw the ragged remnants of the International Brigades march through Barcelona toward the French border, he sadly commented, "The whole revolution is going home."

He wasn't going home himself—not yet. Although Marion left in October and the French camera operator disappeared in November, Malraux continued to shoot literally until two days before Yague's forces reached the suburbs of Barcelona on January 24, 1939. As almost half a million soldiers and civilians fled the city for the French border, André, Josette and his cast and crew packed the last rolls of exposed negative in the trunks of three antique cars and at 4:00 A.M. headed north. The

207

scene at the border was one of fugitives worn out by hunger and fatigue, their clothes damp from rain and snow but their faces laughing with happiness as they marched into safety. At one point, Malraux thought of filming part of the exodus to use it for establishing crowd shots in the Descent to Linares sequence. Most would-be filmmakers might have abandoned the project here. Only a little more than half the shots outlined in the screenplay had been filmed and most of the sequences were incomplete. The negative was safe in the Pathé Laboratories vault, but most of the sound was so bad it would have to be rerecorded. And the Republican government, locked into the fourth of Spain lying southeast of a now near-starving Madrid, could no longer bankroll this film, which had even lost its political *raison d'être*.

Once in Paris, however, Malraux refused to consign *Sierra de Teruel* to the graveyard of noble but unsalvageable filmic failures. Instead, he let go of his considerable persuasive powers and a week after Generalissimo Franco had accepted the surrender of the last Republican armies, his cameras were rolling again.

The rescuer had been Edouard Corniglion-Molinier. The flying ace and one-time senator was now a film producer of two elegant box-office successes—*Courrier-Sud,* an adaptation of his friend Antoine de Saint-Exupéry's novel about pioneer commercial flying, and *Drôle de drame,* Marcel Carné's sparkling comedy. After screening all the footage shot in Spain, Malraux, Corniglion-Molinier and Joinville Studio's chief editor George Grace established a work plan. Hopelessly deficient scenes were eliminated and the plot line rewritten around the gap, absolutely essential connective exteriors were filmed in southern France and back-projections were used for studio-made matching shots. The sound was rerecorded and Max Aub, who had followed *Sierra de Teruel* in exile, got to dub several voices. With Grace at the Moviola, André cut the picture. A few title cards were inserted to bridge the most obvious narrative gaps and Malraux finally asked Darius Milhaud to write a score for the Descent to Linares ending, the only music he wanted in the film.

In July, *Sierra de Teruel* was previewed for Juan Negrín and members of the Republican government, now in exile in Paris. The commercial premiere was set for September. Two days before the scheduled opening, World War II broke out.

Two weeks before Britain and France declared war on Germany, the Edouard Daladier government had banned *L'Humanité* and *Ce Soir,* the two communist daily newspapers in Paris, largely for their knee-jerk welcoming of Stalin's Nonaggression Pact with Hitler as "saving the peace." Wartime censorship banned *Sierra de Teruel,* a revolutionary film. Malraux appealed directly to Daladier, with whom he had shared a Popular Front speakers platform three years earlier. But Daladier decided it was not the moment to add an irritant to Franco's hostility and

208

Det danske Filmmuseum

L'Espoir—scene from the Descent to Linares

Sierra de Teruel remained in the Joinville vault. During the German occupation, the negative and all release prints of the film were destroyed. A unique laboratory internegative survived because it was in cans mislabeled "Corniglion-Molinier's *Drôle de drame.*"

After the war, Corniglion-Molinier, now an air force general, sold the rights to a distributor who retitled the film *L'Espoir* and had Denis Marion change the title cards (in 1930s Loyalist terminology the film referred to the fascists as the rebels, but six years of seeing newsreels of Spain's dictator made audiences believe "rebels" meant Franco's adversaries). With a third of the Descent to Linares cut out and with popular Liberation politician Maurice Schumann underlining the similarities between the Spanish Republicans' fight and the French Resistance struggle in a filmed prologue, *L'Espoir* was released. Despite generous reviews, the film was a flop. In 1945, the Spanish Civil War was ancient history.

A dubbed version reached New York two years later and, in *Time,* James Agee gave it a glowing review.

After pondering why the only movies whose temper could possibly be described as heroic or tragic, or both, had been made by Leftists, Agee called *Man's Hope* "a great Leftist film, and one of the finest." Not everything was successful but the ending, he said, was powerful in emotion and meaning, standing "with the few great classical passages which have been achieved in film, through the perfect identification of melodramatic suspense with meanings which are normally far above the proper use of melodrama." [13]

[13] *Time* (Feb. 3, 1947); and James Agee, *Agee on Film: Essays and Reviews* (New York: Grosset & Dunlap, 1969).

> A road that is always the same, bordered by trees
> that are always the same, and the stones of Flanders always
> as hard under the tracks of our tanks.

> *Antimémoires*

17

With Josette, André spent the late summer of 1939 studying medieval art in Beaulieu-sur-Dordogne in south-central France. Since 1935, he had had in mind to write a book that would grasp the whole of art in one intuitive movement and see art not so much as an expression of beauty but as an age-long attempt at defying human destiny, as a means of escaping implacable fate. In 1938 he had written to Robert Haas to ask if Random House would be interested in an American edition of *La Psychologie de l'art,* as he called this nonfiction work. Josette and André found a lovely hotel-pension in Beaulieu, a sleepy village in the Corrèze *département* midway between Lyons and Bordeaux. "The church in Beaulieu," he was to write in the *Antimémoires,* "has one of the finest of all Romanesque tympanums, the only one in which, behind the arms of Christ stretched out to embrace the world, the sculptor has depicted the arms of the cross like a prophetic shadow."

Art, he was realizing, was dynamics in human history, challenge and defiance, intelligence imposed on matter. Art was not the result of social condition, but of pressure from within the artist and as such was testimony to the transcendence of the human adventure. Spanning time and cultures, art was proof of a deep human communion. What interested him in Romanesque sculpture was the change it denoted. Like the Greco-Buddhist art he had admired so much in Afghanistan in 1931 that he had smuggled a few pieces through half of India, Romanesque sculpture was art in transition, leaving behind it the frozen forms of Byzantium and anticipating the Gothic cathedrals and the warm humanity of the Renaissance. Change, he felt, was of the essence in art, a notion that was to make him realize that art didn't so much live by what it copied as by what it absorbed and, better, by what it challenged. Artists grew by challenging the forms earlier artists had imposed. Not that *all* evolution

211

was a forward thrust. The decline and fall of Rome could be traced in the dusty coin collections in Nîmes and other provincial museums. The coins showed the harrowing descent into medieval barbarism, the fall from Greco-Roman free form to dislocation of structure to total regression.

It was hard to keep the mind on Beaulieu's eleventh-century church sculpture. A radio was always blaring at the hotel and the personnel could not be kept away from the newscasts. One morning André passed two of the old maids on the stairs. Tears were streaming down their faces as they told him the Germans had invaded Poland. "Decidedly, each time I want to finish *La Psychologie de l'art* a new war breaks out," he wrote to a friend a couple of weeks later.

The news was almost anticlimactic. In May, Malraux had attended an international antifascist conference in Paris with Ilya Ehrenburg, Louis Aragon and other communist figures, but in August Stalin and Hitler had signed their Nonaggression Pact, throwing Western communists into disarray and causing several fellow travelers to ask for a painful revision of the broad Leftist alliance. Léon Blum was sure the French Communist Party would be torn apart by Stalin's about-face, but the Dáladier government suppressed the communist press and a little later the Party, thus rescuing it from its profound embarrassment and opening to it the vast advantages of going underground.

The May meeting had been a gloomy exercise in futility. Malraux had made the acquaintance of a shy philosophy professor with a furtive look, Jean-Paul Sartre, who lived with Josette's friend, Simone de Beauvoir, but the speeches had been empty repetitions of things said so many times. The conference had been haunted by Spanish intellectuals who rallied around Picasso. But even he was losing his spirits. For the first time in his life, he told Ehrenburg, he found it difficult to paint. Ehrenburg had found Malraux absentminded and reserved, but the author of *L'Espoir* refused to join any anticommunist stampede. When Raymond Aron urged him to lend his prestige to a demand for a "clarification" of communist intentions, he declined, saying, "As long as communists are in prison, I will say nothing against them." The wealthy classes had no desire to fight fascism, which they secretly preferred to any Popular Front, and now the Right was joined by the millions of communists who felt betrayed by Stalin and resented the harassment of police, the courts and the government. Workers and the middle class had little confidence in the Daladier administration and couldn't follow the reason why it was necessary to fight for Poland after having deserted socialist Austria and Czechoslovakia. The general opinion during those September days was that there would be very little fighting and that, in any case, France was safe behind the Maginot Line fortifications. The joke was that France would get back the immense cost of the Maginot Line after the war because Maginot would become the largest tourist attraction in Europe.

212

When the mobilization posters went up on Beaulieu's church square two days after France and England had declared war on Germany, Josette and André left for Paris. They stopped over in Moulins, where Simone de Beauvoir asked André to do something on behalf of foreigners, especially Spanish Republicans who were forced to join the Foreign Legion or herded into internment camps. Once in Paris, he managed to have a few Spanish friends freed from the Vernet camp.

Malraux's intention was simple: "If you have written what I have and there is a war in France, you fight," he told journalists as he sought to join the air force. If nothing else, he knew aerial combat. He had commanded a squadron and as a gunner-bombardier had personally flown sixty-five missions that included combat with both Italian and German war planes. Because of the "cardiac trouble" noted in his military records following the 1922 induction physical in Strasbourg, he was rejected.

For a moment, he thought of joining the Polish army ("Can you see me wearing a shapka?" he wrote his childhood friend Louis Chevasson), but Poland was crushed by the overwhelming might of the German Army in one week and the conflict settled into the long lull that was soon called "the phony war." Finally, he succeeded in getting into an armored unit and while awaiting the call-up moved into a furnished apartment in the Rue le Marois to settle his civilian affairs. Gallimard's was disorganized by the mobilization of its principal collaborators and all major business decisions had to be postponed. In a long letter to Haas, Malraux tried to settle his American affairs. Although Random House had already advanced him $1,000 on an as yet unspecified book, he asked Haas to advance another $250 and send the money to Miguel Negrín at the Cheshire Academy in Connecticut. The teen-aged son of Republican Spain's last prime minister was safe in the U.S. but totally without funds. After telling Haas to hang on to the French subtitles to *Sierra de Teruel,* sent to Random House to be forwarded to Hemingway for translation and adaptation, and telling him the film might actually be distributed outside France by Metro-Goldwyn-Mayer, André told the editor about his new project, a novel about this war. "The same 'raw material' as *L'Espoir,* but in a more metaphysical mold and with less politics," he wrote. "I am dropping the second Spanish book which I told you about, but its themes will be transferred to the French book: problems of war, life and death are not national. . . . No doubt such a book will find an audience in America. I would want to forward it section by section so that it can be translated as I go along, or, if you prefer to have the translation done in France, please let me know. It would be a pity, I feel, to lose a year translating such a book." [14] This letter, dated September 27, was the last one Haas

[14] Walter G. Langlois, *André Malraux, 1939–1942, d'après une correspondance inédite* (Paris: La Revue des lettres modernes, 1972).

would receive from Malraux for more than a year. As André joined his unit, the DC 41 regiment, Josette became pregnant.

The tank regiment appealed to Malraux because it had been his father's unit in the First World War and because he felt armor would play a decisive role in this new conflict. The DC 41 regiment was based in Provins, a charming medieval town fifty miles southeast of Paris, with eleventh-century ramparts, a thirteenth-century donjon called Caesar's Tower, and eleventh- and sixteenth-century churches. The DC 41 spent the eight months of the Phony War in Provins, going to the bistros, taking turret machine guns apart and assembling them again. The magnificent tank battles of May 1940, which were to become just as magnificent pages in the new novel, occurred hundreds of miles north of Provins. The stories of tanks falling into antitank ditches, metal belts thrashing in empty air, and of a tank commander in his turret "directing" his ear-damaged driver below with strings attached to the driver's thumbs belonged to Fernand Malraux's war. The men of DC 41 never saw action. On May 16, when General Erich von Manstein's armor outflanked the Maginot Line by dashing through Belgium and broke into the heartland of France, they were all German prisoners. When the government scrambled out of Paris for Bordeaux, they were being marched south to form an ever-growing number of prisoners. When on June 17, Marshal Henri Philippe Pétain's hastily formed government, soon to set itself up in the spa city of Vichy, accepted Hitler's terms for an armistice, they were ten thousand in a makeshift camp in Sens, an archbishop's seat with a twelve-century cathedral. After a couple of weeks, this mass of defeated men who had no means of shaving turned into a gothic crowd, as Malraux was to write in his new novel.

The ten thousand captive men were actually not so much a haggard body of soldiers as an amorphous herd of men with defeat written all over them, ten thousand hungry, dysentery-ridden men with only two obsessions —when would they be set free and what would they eat next? They told each other it would only be weeks before the Germans would send them home and invented fabulous gourmet meals. The war was over. Women began to appear outside the barbed wire, looking for husbands and throwing food and scraps of news over the fence. The Germans were occupying only the northern two-thirds of France. The Southeast constituted a demilitarized "free zone" under Pétain's Vichy government.

Life in the camp was tolerable, André wrote to a friend toward the end of July, "not to be recommended for vacations, but nothing should be exaggerated." Each man organized himself, constructing a domain with bricks, cans and pieces of wood, "man's age-old sense of property." In his mind, André was now writing his book, to be called *La Lutte avec l'ange* (The Struggle with the Angel), which would express the universality of man across time—with death and with the dead of other cultures. It would be his first novel to cover any considerable timespan

214

and would be not so much the story of individuals in the mid-twentieth century as a reflection on the eternal endurance of mankind, the permanence of man.

In September, his half-brother Roland showed up at the fence and, when other prisoners had located André, shouted a warning across. To counteract U.S. propaganda, the Germans were planning to free a number of notorious intellectuals. Malraux and Gide were on the list of detainees whose liberation should prove the extent of German humanism to American public opinion. This meant that the German high command was actually looking for him. And if Roland could find out in which POW camp he was so could the Gestapo.

The poet Jean Grosjean, who was to become a co-director of Gallimard, ran into Malraux at a chow line. André immediately asked him why they had lost the war. The next day they met again and talked, stepping over men lying in the grass, mentally eating *fois gras* and stuffed partridge. What surprised Grosjean was that Malraux saw the war becoming much larger than it was, eventually involving Asia, the Near East and the United States. Another day someone handed them the printed appeal of a little-known tank commander—General Charles de Gaulle—who in the dying hours of the Bordeaux government had been named undersecretary of defense. Now in London, de Gaulle called on his countrymen to fight on. He reminded them that "overseas France—nearly half of Africa, Indochina, the Caribbean islands—was not in enemy hands, that most of the navy was safe in Algerian and Moroccan ports, that in the gallant Dunkirk sealift whole divisions had made it across the straight of Dover with the British expeditionary force in Flanders and that England had not given up. With Prime Minister Winston Churchill's support, de Gaulle was constituting a "France libre" government-in-exile. Malraux found de Gaulle's ideas interesting; Grosjean didn't.

In October, when a German edict ordering all Jews to declare themselves was followed by the Vichy "Jewish statute" debarring all Jews from public office and liberal professions, the kommandant demanded volunteers to help with the local harvest. Malraux, Grosjean, a chaplain and eight others immediately stepped forward, certain that as volunteers they would be under sufficiently relaxed supervision to escape. They were assigned to Collemiers, a village five miles from Sens. Their German overseer was a Lieutenant Metternich, who didn't think his POWs should sleep in a barn and arranged to have them billeted at Mayor Courgenet's house. Courgenet, it turned out, was a radical socialist and after a while Malraux told him of their plans. Courgenet agreed to help them with disguises and a little money for railway tickets. As Josette gave birth in Paris to a boy she named Pierre-Gauthier, Malraux, Grosjean and the chaplain slipped away—André in painter's overalls and in too-small shoes that had his feet in flames after two miles of cross-country marching.

They were headed for Vichy France and in order to avoid being spotted split up at the first railway station. André got on a local and while awaiting a change of trains in a larger town ducked into a moviehouse where a newsreel showed the German capture of Warsaw, as he was to remember in *Lazare*. A cat followed him at the edge of the forest marking the demarcation line between occupied and Vichy France, arousing the suspicion of the German patrol.

Would he ever be on any winning side? The fascism he had fought at home and abroad for more than a decade was triumphant everywhere. Nazi Germany ruled Europe from Norway to the Mediterranean, from the Atlantic to the Black Sea, its Japanese ally was debarking in China while Italy, the third member of the triumphant axis, mopped up Greece and in Africa plunged into Somalia and Libya. In Spain, Franco consolidated *his* New Order while the Soviet Union, the hope and focal point of so many progressive passions and dreams, occupied the Baltic states and prepared to sign a Nonaggression Pact with Japan. At home, the doddering father figure Pétain and his Premier Pierre Laval not only resigned themselves to knuckle under to Hitler but by emulating his regime hoped to curry enough favor with the dictator to lead him to go easy on the French. In the atmosphere of threats and fears, defeatism and confusion, they abolished the Republic and instituted *L'État français,* made Pétain Chief of the French State, Laval vice-president and assumed all powers.

Limping in the tight shoes, he made it through the woods to the Vichy zone. Next November, he would be forty years old.

Part Two

18

With their newborn son, Josette joined André on the Riviera in December 1940. Both were totally destitute but the Clotis family offered them shelter. Josette's father was the mayor of Hyères, a village between Cannes and Toulon, and despite rationing and shortages of all kinds, he could accommodate them. Not that they were exactly welcomed with open arms. Their "situation" as unmarried couple, now with an illegitimate child, was not exactly the kind of arrangement that enchanted provincial families. Before the war Clara had refused to divorce André and now he was more than reluctant to begin divorce proceedings against a wife whose maiden name was Goldschmidt and who was born in the Reich.

Money and escape from the Clotis family home became his major obsessions. No money could be sent from Gallimard since the publishing house was in occupied Paris, but the Riviera was full of empty villas, domains left with caretakers by owners who found it prudent to put more distance between themselves and Europe's new masters. To look for Gide and other Parisian escapees known to be on the Riviera, André made scouting trips to Marseille, Cannes and Nice. One day in December in a Nice streetcar a young man tapped his shoulder and introduced himself —Varian Fry of the Emergency Rescue Committee, a private American organization set up in Marseille to assist refugees in difficulty and to organize the departure to America of threatened personalities. They had met in New York in 1938, Fry told Malraux. They got off the tram together.

Marseille was teeming with refugees running out of territory— German and Austrian socialists and communists, Russian revolutionaries out of favor with Moscow, Spanish Republicans, some on their fourth exile, some at their seventh flight in twenty years, stateless persons and Jews of all nationalities, rich Jews selling, buying and selling back documents, visas, currency and titbits of information and poor Jews running through

219

daily routines of terror and glimmers of hope. "In our ranks are enough doctors, psychologists, engineers, educators, poets, painters, writers, musicians, economists to vitalize a whole country," Victor Serge, the journalist-anarchist recently released from Stalin's camps, was to write. "Here is a beggars' alley gathering the remnants of revolutions, democracies and crushed intellect. We sometimes tell ourselves that it would be tremendous if only five in a hundred could manage to across the Atlantic and there rekindle the flame of battle in their hearts. If it had not been for Varian Fry's American Relief Committee [sic], a goodly number of refugees would have had no reasonable course open to them but to jump into the sea from the heights of the transporter-bridge." [1] As did Walter Hasenclever, the German expressionist poet and Bertolt Brecht's mentor.

At Fry's office, Malraux met Victor Serge, whose imprisonment by Stalin had nearly wrecked the 1935 antifascist conference when Gide and Malraux had allowed Serge-defenders to be heard despite the objections of Louis Aragon and the Russian delegation. Serge was Belgian by place of birth and upbringing, French by affinity and literary expression, Russian by parents and for a while by citizenship. Now he was stateless (for the purpose of funeral documents, when he died in Mexico in 1947, he was put down as a Spanish national) and bitterly denounced the trickle of visas the United States and Latin American governments granted. Visas for practically every American nation were blackmarketed at exorbitant prices and Vichy officials conducted their own trade in exit permits. "A fine trade this," Serge railed after he got out with three hundred others on the last ship to Martinique, "selling lifebelts on a shipwrecked continent." *

With the exception of surrealist founding father André Breton, few French intellectuals or even militants took advantage of Fry's offers. Although Vichy police sacked Marseille's socialist city council and rumors were flying that the Germans would soon occupy all of France, most of them were not anxious to cross the Atlantic—not yet. When Fry pressed Malraux to leave, telling him that as a notorious antifascist he was probably high on the Germans' list, André was evasive and instead talked about his financial troubles and about establishing contact with de Gaulle's "Free French" in London. Fry offered to act as an intermediary and to get letters to Haas in New York. Through a British agent, he could also communicate with London, he said.

Malraux was elated and in January 1941, two chapters of the new

[1] Victor Serge, *Memoirs of a Revolutionary* (London: Oxford University Press, 1963).

* Others aboard this ship of fools included German Stalinist Paul Merker and André Simone-Katz. In exile in Mexico Merker slandered Victor, went to East Germany when it was all over only to be arrested and imprisoned as part of the "lessons of the Prague trials." Simone-Katz, allegedly recruited by Noël Coward as a British intelligence agent, returned to Czechoslovakia after World War II and was hanged in the 1953 Prague purges.

novel went to New York, via Lisbon and diplomatic pouch, together with a long letter to Haas, asking the editor to try to serialize the text in the Americas by sending copies to José Bergamín in Mexico City and to Victoria Ocampo, editor of *Sur* and *Nación,* in Buenos Aires. The best U.S. magazine André suggested, was perhaps *Fortune,* now edited by Archibald MacLeish. The two chapters were entitled "Tank Ditch" and "The Camp." "I consider 'Tank Ditch' the most important and only forward 'The Camp' because of its newsworthiness. The next batch will be more important than this one." Impatiently, he wrote Haas again two weeks later, saying he had learned that MacLeish no longer was an editor at *Fortune.* He was sure MacLeish was still in contact with the magazine and, in general, knew the editors of all major publications, and added that "Tank Ditch" might be better suited for *Saturday Evening Post* or *Atlantic,* "better *Collier*'s maybe, than *Life.* These magazines pay well and the situation here is very difficult." On February 28, Haas wrote back that the manuscript had not yet arrived but happily announcing that because of a change in U.S. monetary regulations, Random House would now be in a position to send him seventy-five dollars every month. Malraux was more than grateful and quickly wrote a thank-you note. Until Pearl Harbor, the seventy-five monthly dollars, forwarded through Fry's Emergency Rescue Committee, kept André, Josette and the baby alive.

Malraux was less lucky in establishing contact with London. He gave Fry a message addressed to de Gaulle, offering his services to the *Forces françaises libres* (FFL), imagining, as he was to write in the *Antimémoires,* that the Free French weren't exactly deluged by offers from men with aviation expertise. As he didn't receive a reply, he believed his political reputation had caused the FFL chief to reject him and for years his attitude toward de Gaulle was to remain cool. It was only twenty years later that he learned the woman who had taken his message to the British agent had been caught in a police razzia and been forced to swallow it.

Life was becoming tolerable again. André Gide was in Nice and Roger Martin du Gard in Cap d'Ail. In January, Josette, André and their little boy managed to escape the quarrelsome hospitality of the Clotis family and to move into a magnificent villa in Roquebrune Cap-Martin, twenty miles east of Nice toward the Italian border. The Villa La Souco belonged to British friends of Martin du Gard, the painter Simon Bussy and his novelist wife Dorothy Bussy, who there had entertained Rudyard Kipling and T. E. Lawrence. The villa came complete with Luigi, an Italian butler, who treated the disasters of war with a studied indifference. When chain-smoking André was out of cigarettes—and this happened often—Luigi made his way across the Italian border and returned with a fresh supply of *Nazionale.*

Here, Malraux set down to write. Simultaneously, he plunged into

With André Gide at Cap d'Ail, 1941

three books—*Les Noyers de l'Altenburg,* which was to be the first half of *La Lutte avec l'ange, La Psychologie de l'art* and an extended study of Lawrence of Arabia. *The Walnut Trees of Altenburg* was new territory for him, the first novel to cover any considerable timespan, the story of the father and son of an Alsatian family each fighting on a different side in the two World Wars. As he had told Haas, "Tank Ditch" and "The Camp" were only fringe chapters. The center of the book would be a colloquy held in the Berger family's Alsatian hometown of Altenburg. Here, leading intellectuals would debate the ultimate philosophical question—*Is there a meaning to life at all?*—but the colloquy would be set on the eve of the First World War and thus be swept away by events outside the control of the intellect. In 1914, Alsace had been German and Vincent Berger had served in the German army; in 1939 Alsace had been French and his son had been in a French uniform, taken part in the 1940 campaign and been imprisoned in a makeshift POW camp. Human experiences would be presented as the same for all soldiers, whether French or German.

Malraux felt detached from current events, tired even, of a decade of political action that had led nowhere. Instead, he plunged into the non-topical contradiction at the core of his book. Purely intellectual responses to the question, *Is there a meaning to life at all?* seemed to yield a negative answer whereas an intuitive approach to life tended to lead to a power-

222

ful emotional affirmation. To Europe's leading minds gathered at Altenburg to try to find a meaning to man, the towering walnut trees outside the library were an answer as was the flight of migrating birds above the trenches. While one of the delegates would come to the conclusion that what made Man divine was his capacity for questioning the universe and another participant decided the best way to understand humanity was to contemplate an anthill, Vincent Berger would go off through the fields and in a setting sun contrast intellectual arguments with fundamental life.

Work on *La Psychologie de l'art* was difficult. Malraux was not only far from important museums but also from his friends, Bernard Groethuysen, Pierre-Eugène Drieu la Rochelle, Eddy du Perron and Pascal Pia, with whom he could talk art into the wee hours of any night. "Groot," Pia and Drieu were in Paris—Drieu fast becoming the principal Nazi collaborator. Du Perron, Malraux now learned, had died in Amsterdam of a heart attack, or committed suicide, the day the Germans overran Holland. The book on T. E. Lawrence, Malraux wrote to Haas, would be called *Le Démon de l'absolu.* "It is hard to sum it up, but I don't think I'm totally conceited when I say this will be the most important book on him, because so far nothing very important had been published."

To Gaëtan Picon, a young admirer who was to write the first Malraux biography, André wrote that Lawrence didn't "fascinate" but puzzled him. T. E. Lawrence's life, he felt, was one big accusation. "It is not exemplary and doesn't try to be." Although he had only met Lawrence once—in a gay bar in Montparnasse—Malraux had been haunted by the man who had written, "I have dreamed of hustling into form, while I lived, the new Asia which time was inexorably bringing upon us. Mecca was leading to Damascus; Damascus to Anatolia, and afterwards to Bagdad; and then there was Yemen." Malraux had had Gaston Gallimard bring out a French edition of *The Seven Pillars of Wisdom,* had written the foreword himself and flown over Yemen, perhaps as much in search of the ghost of Lawrence as for the Queen of Sheba's lost city. As Lawrence in Arabia, Malraux in Spain had tried single-handedly to divert, if only for a short while, the course of history. He saw Lawrence, after leading his armies in triumph against the Turks to Damascus, confronted with the absurdity of his own life and the discovery that all his acts, even the most noble and daring, were flawed because the British government had made him the spokesman of promises that London never intended to keep. A stranger among the Arabs, an outcast among the British, detesting himself, he wrote *The Seven Pillars,* Malraux said in the foreword, not as a confession but as an act of penance.

Lawrence, one of the most religious intelligences of his time, if one means by religious someone who knows the anguish of being a man in the very depth of his soul; Lawrence, who had received a religious education in England, who had attended Jesuit schools in France, whose

223

brother and mother were missionaries, who called *The Brothers Kara-mazov* the fifth gospel, and yet there is not to be found in the nine hundred crowded pages of his letters—nor in his books—more than fifty lines on Christianity.

Thirty years later, Malraux told of his meeting with Lawrence.

We were not equal. He had in his pocket the *Seven Pillars,* his work with Churchill during the 1918 Peace Treaty, his breaking off with the world plus the special halo of mystery which Intelligence Service work gave him. Of course his real mystery wasn't there. I was a little French writer who only had the Goncourt Prize. Not much. He was extraordinarily elegant; an elegance of today, not of his era—turtleneck and a kind of off-handed nonchalance and distance. I can't remember what we talked about; all I remember is that he was passionately interested in engines, motorcycle and boat engines. It was a short time before his death. Did he want to die? I've often asked myself, but never found an answer.[2]†

The pre-1914 disintegration of the Ottoman Empire under the pressure of nationalism became connective material linking *Le Démon de l'absolu* and *Les Noyers*. As Lawrence in 1911 had set out on an archaelogical expedition to Syria to become embroiled in local revolt against Turkey (and André in 1923 had traveled to Cambodia in search of Khmer art only to become committed to nascent Vietnamese national aspirations), the fictitious Vincent Berger becomes involved with a historical character, Enver Pacha (1881–1922), the general who commanded the Turkish army in Caucasus in 1914, defended the Bosphorus and was killed while leading a Moslem uprising against the Soviets in Turkestan. Malraux used a little-known episode of the Italo-Turkish War of 1910 to graft Vincent into authentic events. As in *The Conquerors* Garin became a lieutenant to Borodin, Vincent in *The Walnut Trees* is a friend of Enver and takes part in the pro-Turkish revolt of Senussi tribes in Cyrenaica where he practically invents guerrilla warfare. But despite his youthful admiration for Enver and the general's dream of a new Turkish Empire with Samarkand as its capital, Vincent's Asian involvement ends in utter failure. He realizes that because the people of Central Asia have a religious not a racial kinship, Enver's dream of bringing together all the Turkoman races in a blood alliance is even more absurd than the Panislamism preached by the despotic sultan, Abdul Hamid. Following an attack by a lunatic, Vincent turns his back on "this stupid central Asia, with its lies" and returns, disillusioned and sick, to Europe, realizing the disproportion between effort and result.

People showed up. Jean-Paul Sartre and Simone de Beauvoir had

---

[2] *L'Express* (March 22, 1971).
† Lawrence was fatally injured on his motorcycle, swerving to avoid two boys on bicycles, while returning to his Royal Air Force base at Camp Bovington after sendin a cryptic telegram to a friend in May 1935.

bicycled most of the seven hundred miles down from Paris and when they came for dinner were overwhelmed by the fried chicken Josette and André managed to serve. Sartre was canvassing support for *Socialisme et Liberté*, an embryonic resistance movement, but like Gide, Malraux was not interested, saying that for time being he counted on Soviet armor and American bombs to win the war. Two weeks earlier, Hitler had invaded the USSR and André felt it was only a matter of time before the United States would be sucked into the conflict. Once back in Paris, Sartre was to feel some of the pangs of Malraux's fictitious Vincent Berger when the Gestapo arrested two Socialisme et Liberté members, but without his group having any accomplishments to show for the sacrifice.[3]

"Do you have any arms?" was Malraux's pragmatic question to intellectuals eager to become guerrilleros. Roger Stéphane was one such young, energetic journalist, who showed up to ask the former Spanish Civil War commander for help. Instead, he got an earful of Malrucian geopolitics. To Stéphane's surprise, Malraux saw the outcome of the war in terms of who had the edge in technology. Although Nazi Germany was triumphant on all fronts—steamrolling into the Ukraine and toward Moscow, dashing through North Africa toward Egypt and subjecting England to the relentless blitz bombing—Malraux said the German forces were already beyond their peak and that Germany's defeat would mean a victory for the Anglo-Saxons "who will colonize the world, France included." British bombs were superior to German bombs and "no German success in Russia can be definite because one day antitank weaponry will annihilate armor." [4]

Stéphane felt Malraux was anxious to join the war, but when he returned again in September, he found the author of *L'Espoir* cautious. Malraux warned that he was probably under surveillance, said he approved Stéphane's resolve to act but told him he didn't believe in nationalism, nor in revolution that gave the masses more dignity but not more to eat. What would the postwar world look like? An American victory would mean a European New Deal, a federated Europe, but without the Soviet Union. Emmanuel d'Astier, aristocrat and diplomat who had married a Soviet commissar's sister, also visited and tried to recruit Malraux. He came away feeling Malraux would in due course have his own resistance movement. In January 1942, after Pearl Harbor had brought America into the war, yet another budding *maquisard,* Francis Crémieux, showed up with a concrete proposal—the leadership of the "secret army" in Toulouse, which would include a good number of Spanish Republicans now living underground in the Pyrenees. "I thought he would accept," Crémieux was to write after the war. "We had no arms, few men

[3] Simone de Beauvoir, *The Prime of Life,* trans. Peter Green (New York: World Publishers, 1962).
[4] Roger Stéphane, *Chaque homme est lié au monde* (Paris: Sagittaire, 1946).

and everything was still to be done. I was still coasting on my youth and imagined that Malraux was a man ready for the humblest of tasks. He answered point blank that the French people didn't inspire confidence, that his Spanish experience had disappointed him and that he couldn't believe in birth of a popular force in an occupied country. 'For me, there are only two things that count—planes and tanks,' [he said]. 'If you can guarantee that we'll have arms, I'm with you. I've got to be able to refuel. Will we have refueling supplies? It seems to me you're playing boyscouts. That's not what it's all about.' We were looking for men and arms; he dreamed about planes and tanks. I said partisans; he answered boyscouts. Then he made me understand he would like to talk to serious people— British or American officers, people from the Office of Strategic Services (OSS) or the British Intelligence Service." [5]

Meanwhile Malraux continued to work on *Les Noyers* and when he visited Gide, now seventy-three years old, at Cap-Martin, he read a long excerpt to him. Gide didn't like it and told Malraux his disappointment was caused both by content and form—Malraux's fragmentary narrative and forced locutions were not easy to follow. Apparently, Malraux paid no attention. Reading the published work in 1944, Gide noted in his *Journal,* "I recognize what he read to me in Cap-Martin. Again I find the weaknesses of form which I had drawn to his attention then."

In October 1941, Malraux established a new route for corresponding with New York—"one of Lisbon's leading journalists," as he notified Haas. José Augusto de Santos had been a war correspondent in Republican Spain and besides finding a Portuguese publisher for André's new novel agreed to take letters to Haas to the U.S. embassy in Lisbon for forwarding via diplomatic pouch. In early December, Malraux sent the finished manuscript to de Santos who forwarded the package, via Portuguese navy ship, to Bermuda, and wrote a note to Haas telling him to have someone pick it up in Hamilton. The United States entry into the war on December 8 upset the elaborate plan. The note never got to New York and no one met the Portuguese warship in Hamilton. The package went back to Lisbon —to be returned to Malraux at the end of 1942. A copy of the manuscript, however, had been sent to neutral Switzerland, where it was published in a limited edition in Lausanne in 1943. America's entry into the war, however, did not immediately sever the Lisbon connection and Malraux was able to correspond with Haas until September 1942.

The Walnut Trees of Altenburg is unlike any of the other novels. Written, like *L'Espoir,* in midwar, it proclaims the universal brotherhood of all men rather than partisan righteousness. In rhythm it is musical, almost symphonic. Malraux's British biographer Robert Payne was to call it one of his greatest achievements, "like Goethe's *Dichtung und Wahrheit,*

[5] *La Marseillaise* (April 23, 1947).

the work belongs to that category of books that are neither novels, nor autobiographies, nor essays but are all of these." Jean Lacouture was to say that the pages telling of the poison gas attack on the German-Russian front in 1915 are stirred by "the breath and something of Tolstoy's vital essence." Critics in favor of the novel usually equate its literary value with its intellectual content and those opposing it hold that it is too fragmentary and echo Groethuysen's assessment that in *Les Noyers* "Malraux is in full possession of his shortcomings."

Malraux chose the name Berger because it is both German and French (*ber-gher*, German = mountain man; *berzhay*, French = shepherd). The opening section sets the tone for the whole novel as being based on experience rather than events. Young Berger (he never has a first name) is one of thousands of French soldiers interned in 1940 in a German POW camp at Chartres—Chartres, rather than Sens, perhaps because of the historical and artistic associations of the cathedral city. The camp makes the tank commander think about war and human solidarity. Despite bloodshed and destruction, war strips away the veneer of individuals and reveals the common essence of people—surrounded by barbed wire, each soldier begins to construct a "territory" for himself with bricks, cans or whatever other materials are at hand. Snippets of conversation between the German guards reveal they are talking about the Bamberg cathedral as "the German Chartres." Berger also thinks about his father, Vincent Berger, who in the First World War had been a German soldier. To keep his sanity in the camp, young Berger begins to write about his father as he recalls his childhood, his grandfather Dietrich who committed suicide, his uncle Walter and their ancestral home in Reichbach. Walter, who is described as looking like "Michelangelo at the end of a long university career," had been a friend of Nietzsche. Mixing facts with fiction, Malraux tells the well-known story of how the mad Nietzsche is being brought back to Basel from Italy, making Walter the charitable friend who assists Nietzsche's real-life friend and former colleague Franz Overbeck.

"It was a long journey, from Turin to Basel. The train was practically full of poor people, Italian workers. His landlord had to find three seats. I remained standing in the corridor, Overbeck sat on Friedrich's left, Miescher, the dentist, on his right, and there was a peasant woman next to him. She looked like Overbeck, the same grandmotherly face. A hen kept poking its head out of her basket, and she kept pushing it back again. It was enough to make one go berserk—literally berserk. What it must have been like for a . . . sick man! I expected some appalling incident.

"The train entered the St. Gotthard tunnel, which had just been completed. In those days it took thirty-five minutes—thirty-five minutes —to get through and the third-class carriages had no lighting. In spite of the rattle of the train, I could hear the hen pecking at the wickerwork,

227

and I was on tenterhooks. How to cope with a fit of violence in the darkness?"

Except for [Walter's] flat lips, which scarcely moved, his whole face was still motionless in the theatrical light. But his voice, punctuated by the raindrops falling from the gutters, betrayed the vindictiveness that underlies certain forms of pity.

"And suddenly—you know, of course, that a number of Friedrich's writings were still unpublished—a voice rose in the dark, above the clattering of the wheels. Friedrich was singing—with perfect articulation, although in conversation he used to stammer—he was chanting a poem which was unknown to us; and it was his last poem, 'Venice.' I don't much care for Friedrich's poetry. It's mediocre. But this poem was . . . well, by God, it was sublime."

To Walter, the mad Nietzsche singing in the St. Gotthard tunnel is a symbol of man's power to conquer his destiny. "And in that railway car, you know, and sometimes since—I merely say sometimes—the infinitudes of the starry sky have seemed to me to have been blotted out by man as our petty destinies are obliterated by the starry sky."

Young Berger writing about his father, his uncle Walter and the Altenburg colloquy in the third person gives the central section a unique tone in Malraux's work. The elder Berger is a lucid adventurer and an intellectual fascinated with power and propaganda who as a young man had been to Turkey. His involvement with Enver and the Young Turks movement had ended with disillusionment, a feeling that now grips his son in the Chartres POW camp. Vincent's return to Europe in 1913 had given him a feeling of freedom from the past and a new awareness of the individuality of European life.

Vincent's experiences in Asia Minor are a prologue to the book's central episode—the Altenburg conference.‡ Inspired by the Pontigny meetings which Malraux—with Clara in tow—attended in the early 1930s, the Altenburg colloquy bursts with ideas and is peopled with fascinating characters. The most remarkable participant is Möllberg, an erratic and emotional ethnologist and *kulturphilosoph,* who, like Spengler, had developed ideas of "cultural complexes" into a theory of "cultural cycles" and started his own Research Institute for the Morphology of Civilizations. Malraux's models for Möllberg were both his artist friend Leopold Chauveau and Leo Frobenius (1873–1938). Möllberg physically resembles Chauveau and like him carves small, sad, half-human half-gargoyle figurines that all look like him. Frobenius was a far-out name in ethnology, the author of many books and much research into prehistoric man in the Alps, Spain, Libya, Rhodesia and bushman caves in South Africa, who, like young Malraux, was not above using dubious means to obtain objects

‡ There is no Altenburg in Alsace and the name seems a tribute to Nietzsche, whose father had been a private tutor to four princesses of Saxe-Altenburg.

for his museum. Between 1904 and 1935, he made twelve expeditions to Africa and was one of the principal discoverers of the former existence of an indigenous African civilization. He combined a deep respect for this past with a biting contempt for living Africans and for what he considered the excessively soft treatment of them by missionaries, especially British evangelists. The Berlin-born scientist was one of the founders of the diffusionist school of anthropology which holds that cultural developments are not invented independently in different cultures, as evolutionists believe, but pass on from one to another. In the ritual slayings of kings which he had witnessed in southern Africa, he saw a mark of a "culture complex" with its primary origin in India.§ Möllberg used to believe in Hegel's dictum that man is a strict continuity and that history is an enduring framework for the human adventure, but Africa had unsettled him.

Besides Möllberg, Walter and Vincent, the participants include Ravaud who sees art as the key to the eternal, and Thirard, who holds that there are two kinds of knowledge—formal knowledge, which tries to reduce man to a system of psychological laws, and intuitive knowledge as displayed by such writers as Stendhal, Tolstoy, Meredith, Dostoyevsky and Montaigne. Also there are Walter's assistant Hermann Müller, described as an aging gigolo with frivolous neckties, and Steiglitz, a pugnacious professor who calls the knowledge of novelists artificial and contrived. Steiglitz has a friend who has spent time in a penitentiary and who claims only three books stand up to the test of being read in prison—*Robinson Crusoe, Don Quixote* and *The Idiot*. Although neither Defoe, nor Cervantes nor Dostoyevsky had undergone the experiences they wrote about, all three had suffered isolation from others, humiliation and shame since Defoe had been in the pillory, Cervantes had been a slave and Dostoyevsky a convict.

Steiglitz makes a fundamental challenge to psychology which brings Vincent to tell about his Asian experiences. Only Westerners need psychology, Vincent says, because Western thought is in opposition, not in harmony, with the Cosmos and with fate. Steiglitz interrupts to say psychoanalysis is the old idea of original sin dressed up in new clothes, since the unconscious is always considered evil. The West, he says, always confuses knowledge of man with knowledge of his secrets.

This brings the conversation to the central thought of Malraux's philosophy—art as man's supreme way of escaping his fate and even of dominating it. "Essentially, our art is a way of humanizing the world."

Möllberg begins the discussion on the theme, *Is there any meaning to the idea of man?* by wondering whether it is possible to dig under the variety of cultures, under the masses of divergent myths and beliefs,

§ According to Denis Boak, op. cit., Frobenius' unorthodox approach to primitive societies, combined with "perhaps a streak of paranoia and charlatanism in his character" and the waning of interest in diffusionist theories may explain why he is little known in English-speaking anthropological milieus.

through the different mental structures and "isolate a single permanent factor which is valid throughout the world, valid throughout history."

Saying "we must have a world we can understand," he argues that only history had given a meaning to the human drama and that man is only human because he can think. "If mental structures disappear forever like the plesiosaurus, if civilizations succeed each other only in order to cast man into the bottomless pit of nothingness, if the human adventure only subsists at the price of implacable change, then it's of little importance that for a couple of centuries men can transmit their ideas and techniques because man is a fluke and, fundamentally speaking, the world is made of oblivion."

Möllberg's argument impresses the others. Steiglitz takes up Möllberg's pessimistic conclusion by saying that even between modern Western man and medieval man there is a huge difference in mental structure, as seen in their different attitudes toward miracles. Thirard wonders whether this difference in mental structure is valid for simple peasants as well as for members of more specialized occupations, to which Möllberg replies that the millions of peasants throughout the ages may be alike, but that they are not, ultimately, significant. "Man isn't in himself interesting, it's only what makes him human that makes him interesting." This makes Vincent Berger ask *what* fundamental man is and Möllberg to answer that beyond thought there is no residue of fundamental man. "A civilization is not some sort of ornament," he argues, and "there is no such thing as fundamental man, enlarged, according to different epoques, by what he thinks and believes—there is man-who-thinks-and-believes or nothing at all." Ravaud maintains that man's capacity for thought is his supreme achievement and the gift that makes him approach eternity, but Möllberg retorts that "Sisyphus is also eternal," and that humanity's successive psychic states are different. "When it comes down to the essentials, Plato and Saint Paul cannot agree, nor convince each other; only convert each other," which is why, he says, that after many years work, he has thrown the sheets of his *magnum opus* to the winds as he crossed Africa. His last words express his bitterness and irony: "there is no better way to understand humanity than to watch an anthill."

The humanism of the Altenburg meeting is utterly swept away by the First World War. The fourth section of the book opens with Vincent Berger on the Russian front, on June 11, 1915, when the Germans launch an experimental gas attack. As Boak was to note, atomic weapons have since overshadowed gas warfare, but when Malraux wrote Les Noyers, it was still the most terrible and deadly weapon of war so far developed and used. Malraux writes magnificently of this horror gas that is so deadly that it kills even vegetation.

Vincent meets Professor Hoffman, the expert on poison gases, a deliberate caricature of the dehumanized scientist, for whom the deaths of enemy soldiers merely represent a successful experiment. Before the attack Vincent is with the soldiers in the trench, for the first time beginning to know ordinary men. "Eavesdropping on this living darkness, my father heard for the first time the German people. Just people—a voice close by in the primitive obscurity, a silhouette barely outlined in the darkness. Soldiers had always had a false rapport with him, the relationship of men with officers who are not their own direct superiors."

The gas attack is so devastating that the German soldiers recoil in horror themselves, as summed up in the scrap of a sentence one of them utters staggering back toward his own lines with a stricken Russian on his back, "Gotta do somethin'." Watching in field glasses, Vincent's full realization of the effect of the gas is shown by the image of a dead tree— dead for years already—which seems the only trace of life. A horse, running wild in no-man's land, its sudden wild neighing contrasting with the prevailing silence as the gas creeps forward and reaches the Russian trenches. The silence is broken by frantic gunfire. The Russians shoot at the gas as they would try to pulverize advancing troops. The shooting stops as suddenly as it started, as Vincent repeats to himself the symptoms Professor Hoffman has enumerated—"the cornea of the eyes turning blue, wheezing effect while breathing and the pupil, and that's very curious, becomes almost black," and repeats to himself the first warning signs of bitter almond taste and wheezing breath. German soldiers, wearing gas masks, advance, get clumsily caught in barbed wire, then disappear into the Russian trenches. Suddenly a man in shirtsleeves and without a mask comes up from the trenches, stumbles forward and falls.

Jumping into the saddle of a horse, Vincent rides toward the trenches and meets the first returning Germans who have dropped their rifles and can only manage to shake their masked heads before the horse caves in under him, throwing him into a bush. When he gets up, the animal is dead. Further on, he sees a German drop the Russian he is carrying as soon as he realizes that the poison has begun to contaminate him. Vincent's next thought is cruelly ironic: "there is only one thing man doesn't get used to, to die." At the same moment, as he helps a Russian, he is himself poisoned.

In the fifth and final section, we are back with young Berger in the POW camp at Chartres, ruminating about *his* war experiences prior to imprisonment—the outbreak of the Second World War, life in the barracks and his only combat experience, a dead-of-night tank offensive against a never-seen enemy. "There is no word to describe the sensation of advancing on the enemy, and yet it is as specific and as powerful as sexual desire or pain," young Berger recalls. "The whole world becomes an undifferentiated menace." Berger and his men are all one in their tank, Pradé the driver watching his dashboard, Léonard the radioman trying to guide them in the night, and Bonneau the gunner glued to his periscope as Berger himself is glued to his viewing slits in the armor plating. What they dread most happens, they fall in a tank trap presumably with an enemy artillery piece pointed at them.

By the flash of an explosion, they see that one of the walls of the ditch is on a slope and with Pradé fixing treetrunks as an emergency beam under the tracks, they manage, "engine racing, the mass of steel churned into the treetrunks," to climb out of the pit. By the time they reach the designated target village, the Germans have evacuated it. In a morning "as pure as if war didn't exist," they stop at a deserted farmhouse and splash cold water on their faces. Berger is struck by the orderliness of the farmyard, wood gathered for the winter, wooden clothespins holding wash not yet dry, "thread-bare stockings, working gloves, blue overalls; in the midst of this desolation, this disaster, the towels bore initials.

> We ourselves, and the Germans facing us, were no longer good for anything but manipulating our murderous pieces of machinery; but the old race of men which we had driven off and which had left behind its tools, its washing and its initialed towels, seems to me to have risen, across the millennia, from the shadows of the night just past—slowly, laden like misers with all the paraphernalia it had now abandoned in our path, the wheelbarrows and harrows, the biblical plows, the dog kennels and rabbit hutches, the empty ovens.

Malraux never wrote the continuation, but transferred the pages on Möllberg, Nietzsche's madness and the tank ditch to the *Antimémoires* and the gas attack on the Russian front to *Lazare*. In a preface to a 1948 edition of *The Walnut Trees,* he wrote that "the continuation of *The Struggle with the Angel* has been destroyed by the Gestapo" and indicated he still hoped to finish the work. Most critics have tended to doubt the story of the Gestapo destroying the manuscript (Boak: "The manuscript may even have survived, since it was the Gestapo's custom to file documents rather than to destroy them, and it seems difficult to know how Malraux—at the time, if his home had been raided, presumably on the run—could have discovered the precise fate of his work." Lacouture: "His departure from 'La Souco' for the Allier *département* and the Chevassons, then for Corrèze at the end of 1942 were not so precipitate that he couldn't have found a secure shelter for manuscripts he must have been attached to.") Instead, they feel that the real reason why he never rewrote or continued *Les Noyers* was the evolution of his basic attitudes and the changing events of the war. "After 1945 his interests—like those of Aldous Huxley slightly earlier—seem to have moved to general ideas." Boak was to reason: "He now evidently began to see himself less as novelist than as philosopher; and he may have found imaginative work less attractive, or perhaps thought that he was unlikely to achieve again such a widely acclaimed success as *La Condition humaine.* In 1948, as we have seen, he appears to have intended continuation of *La Lutte avec*

232

l'ange, but the success of his *Psychologie de l'art* may well have encouraged him to pursue this new line of development and drop *La Lutte.*" Picon, who was close to Malraux during the early war years, was to feel that *Les Noyers* was almost written in the margin of the art books and that Malraux's overriding obsession was to discover the power capable of giving the human adventure a meaning. To Lacouture, *The Walnut Trees of Altenburg* was temple ruins like Banteai Srey, where the author would supply himself with new building blocks. In 1975, Malraux told this writer he had abandoned the second half of the planned *Struggle with the Angel* because he had only begun to write again in 1969 and that, in any case, the essence of what he had wanted to say had passed into the *Antimémoires.*

Volume II of *La Lutte avec l'ange* was not the only book discarded in 1942. With the exception of one chapter appearing in 1946, || *Le Démon de l'absolu,* the essay on Lawrence, was never published. However, the letter to Haas saying the book would be finished in August and that "it is hard to sum it up," seemed to indicate the book was actually written and Picon saw it on Malraux's worktable in Corrèze in early 1943.

With Josette and little Pierre-Gauthier, to whom *The Walnut Trees* was dedicated, André spent part of September 1942 with his childhood friend Louis Chevasson and the latter's wife, Germaine, at Commentry, near Vichy, in Allier *département.* Louis was the caretaker boss of a small instrument manufacturing plant owned by Jews, a legal ploy that avoided German seizure of the little factory. While in Commentry, André met with the British officer heading the Allier section of the so-called Buckmaster network. The meeting with a British underground leader indicated the ease with which Malraux moved underground and the confidence London placed in him.

A month later, Germany put an end to the fiction of two "zones" by occupying Vichy France. German soldiers in the streets of Nice made life "aboveground" precarious for the notorious antifascist, fellow traveler and freedom fighter in Spain and the Malraux household prudently left the Riviera for a Disneyland setting in Gascony where Emmanuel Berl and a good number of people who had little desire to be known to the Gestapo led very discreet lives. A notary public in Saint Chamant, a village on the limits of the Corrèze, Dordogne and Lot *départements,* suggested that Malraux rent the local castle and for the next eighteen months, André and his family lived in this stage operetta château with its medieval tower and French garden surrounded by chestnut, pine, birch and walnut trees overhanging a fairyland tributary to the Dordogne River. The notary public, Frank Delclaux, and his wife, Rosine, became friends

|| "N'était-ce donc que cela?" published in an edition limited to 80 copies by Editions du Pavois, 1946; and in *Liberté de l'Esprit* Magazine (April, May and June, 1949).

—at a time when nothing was more precious than trustworthy friends. Few old acquaintances visited André, Josette and little Gauthier—the "Pierre" part of the hyphenated name had been dropped. Gaetan Picon showed up sometimes as did Berl, who as *Marianne*'s editor back in 1932, had been the unwitting matchmaker of André and Josette.

They saw André's half-brother Roland, who was a resistance fighter in Corrèze, and deputee to a British major. Now aged thirty, the handsome, blue-eyed Roland Malraux, who during his period in Moscow had had a mistress called Princess Galitsin and was still a militant communist, had recently married. His wife was Marie-Madeleine, née Lieux, the daughter of a textile manufacturer in Toulouse. She was a girl of grave beauty and an accomplished pianist who had studied at the Paris Conservatoire. André's other half-brother, Claude, was in the maquis in Le Havre. Now twenty-two, bachelor Claude was a daredevil and a dynamite expert. Together with his group of three hundred men, he had sunk one ship in Le Havre harbor and destroyed a power substation outside Rouen.

Josette loved Saint Chamant and the Black Perigord they lived in— black because of its forests of chestnuts, beeches and elms, as opposed to White Perigord's wheat fields. In November 1943, a second son, Vincent, was born. This time, Josette joined her family in demanding that André marry her. He refused. In 1943, it was even more dangerous to begin divorce proceedings against already victimized Jews. To protect Clara he resisted the formidable pressures of the Clotises who were now convinced the rogue would never marry their daughter.

In March 1944, the arrests, in totally unconnected incidents, of both Claude and Roland brought home to André the rude message of war. Early in the month, Claude had been caught red-handed planting explosives aboard a German ship in the Seine estuary and on March 22, the Gestapo raided the Corrèze maquis headquarters as Roland, the British major and two others were radioing London.

A week later, Picon received a laconic postcard from Malraux saying "I no longer have an address."

234

> And suddenly we all looked at each other, words
> and gesture suspended in midair—in the prison yard,
> women's voices were yelling the *Marseillaise*.
>
> *Antimémoires*

19

In the spring of 1944, the year that saw the turning of the tide for Allied forces everywhere, Black Périgord sheltered an exceptionally high number of partisans of varied political stripes, ranging from Spanish Republicans and communists, to radical saboteur groups, patriotic middle-of-the-road maquisards, right-of-center formations, plain armed bands and, besides the British Special Operations Executive (SOE), the forces of de Gaulle, organized and supplied from London and—as the Allied war machine became increasingly formidable—from "national territory" in Algeria and, finally, France. In all, they were over fifteen thousand maquisards in the R5 resistance zone, the sixteen thousand square miles of arid plateaus gashed with fertile valleys on the western slopes of Auvergne's Massif Central mountains. If they all wanted the defeat of Nazi Germany, their ideas about the future were ideologically light-years apart. The communists, who were the first to fight and who sustained the heaviest losses, wanted if not an outright Marxist regime at least a Popular Front after the war. De Gaulle and his "government in exile" obviously had different visions for the future of France.

Malraux's legend, charisma and authority again made him a natural leader and his first effective intervention in the guerrilla movement was as a healer of factions and as rallying point. Although a latecomer and a "foreigner in Périgord," his liquid ideology and persuasive powers allowed him to move freely among the factions and, as he got to know each, trade on this knowledge and, finally, to impose himself, if not on everybody at least on a good majority of the forty-odd leaders of the R5 operation zone. Always a man with connections, he made contact with the British underground agents and within three months could impress communist cells by organizing British parachute drops of weapons and ammunitions. The nom-de-guerre he chose for himself was "Colonel Berger."

Colonel Malraux, October 1944

Roland Malraux had been a part of the Buckmaster network and André made his first contacts with a "Colonel Jack," who had replaced the British leader picked up by the Germans together with Roland and two others. All four, André learned, had been taken to the Tulle prison. The fate of Claude was probably worse. His capture, weapons and dynamite in hand aboard a German ship, made him a terrorist subject to instant execution. Before imposing himself as an underground leader, André brought Josette, Gauthier and new-born Vincent to Domme, a village near Sarlat in eastern Dordogne. There, André and Josette met up with André's sister-in-law, distraught by Roland's arrest. Madeleine was expecting and André and Josette told her they would stay in contact. They didn't tell her they had learned that Roland had been deported to either Naungamme or Buchenwald concentration camps.

Colonel Berger's self-styled "inter-Allied" headquarters were usually set up in one of Périgord's hundreds of castles. Although he moved often, he was not very secretive and, as one maquis leader was to remember, if anyone asked in the village, "Where's the inter-Allied H.Q.?" any kid would answer, "At the château, Monsieur." Malraux lived practically without armed protection and covered the R5 territory without taking any particular precaution. "Those who met this strange Berger then cannot possibly forget him," Pierre Viansson-Ponté, future political commentator, was to remember. "Sporting an Al Capone fedora or a beret screwed

236

stiffly on the head and lighting one English cigarette with the other (smoking British cigarettes, found at the bottom of parachute containers, was a visible sign of importance in the underground), he soliloquized, jocular and strutting, on his 'buddies,'—'Old Man Churchill' and 'that guy de Gaulle,' finished each talk span with 'Your turn,' an interjection no one should take as an invitation to speak." [1] In mid-April, the maquis leader Antoine Diener first heard of an "inter-Allied officer," who because of his contacts with London could perhaps provide his unit with more arms. When Diener showed up at the Urval castle, he was received by a tall, frosty man in uniform who talked only figures, communications and logistics. Like T. E. Lawrence, Malraux imposed himself by never hesitating to make a decision and by delivering on his promises of arms. A month later, Diener received the visit of Berger, who wanted to know whether Diener's group could protect a parachute drop in the Domme area. Once their official business was taken care of, Berger asked to inspect Diener's men. The maquisards were lined up and while everybody tried to sing the *Marseillaise* in key, a French flag was run up a flagpole. When Diener caught a glimpse of the visiting colonel, he saw him salute the flag with a clenched fist. A reflex from Spain? Retelling the incident to Lacouture twenty-eight years later, Diener still remembered his astonishment at seeing the inter-Allied liaison officer with his London connections give the national anthem the "red" salute.

As it were, the communists were the ones who balked the most at Malraux's attempts at federating all resistance units. Diener and his men belonged to the middle-of-the-road *Armée secrète,* which, if anything, hoped a heavy Anglo-American presence would be a countervailing force to the communists after the Liberation.

Colonel Berger's strategy was to be part of the British-American invasion, now rumored to be imminent. The whole coastline, from Belgium to Spain, was one long German fortification. The "Atlantic Wall," as Nazi propaganda called it, bristled with barbed wire and enormous reinforced concrete structures, built by French forced labor under the direction of German engineers. If these blockhouses were impregnable and beyond the assault capacity of guerrilla forces, their hinterland lifelines were not. The Germans brought practically all their supplies to the Atlantic Wall via railway and railway track was the easiest thing to blow up. "Do you have any arms?" André had insisted since 1941. Now, his first objective was to get weapons—lots of them. Together with Cyril Watney and George Hiller, two British intelligence officers, and—soon to be parachuted in—U.S. Army Lieutenant Richard Atkinson, Malraux pressured London for an intensification of parachute deliveries. But the air-dropped weapons had to be stored in secret places. Fortunately the Dordogne area was honey-

[1] *Le Monde* (Sept. 27, 1967).

combed with ancient caves. It was in the beam of a flashlight that Malraux first saw the prehistoric wall paintings in Lascaux and Les Eyzies. The gigantic aurochs, friezes of swimming stags and figures grouped in anecdotal scenes, had been discovered in 1940.

Colonel Berger's ascent was momentarily challenged by Pierre Jacquot, a vivacious and husky little professional soldier constantly cracking jokes. A former Leftist radical who had held a post in the Defense Department during the Daladier administration, Jacquot soon became a friend and an ally. He liked Malraux's overall plan and Malraux appreciated Jacquot's vivid intelligence and constant flow of suggestions, schemes and ideas.

The Allied landing in Normandy June 6 electrified the resistance movement and, indirectly, strengthened Malraux's hand in the underground power play. The vast Anglo-American armies with their integrated command—under Supreme Allied Commander Dwight D. Eisenhower—gave the expression "inter-Allied headquarters" credence and prestige, and German military reaction to the invasion immediately made the coordination of R5 guerrilla activities imperative. On June 7, Field Marshal Gerd von Rundstedt ordered the crack SS *Das Reich* Division to move up from Toulouse. When the heavily armored division entered the R5 zone at Cahors, the entire resistance movement, now under the overall leadership of a Commandant Collignon, a professional soldier, went into action. Bridges were blown up, railway track torn up and tanks were harassed with that newest and deadliest of Allied weapons—bazookas. At Malraux's request, British liaison chief Cyril Watney radioed London and insisted on air strikes. The German reaction was reprisals against the civilian population, notably the rounding-up and execution of fifteen hundred men, women and children in Tulle and Oradour.

Ten days behind schedule, the *Reich* division reached the Normandy front so disorganized that its use was discarded by Rundstedt and Field Marshal Erwin Rommel in their defense plans for the first crucial battle shaping up around Cherbourg.

On July 14—Bastille Day—two hundred U.S. and Royal Air Force planes relayed each other for six hours dropping supplies in a fifteen-square-mile zone marked off in the middle by all the region's sheets spread out in one enormous Z. Dodging German roadblocks and intersection "hot points," fifteen hundred men and women surrounded the site and carried the supplies to safety as fast as they were dropped. The organizer of this coup—the biggest Allied operation of its kind since British parachute drops in Norway in 1940—was Colonel Berger. Three days later, he called together at his Urval headquarters all the R5 chiefs. If several communist leaders were missing, Collignon was there, with the Armée secrète cadres, with Watney, Hiller, Atkinson and Jacquot.

On July 23, Collignon, Hiller and Malraux inspected a radio transmitter belonging to the Veny network in the Villelongue Forest and met with communist cadres to coordinate future actions. After the meeting, they set off for Cahors, driving in an old Citroen with FFI markings on the side and a French flag painted on the hood. Next to the driver sat two armed maquisards while Collignon, Hiller and Malraux were massed together on the backseat. As they entered the village of Gramat, they encountered a motorized German column. The Germans opened fire and the Citroen careened into a ditch. The driver was killed instantly and the other maquisard was hit in the stomach as they all tried to flee. A second later, Malraux was hit in one leg. As he fell, he was hit in the other leg and passed out. The Germans didn't pursue the others through the field but cut down Hiller in a machine-gun burst. Hiller was to spend eight hours behind a haystack with an open stomach trying to stop the hemorrhaging by stuffing his necktie and two handkerchiefs into the wound. Alerted by Collignon, Watney was to find him after nightfall, in a coma, and bring him to a nearby parsonage where a Cahors surgeon, ordered out of his bed at gunpoint, operated and saved his life.

When André came to, a German officer stood over him ready to begin a first interrogation. Two German soldiers carried him on a stretcher the few hundred yards to Gramat and into a small barn. He was so sure that within hours he would be taken to a ditch and shot he actually told the German NCO that he was André Malraux. Feeling dazed when he tried to stand up, he was taken to a first aid station where a medical officer and orderlies dressed his leg wounds. The road and the town was one long line of German tanks. Later, he was taken to the Kommandantur, set up at Gramat's only hotel. He was questioned twice during the evening and left, under guard, to collapse into feverish sleep. The next morning, the proprietress kneeled in his blood and handed him a cup of ersatz coffee before the Germans changed his bandages. In an armored van, he was moved with the armored column thirty miles to the south. When the column halted in Figeac, he was allowed out. Mutely, an old man handed him a stick to use as a cane. Every French glance told him he was a condemned man, but he realized that he would live until after another interrogation or trial. This transfer had to *mean* something.

The column halted for the night in Villefranche-de-Rouergue, where he recognized the almost Spanish church as the one he and Edouard Corniglion-Molinier had used as a stand-in for Teruel in the footage they had shot in order to complete *L'Espoir*. Under guard, he was put up at a local convent. The mother superior was allowed to bring him his first food in almost three days and left him with a Bible. During the night, he wrote his will on the frontispiece, leaving whatever he had to Josette. He tried to read the Gospel according to St. John, but failed to feel moved.

The next day they continued south. At Albi, the sentry guarding him pulled out two photographs from his pocket—one of Marshal Pétain,

239

the other of de Gaulle. Placing his finger on the one of Pétain, he said, "Very Good!" Then reprovingly, with his finger on the one of de Gaulle, "Terrorist!" A moment later, he pointed to the likeness of de Gaulle, saying, "Tomorrow, maybe very good?" Then on to Pétain, "Perhaps terrorist?" Then he made a gesture that meant, "You never know," shrugged his shoulders and went back to his post.

At Revel, where, leaning on his stick, André was now able to walk a little, he was blindfolded and taken to the local château. While a kind of surreal dance of officers and female auxiliaries of the Occupation forces went on, he was taken to a huge room where, behind a Louis XV desk, a white-haired German major with Iron Cross and dark glasses conducted a rambling interrogation.

The transfer ended in Toulouse, where Malraux was handed over to the Gestapo, and, still wearing the uniform he had been captured in, shoved into a big cell already occupied by a dozen other prisoners. Everybody wanted to hear the latest about the Allied invasion. He, in turn, learned he was in the old Saint Michel prison, a halfway house. Every month, a convoy left for camps in Germany. The oldest inmate had been there months, the newest three weeks. Here, they warned him, new prisoners were taken to the basement at dawn and tortured until they told everything they knew.

Nothing happened the next day or the next. When André was beginning to hope the Gestapo had forgotten about him, he was called out of the cell and led downstairs. His mind raced ahead. What could they want to torture him for? He had been under arrest too long to possess still valid information since his arrest had triggered the automatic reorganization of the command structure. In a guardroom, he saw a haggard woman prisoner try to introduce a spoonful of tea between the teeth of a prisoner whose features had been beaten into pulp. A soldier was making a fantastic din by hammering on a piece of sheet iron with a chain, apparently to drown screams. Suddenly handcuffed, André was led through a hallway where open doors revealed glimpses of two men being battered by booted feet. In spite of the din, he thought he could hear the thud of blows on naked bodies. As he was to retell it in the *Antimémoires,* he was pushed into a room. A man with curly blond hair sitting behind a desk, began:

"Don't give me a lot of stupid answers; Galitsina is working for us now!"

What was he driving at? It could be a good thing that he was on the wrong track. The important thing was to keep a clear head in spite of the atmosphere, the uproar, and the feeling of having only one arm.

"You spent eighteen months in Soviet Russia?"

"I haven't spent more than three months outside France for ten years. That can easily be checked through the passport office."

"You spent a year in our country?"

He was obliged to shout, as I was.

240

As the interrogation about this identity continued, he suddenly realized he was being mistaken for his brother. It was Roland's dossier that the Gestapo headquarters had sent to Toulouse. Roland had lived with a Princess Galitsina, Roland had spent eighteen months in the Soviet Union. Before that, Clara and he had sent Roland to Magdeburg to stay with the Goldschmidts and learn German. But Roland was already in German hands. If the Gestapo had not located the Malraux, André, dossier it was because on his birth certificate he had been registered as Georges André. Since he had more than thirty cousins called Malraux in the Dunkirk region, the Paris Gestapo headquarters obviously had forwarded the dossier of the most notorious of the Malrauxs.

His cellmates were stunned—and suspicious—when he was returned without having been tortured. "Match postponed; they had the wrong dossier," he told them. Through the "wall telephone," the tapping of messages from cell to cell like in *Le Temps du mépris,* neighbors congratulated him and told his cell that the Allies had reached Nantes and Orléans. At night, they heard long, drawn-out rumblings, faint and muffled and wondered whether it was distant artillery or guerrilla sabotage. The next day there were explosions so close and so violent they believed Toulouse was being bombed. Some of the men guessed it was long-range artillery since there was no sound of aircraft, others thought the Germans were blowing up their own ammunition dumps in preparation for a retreat. Suddenly, a guard opened cell doors and shouted, "Everybody below with your belongings." In theory, "with your belongings" meant deportation to Germany.

They were soon five hundred in a big room, each with his shabby bundle, all told to sit on the cement floor—a scene that resembled the school hall in the end of *La Condition humaine* where Kyo, Katov and two hundred others wait to be taken out and shot. Wild rumors spread like wildfire—Germany or summary execution. André thought it was too late for deportation because the resistance had blown up too much railway track and that it wouldn't take many machine guns to kill them all. After three hours, they were herded back to their cells.

No evening meals were served and guards silenced the few prisoners who dared to bang on their doors with a few random shots down the corridors. All night long, they heard troops pass by, followed by the clatter of tanks. Either there was fighting to the north of Toulouse, they theorized, or the Germans were evacuating the town.

> And suddenly we all looked at each other, words and gestures suspended in midair—in the prison yard, women's voices were yelling the *Marseillaise.* It was not the solemn chant of prisoners on their way to the extermination camp; it was the roar that perhaps was heard when the women of Paris marched on Versailles. There could be no doubt about it, the Germans were gone. Had the women found some keys? Men were running in the corridor shouting, "Out, Out!" On the ground floor,

a colossal wooden gong sounded slowly, then developed into a rapid tom-tom. Suddenly we got it. In each cell there was only one piece of furniture—the table, thick and heavy as in all the old prisons. All of us took hold of ours.

Using the table as a ram, they battered and battered the heavy door until it came down—as did the prisoners in all the other cells. The whole prison shook. The first men were already in the prison yard below and storming toward the gate when a parting German tank swung its turret around and fired a machine-gun burst into them before rumbling on. A grisly sight greeted André when he and his cellmates reached the yard. Since his uniform gave him some kind of instant authority, "Colonel Berger" climbed on a packing case, ordered the hundreds of prisoners to form up in lines and located the doctors and orderlies among them. When one of the doctors asked Berger what he and the three other physicians should do with the wounded, all he could say was, "Whatever you like. Move!" Next, he sent men to the towers at the four corners of the prison walls. The women who had been chanting were the wives of prisoners. When they had seen the German soldiers leave Saint Michel, they had run up and found the gate unlocked. One of the men in one of the towers yelled that Paris had been liberated. Nine more German tanks rumbled past the prison, one of them taking a potshot at it.

The news that Paris had been liberated proved to be premature. The Germans retreated from Toulouse—and the prisoners broke out of Saint Michel prison—on August 18. It was only a week later that General Philippe Leclerc's Second Armored Division rolled into Paris, via Porte d'Orléans and down Boulevard Raspail to Montparnasse—that Paris should be liberated by French troops was one concession de Gaulle had extracted from Roosevelt and Churchill in 1943.

If Paris was liberated August 25, André was there on the 28th. So was everybody. After learning of his arrest at Gramat, Josette had gone into hiding. She now rushed to Paris, leaving Gauthier and Vincent with Frank and Rosine Delclaux in Saint Chamant for this first dash through the newly liberated half of France. They ran into each other's arms in André and Clara's old apartment house in the Rue du Bac, where, instinctively, they had thought of looking for each other. Although he was only to find out later, Clara—and Florence, now eleven years old—had also survived.

Malraux dashed over to see Gaston Gallimard, visited "uncle Gide" and, in the newsroom of the newly surfaced Resistance paper, *Combat,* met its editor, Albert Camus. A journalist, Marcel Duhamel, took him to—of all the Spanish Civil War friends and acquaintances—Ernest Hemingway. *Collier's* war correspondent was surrounded by an odd bodyguard of hangers-on and holding court in his room at the Ritz Hotel in the Place Vendôme. The French press delighted in retelling and improving the Hemingway "liberation legend," especially how he had found a group of maquis near Rambouillet and how they had insisted on placing themselves under his command. He had clothed them in uniforms from a dead cavalry reconnaissance outfit and armed them from U.S. division headquarters, taken a village and defended it against fifteen German tanks and fifty-two German cyclists. They had entered Paris via the Port Maillot and L'Étoile and proceeded to liberate the Café de la Paix.

According to Hemingway, he and his maquisards were fieldstripping and cleaning weapons, when his rival from Spain walked in, resplendent in colonel's uniform and with gleaming cavalry boots. Hemingway loved to tell the story, which his biographer Carlos Baker said got better with each passing year. To his "Bonjour, André," Malraux replied by asking how many men Ernest had commanded. Hemingway's answer was typically modest as he went from ten or twelve to "perhaps two hundred." Malraux's thin face contracted in the famous tic as he said, "I commanded two thousand."

Hemingway fixed his guest with his coldest stare as he replied that it was a pity he and his men hadn't had the assistance of Malraux's force when they took "this small town of Paris." André's answer was not on record, but one of Hemingway's partisans beckoned Ernest into the bathroom and asked him whether they should kill this idiot. No, said the author of *For Whom the Bell Tolls,* they should just offer the man a drink and he would leave without bloodshed. So they offered him a drink and went on with their soldierly work, leaving their distinguished visitor, as Baker was to retell it, "to preen, jerk and twitch until he rose to depart. This at any rate, was Ernest's version of the event." [2] Malraux was only to mention Hemingway once in his *Antimémoires*—as an example of a writer who foreshadowed his own fate, beginning as a young man in love with an older woman and ending, after no one knows how many moments of impotence and suicide, as a sixty-year-old lover of a young girl.

But the war was not over. Nazi Germany still held half of France, including Alsace-Lorraine, which, since *The Walnut Trees of Altenburg,* Malraux had made his. For the remainder of the war, this Parisian of Flemish and Italian blood was to become the Lawrence of Arabia of these bleeding borderlands, which through history had alternately been German and French and had always suffered more than other regions.

[2] Carlos Baker, *Ernest Hemingway: A Life Story* (New York: Charles Scribner's Sons, 1969).

Yet Josette, who knew I would be coming from the front and who had asked that her face be made up before my arrival, used the same phrase as my wisest friend, Bernard Groethuysen, who, with terminal cancer, said, "I wouldn't have thought it would be like this, to die . . ."

Lazare

20

Antoine Diener, the partisan leader who had been startled at seeing Colonel Berger salute the tricolore with a clenched fist, was an Alsatian. So were the Catholic priest turned maquisard Pierre Bockel, the doctor Bernard Metz, a Colonel Detinger parachuted into Black Périgord a month earlier, and a lot of others who had met Malraux during his months as self-imposed "inter-Allied" liaison chief in combat zone R5, men with family names like Muller, Fischer, Sigrist, Pleis, Riedinger and Steicher. In early September, Bockel, Metz, Diener and Detinger met at Brive, in Corrèze *département* where they were still located, and kicked around the idea of some sort of autonomist brigade of "landsmen" essentially dedicated to the liberation of their homeland. Bockel had fought in the underground since 1940, first in Lyons and later in and around Toulouse, Dr. Metz had transformed a suburban Lyons clinic into a resistance headquarters and Diener was now the leader of over five hundred compatriots here in Périgord. In all, the four men were the leaders of some fifteen hundred well-trained partisans of Alsace-Lorraine origin.

What they needed, they felt, was someone who could both push the idea of an autonomist military formation with de Gaulle, Leclerc and the military powers that be, and, if the idea was approved, be the supreme commander. Bockel suggested Detinger, but Metz felt they shouldn't only play the ethnic angle but simply find an intelligent and energetic leader with clout. What about Lieutenant-Colonel Pierre Jacquot? But Metz wondered if the former Daladier government cabinet member wasn't too Leftist, too anticlerical. What about Colonel Berger? Diener asked, adding that in his sector Berger, who was really André Malraux and had just been liberated from prison in Toulouse, had been very effective in obtaining both Anglo-American attention and arms. Metz said he loved *L'Espoir* passionately, to which Father Bockel answered that the best Malraux novel

244

was of course *La Condition humaine*. After convincing Detinger to bow out gracefully, they all drove to Jacquot's headquarters at Aubazine, twenty miles from Brive. In half an hour, everything was settled: Malraux-Berger would be the leader and Jacquot the deputy of his Alsatian "brigade"— André loved the word with its echoes of Spain.

The military chief of R5 refused to let Diener's unit leave—their departure would leave the communists in military charge of the region. By chance, the "conspirators," as they called themselves, ran into André Chamson, another literary freedom fighter. Malraux had first met Chamson in 1927 when both were writing for Daniel Halévy's *Cahiers verts*. They had argued art and morals at Pontigny, had shared the dais of the 1935 antifascist congress in Paris and had both attended the 1938 "roving circus" Writers' Convention in Spain. If Chamson was now in Aubazine it was because his arts expertise had made him the maquisard in charge of bringing national museum treasures to safekeeping in secret reserves. In 1939–40, Chamson had been a liaison officer with the staff of General Jean de Lattre de Tassigny, who since the August 15 Allied Seventh Army landing in Provence was the commander of all French forces on this ballooning "second front."

Within ten days, the Alsace-Lorraine Brigade was on its way to Lyons to put itself under de Lattre's command, a move Chamson had organized. The general had expected "a couple of hundred lice-infested brigands" and was flabbergasted to see an army of two thousand men, commanded by a writer, presenting arms. Not that the brigade was particularly martial looking. The three battalions—commanded respectively by Diener, Bockel and a Captain Pleis—had no uniforms, and the men, mostly volunteers "recruited until the liberation of the home territory," were dressed in a nonchalant mix of civilian clothes and scraps of uniforms scavenged from several armies. The commander himself sported his own sartorial defiance, topping his French army officer's uniform with the black Basque beret of the Spanish Republicans.

Colonel Berger was an uncommon commander. He tried to obtain the intelligent participation of the men. He was a chief who treated his subordinates as friends, but seemed timid in the presence of private soldiers. It was not the number of men that mattered, but the stuff they were made of, he said, and he commanded with a combination of reasoned enthusiasm and psychological insight that made more than one observer think of Trotsky organizing the Red Army in 1917. His disciplining was decidedly unmilitary. When a regular officer refused to lead poorly trained newcomers into battle, Malraux refused to court-martial him and instead told Jacquot to take the man to the nearest railway station and send him home. Not all officers had confidence in Malraux and considered him above all a partisan.

Malraux conceived the command of men in war in the spirit of

245

traditional courage and was always in the front line himself. During the Dannemarie offensive, he and an officer set off alone to blow up a bridge. During the same engagement, he answered a general asking for some of his men to neutralize an armored train, "Never mind, I'll go myself." And he did. To Jacquot, who in two months was wounded three times, he one day said he had a feeling he was invulnerable. When a *Combat* correspondent sent out by Albert Camus expressed his surprise at seeing so many officers on the front line, he was told combat founded on moral principles required this. In his discussions with his officers he refused to speculate about France's political future. He had only one objective, he said—to drive the enemy from French territory. In staff conferences, he would generally opt for the most direct, and least orthodox, solution to a problem. The no-politics rule didn't mean he was personally without political ideas, it merely served to unite such politically diverse men as Father Bockel and Jacquot.

Incorporating the brigade into the French Army forced its commander to make one concession to nationalism. With reluctance, Colonel Berger let go several Alsatians who were deserters from the Wehrmacht, a Belgian captain and a few other foreigners. But he refused to see police records of any of his volunteers who included a number of men with questionable pasts (one of the times when Jacquot was taken to a field hospital by a couple of privates, his wristwatch was missing upon his arrival).

The brigade became operational September 22, attached to the First Armored Division and thrown into action on the Moselle front, south of Epinal in the hilly uplands of the Vosges mountains. For the first two weeks, the brigade took very heavy casualties—ironically at the hands of other Alsatians, "Hitler-fanaticized" cadets of the Colmar military academy. The fighting was so heavy that on October 10, the unit was pulled back for a week's rest.

In mid-October, the rains started and, it seemed, never stopped. Also, the closer the Allies drove their enemy toward his own border the harder became his resolve. General George S. Patton's Third Army wormed its way deeper into Lorraine, but the welcoming crowds thinned out and hostility increased. Among the civil population were thousands of die-hard Nazis planted there after 1940 when thirty-five thousand French-speaking citizens had been expelled or deported. Slowly, the war of movement that General Omar Bradley had ushered in after Paris turned into a war of position. All around were signs of enemy-delaying actions to harass the flanks of advancing American and French columns. To the north, a daring British push into Holland proved costly. Patton's steamroller got stuck in the mud around Metz.

In December, the Battle of the Bulge was on; Hitler's major and carefully conceived offensive to avert defeat was a blow to the Allies of unsuspected strength. On December 16, two hundred thousand Germans attacked through the snow with all they had, from specially souped-up tanks to spoiling side attacks, making deep penetration before Eisenhower knew what to make of the situation. The German high command accurately assessed and hit the weakest point on the four-hundred-mile front—the eastern Belgian market town of Bastogne. It was not until mid-January that the Battle of the Bulge was won—at the cost of 176,000 casualties, 76,000 of them on the Allied side—and the push through the snow to the Rhine was resumed.

In early November, the Alsace-Lorraine brigade was moved to the southern flank of the bulge and thrown into the battle for Altkirch, the southernmost Alsatian town of any importance, situated less than twelve miles from the border of neutral Switzerland and twenty miles from the Rhine and Germany. Attached to the Fifth Armored Division, the brigade played the ungrateful role of infantry support and again suffered brutal casualties. When it took Altkirch on November 11, Malraux received the cruelest of news.

Back in Saint Chamant, where Josette and the infant boys were waiting out the end of the war and André's return, she had put her visiting mother's luggage aboard the local train and, with her friend Rosine Delclaux, stayed with her mother until the little train began to pull out. As she hopped down, she was hampered by the thick-soled wartime shoes and fell between two cars. Because Winston Churchill was visiting the Alsace front communications were improved and Malraux received the telegram almost immediately. Josette had been transported to a hospital in Tulle where she died ten hours later, horribly mutilated but lucid to the end. André reached Tulle the following evening.

Too numb to feel the pain, he mechanically went through the motions of arranging for the funeral of the mother of his sons he had never married, and to have the Delclauxs care for four-year-old Gauthier and one-year-old Vincent. His very pregnant sister-in-law Madeleine joined him. They left together for Paris to seek news of Roland. At the Hotel Lutetia, requisitioned by the army to serve as a receiving center for homecoming deportees and clearinghouse for information about them, they were told that Roland had died. That evening, Malraux drifted over to Gide. Gide was not home, but his oldest friend, Mme. Théo van Rysselberghe, and her daughter Elisabeth were there. Together they ate a gloomy dinner. Talking about war's end, Malraux foretold that Berlin would become another Stalingrad, reduced to ruins, that Hitler would launch any number of desperate counteroffensives and finally commit suicide. Before returning to the front, he visited the editorial offices of *Combat*. A photo of him, Camus and his old surrealist friend Pascal Pia snapped in the newsroom showed him ravaged and devastated. Much later, he was to write that only mature men who have lost young wives could understand.

The war soothed him. Father Bockel, who knew André was an

agnostic yet said his passionate love of men and liberty revealed new depths of faith in those who believed, respected his silence. So did others. When Roger Stéphane spent several hours questioning and listening to Malraux in early February, he only heard one fleeting allusion to Josette's death.

The brigade had some of its heaviest fighting ahead of it. As General Leclerc's Second Armored Division liberated Strasbourg November 23, the brigade suffered fifty dead in less than two hours of combat near Dannemarie, seventy miles to the south. In biting cold, the brigade approached Dannemarie, but took seven days to advance seven miles. The town was defended by an armored train. Diener was wounded, but on the morning of the 28th, the train was gone. In early December, Malraux was in Strasbourg, bringing with him from the Haut-Koeningsburg caves Grünewald's celebrated Isenheim Altarpiece, one of Alsace's most famous art treasures and of all medieval art the work André admired most. He attended the rededication of the Strasbourg Cathedral and wrote to Rosine Delclaux that the music played to celebrate the brigade's entry into a village seemed to have been written for Josette.

But on Christmas Day, von Rundstedt launched the Ardennes counteroffensive and by New Year's Day, 1945, the German impact had been stunning. Crack armored and infantry divisions drove forward behind massive artillery barrages, paratroops landed behind U.S. lines and resurgent Luftwaffe bombers and fighters supported the ground attack. East of Malmédy, the Germans overran the U.S. positions, advancing five miles into Belgium. On January 5, the enemy pressure was still growing along the Rhine front below Strasbourg where the Germans held Colmar. Supreme Commander Eisenhower wanted to shorten the front by abandoning Strasbourg, a strategically defensible solution but one that most Frenchmen found unacceptable. De Gaulle summoned Churchill to change Eisenhower's mind and without waiting for a decision ordered Leclerc to defend the city. Most Strasbourgeois feared that atrocious reprisals would occur should the swastika, as attacking General von Maur said it would, again fly over City Hall. For the Alsace-Lorraine Brigade its finest hour was at hand.

Between the First Free French Division and the Seventh U.S. Army, the brigade was ordered to hold a ten-mile stretch of front running from suburban Plobsheim to the near-frozen Rhine. During the night of January 3, when an American regiment was ordered back, the brigade spread itself thinner to defend this stretch also, inheriting several artillery pieces and antitank mortars from the departing GIs. Malraux ordered his men to hold until all ammunition was exhausted, then to fall back into Strasbourg, "where we will fight, street by street and house by house." [1] Streetcars had been overturned and filled with cobblestones to help stop the dreaded new

[1] Pierre Galante, *Malraux,* op. cit.

248

Alsace-Lorraine Brigade commander, January 1945

German Tiger tanks if the fallback became necessary. On January 7, the German counteroffensive units reached Erstein, twenty miles south of Strasbourg, and the Tigers began to appear. On the 8th, the enemy pressure continued unabated as the brigade began to run out of ammunition. On the 9th, when the temperature dipped to −4° F, one of the brigade's three battalions was cut off on a small island between the so-called Old Rhine and the main river. Two volunteers stripped, broke the ice and swam across to the islet to make contact with their comrades, then vanished to reappear some hours later at Jacquot's headquarters in a farmhouse. Their feet were frostbitten and they were more dead than alive but they still carried their weapons. At one time Malraux thought of making a film about the brigade and one of the most important scenes would have shown the frozen and naked men making their way across the river. To escape, nearly a thousand men, bundled up like Genghis Khan's men fighting on the frozen Yangtse River, finally crossed the inlet where the iceflows were the thickest.

By the end of January, American divisions hammered the Bastogne bulge flat again and along a forty-mile front resumed the forward thrust toward the Siegfried Line and Germany's border. At the same time, the German pressure on Strasbourg eased up and Malraux made a dash to Paris.

Irresistibly, he was sucked into politics and into the groundwork being laid for the first elections. On January 27, he broke with the communists before two thousand delegates attending the founding convention of the short-lived *Mouvement de Libération national* (MLN). Three days later before returning to the front, he met for the first time with the provisional chief of state, Charles de Gaulle.

Theoretically, the creation in 1943 of the National Resistance Council had brought all partisans and maquis organizations under de Gaulle's authority. Until 1944, de Gaulle had had only enemies to the Right, the Vichyizing *grande bourgeoisie* which had largely ignored his Siren calls from London for armed uprising and open revolt. With the Liberation of Paris, however, his support shifted imperceptibly back toward the right-of-center, toward that majority of Frenchmen who expected him to safeguard French society. For them, this career soldier with his general's stars, his "little nobility" ancestry, his taste for authority and sometimes haughty opportunism, began to emerge as the savior, as the law-and-order man who, once the enemy was driven from the national territory, would know how to disarm the millions of communists and fellow-traveling maquisards. In January 1945, the general had not yet made up his mind but was weighing his options. He realized that despite his glory and his constant appeals for "national unity," his political power base rested on delicate compromises. He also realized that an era was drawing to a close and that his forty million countrymen were looking toward the future.

250

The MLN convention in the old Mutualité Hall was closely watched by everybody trying to read the political tea leaves of the immediate post-war future. The MLN, which had asked Malraux to join its executive committee, was an umbrella organization of some one million noncommunist but generally Left-leaning partisans. The principal members were anticapitalists out of indifference to money and out of contempt for Vichy and for everything that reminded them of prewar politics and politicians. They were also anticommunists, but their hostility, as Malraux noticed, was not so much toward Marxism as toward Stalinism. But the communists, who had fought hardest and suffered heaviest in the four-year resistance against Nazi Germany, wanted *their* slice of the postwar pie. The French Communist Party was determined to gain control over all resistance organizations and at the MLN convention lobbied secretly and aboveboard for a merger with the Front National, the other major council of resistance groups firmly controlled by communists but also comprising such "reassuring" personalities as Catholic François Mauriac.

Two tendencies immediately became apparent at the convention. A number of leaders wanted to realize the old dream of a French labor party. Others sought to bring de Gaulle onto their side through a broad-based middle-of-the-road alliance, while still others like François Mitterand, who thirty years later was to lead a socialist coalition to within a hair's breath of victory over de Gaulle's heirs, were keeping their options open. All theses at the convention were discussed intelligently in *Combat,* the main resistance newspaper and now a Parisian daily, and commented upon in Camus' unsigned editorials.

On the third day, Malraux strode to the speaker's podium, where he had defended Thälmann, Dimitrov and so many other communists, and in a somewhat cryptic speech tipped the scales against the communist merger proposal.

As the Red Army captured Breslau—which, in eastern Europe's New Order, was soon to become Wroclaw—Malraux paid tribute to the communists with whom he had traveled so long, but told his audience that a new Resistance was in store. Dressed in his self-styled colonel's uniform and brushing the familiar lock from his "pale" face (as *Combat*'s reporter noted), he called the MLN assizes a vulnerable conscience of France, quoted Hitler's phrase that "when weaponless men want to fight, weapons grow out of their hands," demanded nationalization of credit but asked that the MLN back the provisional de Gaulle government until the end of the war. He said France needed the deepest of reforms and urged the delegates to learn from the communists how to maintain their energies mobilized during difficult times. Saying he felt most of his fellow delegates seemed to be against the merger proposal, he pleaded for action. "We either don't want to act in which case we negotiate, meaning that we add new cadavers to old ones, or we seriously want to do something. If so, we must tell ourselves without illusion that a new Resistance is shaping up. And I must tell those of you who began the first Resistance empty-handedly, you can do it again, now that you have everything in your grip." [2]

Although he didn't clarify what he meant by a "new Resistance," the speech was applauded and, by a 250–119 vote, a "Malraux motion" was carried, effectively blocking a merger with the Front National. Did Malraux call for a resistance against the communists? Most delegates understood it that way and communist commentators wondered whether the author of *L'Espoir* had in mind to create a new party which might start as "neosocialist" and end up neofascist by provoking demagoguery and anarchy so as to bring about the "rule of the savior—dictatorship." [3]

The meeting with de Gaulle took place at the grimy old Defense Ministry building on Boulevard St. Germain. It had been arranged by Edouard Corniglion-Molinier, André's flyboy friend and former movie producer who was now a general; Gaston Palewski, a former ambassador and intimate of the general's entourage; and by Captain Claude Guy, a friend of Malraux's who was acting as aide-de-camp to de Gaulle. On Guy's agenda, Malraux was down for a ten- to fifteen-minute interview. It lasted an hour and a half and on the way home afterward, de Gaulle suddenly turned to Guy, sitting beside him in his limousine, and announced, "He's great, your Malraux!" [4]

"First of all the past," de Gaulle began, forcing the momentarily surprised Malraux to give a résumé of his own life, which led to his summing up of the MLN convention and to de Gaulle interjecting that France no longer wanted revolution.

Malraux was struck by de Gaulle's neutral tone—"he might have been talking about the Roman Empire," he was to note in the *Antimémoires*—and realized how trifling the supreme values of others, even of those who were not his opponents, seemed to the general. De Gaulle told him credit, railways, light and power would be nationalized before the end of the year, "not for the sake of the Left but for the sake of France," and asked what the feeling was among intellectuals.

Malraux was fascinated. As he walked along Boulevard St. Germain, he tried to analyze what it was that had impressed him. He had known de Gaulle from newsreels where the general always spoke. Here, he had been face to face with a man who asked questions and whose strength was in his silence and in a certain remoteness. De Gaulle established with the person he was talking to a very powerful contact which afterward seemed inexplicable and his silence, Malraux felt, was an interrogation. In exploratory talks with Palewski, Malraux had said he had no desire to run for public office and that the only expertise he could offer was a pet project—to use audiovisuals to teach, to have famous poets

[2] *Combat* (Jan. 28, 1945).
[3] Pierre Hervé, *Action* (Jan. 28, 1945 and Feb. 16, 1945).
[4] Pierre Galante, op. cit.

252

broadcast lessons on poetry and to replace geography lectures with geo-graphic films. But de Gaulle had not asked anything of him and their talk had not touched modernization of education. Instead, Malraux felt he had given an account of himself to someone who had seemed preoccupied with a destiny for France that he had not yet discovered or asserted. "I was trying to get to the bottom of a complex impression—the man lived up to his myth, but *in what sense?"*

As he went to Alsace and his men, now in Illkirch ten miles south of Strasbourg, Malraux suffered pangs of guilt for having turned against his former allies. He had told de Gaulle he felt the essential lesson of the past twenty years had been the primacy of the nation-state, including the Soviet fatherland, and paraphrasing Clausewitz he had warned the general that for the communists, politics was a continuation of war by other means. "But on my way back to the front through the snow-covered countryside of Champagne, I thought of my communist comrades in Spain," he was to write in the *Antimémoires,* "of the epic of the Soviet achievement in spite of the secret police; of the Red Army, and of the communist farmers of Corrèze, always ready to help us in spite of the Vichy *milice* on behalf of this Party which no longer seemed to believe in any other victories than those won by stealth."

The brigade pushed south toward Sainte-Odile on the Vosges heights with its abbey—where Malraux had placed his fictitious Altenburg —and toward Colmar with its Maginot Line-stronghold still in enemy hands. The brigade's fame grew in strange leaps and bounds. One day a jeep rolled up with Alsatian-born U.S. Air Force major and Hollywood filmmaker William Wyler and, as his chauffeur, Leicester Hemingway, Ernest's kid brother. The trilingual native of Mulhouse had heard about the Malraux brigade in Luxembourg at General Bradley's headquarters. Now making air force documentaries, the director of *Mrs. Miniver* was impressed by the novelist-commander and his wild bunch, all dressed dif-ferently, who had one tank and all loved their Colonel Berger.

"Malraux got his supplies from the Americans and the French Army, but he would have nothing to do with either of them," Wyler was to recall. "He ran his own war. He took me to several of his posts and together we crept to the edge of the Rhine and looked across at the Ger-mans on the other side. There was a fierce loyalty to him wherever we went; all these fellows with old-fashioned rifles and that one tank showed they loved him." [5] Major Wyler had earlier met Ernest Hemingway and his party and heard the story of how he had tried to get General Patton to give him explosives to mine a road no Germans traveled and how he shot heads off chickens and had French villagers make chicken fricassee. Like Hemingway but in a different way, Wyler felt, Malraux loved war. Before Wyler tooled off again in his jeep toward his hometown, whose liberation

[5] Axel Madsen, *William Wyler* (New York: T. Y. Crowell, 1973).

253

he wanted to be part of, he and Malraux talked about movies. André said he was very interested in making a documentary about the war and made Wyler promise they would meet again after the war. They never did.

Roger Stéphane arrived February 3 and stayed several days. Malraux talked for seven hours, answering all questions and giving the twenty-five-year-old journalist a detailed exposition of his moral, political and intellectual ideas. Stéphane wrote everything down and ten years later published a thirty-page account of Malraux in the snows of Alsace three months before war's end.[6] Stéphane had read Malraux's speech at the MLN congress and began with politics. Malraux told him he had been offered the presidency of the Mouvement. "So what?" the journalist asked with youthful impertinence. "So what? I don't know, but I want to do something concrete. Don't talk to me about workers' soviets in France which Frenchmen are incapable of making happen or only in a thousand years. Maybe it's impossible to conduct a war and a revolution at the same time. Since it is out of the question to adapt Russian-style socialism, we can try Anglo-Saxon laborism." When Stéphane wondered whether deportees returning from the camps wouldn't give France both a sense of direction and a taste for revolution, Malraux said liberated prisoners would be more than happy just to find their wives and their bicycles again.

Malraux changed the conversation by asking his visitor what he thought of the brigade. Stéphane refused to judge anybody but admitted a meal eaten with the officers had been a bore. "With the exception of your family, with whom can you eat ten consecutive meals without being bored?" was the answer. After listening to a newscast with Jacquot and dining with the general staff, where Malraux spent his sarcasm on the quality of the food and the absence of wine, Stéphane expressed his fears that Malraux was drifting toward fascism and quoted from L'Espoir: "A man who is both an activist and a pessimist is or will be a fascist, except when he has loyalty behind him." "I've got loyalty behind me," Malraux answered curtly. "My fidelity is to blowing things up." When the subject came up again, Malraux said more seriously, "I know I won't be a fascist because I know who I am and that's enough." When they were alone again, Stéphane brought up the real reason for his visit—he would like to write a book about T. E. Lawrence, E. von Solomon, Alberto Moravia and Malraux, four writer-adventurers, each both a product of and in conflict with his nation's identity, its beliefs and aspirations.[7] Malraux immediately launched into a heady analysis of Lawrence of Arabia, talking about his book on Lawrence and saying that what made Lawrence remarkable was his zest, his lucidity, ingenious mind and precise knowledge of what he was

---

[6] Roger Stéphane, *Fin d'une jeunesse* (Paris: Table Ronde, 1954).
[7] Dropping Moravia, Stéphane five years later published his essay: *Portrait de l'Aventurier, Essai sur T. E. Lawrence, A. Malraux et E. von Solomon,* preface by Jean-Paul Sartre (Paris: Sagittaire, 1950).

254

talking about. He said he didn't subscribe to the theory of Lawrence's homo-sexuality, claiming instead that Lawrence had been impotent although he had lived in the only two milieus where homosexuality was tolerated—the colonies and the British aristocracy. Lawrence was born out of wedlock and his mother ended her life as a deaconess. He died on the way to the post office to send a telegram in which he agreed to meet Hitler—details that Stéphane in his research was never able to confirm or deny.[8] When Stéphane talked about the renunciation and disavowals of Lawrence's last years, Malraux said, "He had the choice between that and suicide—they had offered him to become viceroy of India or governor of Egypt. He couldn't accept to become part of an administration he hated and he didn't want to deceive the Arabs any longer." When Stéphane said he found it curious how some men wanted to plunge into certainties and evoked a friend who, paradoxically, hesitated between conversion to Catholicism and adherence to the communist party, Malraux said, "It's the same thing, the same will to renounce combined with a desire for justice and a desire to be of help to others." Lawrence's admiration for Bernard Shaw, Malraux felt, was because he thought masterpieces were written with formulas. "He didn't know that you only discover that after the fact."

The next day after lunch when a private played Beethoven on a piano in a hallway, Malraux leaned toward Stéphane and asked him what he believed was a work of art. When Stéphane said it was a mix of beauty and harmony, Malraux said, "Not necessarily. If art is only beauty, then Goya isn't an artist. There is something to be said on ugliness in art," in-timating that he would say it himself in *La Psychologie de l'art*.

In mid-February, the Brigade took part in what turned out to be its easiest campaign—the capture of Colmar. Instead of continuing south to Mulhouse for mop-up operations, it was ordered east into Germany. If the Americans crossed the Rhine at Remagen, Malraux's men crossed on the Kraft Bridge at Strasbourg and after action in Baden in March con-tinued to Wurtemberg. In April—as the Allies occupied most of southern Germany—the Brigade ended its active campaign at Stuttgart. On May 5, Hitler committed suicide in his Berlin bunker and two days later the Wehrmacht capitulated.

Malraux was in Stuttgart when General de Lattre pinned decora-tions on him and his comrades, but since February he had left the actual command to Jacquot. Shortly after his meeting with de Gaulle, he had been asked to join the general's staff.

---

[8] The telegram to his friend Henry Williamson, postmarked May 13, 1935, read LUNCH THURSDAY MEET FINE COTTAGE ONE MILE NORTH BOV-INGTON CAMP. *The Essential T. E. Lawrence,* selected with a preface by David Garnett (New York: The Viking Press, 1964).

One of Napoleon's phrases which has always
disturbed me because it is magnificent and
incomprehensible, is: "I make my plans with the dreams of
my sleeping soldiers."

Felled Oaks

21

Yes, General Charles de Gaulle told the fuming and frustrated
Consultative Assembly in March 1945, he would gladly confer with them
about his ministers. When seventy leaders of the advisory parliament met
with him, he listened politely. He had heard their complaints before—his
Justice Minister didn't prosecute collaborators vigorously enough, his Food
Minister was too slow in allaying hunger. Then he replied: "You are not
elected and neither am I. So we must do our best and just try to get along
until popular elections have decided for all of us. Until universal suffrage
will be functioning, I, alone, am responsible before the country."

The "I, alone" was deceiving. In April, as street lights gleamed
along the Champs-Élysées for the first time in five years and more than
two million Parisians marveled again at their City of Light, de Gaulle ran
head-on into his first political roadblock. With his provisional government,
he tried to come to grips with the nation's economic problem—the disastrous gap between productivity (a third of the 1938 output) and the ocean
of money the Occupier had kept printing. In provisional finance commissioner Pierre Mendès-France, de Gaulle found someone energetic enough
to propose the experiment successfully carried out in Tunisia and Belgium
—the authoritarian reduction of money through an exchange of bank notes.
But others urged the general not to attempt such radical surgery. They
argued that this was not the moment to inflict such a brutal cure on people
who had already suffered enough and that inflation, in any case, would
stimulate economic reconstruction. Socialists and communists surprised
him by also backing less brutal solutions, stressing that a wage and farm
product freeze, which was part of Mendès-France's plan, would be very
unpopular. De Gaulle wavered. Mendès-France resigned, to be replaced
by René Pleven, and the slide back into prewar politics was beginning.

Whether de Gaulle liked it or not, he headed a Leftist caretaker

256

administration, whose Leftist majority accurately reflected popular sentiments. The National Resistance Council's economic program demanded a heavy participation of the State in rebuilding the country, but Leftist "planification" didn't scare the Right as much as many politicians thought. If anything, astute business leaders realized that planification meant the State would pick up a large part of the tab for reconstruction, even in the private sector.

It was not so much nationalization of credit, railways and energy as the specter of left-wing purges that left the *grande bourgeoisie* uncomfortable. While popular wit gave a new definition to a collaborator—"anybody who collaborated more than you did"—de Gaulle was faced with popular impulses that threatened to overwhelm him. By nature he favored the respect for the law—even recently enacted laws—as the only means of stemming popular wrath and he felt justice had to be an integral part of a reconstructed society. To prevent popular vengeance, he believed the justice of the State had to be severe. In July, the treason trial of Marshal Henri Philippe Pétain began and in August, hard-pressed Generalissimo Franco handed over Pierre Laval, who had fled to Barcelona. De Gaulle commuted eighty-nine-year-old Pétain's death sentence to life imprisonment but let Laval face the firing squad in Fresnes prison outside Paris, the way-station for so many Frenchmen to the death camps of Germany. Yet thousands of Frenchmen who had been guilty of what de Gaulle himself called the most odious of crimes—informing on patriots—went free.

De Gaulle was more successful in imposing his country's authority among its towering allies, but in the far-flung corners of the Empire long fuses were lit. If a trip to Moscow in November 1944 hadn't earned him an invitation to Yalta, he managed to convince Churchill to convince the dying Roosevelt and Stalin to let France become one of the Big Four occupiers of Germany and a Security Council member of the United Nations, chartered to safeguard international security. Although he brushed off an invitation to meet Roosevelt in Algiers on the U.S. president's return from Russia in order not to seem to ratify the Big Three's Yalta decisions, de Gaulle managed to have Leclerc aboard the S.S. *Missouri* to countersign Japan's capitulation. But in Algiers, a VE-Day celebration turned into an ugly riot just as hideously repressed, and in Indochina, where Japanese forces had eliminated all traces of French authority in 1942, the returning French administration and *colons* paid little attention to promises from Paris of a future autonomy status and little was done to prevent anti-French riots that exploded in Hanoi in August and in Saigon a month later. Nor did anyone pay much attention when from the balcony of the Hanoi Municipal Theater a former schoolteacher who called himself Ho Chi Minh proclaimed an independent Vietnam on September 2.

But de Gaulle's biggest battle was the new Constitution. Pétain and Laval had abolished the Third Republic—the First Republic of 1792 had

257

lasted until Napoleon had made himself emperor in 1804; the Second Republic of 1848 had ended with the reestablishment of monarchy in 1852 and the Third Republic had lasted from 1870 to 1940. The communists wanted a Fourth Republic governed by the masses through the direct election of an Assembly that would both write the new constitution and sit as a first parliament. The socialists and the radicals—despite the name the latter were the French equivalent of the Social-Democrats emerging in Italian and German postwar politics—wanted to revive the parliamentary system of the Third Republic by readapting the 1875 Constitution, while de Gaulle, with the reluctant support of the Right and "his" party, the *Mouvement républicain populaire* (MRP), the democratic-catholic party which grew out of the Resistance, proposed a constitution with a strong executive branch. From the politicians, he obtained the promise that a popular referendum would decide. On October 21, twenty-four million Frenchmen and Frenchwomen trooped to their first free election since 1936 and chose a Constituent Assembly, ordered it to frame the new Constitution and approved a strong executive interim government. The vote gave a solid mandate to middle-of-the-road socialism. It witnessed a triumph of prewar tripartism, with the communist, socialists and the MRP the winners, but also saw the collapse of such prewar formations as Edouard Herriot's Radical Socialist party. Although the Communist Party polled the most votes, the socialists and MRP together received sixty percent of the ballots cast. By voting for a strong interim executive, the electorate showed its support for Provisional President de Gaulle.

The election was a qualified victory for de Gaulle and on November 13 the new National Assembly voted unanimously to make him head of state, eliminating the "provisional" of the title. The communists voted with the others. Despite right-wing opposition, de Gaulle had allowed Party secretary-general Maurice Thorez to return from wartime exile in Moscow and the communists had accepted the dissolution of their paramilitary "liberation committees." Since as a party they had polled the most votes, they wanted to name their own people in the key posts of Foreign Affairs, Interior and Defense. De Gaulle refused but offered them three lesser cabinet posts. When Thorez accused him of desecrating "the memory of seventy-five thousand communists who had died for France and freedom," de Gaulle took to the airwaves and told a national radio audience he didn't believe he could confide to communists "many of the levers that control foreign policy—the diplomacy that expresses it, the army that sustains it and the police that protects it." A week later, a tense Assembly met in an atmosphere made tenser by the presence of heavily armed guards, voted down the communists, 400–163, and directed de Gaulle to continue his efforts to form a coalition government. The general got his way, kept the three ministries out of the communist hands and instead gave them three lesser departments—Labor, National Economy and Industrial Production

258

and named Thorez Assembly speaker. André Malraux became Minister of Information, at forty-four the youngest member of the cabinet.

Fascinated but not captivated. To the general's "He's great, your Malraux," the author of *Man's Fate* in November told Claude Mauriac, his new colleague (and son of *Le Figaro* commentator François Mauriac), that de Gaulle was a "prodigious thinker, unshakeable like rock, fascinated by principles and therefore invulnerable in a world without principles." The general's asset, he felt, was the extraordinary care with which he rebuilt the top levels of government, while his drawbacks were his fascination with the Rhine, "an obsolete exigency," and his ignorance of little people. "What a weakness never to have broken bread with a worker!" [1] Becoming a minister of de Gaulle and, later, in the general's self-imposed exile, the friend of a man not given to close friendships, was both challenge and logical consequence of maturity and changing times. "Adventure only exists now at the level of governments," he told Nino Frank, who came to see him during the summer.[2] To be a minister was in itself a considerable adventure, Father Bockel observed when interviewed about the new Secretary of Information. "In the life of a man like him there is a time for nomadic adventure and a time for sedentary adventure, a time for the barricades and a time for the memoirs, a time for tearing down and a time for building." [3]

De Gaulle welcomed him. If the general didn't appreciate Malraux as a writer as much as Georges Bernanos or Paul Claudel, he was sensitive to an international fame that rivaled the reputation of his elders, Gide and Claudel. He recognized that in the person of Malraux he was associating himself with the most brilliant and generous features of the intellectual Left. He liked in Malraux the man of action and the resistance figure. Their affinities were deep. They both believed in grandeur, in a kind of fatality and a tragic view of man. They both read history the same way and wanted to re-create new postwar structures. They were both devotees of the rostrum, a certain theatrical pathos and believed in marks of destiny. Both were realists with a penchant for transcendence.

Revisionist historians were later to charge that what brought them together was anticommunism. But in the fall of 1945, de Gaulle was not yet—like Churchill and Harry S. Truman—convinced of the inevitability of World War III, and Malraux was not yet—like Arthur Koestler—reminding people that history's most formidable war machine, the Red Army, was less than a hundred and seventy miles from Strasbourg. (When André was later to warn Gaullist rallies of the proximity of the Russians in their East Germany occupation zone, he would say, "the Cossacks are two Tour de France bicycle racing laps away."). In 1945, de Gaulle headed the most

---

[1] Claude Mauriac, *Un autre de Gaulle* (Paris: Hachette, 1970).
[2] Nino Frank, *Mémoire brisée*, op. cit.
[3] Pierre Galante, *Malraux*, op. cit.

Leftist government France had ever known since the communists were in the administration. Thorez sat in on cabinet meetings and Party members were ministers of Labor, Productivity and National Economy. The first legislation was the enactment of the Resistance movement platform—nationalization of the railways, natural gas and electricity and partial state-control of credit—measures that went far beyond anything Léon Blum's prewar Front populaire had dared dream of. De Gaulle disliked the communists' "double allegiance" and in discussions with Thorez tried to convince him to put a certain distance between the *Parti communiste français* and Moscow, but did not believe in a communist putsch or even a general strike leading to a new insurrection. De Gaulle did not yet find communists despicable, only exotic and perhaps anachronistic. Malraux, who at the height of his flirtation with Stalin was a friend of Trotsky (and in Moscow in 1934 had dared to propose a toast to Leon Davidovich), admired Stalin's Machiavellian rule. Yet, he also felt the new European order would change communism and that Russia's might would inevitably make the USSR into an imperialistic superpower.

Malraux had expected a more important cabinet post—Foreign Affairs, apparently—but as Minister of Information energetically set out to make *his* reforms. He was full of ideas—*maisons de culture* in every major town in France so as to decentralize culture, mass education through radio and cinema which would make it possible to have the best minds in every field teach in all colleges at the same time. Education, he soon discovered, did not fall under his jurisdiction. But dissemination of culture did, he decided. One of his first ministerial decisions was to order art into every schoolroom and, possibly, every factory lunchroom. What art? He ordered full-size and full-color reproductions made of four of the Louvre's glories —Renoir's *Le Moulin de la Gallette,* the Avignon *Pietà* by an unknown fifteenth-century artist, Watteau's last important work, *L'Enseigne de Gersaint,* which André had admired as an eight-year-old, and Cézanne's *Château noir.* Full-sized color reproductions were unusual—and expensive —in 1945, but Malraux cleverly defended his department budget in cabinet meetings and in the Assembly.

He also surrounded himself with able people. His undersecretary was Jacques Chaban-Delmas, a young maquis general of Christian-Democrat leanings, and first secretary was Raymond Aron, whom he had met in Pontigny back in the late 1920s and who had become a philosophy professor and had spent the war years in London. Malraux also kept a high profile in the cabinet, taking an active part in the "morning sessions" where the ministers prepared the general's work. Although the "subversive" of these meetings, according to Gaston Palewsky, was a schoolteacher named Georges Pompidou, Malraux didn't stick exclusively to cultural affairs, but entered political debates with passion.

He also received important foreign journalists for both on-the-rec-

260

ord interviews and "backgrounders." Cyrus Sulzberger, the head of *The New York Times'* foreign service, was one such roving correspondent and intimate of statesmen, diplomats, generals and presidents who met de Gaulle's Minister of Information on January 7, 1946, and who was fascinated and came back for more. Sulzberger jotted down his impressions and the essence of his interviews as soon as he had left his VIP subjects and in 1969 published his diaries under the title *A Long Row of Candles.* He was on his way to Moscow when he first met Malraux and afterward wrote in his staccato style:

He was extremely nervous and rather dissipated looking: very thin, with dark shadows under his eyes and a long nose and face. He smokes American cigarettes constantly and refuses to sit down, walking about all the time. He said he had no time to write these days. He is very assertive and sure of his opinions. He told me he knew Tito in Spain. . . . Malraux said all political parties in France were extremely weak which was a sign of feeble conditions in France these days. The strength of the communists was greatly exaggerated . . . thinks the communists do not wish to really get power in France. He does not foresee any communist effort at an armed coup. What the communists want is to gain control of the Assembly and subject the administrative and executive powers of the President to the orders of the Assembly. If the president refuses to carry this out, they will withdraw their support. De Gaulle wants an American-type democracy and more executive power for the president. Malraux expects a very serious crisis long before May when the Constitution will be completed. He does not know whether de Gaulle will resign and form his own party or not. He says it is possible but not probable. Not even de Gaulle knows yet what he will do.[4]

Malraux's assessment was both candid and accurate but less than two weeks later, de Gaulle pulled a fast one on everybody. On Sunday, January 20, 1946, he summoned the members of the government to meet him at the Defense department at high noon. Wearing his general's uniform, he entered the Hall of Arms at the stroke of twelve and in measured tones told them:

Party politics has reappeared. I disapprove of it. But short of establishing by force a dictatorship I do not want and which no doubt will turn out badly, I do not have the means to prevent this experience. It is therefore necessary for me to withdraw. This decision is irrevocable and takes effect immediately. If you fail at least I will remain intact. I thank each of you for the collaboration you have given me in these historic times. I consider my mission ended.[5]

He rose, shook hands with each of his ministers in turn, strode out

[4] Cyrus L. Sulzberger, *A Long Row of Candles: Memoirs and Diaries, 1934–1954* (New York: Macmillan, 1969).

[5] Charles de Gaulle, *Mémoirs d'espoir* (Paris: Plon, 1970).

261

of the room and had his chauffeur drive him and Yvonne de Gaulle to their newly purchased country home in Colombey-les-deux-Églises in the Haute Marne *département* a hundred and fifty miles east of Paris.

The resignation, with its high-drama theatricality, was a ploy—and a gamble he lost. Party politics, which he was convinced had destroyed the Third Republic and led to the humiliations of 1940, had been with him with a vengeance and contested his rule at every turn. The communists had clashed with him at the referendum and in the squabble over cabinet posts and the right-of-center parties had rallied to his constitutional proposals with a caution that had irritated him. His brush-off of the Roosevelt invitation to an Algiers meeting had provoked criticism in the Assembly and in the press that had shocked him and in January 1, 1946, socialist leader André Philip had asked for a reduction in military spending, a proposal that, coming from de Gaulle's trusted comrade in arms from London, he felt as a personal betrayal. According to the scenario the general and his closest advisers had worked out, chaos would follow the resignation, the communists would be scared and the country would be alarmed. He would be called back and then make his conditions. "My departure is only an abrupt change," he wrote to a friend three days later. "Before coming to any conclusion, wait for the rest of the story." The scenario held true insofar as Thorez became worried and political commentators expressed alarm, but a frightened nation didn't call the general back to power.

If in the Hall of Arms Thorez was sufficiently impressed to exclaim, "Now there's a gesture that doesn't lack grandeur," Malraux, who as Information Minister had known of the general's decision since Saturday night, disliked not so much the gesture as its execution. A few days after the resignation, he told Claude Mauriac, "What's so annoying isn't so much the departure as the holier-than-thou letter accompanying it.[6] In the *Antimémoires,* he called his cabinet post "an interesting job."

> My chief task was to prevent each party from grabbing all the bed covers. Thorez observed the rules of the game, putting the Communist Party at the service of national reconstruction. But at the same time the Party was infiltrating and infiltrating. [Communist Minister of Industrial Production] Marcel Paul's reports were blatantly false and in this tripartite government, false communist statements gave rise to false statements on the part of the socialists and the MRP. After cabinet meetings, the general would make renewed efforts to convince this or that minister, but his arbitration, which he regarded as essential to the working of the State, could not go on being an arbitration between parties and I doubted whether he would put up with this contest in duplicity for long. He seemed to be discovering something which he must always have known, but which the war, the Resistance and perhaps his familiarity with British democracy had obscured, that our democracy is a struggle between parties

[6] Claude Mauriac, op. cit.

in which France as such plays a subordinate role. He had been disconcerted by the refusal first of Herriot and then of Léon Blum to join the government to help in the national reconstruction on the grounds that their first duty was to their parties. All the more so because he knew, at least in Blum's case, that party allegiance stemmed from something more than a desire to be boss.

A few days before de Gaulle's strategic fallback, he had invited Malraux and Blum to dinner and, half seriously, half ironically, asked the old socialist leader to convince his Information minister that it was possible to have confidence in communists as ruling coalition partners. But Malraux objected that real communists couldn't take the present coalition for anything more than a weak caretaker administration, something like the provisional government of Alexander Kerensky which Lenin's Bolsheviks swept away in 1917 or the 1918 Polish government of Josef Piludski also dislodged by more radical elements.

"How can you expect true communists not to take us for another Kerensky or Pilsudski government?" I asked. "It's simply a question of who shoots first. This is no longer politics but a western movie. Remember the Popular Front."

"But the Popular Front worked. Léon Blum turned his long delicate face toward us, and pressing his hands together, repeated firmly, in a frail and slightly disillusioned voice that contrasted with the general's deep voice, "It worked."

"Yes," the general answered bitterly. He was probably thinking "And then what happened?" For Léon Blum, in spite of his moral courage which was considerable, politics was the art of conciliation.

With de Gaulle's resignation came the automatic resignation of his cabinet. Malraux cleared out with a rolled-up print of *Le Moulin de la Galette* which he hung in his new apartment in Boulogne-sur-Seine on the western outskirts of Paris. Among his varied attributes, he could now add the title of former cabinet minister.

> Experience has taught our century that revolutions
> are *also* revolutionary.
>
> Foreword to *Saint-Just*

22

The whole thing had lasted two months. It was hard to concentrate on the solitary métier of writer after the heady days in the corridors of power and Malraux was rumored to be seeing a lot of people and attending the weekly "barons' lunches," the Gaullist brainpower reunions where—without the general—Gaston Palewsky, Georges Pompidou, Roger Frey, Christian Fouchet and Jacques Chaban-Delmas evaluated the political situation to plot their own return to power on the tall man's coattails. But it would not be until 1958 that a France on the brink of civil war over a disastrous colonial adventure would call back the general. Then, Malraux would call the intervening twelve years "the crossing of the desert."

For Malraux, the crossing of the desert was to be both the period of political disappointments and his greatest years as a humanist. During the late 1940s, he lived yet another failure—de Gaulle's failure to unify his country in peace as he had rallied an ever-swelling number of his countrymen in war. This failure removed the general further and further from power and allowed Malraux—finally with a sense of relief—to escape toward the inner self. Again, he would be just a writer. Between 1947 and 1957, his meditation on creativity was to result in eight books on art, including *The Voices of Silence,* which was also to be the means of his own liberation.

The war had taken its toll. The news of Roland's death that he and his sister-in-law Madeleine had received in Paris after Josette's funeral had proved to be premature. Roland had been alive when Madeleine had given birth to their son, Alain, and had only died in one of those absurdly cruel incidents that marked the last hours of the war. In April 1945, he had been one of twenty thousand concentration camp prisoners that a number of desperate Nazi leaders had thought they could use to buy their own freedom from the victorious Allies. Twenty thousand men and women

264

Florence with Madeleine Malraux

had been marched from central Germany to Lubeck on the Baltic coast and stocked into the holds of three freighters which were to sail to Sweden had a bargain been struck. With ten thousand others, Roland was on board the *Cap Arcona,* the biggest of the three ships. On May 4, the *Cap Arcona,* flying the swastika, had been off the coast of Germany when U.S. Air Force bombers had strafed it. Instead of raising the white flag, the Nazi guard and crew had put the lifeboats overboard and rowed away when the Americans had come in for the bombing run. Of the ten thousand prisoners, only two hundred survived, most of them burned beyond recognition by exploding fuel oil.

Young Claude, caught in a sabotage attempt aboard a German ship in the Seine estuary, had been executed. The date of his death was never established.

In 1946, Malraux moved into a duplex apartment in a big house among the elegant mansions of Boulogne-sur-Seine and a short time later asked his sister-in-law to be his house guest. Together they brought the three boys to Paris to live with them—Pierre-Gauthier and Vincent now six and three, and two-year-old Alain. Malraux had finally divorced Clara, with whom he was to remain on easy if not devoted terms, seeing their now teen-aged daughter Florence quite often. In 1948, he married his brother's widow. A natural intimacy had grown between him and this dark, attractive sister-in-law and an adult affection united them, sustained by

265

Father and sons with Hopi dolls from Arizona. Left to right: Vincent, Gauthier and their nephew, Alain, the son of Roland.

their responsibilities toward their half-orphaned children. The civil marriage was held in Riquewihr in Alsace with Father Bockel and several veterans of the Brigade in attendance.

Friends guessed that he was happy. Visiting the Malrauxs in their big studio apartment with the family studio-salon, built from André's design, two stories high, white, handsome and modern dominated by Madeleine's concert piano and the *Moulin de la Galette* reproduction and with choice ornaments such as a Khmer sculptured head wedged in among books and Dubuffet and Jean Fautrier paintings, the astute Nino Frank felt "another life" behind the official Malraux, "which he doesn't display, and which one can only guess—other lives actually, childhoods near him that take shape, a new pact with earth." [1] Janet Flanner, whose Letters from Paris had now periodically graced the pages of *The New Yorker* since 1925, visited in the mid-1950s and came away with a more explicit account of the Malrauxs:

> Theirs is a curiously overlapping dynasty, since the boys are at once, in due proportion, their parent's sons, nephews and stepsons. Malraux is a prodigal, inventive and stimulating father, lavish with gifts and with private jokes that suit all their age levels, and his own as well; "I suppose I am really a sad type," he recently wrote to an acquaintance about a gloomy photograph of him that neither liked, "yet I recognize

[1] Nino Frank, *Mémoire brisée,* op. cit.

266

myself only in pictures where I look gay"—his rarest expression. In casual conversation, his humor consists of raillery, paradox, astringent French wit and occasional extravagances, created all of a piece and like exaggerated baroque. He has always drawn amusing, skillful little animal grotesques—like one recently published in *Malraux par lui-même*,[2] which resembles a cross-eyed donkey and is captioned "Le Dyable de la Critique d'art"—and quantities of spare, high-tailed cats (cats are his favorite creatures, though he says they will not often have anything to do with him), and he invariably draws something of the sort in books he gives to children, and sometimes in those volumes of his own works he presents to adults—for he is a steady bookgiver. His daughter Florence was only six when the war started, during which he did not see her, but a few years ago they came together again. Attractive and extremely intelligent, she is now his confidante in his literary projects and has been working in the art department at Gallimard. Malraux plays the piano—not well, he insists, but well enough to play two-part pieces on a grand piano with two keyboards, specially made by Pleyel, with Mme. Malraux, who is expert, having formerly been a concert pianist.[3]

Malraux received many journalists at Boulogne. Cyrus Sulzberger, who in 1947 said the apartment was still in the process of being furnished, made it a habit of including Boulogne in his Paris touchdowns. Jean Lacouture, who had just spent over a year in Hanoi and Saigon, was invited to come and talk Indochina ("It was *he* of course who talked"). At the end of 1945, Gaëtan Picon's Malraux biography had appeared,[4] the film *L'Espoir* received the Louis Delluc prize following its short run at the Max Linder cinema and Gide's vivid portrait of Malraux had been published in a new weekly magazine. To the now seventy-six-year-old Gide, who was shortly to receive the Nobel Prize, Malraux was a man in love with the beautiful and tragic in the human adventure.

Malraux is open to everything and everybody, always receptive and, I would say, pervious if I didn't know he could resist what might bend his decision or broach his will. Right away he acts, becomes responsible and exposes himself. Wherever a just cause needs a defender, wherever a beautiful combat is fought you will find him. He knows how to give himself and to dedicate himself without haggling and even with something that is both boldness and despair. He is first of all an adventurer and it seems to me that he threw himself into his dazzling career by petulance, before measuring anything, before weighing what was in it for him. With him the word "adventure" takes on its fullest, its most beautiful, its richest and most human meaning.[5]

[2] Gaëtan Picon, *Malraux par lui-même* (Paris: Seuil, 1953).
[3] Janet Flanner, *Men and Monuments* (New York: Harper and Row, 1957).
[4] Gaëtan Picon, *André Malraux* (Paris: Gallimard, 1945).
[5] *Terres des Hommes* (Dec. 1, 1945).

267

The Cold War darkened Malraux's vision. The Stalinist coup in Czechoslovakia and the Berlin Blockade which sent the Iron Curtain clanging down the middle of Europe not only hardened his view of the Soviet Union but made him feel Europe was living in its final twilight. Europe's only chance, a coalition around France and Britain, was no longer possible, he told Claude Mauriac in March 1946. Facing the monstrous empires, dependence was inevitable and any policy not taking the new geopolitical facts into account was absurd. When Sulzberger came to see him in February 1947, he told *The New York Times* editor that the U.S. and Russia had reached an understanding to divide the world into spheres of influence and that he could foresee no World War III. The only possibility of a Big Two war would be unexpected events inside the Soviet Union or an inflammatory act by some satellite country disobeying Moscow.[6]

Tragic humanism, he was increasingly coming to believe, was the only possible humanism. The nineteenth century had been the zenith of optimistic humanism—God, Nietzsche had said, was dead, but the kingdom of man had replaced Him, the world had progressed in manners and morals, customs and arts, under the guidance of reason and science. In the twentieth century, two holocausts had displayed such horror, suffering and human degradation that the optimistic world view had been slaughtered along with the tens of millions. The only answer was a tragic humanism, the realization that no change in the material and political conditions could substantially alter the terrible isolation of every individual while at the same time admitting that under certain political conditions certain political and ethical choices could provoke emotions that could mitigate the human predicament.

To address the founding session of the United Nations Economic, Scientific and Cultural Organization (UNESCO) in November 1946, he found the most vibrant tones to express this belief. The lead-off lecturer at the main Sorbonne University amphitheater symposium, chaired by Stephen Spender, he said that culture had become an adventure in freedom but that humanism was necessarily tragic since we would never know where the human adventure was going.

The speech, defensive in its resolve yet soaring in expressing the hope that man might once more be able to build himself from clay asked "What are the values of the West today?" and proceeded to answer that with Europe in ashes it could surely not be said to be reason or progress, but perhaps the stoic acceptance of a kind of open-endedness to the human adventure. Modern man, he said, was as much eaten away by mass psychology as by excessive individualism, both of which begged false questions, when the taste of each individual was first of all to conceive himself. Western man's first assets were his own self-awareness and the willingness to

[6] Cyrus Sulzberger, op. cit.

discover, as shown in the age of the great navigators, in the succession of forms in the evolution of the arts, in the permanent struggle between psychology and logic as seen in the novel and in the creations of the mind. The speech, as most of Malraux's public utterances, angered communists. As official Party delegate at the UNESCO conference Louis Aragon objected to Malraux's wondering whether European man was dead and assailed the author of *L'Espoir* for commending Churchill while forgetting Stalin and the Red Army which alone, he said, had saved Europe from tyranny. To communists in general and France's new intellectual star, Jean-Paul Sartre, in particular, Malraux was now the big turncoat and false prophet who had betrayed his past, abandoned the Left and had embraced fascism by joining de Gaulle, that "gravedigger of democracy," as Simone de Beauvoir called the general.

The Cold War sharply divided intellectuals and created strange bedfellows. If Arthur Koestler was the staunch bulwark of a Left disenchanted with communism, Sartre was the brilliant rampart of Marxist ideology. Koestler's novel *Darkness at Noon,* the story of an old-guard communist falling victim to Stalin's purges, actually written in 1940, became a postwar phenomenon in France. Translated as *Zéro et l'infini,* it assumed a symbolic actuality and an allusive relevance and broke all records in French publishing, selling a quarter of a million copies. Sartre's influence was not limited to one book, but spanned the media, from the theater, where his plays *Les Mouches* (1943), *Huits Clos* (1945) and *Les Mains sales* (1948) and their filmization had made him a millionaire, to his novels and his magazine *Les Temps modernes* (published by Gallimard), which catalyzed his philosophical thinking and on whose editorial board all his friends and disciples were to be found. While trying to humanize Marxism, Sartre's monthly followed the general Cold War party line of calling anyone who criticized the Soviet Union a fascist. It defended every measure of the Soviet regime—including the 1939 Stalin-Hitler pact—as an "historical necessity."

Between Koestler and Sartre stood that other new commanding postwar figure, Albert Camus. In 1946, Camus wrote in *Combat* a series of articles expressing the hope that mankind could somehow bring an end to "ideologies, that is to say, to absolute utopias which destroy us by the historic price they end up costing us." [7] Camus refused the Marxist view of history, saying the goals of Marxism were "undiscernible" and murder, even in the name of progress, was inadmissible. The existence of Soviet concentration camps was at the center of 1940s and 1950s debate—to be revived again in the 1970s by Alexander Solzhenitsyn, and it was also the core of a celebrated disagreement between Sartre and Camus. This debate, which was soon to be seen as absolutely central to the concerns of the

[7] Albert Camus, "Ni victimes ni bourreaux," *Oeuvres complètes,* Vol. II (Paris: Pléiade, 1962 and 1965).

century, began with a review by Francis Jeanson in *Les Temps modernes* of Camus' book *L'Homme révolté* (*The Rebel*).[8] Camus condemned some aspects of Marx, especially his historical determinism, and came down hard on the Siberian concentration camps on the grounds that no ends could justify unjust means. He drew unwelcome attention to the "fascism" that came in the wake of the French and Russian revolutions and to the "Caesarism" that revolutionary action invariably seemed to flounder into, and, in effect, postulated a nonviolent, liberal and pluralistic alternative to communism. Jeanson's review said that while Russia was imperfect, it was nevertheless the only Marxist state and therefore privileged. Camus replied arrogantly and injudiciously, ignoring Jeanson and addressing himself to Sartre, rejected the idea that the USSR was "privileged" by any historic Absolute. Sartre's reply was far from clear and never spelled out whether he believed History possessed the direction and meaning Marx gave it, or indeed any direction or meaning at all. "The question is not whether History has a meaning and whether we should participate in it," Sartre wrote, "but once we're in it up to here, whether we should give it the direction we feel is the best." [9] If, according to Camus, the Soviet leaders were to be judged on their acts, Sartre said they should be judged on their intentions. If, as Camus charged, the Gulag Archipelago condemned the Soviet Union, Sartre was embarrassed and could only say that the way anticommunism exploited the camps was no less justifiable. Retroactively, he was to agree with Camus and, in 1968, eloquently condemn the Soviet Union for sending tanks into Czechoslovakia to put an end to the "spring of Prague."

While not a party to the Camus-Sartre polemics, Malraux was to give his political commentaries to their exemplary debate in numerous speeches and his philosophical answer in a 1953 foreword to a biography of Louis de Saint-Just, the theoretician of the Terror of the French Revolution who himself died on the guillotine with Robespierre when he was twenty-six years old.

During the second half of 1946, de Gaulle had, with difficulty, kept silent, refusing to condemn various initiatives to form a Gaullist party while at the same time talking against party politics. Malraux was not in the general's entourage during these months but working on *Scènes choisies* and *La Psychologie de l'art. The Selected Scenes* was a Gallimard reprint of *Esquisse d'une psychologie du cinéma,* Malraux's reflections on the movies following the making of the film version of *L'Espoir,* originally published in *Verve* magazine in 1939, followed by a large excerpt from *Le Temps du mépris,* that slim 1935 novel-tract against fascism that he pretended to disdain. But in December 1946, de Gaulle could wait no longer. After public appearances and speeches against a constitution

8 Francis Jeanson, "Pour tout vous dire," *Les Temps modernes* (Aug., 1952).
9 Jean-Paul Sartre, "Réponse à Albert Camus," *Situations IV* (1952).

giving France a strong legislative branch failed to prevent the passage of precisely such a "parliamentary sovereignty" constitution, the general and his braintrust came up with a barely legal plan to regain power. The idea consisted of applying public pressure on newly elected President Vincent Auriol—under the new legislative-oriented constitution a weak chief of state—to force him to call on de Gaulle to form a government. De Gaulle would only accept if he were given "full powers" in order to achieve certain specific objectives outlined in a fifteen-point program. Next, Prime Minister de Gaulle would ask the people to approve, in a national referendum, a new constitution with a strong executive branch.

On April 7, 1947, de Gaulle "crossed the Rubicon," as Malraux would say. On the balcony of the Strasbourg City Hall, flanked by Malraux and Jacques Soustelle, his wartime secret service chief, de Gaulle announced the creation of the *Rassemblement du peuple français,* which, in the mind of its leader, would rally national energies more than would a political party. At home, the Rassemblement should save the republic from strife and division and abroad it should reassert France in a West trying to melt her down in the European magma and against a now unmasked East. So many people had asked him to throw the weight of his immense glory into the national debate.

From the balcony, de Gaulle said France would have to learn new words—efficiency, harmony and liberty—or the country would end up an impotent and disillusioned dictatorship. The year 1947 saw the creation of the Marshall Plan whose rejection by Russia and its "satellites" established, together with a monetary reform in the western zones that the Soviets refused to join, the partition of Germany, followed a year later by Stalin's attempt to dislodge the western Allies from Berlin, the formation of the North Atlantic Treaty Organization (NATO) and the division of Europe. During the next six years de Gaulle would create and sustain within the RPF a virulent anti-communism and the grand theme of his public appearances on behalf of this party born of the great Fear of 1947 was planetary catastrophe, the near-certainty of world war and, unless he was brought to power, the collapse of France.

"The RPF is like the *métro,"* was Malraux's slogan, "you meet all kinds." Named "delegate in charge of propaganda," Malraux shared de Gaulle's fear of the Soviet Union and his apocalyptic world view, but wanted to pull the RPF to the Left. The demographic breakdown of the party membership was eighty percent workers, small businessmen and civil servants, but the party cadres were men whose ideas, style and electoral "clientele" belonged to traditional right-of-center politics. Malraux was embarrassed, as he told Cyrus Sulzberger, by de Gaulle's right-wing sympathizers and immediately set out to create a left flank for the party. As delegate in charge of propaganda, he created a monthly bulletin called *L'Etincelle* (*The Spark,* as the title of Lenin's journal) and at offices near the Paris Opéra tried to bring together a braintrust. Headed by Christian Fouchet, one of the "barons" and a nephew of the general who soon dropped out, the "propaganda" section, where everybody from secretaries to notables called the boss André, when they didn't use the shockingly informal diminutive "Dédé"—*L'Etincelle* was soon replaced by a weekly magazine, *Le Rassemblement*. The editorial triumvirate in charge was two young self-proclaimed Gaullists—the historian Albert Ollivier and Jean Chauveau, the son of Leopold Chauveau who had stood in for part of the portrait of Möllberg—and Pascal Pia, Malraux's old friend from the days of Florent Fels and Max Jacob, who together with Camus and Raymond Aron, Malraux's ministerial secretary during his two months in power, had made *Combat* one of the best postwar daily newspapers. Aron was also a friend of Sartre (having helped Sartre to get a cushioned job in the army during his 1931 military service), but it was Koestler who brought Sartre, de Beauvoir and Camus together with Malraux to mend old acquaintances and to attempt a patchup of old Leftist alliances.

The meeting took place at Koestler's apartment in the spring of 1947, and, the author of *Darkness at Noon* was to remember, Sartre and de Beauvoir hadn't needed too much convincing to come and meet Malraux. Camus began the conversation and stumbled on the word "proletariat." Malraux cut him off, asking him to define the term. Camus became nervous and got tangled up in his definition. Sartre got angry. He and Malraux would not see each other for a long time. In *Tout compte fait,* de Beauvoir was to write about Malraux with rancor. Still, when it was announced that Camus had won the 1958 Nobel Prize, he was to exclaim, "Malraux should have gotten it."

Although André feigned haughty disdain for "those people at Café Flore"—the new "in" hangout on Boulevard St. Germain where Sartre and de Beauvoir were now celebrities—it hurt him that the French intelligentsia would not join the Gaullist ranks. When Sulzberger met him and Soustelle in May, Malraux told the American that the RPF was finished if it couldn't successfully appeal to the Left, adding "we are embarrassed by some of our right-wing supporters. There is nothing we can do about it." This admission led to what Sulzberger called a "curious confession." If there were a Trotskyist movement in France today, a movement which stood some chance of success instead of the tiny handful of Trotskyites bickering with the communists, Malraux would be a Trotskyite and not a Gaullist. A month later Sulzberger was back and, under a June 12, 1947, entry noted:

> Lunched again with Soustelle and Malraux. Both extremely vague and confused about de Gaulle's movement. Malraux had a few interesting things to say on other subjects, however.
>
> He used to know Maxim Gorky, who was the only "mammoth" he ever knew besides de Gaulle, a heritage from man's ancient past. He said Gorky was a huge man, but had the teeth of a six-year-old child—

272

small, white and evenly spaced. He was astonished when Gorky opened his mouth to laugh. The one time he met Stalin was at Gorky's house. He said Stalin adores Shakespeare and never misses a performance. His other hobby is the dance—to watch other people dance. Stalin told him that the way he destroyed Trotsky was by making him write.

Malraux said Gorky paid a pension all his life to four old friends, one was a waiter in a café at Capri, another was a Romanoff princess. He said the greatest intellect of the revolution was Trotsky's.[10]

All of this Sulzberger reported to President Truman when he saw the president in Washington five months later.

A joint broadcast interview in which de Beauvoir called de Gaulle a gravedigger of democracy to be compared to Spain's Franco, and Sartre backed her up by expounding the theme of de Gaulle as a Roman despot and future liquidator of human rights in France, led to a very real break between Malraux and the two existentialist authors. The broadcast, which caused a sensation and had wide repercussions in both literary and political circles, had the tacit approval of the government of Edouard Herriot. But to call de Gaulle a fascist and a would-be dictator was, to Malraux, an insult. Instead of asking Sartre and de Beauvoir for a retraction in *Les Temps modernes,* Malraux confronted Gaston Gallimard with an ultimatum—either Gallimard dropped publishing *Les Temps modernes* or Malraux would quit, and with him would go Gide and most of the elite of the house. The matter was settled in twenty-four hours. Sartre would remain a Gallimard author, but *Les Temps modernes* would go—eventually to the sponsoring of René Julliard, an up-and-coming publisher who would make his name and fortune by discovering Françoise Sagan. Malraux, Sartre and de Beauvoir were not to find themselves on the same side of an issue until ten years later when, under Soustelle's governorship, an Algeria in revolt would denounce French army torture of Algerian guerrillas and terrorists.

But what was the RPF to Malraux?

At rallies and in interviews, he hammered home the need to defy communism and to unite in the defense of the republic, both conceived as moral challenge and physical confrontation and both often expressed in the stirring rhetoric of Danton, Saint-Just and Robespierre of the 1792 First Republic. "You can have no democracy where one partner cheats," he told an audience in Nancy. "To kick over the chessman is not a peculiar way of playing chess. There can be no fair play with Stalinians whose only objective is to shuffle the cards so that this pseudo-democratic game plays into the hands of Russia." More strident, he told a Paris audience filled with Leftist hecklers that "we of the Left were not given to understand that the chants of tomorrow hailing the triumph of socialism

[10] Cyrus Sulzberger, op. cit.

273

should turn out to be the howls of the convicts of Stalin's concentration camps."

As the municipal elections of October 1947 approached and the RPF fielded candidates in a thousand precincts, de Gaulle and his "delegate for propaganda" had perfected a campaign routine that the general would stick to for the next three years. As stage-directed by Malraux, the rallies would have the audience plunged in near darkness and de Gaulle appear on a podium that was draped in a French flag. Under an immense Croix de Lorraine, he would speak over a booming public address system. Music, lights, crowds in the shadows shouting their expectations and their anger, muscular security guards and summary slogans all gave the rallies a militant and quasi-sacred aura and shot up the adrenalin in the crowds, usually composed of masses of faithfuls and also organized hecklers. When Malraux shouted "Gaullism is where you learn energy" to a Marseille party convention in April 1948 infiltrated by communists, fist fights broke out. Before de Gaulle came on stage, Malraux would speak in ringing tones, making hypnotic images clash in fireworks of incandescent suppositions and judgments.

> Our propaganda is this—this poster formerly designed by Rodin, this Republic shouting her hope in France on all the walls in the city, a poster unavailingly slashed and torn. There are no better posters than torn posters. There are no more beautiful faces than faces wearing their wounds!

On communism, he would say that "Marxism is not to our Left, it is to the East," or "We are on this platform and we won't forswear Spain; let us see a Stalinian ready to defend Trotsky," or "the essential question is how to prevent psychotechnicians from destroying the quality of the mind." The goals of Gaullism he defined as "giving France architecture and efficiency."

> We don't say that we will succeed, but we say that our opponents cannot succeed. Don't forget that Gaullism is not a theory like Marxism or even fascism, it is a movement for public salvation.

In a March 5 speech in Paris' Salle Pleyel, Malraux warned of Soviet tyranny with Michelangelo's words, "If it be to open your eyes upon tyranny, may you never awaken," from the pedestal of the *Night* sculpture in the Vatican. The Soviet structure, Malraux warned, despised Europe's past, detested her present and accepted from her only a future in which exactly nothing remained of what she once was—Chartres cathedral, Michelangelo, Shakespeare, Rembrandt. Stalin was the enemy of art. He had no use for artists unless they served the state, with the result that Soviet sculptors and painters were compelled to create vast images of Stalin. Malraux reprinted the speech as an afterword to a new edition of *Les Conquérants* in 1949.

274

The October municipal elections had given the RPF thirty-eight percent of the ballots cast, the party's biggest victory. In senatorial elections in 1948, RPF candidates managed to capture thirty-seven percent of the popular vote, but in district elections the following year, the party's slice was down to twenty-five percent.

If journalists didn't know whether to be appalled or to admire, Malraux's friends, fellow-intellectuals and old comrades-in-arms were baffled, conceding that his pessimism and taste for pathos made his Gaullism logical. Less kind friends attributed his rallying to an authoritarian cause to a renewed attack of heroic romanticism and a taste for power. But, said *L'Esprit*'s founder Emmanuel Mounier, Malraux had not chosen an easy role for himself. Mounier threw open the pages of his monthly magazine, which expressed a low-key, interiorized Catholicism turned toward social equity but hostile to Marxist materialism, to an "interrogation" of the Malraux case and devoted its entire October 1948 issue to the author of *La Condition humaine*. Lined up for the defense were Gaëtan Picon and Roger Stéphane repeating Malraux's Alsatian words, "When you have written what I have, you can't be a fascist."

Albert Béguin, the Swiss essayist, Pascal authority and *L'Esprit* publisher, wrote that Malraux was, "in a sense, the only authentic French fascist" but certainly no vulgar opportunist. "In this country where reactionaries, conservatives and people whose minds stand still are called fascists, he is more or less the only one who has followed the classical road of the revolutionary who has remained a revolutionary but who, because of failures witnessed or a congenital bent, has come to find humanity hopeless." To Mounier himself, Malraux was battling impossible windmills:

> If he really believes that, by the sole flintiness of his solitary energy, he can triumph over the accumulated mediocrities of these congregations (*rassemblements*) of rout which a European middle class, no longer capable of invention or initiatives takes for heroic advances, we cannot deny that he continues to do battle on the outer limits of feasibility. But if this hypothesis is exactly what saves Malraux, won't he find in this paradox of action, in this obscure and lyrical gap between revolution and conservatism something of his old taste for paroxysm and absurdity? Lyrical illusion can have many faces. To listen to some of the disturbing pathos of his public utterances, one can only anxiously ask oneself if some obscure mix of fervor not pursued and hopelessness not overcome are not threatening to throw the living forces of *L'Espoir* to the chilly Europe belonging to the plotters of fear.

With some justification, Malraux would say in 1953 that it was not he who had changed but the world and, most of all, the communists. At one point in time, his and their goals had overlapped and an alliance had increased their chances of success. Later, their goals had no longer coincided and he had sought a new alliance. He had consistently placed human and subjective values above historical and objective importance and his goal—cultural as much as political freedom—had not changed much since Clara, Paul Monin and he had tried to take on the Saigon colonial establishment or since the specter of fascism had made him travel to Moscow, and Madrid. He believed, with Trotsky, that the purpose and ideal of revolution had been betrayed by Stalin. After World War II a victorious Soviet Union had radically altered the world and, in France, made communists thoroughly suspect as allies. He had embraced Gaullism insofar as de Gaulle's goal of national regeneration, which had animated the Resistance, coincided with his own demand that postwar France give herself the deepest of reforms. His new nationalism was never vulgar since he argued that France had always been greatest when most generous, outward-looking and universalist. Nationalism, as he had told de Gaulle at their first meeting, was justified by the primacy of the nation-state, including Russia, which Stalin had transformed from the first "privileged" state of a worldwide communist community—humanist and egalitarian in its goals—into a Soviet fatherland.

"Culture," he would write in 1952 in *Confluence,* a new American "think tank" quarterly founded by a Harvard political science graduate named Henry Kissinger, "would seem, first and foremost, to be the knowledge of what makes man something other than an accident of the universe, be it by deepening his harmony with the world or by the lucid consciousness of his revolt from it." [11] All political and cultural action was double-edged, in harmony with, and in opposition to, present structures.

Imperceptibly, he was drifting away from politics. "Art excites me five hundred times more than politics," he told visiting American political writer Theodore White.[12] In the RPF publication *Liberté de l'esprit,* he wrote that a political indictment of a social situation led to the destruction of the forms that expressed it, whereas in art an indictment of the human situation led to the destruction of the forms that took it for granted.[13] Overseeing the RPF public relations machine was not a full-time job and in his Boulogne studio he worked on his books. In 1947, Skira, the Swiss art publishers, had brought out his essay on Goya, later reprinted under the title *Saturn* (so called after the figure of a giant devouring his son, probably the most fearful of Goya's nightmarish paintings). Goya had

[11] *Confluence* (Sept., 1952). To launch his journal, funded by a Rockefeller Foundation grant, Kissinger solicited and received contributions from Malraux, Alberto Moravia, Reinhold Niebuhr and Enoch Powell. *Confluence* survived only a dozen issues and folded when Kissinger took his first leave of absence from Harvard in 1955. Malraux's contribution was a reprint of a speech delivered at the Congress of Cultural Freedom, June 6, 1952.

[12] Theodore White, "The Three Lives of André Malraux," *The New York Times Magazine* (Feb. 15, 1953).

[13] "N'était-ce donc que ça?" *Liberté de l'esprit* (April-June, 1949).

begun his work in the Italian style but, in forty years of evolution, had repudiated everything he had learned to end up creating great art as a defense against the Absurd. Goya was the intellectual ancestor of modern man. For Goya, the Enlightenment idea of man had utterly collapsed, to be replaced at best by a question mark. In 1949, Skira published *Le Musée imaginaire*, the first of three volumes comprising *La Psychologie de l'art*. The "imaginary museum" immediately entered the French language in its Malrucian meaning—that through photography and the modern printing techniques twentieth-century man was heir to a ubiquitous imaginary museum containing the art of all times. That this new familiarity with all art was the starting point for a modern universal humanism. In 1949, Skira published the second volume, *La Création artistique* and the following year the third volume, *La Monnaie de l'absolu*.

Malraux's workroom was a vast study on the top floor at Boulogne, a room like a painter's studio with bay windows opening on the Bois de Boulogne. He was not well and gave up the habit he had had since youth of only writing at night and carefully reorganized his life for working by day. During the summer of 1950, he suffered a paratyphoid fever attack that kept him bedridden for nearly two months.

The illness and long convalescene that followed removed him further from party politics and made him reassess his position. The faction he liked least, the party tacticians, were winning out. In 1951, the party's decline was conspicuous. At that year's important parliamentary elections, RPF candidates managed to capture only twenty-one percent of the vote. After de Gaulle's candid assessment of his movement's slumping electoral fortunes, Malraux felt free. Yet he was still there next to a suddenly aged de Gaulle at a Paris rally in 1952 and again the following year when the general admitted to his faithfuls that their political action had not borne fruit.

Culture and art, he felt, were expressions of the most fundamental of liberties. Culture was the sum of all the forms of art, of love and of thought, which, in the course of centuries, had enabled people to be less enslaved. During his convalescence, he decided to rework the three long essays of *La Psychologie de l'art,* to deepen their tone and to say that modern art, starting with Manet, contained a tremendous philosophical and moral message because it represented, for the first time, a deliberate decision not to create a world in harmony with nature but with ideals. As he had indicated in *Les Noyers de l'Altenburg,* only action that was finally creative was justifiable. The artist was perhaps the greatest conqueror of them all.

As Gide died peacefully at the age of eighty-two, Malraux started to work on *The Voices of Silence.* Emaciated and hollowed out by illness and with the perennial cigarette dangling from the corner of his mouth, he sat in his old bathrobe on the floor of his study surrounded by hundreds

277

and hundreds of photographs, choosing them, drawing them together, permitting them to illustrate and reflect one another, arranging them so they would show themselves to their most illuminating advantage and reveal the tension between the irrational and the rational and perhaps the hidden meaning of evolution.

> "This world of ours," Mallarmé once remarked, "has all the makings of a great book."
>
> *The Voices of Silence*

23

Les Voix du silence is a hymn to man and his infinite possibilities. Art is the most triumphant form of human expression and the creative process is the song, not the newsreel, of History. Culture is the soul of a civilization and the art of all societies expresses man's defiance of the Absurd. In the vast twentieth-century synthesis, it is a bond, both to other men and to our past, and as such a means of overcoming differences and of destroying that past. In every age the artist is alone because genius is neither fidelity to appearances nor old forms rearranged, but invention. In rejecting the dominance of historical conditions and influences, the artist frees himself and, in so doing, frees us. No doubt the artistic manifestations of mankind are countless, their telltale archetypes are nevertheless few. Art is the only true revolt against the feeling of being marooned on an insignificant planet, a mere by-product of an indifferent universe.

The Voices of Silence is not a book for beginners. It assumes that the reader has a solid knowledge of art, esthetics and history as well as a vast general culture. Intensely personal, *The Voices* is more polyphonic dynamics than a formal system of esthetics or even art history. It is written in Malraux's leaping style and knotted images and is full of startling connections and dramatic ellipses that force the mind to associate the familiar with the remote in a Promethean clash of ideas as Goya and Polynesian mask carvers, Leonardo and cathedral builders, Takanobu and Caravaggio wrestle with themselves and with fate to impose human intelligence on the forms of our planet, thereby to give human adventure a meaning. "You will find my lyrical passages frequent and fatiguing; just do the best you can with them," Malraux told Stuart Gilbert when the former colonial judge from Burma embarked on the translation, which to Doubleday represented an investment of close to $200,000 by the time the 650-page volume with its 400-odd illustrations came out in English in the fall of 1953.

279

Preparing *The Voices of Silence*

The publication in Paris was the literary event of 1951. The sale of the Gallimard de luxe edition was phenomenal and in America nearly fifteen thousand copies were sold by Christmas 1953 at $25 a copy, providing Malraux with the richest immediate royalties he had ever known.

When an acquaintance asked Malraux in 1957 how long he had worked on his art book, he answered, "All my life." *Les Voix du silence,* dedicated to Madeleine, was essentially a thick, one-volume revision and expansion of *Le Musée imaginaire, La Création artistique* and *La Monnaie de l'absolu,* which Gilbert translated as *Museum Without Walls, The Artistic Act* and *The Twilight of the Absolute.*

Here is a synopsis:

Although much of what Malraux says in *Museum Without Walls* about the changes in the way we understand art is somehow obvious to a 1970s mind familiar with mixed media and global village input, it is both fundamental and illuminating. A Romanesque crucifix was not regarded by its contemporaries as a work of sculpture, Malraux begins. Museums are no more than two hundred years old and the whole idea of hanging paintings side by side is a modern notion. Juxtaposition meant discovery of style and evolution, but the real metamorphosis has come in our century. Photography means wider comparisons, not only by allowing us to compare paintings that are centuries and continents apart, but by bringing tapestry, stained-glass windows and bronze miniatures onto the same flat surface. Blowups, angles and layouts can give ancient works of sculpture a startling, if spurious modernism. Reproduction has revealed a whole world of sculpture. It has multiplied accepted masterpieces, promoted other works to their due rank and launched some minor styles—in some cases even invented them. The original meaning (mostly religious) has disappeared and the miniatures, frescoes, stained glass, Scythian plaques and Greek vase paintings have become ends to themselves. To medieval Christians, a "Virgin" was not color arranged in a certain order, but *the* virgin. By its mere birth, all art modifies the arts that preceded it. Since Van Gogh, Rembrandt has never been quite the same as he was after Delacroix. It is not research that has led to understanding El Greco, but modern art.

Art history turns on the changing concept of function and beauty. Until the sixteenth century, great painters indulged in telling stories on their canvases, in depicting human personality instead of line and color while in the eighteenth century painting became subordinated to the "rational" expression of the person portrayed. No one but the painters themselves and a handful of connoisseurs realized that the plastic art might be a language of its own, like music. Goya foreshadows all modern art and leads to Manet and the disappearance of the "subject" in favor of the artist's right to freely express himself. When the Impressionists began going outdoors, they weren't so much trying to reproduce the outside

281

world more faithfully as to *intensify* their painting. The crucial discovery was then made that, in order to be expressed as painting, the universe seen by the artist had to become a private one, created by himself.

And what became of descriptive art? It found a new medium—the movies. Photography couldn't take over from painting because it has no scope for fiction. It could record a dancer's leap, but it couldn't show the crusaders entering Jerusalem. The desire for descriptive pictures, from saints' faces to great historical scenes, has always been focused as much on what people have never seen as on familiar things. The dynamics of filmcraft weren't discovered by making actors act differently, but by modifying the relations between filmmaker and audience, in short, by inventing the closeup and montage.

Freeing painting from storytelling not only gave us such diverse artists as Monet, Cézanne, Gaugin, Rouault and Picasso, it also threw new light onto other centuries and other cultures with the result that a large share of art heritage is now derived from peoples whose idea of art was quite different from ours and even from peoples to whom the very idea of art meant nothing.

Change is of the essence, says Malraux in *The Metamorphosis of Apollo*. Art doesn't live by what it copies but by what it absorbs, which doesn't mean all evolution is a forward thrust. The decline and fall of Rome can be traced in coins and statues as going from humanistic expression to barbarism, from Greco-Roman free form to dislocation of form and total regression. To third-century sculptors, Aphrodites and Venuses weren't so much ignored as found unacceptable. Christianity in the West and Buddhism in the East transformed Apollo into Jesus and Siddhartha. Both creeds are otherworldly and as art left the public square for convents and temples, gestures became ritualistic and priestly. The history of Buddhist art is primarily the story of the conquest of immobility. If Christendom is dominated by the tragic picture of an execution, Buddhism is expressed by the tranquil picture of a meditation. Buddha's eyelids were lowered, the drawing of his face tightened, movement disappeared and by the time Buddhism reached China, the languid convolutions of Indian lines became ideograms charged with sensibility.

Giotto is the last of the great master craftsmen and the first artist. With him psychology, the frame and composition appear. Figures in his paintings look at each other, not out into space. For the first time, an imaginary window defines the boundaries of painting—Giotto's use of the "frame" was a first safeguard against the risk of disintegration to which an art on the verge of discovering space is bound to be exposed. Depth of field begins with color relations. At the dawn of the Renaissance, style no longer means a set of characteristics but the supreme object of the artist's work. "And so, to the question, 'What is art?', we answer: 'That whereby forms are transmuted into style.' "

282

The subject of *The Artistic Act*—better translated perhaps as The Creative Process—is the different ways of seeing the world, the artist's vision of the Eternal and his growth. The hunter doesn't see the forest the same way as the artist does; to be an instrument-maker doesn't demand musical appreciation. To the eye of the artist, things are primarily what they can *become*, what he can make them into. "The painter reduces form to the two dimensions of his canvas; the sculptor reduces every movement, potential or portrayed, to immobility. This reduction is the beginning of art."

Nearly all artists grow in the same manner. Very young, they are more responsive to the word of art than to the world they share with others. They feel a compelling impulse to paint, though aware that their first works will no doubt be bad. After an early phase of copying near-contemporary masters, they become aware of a discrepancy between the nature of the art they are imitating and the art which one day will be theirs. They have glimpses of a new approach and as they master color, drawing and means of execution, once approach has become style—a new interpretation of the world develops. As they age, they modify and intensify this interpretation. An artist doesn't evolve from his childhood—the gifts of children control them, not they their talents—but grows out of the *conflict* with his predecessors' achievements; not from his own formless world, but from the struggle with the forms others have imposed.

The notion that one of art's chief functions is to resemble life would have surprised a Byzantine, for whom art meant eliminating the personal, as it would have surprised a Chinese classicist for whom resemblance was outside the range of art. The camera possesses total realism, yet it was barely invented before photographers and filmmakers came up against the age-old question of style and composition, eventually learning to isolate realism. Instinct is an uncharted area. Though artists tend to explain their genius in terms of the values of their generation, their triumphs over the darker powers that assail them and to which, in their quest for perfection and ecstasy, they give in, are far from understood. Art is born from the refusal to copy appearances, from the lure of the elusive. To advance is to be driven to impose new forms and patterns and there is also a destructive, almost demoniacal quality to art. The artist wants to destroy the forms that gave him birth.

Malraux pays tribute to all artists, but his most passionate pages are devoted to the solitary giants of the last four centuries who, out of their violent conflict with a growingly secular world and an anguish that would "transform a bouquet of flowers into a burning bush" created works that stripped their contemporaries of complacency. The masters are Rembrandt, El Greco, Goya and Van Gogh.

Great works of art seem to hover, superimposed, over the masterpieces that precede them. Art begins as a break with the past. This break is not in itself art but no art emerges without it. If we are often at a loss to understand the working of the creative process, the reason is our unclear definition of the artist. During the Renaissance, a great artist was necessarily someone who produced "high art," but during the last century ideas of what is meant by "genius" have become blurred. Romanticism has bequeathed a concept of the artist as "interpreter of the great mystery," a notion that invests him with the genius implicit in his work and assumes that he has mastered life with the same compelling power. From Leonardo to Cézanne, however, most artists were conventional people, often saying rather silly things about their work. "Cézanne doesn't necessarily want to change the world or justify God's ways; he wants to challenge existing paintings with paintings that do not yet exist."

Every great artist's achievement of style coincides with the achievement of his freedom. Cézanne's architecturally ordered compositions didn't come from displeasure with nature as he saw it, but from his dissatisfaction with tradition. Schools of art come from a romantic belief that absolute beauty can be taught by great masters, when in fact every great school is a response to change, to the discovery of new significance. Latour took over Caravaggio's cardplayers, musicians, Magdalenes and Saint Francis figures, his Crowning with Thorns, his way of playing red draperies against dark backgrounds and sometimes even Caravaggio's particular shades of red, yet ended up with an art almost the opposite of Caravaggio's. Latour's discovery was that surface can suggest volume.

The relations between art and history are puzzling because different cultures and even great periods of a same culture don't have the same past. The artist in revolt against his own age often tries to belong to no period at all, but standing outside time is impossible. Even a nude can be dated at first glance. Yet artists can anticipate the future, sometimes in startling ways. Thematically, Goya is in step with his time, but his vision belongs to a later perception. The fact that Manet, Cézanne, Renoir and Rodin are contemporaries shows that any age can have complex and unpredictable patterns and that its artistic expressions can be infinitely subtler than its emotions. "Just as the rift between the artist and the period preceding him compels him to modify its forms—and the fissure between himself and his masters to alter their forms—so the difference between his present self and the person he was compels him to constantly change." The personality of an artist takes form and emerges in his work in different ways, depending on whether his art is in harmony with or in opposition to the social order of his time. The artist "filters" what he sees, but life sometimes filters it for him. Caravaggio's passions—he killed a man in a brawl—Goya's illness, life's fateful impact on Hals, Gauguin and Dostoyevsky modified their art and perhaps even their idea of art. In every age certain artists, when they feel death approaching, have been moved to sum themselves up, to paint their last will. Death bestows on

284

all last works a perspective reaching out into infinity and all Western painting seems to be bathed in the evening glow of the last years of Titian, Goya, Rembrandt and Renoir.

Our notion of perfection has undergone gradual but far-reaching change. Every great art rediscovers its perfection and its ancestors. Today, perfect color has stolen a march on perfect drawing and it is possible to be perfect without drawing a human figure. What has survived of great artist's works is the part which has the greatest *density*. A masterpiece is often assumed to be one in which the artist uses all his means. Sometimes, however, he can use all his means to eliminate things. The supreme power of a masterpiece is due to its conquest of the visible world, not to its technique. It always contains an element of the personal and the unforeseen. Time converts certain works into landmarks. Modern art has revived not Turner but El Greco. Delacroix could not have responded to Japanese portraiture like Takanobu's as Braque did. The great artist doesn't stand alone because he is original; he is original because he has broken free with such compelling power that he can illuminate his own liberation.

Malraux begins *The Twilight of the Absolute*—literally, The Small Change of the Absolute—by saying Western art didn't emerge from Christianity but from the fissures in the creed. It is logical that Protestant Holland should give us the painters with whom modern art begins. Hals and Rembrandt inaugurate the conflict between painter and model. Before them, color and brushstrokes were used to serve the model; now the model became painting.

With the seventeenth century, the sense of the Absolute disappears from Western civilization. For the first time, a religion isn't threatened by another one but by science and reason and the decline of Christianity is a transition from the absolute to the relative. In art, however, the Christian absolute wasn't replaced by Reason and political passion. Revolution—and the French Revolution, unlike Cromwell's and Washington's, was not only directed against kings but also against Christianity —didn't lead to Rousseau, David and Ingres, but to Goya and the notion of the artist as a rebel. By the nineteenth century, artist and ruling class stopped having the same values. "The fulminations of the nineteenth-century artists against the bourgeois often strikes us as farfetched and even puerile, because the artists mistook the reason for their grievances. They accused the bourgeois of not knowing anything about art, but had the aristocracy understood it any better? Were Géricault, Delacroix, Corot and Manet appreciated in court circles any more than by the working class? Did workers show any taste for Courbet's pictures? The more the bourgeois came to ask of art a mere pleasure of the eye, the more artists broadened the scope of their revolt."

Artists adopted a kind of clannish aloofness—both contemptuous and creative. Earlier, all arts had tended to accept the same values al-

285

though painters, poets and musicians rarely met. Now as art branched out artists got together to launch concerted attacks on the culture they disliked. Humanism had glorified the culture to which it belonged, now art was an end to itself. When Van Gogh "copied" Delacroix and Manet and Cézanne "copied" Venetian masters, they destroyed poetry in favor of a new divinity—paint. Confronting a culture less and less sure of itself, artists were to be haunted by visions of their own absolute. Cézanne believed his canvases would find their way into the Louvre but not that reproductions would make them known around the world. Van Gogh suspected he was a great painter but not that fifty years after his death he would be more famous in Japan than Raphael.

Agnosticism is nothing new; what is new is an agnostic society. Nowhere has modern civilization built a temple or a tomb. Ours is the first culture to have lost all sense of the sacred. Moreover, modern society no longer trusts Reason and now even refuses to regulate its own irrationality. As a result, the individual knows he counts for very little. Once beyond hedonism, individualism tends to yield to the lure of the grandiose.

Folk art may be the world's oldest art but that, too, has disappeared. There is now a type of novel written for the masses, but not a Stendhal for the masses; there is music for the masses, but not a Bach. The movies' millionaire-marrying-the-shopgirl plot is not a cinematic retelling of *Cinderella,* because the fairytale is not only a success story but a tale of enchantment. Modern crowds don't demand profound emotions from art. On the contrary, the demands are often "superficial and puerile and rarely go beyond a taste for violence, for religious or amatory sentimentalism, a spice of cruelty, collective vanity and sensuality."

Thousands of people may be united in revolutionary fervor but—except in the jargon of propaganda—they are not "masses." Collective virtue comes from a communion not merely from shared emotions. Cathedrals are replaced by movie palaces and the creative imagination is put in the service of entertainment. "It is remarkable that even bad painting, bad music and bad architecture should have only one term, 'the arts,' to describe themselves. The term 'painting' applies equally to the Sistine ceiling and to the most ignoble colorprint." One reason may be that until comparatively recent times, no "bad painting" existed. The difference between Giotto and his feeblest disciple was one of talent, not one of attitude or function.

Consumer art is antiart because of its purpose. Authentic art devotes its means—even its most brutal—to the service of some part of Man, passionately or obscurely sponsored by the artist. More blood is shed in the *Oresteia* and in *Oedipus Rex* than in a sensational gangster story, but in the Greek tragedies, the blood has a different meaning. "The extinction of African and Polynesian arts in all seaports where whites buy fetishes

286

throws a sinister light on what becomes of art when the value of the artist is scaled down to the collector's taste." Significantly we pay no attention to second-string art of a century ago, not because the painters carried out the orders of the people who paid them, but because they catered deliberately and exclusively to the sentimentality and licentiousness of the day. The art of the insane also illuminates this. Like the artist, the madman has broken with the world, but his art—which impresses us because of the mental anguish behind it—is fettered by the predicament to which he owes his seeming freedom. His break with society is not a victory, lunatic art conquers nothing.

Primitive art raises stupendous questions and challenges the very foundation of Western optimism. "Savage art," which has no history, seems uncontrolled and guided by instinct alone, yet we seem to feel that it expresses certain dark, uncharted regions of the human psyche, which is why modern artists try to find in it the primordial matter of art. African, Polynesian and prehistoric art is an indictment, defying not only painting as we know it, but the illusion that the human predicament is amenable to logic. African masks are not a fixation of a human expression; they are an apparition. Their carver doesn't impose a geometrical pattern on a phantom he knows nothing about, but conjures one up by his geometry. For the African sculptor, the best mask is the most potent one and its potency depends on the completeness of its style. "In all parts of the world, the rule holds that a styleless illustration is devoid of 'power.' "

Provided we have art, not culture, in mind, the African mask and Michelangelo are not adversaries but polarities. Today, all art is a *continuum*, a world existing in its own right. We can welcome the fetish into the universal language because we have become a pluralistic, one-world culture. The legacy of archaic man is giving a resonance to masterpieces because his art links us with that incessant *conquest* which is the lifeline of creative expression regardless of whether it allies the artist with the gods or leads him to defy them. The maker of masks may be possessed by his familiar spirits, but he hears in them one of the world's voices and, as a sculptor, he takes possession of them.

Art, finally, has become its own Absolute, a bond that links all men across the chasms of time and civilization, a testimony to the power and glory of being Man. It is certain that painting has a history, but much less certain that creation has one. We are the first civilization to realize that every art has its own significance; until our times forms that did not tally with a preconceived meaning were not connected with *other* meanings. When the Ottoman empire threatened Europe, the West couldn't regard Islam as a hypothesis; only as a deadly peril. In the twelfth century, a Wei statue couldn't be compared with a Romanesque statue since one was an idol and the other a saint. In the past, no art could be separated from the values it served, meaning that all art that didn't serve

287

specific cultural values was, so to speak, invisible. This notion only disappeared when art came to be regarded as having its own value. Although Khmer heads didn't thereby become "modern," they became visible and, compared with other heads, some of them became what they actually are —works of art. If faiths decline and wither away along with the organic life of the cultures that fostered them, arts survive. History may clarify our understanding of the supreme work of art, it cannot account for it. The creative process functions no less potently in the darker tracts of history than in triumphant periods; "all that Versailles could produce in its hours of glory was Lebrun whereas Spain in her darkest hour gave birth to Goya." A culture survives—or revives—not because of what it is but because of the values it transmits. All cultures have a legacy. If it is a strongly developed civilization, it hands down an exemplary picture of man; if it is a weak culture, it passes on *elements* of man.

Culture is the heritage of the quality of the world. Art is not the result of social conditioning, but of pressure from within the artist. However brutal an age, its style transmits only its music. Athens was not the childhood of Rome and our civilization is not the sum total of earlier, now reconciled, cultures, but of irreconcilable fragments of the past. It is not the vestiges of death that touch us in ancient works of art but their echoes of life. The past is not an inventory but a heritage. It is through Greek art, showing us Greece at its noblest, that Greece solicits our love.

Art does not deliver us from destiny, from being mere by-products of the universe, but at times when we feel stranded and alone, it assures us of a deep human communion which otherwise would not exist. Art is human intelligence imposed on the forms of our planet. The artist's victory becomes form and after his death this form starts out on its own unpredictable life.

Les Voix du silence was a confrontation never attempted before. In text and illustrations, the art of prehistoric caves confronted Botticelli and Goya and fetishes of New Guinea headhunters bathed in the passions of Michelangelo while Grünewald's *Crucifixion* illuminated a Vietnamese straw mask and a Piero della Francesca a twelfth-century Buddhist fresco. Malraux had given himself the utmost freedom to develop his ideas and to write about whatever interested him, leaving to others the task of adding the scholarly footnotes. A quotation from Cézanne seemed to short-circuit all criticism and perhaps *The Voices* itself.

> It was Cézanne who said: "There is a logic in colors, and it is to this logic alone, and not with the logic of the brain, that the painter should conform." This clumsy phrase—one of the boldest and sincerest a painter had ever uttered—explains why every painter of genius feels that trying to write about his art is silly.

288

Les Voix du silence was not without its critics. Many art historians were offended by Malraux's intensely personal view. Critics basically called it a grandiose poem, a lyrical hymn to dignity and grandeur with rhetorical passages they sometimes called "Wagnerian" with a flavor of Victor Hugo and Chateaubriand. One art historian, Georges Duthuit, was roused to such fury he began to write a pamphlet against *The Voices* and in time expanded it into a 600-page book, *Le Musée inimaginable,* taking Malraux to task for saying that artistic contemplation and the notion of a museum were alien to Asians and for being at fault in his study of Greco-Buddhist art.[1] In Britain Ernst Gombrich accused Malraux of sweeping aside existing interpretation on the grounds that knowledge of the past was incomplete while at the same time insisting on the correctness of his own interpretation—that myth was no substitute for knowledge.[2] Robert Payne would write that Malraux was taking his readers on a scary roller-coaster ride by abandoning an argument to pursue another "as though the world of art were so full of arguments that all of them must be enjoyed."[3] More interestingly, Germain Bazin, chief curator of the Louvre, put Malraux in the context of art history and cultural theory and assigned to him a place midway between Alois Riegl, Heinrich Wölfflin, Swiss theorists, René Grousset and the American classicist Bernard Berenson. In 1893, Riegl had established *kunstwollen,* or will-to-art, as the active principle behind all artistic development, an *idée force* or dynamic theory characteristic of German philosophy and at the turn of the century Wölfflin had defined "classical" and "baroque" concepts. Classicism is an attempt to strike a balance between forms as conceived by the intellect and the direct observation while baroque expresses uneasiness and a longing for freedom and shows itself in open compositions, fragments rather than wholes and forms that are imponderable, weightless and organic.[4] The Lithuanian-born Berenson, most widely known for his 1930s principle of "tactile values" as a touchstone of assessment and until his death in 1959 the supreme American art theoretician, remained faithful to the traditional, pre-Riegl supremacy of classicism. In his 1946 *Bilan de l'histoire,* Grousset had written the first great synthesis of Western and Eastern cultures, taking works of art into account, though, as evidence of civilization rather than for their own sake.[5] Bazin found Malraux to follow Riegl, Wölfflin and their 1930s French disciples, Elie Faure and Henri Focillon, in the dynamic interpretation of the creative process, to have

[1] Georges Duthuit, *Le Musée inimaginable* (Paris: Corti, 1956).

[2] *Burlington* Magazine (Dec., 1954), and *The Observer* (Oct. 9, 1964).

[3] Robert Payne, *Portrait of André Malraux,* op. cit.

[4] Alois Riegl, *Stilfragen* (Berlin, 1893, 1923) and Heinrich Wölfflin, *Renaissance und Barock* (Munich, 1888).

[5] René Grousset, *Bilan de l'histoire,* English trans. A. and H. Temple Patterson, *The Sum of History* (London: Hadleigh, 1951).

something of Berenson's elitism and especially to share Grousset's enthusiasm for India as creator of great metaphysical ideas and of Greek art's astonishing conquest of Asia, with the Greco-Buddhist art of Gandhara the point where the twain did meet.[6]

In the U.S., where *The Voices* sold more copies in its first year than any other book on the plastic arts, *Time* called it "a brilliant if tantalizingly subjective musing on art through the ages"[7] and Edmund Wilson felt he had to expand in his comment on *Psychologie de l'art* as "not simply one of his best productions but perhaps one of the really great books of our time."[8] Its success led to a string of university press volumes on Malraux. Wilbur Merrill Frohock, a Stanford University French professor, had written the first American book on Malraux in 1952[9] and over the next ten years five other volumes appeared, ranging from Gerda Blumenthal's *André Malraux, The Conquest of Dread* practically exclusively devoted to *Saturn* and Malraux's attempts "to exorcise the demonic or saturnine powers that threaten to destroy modern man" to William Righter's *The Rhetorical Hero*.[10] While Miss Blumenthal found Malraux's vision of the creative process to concur with his vision of human destiny —"both are conceived as movement, as a continuous process from imprisonment to freedom, from deception to mystery, from estrangement to reconciliation"—Righter found that Malraux somehow "dehumanized" art and often tried to identify himself with the artist. Righter's book drew a rebuttal from Wilson: "I differ from Mr. Righter in his insistence that Malraux here is attempting, with tragic failure, to exalt the intellectual by identifying himself with the artist. Is not Malraux himself an artist, who, whether working in terms of the history of art or of fiction based on current history, has, by force of imagination, been re-creating for us our world?"

In bringing his ideas home to the widest of audiences and in trying to grasp the whole of art in one intuitive sweep, Robert Payne was to write in perhaps the best hindsight glance on *The Voices,* "Malraux had broadened and deepened art appreciation and by his tone of passionate enthusiasm had led many who otherwise might scarcely have come to know it to a serious interest in art."[11]

The Voices was not to be Malraux's last art book. A quarter of a

[6] Germain Bazin, *Histoire de l'art* (Paris: Garamond), English trans. Francis Scarfe, *A History of Art* (Boston: Houghton Mifflin, 1959).
[7] *Time* (Dec. 21, 1953).
[8] Edmund Wilson, *The Bit Between My Teeth: A Literary Chronicle of 1950–1965* (New York: Farrar, Straus & Giroux, 1965).
[9] Wilbur Merrill Frohock, *André Malraux and the Tragic Imagination* (Stanford: Stanford University Press, 1952).
[10] Gerda Blumenthal, *André Malraux, The Conquest of Dread* (Baltimore: Johns Hopkins Press, 1960), and William Righter, *The Rhetorical Hero* (New York: Chilmark, 1964).

century later, he was to finish the *Metamorphosis of the Gods,* which he had started as an afterthought to *The Voices* to find out which part of man demanded "a part of eternity."

[11] Robert Payne, *op. cit.*

I would like to understand the witches of my time.

Felled Oaks

24

The mid-1950s was a curiously vacant time for Malraux whose art and life, as Gaëtan Picon wrote in 1953, was "a systematic organizing of courage." It was a time for writing on art, for traveling and, as France's Indochina quagmire oozed over into North Africa, for political reassessment. Torture by French soldiers in Algeria and witch-hunt of scientists in America brought Malraux back to square one, to the youthful years of anticolonialism in Saigon and to the lancing antifascism of *Le Temps du mépris*.

If in 1945 Provisional President de Gaulle had offered Vietnam gradual independence and sent General Leclerc to Haiphong to drink a toast with Ho Chi Minh, his communist-socialist-MRP coalition successors had, in the name of a million Catholics in Indochina, reneged. Ho Chi Minh had cried betrayal and overnight increased his guerrilla forces from thirty thousand to sixty thousand men. In November 1946 a popular uprising provoked by an obscure collision between Vietminh and French customs agents had led to a French "teach-them-a-lesson" shelling of Haiphong. The bombing had cost five thousand lives and the thirty-year Vietnam war was on.

From 1946 to 1950, Ho Chi Minh and his military deputy Vo Nguyen Giap lived according to Mao Tse-tung's maxim: "If the enemy is strong avoid him; if he is weak, attack him." As guerrilla movement, the "Viets" harassed the French expeditionary force without being able to tear away control of the country. Mao's victory in China changed the Asian picture and from 1950 on, Giap disposed of a veritable army and sanctuaries in China. Over the next four years, French garrisons fell like dominos from the Chinese border to the Hanoi delta with General de Lattre trying to save the situation by pulling back toward Hanoi and other coastal cities. Leclerc had said it would take half a million men to win.

292

Paris sent only 130,000 of whom barely 40,000 were Frenchmen. Many were Germans, some barely repentant Nazis in the Foreign Legion; the rest were Algerians, Tunisians and Moroccans who would soon put to practice at home the lessons in guerrilla warfare they were learning in Indochina. With the outbreak of the Korean War, President Vincent Auriol managed to persuade President Truman that both were fighting the same enemy. Henceforth, the U.S. paid forty percent of the war costs, then sixty, then eighty percent. For France, the war was becoming a money-earning proposition—$4 billion in four years. While by 1953 the Americans had had enough in Korea, the Indochina war continued. On the French side the toll was now 10,000 French dead, five thousand legionnaries and six thousand North Africans.

On the homefront, the war provoked *le pourissement*—the "rotting" of public mores that spanned a foreign exchange scandal and a "generals' affair" that splattered police, Socialist Party, government and the presidential Élysée Palace. A new weekly magazine, *L'Express,* tried to touch raw nerves and gave Pierre Mendès-France a platform from which to utter the taboo words, "It cannot continue; the only solution is to negotiate." But before anyone could negotiate anything, the elite of the French expeditionary force, twelve thousand men of ten different nationalites, agonized in a jungle depression three hundred miles east of Hanoi, pinned down by Giap's guerrilla forces. Premier Georges Badault asked Washington for a nuclear strike. John Foster Dulles was for it and a B-29 flew over Dien Bien Phu on a photo reconnaissance mission. Everything was ready when President Eisenhower vetoed the idea. On May 7, the red-blue Vietminh flag with its golden star flew over Dien Bien Phu and ten thousand beaten and humiliated men filed past Soviet cameramen—some to turn up as parafascist "centurions" in Algeria, others to meet them head-on as burning Moslem nationalists when the combat shifted to the hot sands of North Africa. Two months later, Mendès-France was premier and met the North Vietnamese delegation in Geneva to give Vietnam its independence. Shaken, he emerged to tell the assembled press, "They speak French like you and me. They could have been our friends. What a tragedy!" The Geneva Agreement divided Vietnam at the seventeenth parallel and promised national elections within two years to reunify the country.

Mendès-France, the Jewish Parisian who tried to combat national alcoholism by drinking milk at the National Assembly rostrum, was the rallying point of everything that was progressive in France in the mid-fifties. During his seven months in office in 1954–55, he managed to offer audacious solutions to suffocating problems, ranging from giving Tunisia home rule to squeezing through the Assembly, 287–260, France's ratification of Germany's entry into NATO. Together with François Mauriac and Albert Camus, Malraux rallied to Mendès-France's support—from his

293

Colombey retreat even de Gaulle came forward to say that Mendès-France's politics could be adopted without scorn. Jean-Jacques Servan-Schreiber, Mendès-France's best friend and editor of *L'Express,* interviewed the author of *Man's Fate,* who saluted the new Premier's "energetic style" and said the New Left would have to learn to play a winning game and to stop thinking of communism as the only effective opposition to right-wing politics.

If Malraux had been less than eloquent during the distant and, to most Frenchmen, vague and unreal Indochina conflict, he was a courageous backer of "the other side" in that much more traumatic Algerian War which broke out before the signatures of the Geneva Agreement were dry. In 1945, he had warned de Gaulle that none of the colonial empires would survive the European war and two years later he had felt France could negotiate the independence of Vietnam with Ho Chi Minh's nationalists from a position of strength (de Gaulle had thought a "French solution" was still possible). The Algerian War was different. It was complicated by the fact that over a million *pieds noirs*—Frenchmen with a sprinkling of Italians—had settled in Algeria, many of them several generations ago. To them granting the Moslem majority independence was tantamount to betrayal and Mendès-France and all the other precarious coalition governments of the Fourth Republic shrank away from any and all courageous acts in Algeria. The powerful ally of the settlers was the French army. Whole classes of Saint Cyr graduates had disappeared in Vietnam and officers and career soldiers all felt they had been sold down the drain by a weak civilian government. They were animated by a "never again" resolve, a contempt for democratic compromise and a morbid respect for the merciless efficacy of "national liberation fronts," be they Vietnamese or Algerian. As soldiers and as Europeans they felt they had to adopt their enemy's ruthless tactics and resort to mass punishment, indiscriminate terrorizing of civilian populations, and, in the day-to-day combat with an enemy that all too easily melted into an anonymous Arab crowd, to torture in order to obtain information. Only highly paid volunteers and career soldiers had been sent to Indochina; the Algerian conflict was fought with draftees, supported by professional units such as the khaki-clad elitist paratroopers who served as a copy for the U.S. Army when it made the Green Berets specialists in Third World counterrevolutionay warfare. Algeria split French society down the middle, with the Right supporting the conflict—and the ultra-Right resorting to violence—and the Left slowly drifting toward open opposition while for a long time shying away from the taboo word of independence for Algeria.

The war made Malraux—and his daughter, Florence, now a Gallimard arts department employee and *L'Express* contributor—move from Mendès-France's liberalism to outright condemnation of the French army. In 1958, he cosigned a resounding protest against torture and censorship and four years later was the object of a right-wing assassination attempt that halfway blinded a four-year-old girl. "We're making war because we've got no ideas and we continue it because it's an answer to housewives protesting higher prices," he told journalists in early 1958. "And because we have no ideology, we let ourselves go—even as far as torture." When the newsmen asked if *he* had a solution, he said yes, a temporary one.

> In order to make Europe survive [in North Africa] and at the same time to yield to Arab nationalism, we must immediately start a model zone . . . In this pilot area we do everything—Stakhanovite incentive programs, agrarian reforms, kibutzim, Arab model villages, dam projects, the works. And at the same time, we spruce up what's Arabic and Muslim to the point where even in Egypt people will talk about this model zone as a Mecca. We must make Algerians proud of cooperating with France and make all other Arabs, in Algeria and elsewhere, jealous of the people living in this zone. This doesn't mean we shouldn't negotiate and it doesn't cancel political decisions, but it creates a mystique of accomplishments, the only weapon that we have against the "allure" of the *Front de liberation national* (FLN). Later we can then build a Franco-North African federation because for a change the peoples of North Africa will have seen the advantage of cooperating with us. At the same time, we can rebuild France by giving ourselves a goal.

As in Saigon in 1924, Malraux didn't propose revolution but reform with bite, shine and hope. In April 1958 when *La Question*—a book in which Henri Alleg, a communist militant fighting with the FLN, described the torture he had been subjected to—was banned, Malraux signed with Roger Martin du Gard, Mauriac and Sartre (Algiers-born Camus refused to join them), a "solemn address" to President René Coty.

The mid-1950s were also a time for travel and for writing. After trips to Greece, Egypt and Iran in 1952, he and Madeleine were in New York the following year, attending a Columbia University anniversary and the inauguration of new Metropolitan Museum sections. When someone asked him if he agreed with Rebecca West's *mot* that America's cathedrals were its railway stations, he amiably answered, "No, America's cathedrals are its museums."

The Oppenheimer Case brought him into the orbit of American Cold War politics, with Haakon Chevalier providing the link and the "father of the atom bomb" the object-lesson in intellectual bewilderment. André's translator and prewar guide to West Coast radical chic was now a UNESCO interpreter in Paris. Chevalier had remained a friend of Kitty and "Opje" and when he had married, the Oppenheimers had sent him and his bride Carol a magnificent mahogany salad bowl from the Virgin Islands together with the wishes that the four of them might eat a salad from it before long. When in December 1953 Chevalier heard the Oppenheimers were coming to Europe, he invited them to come and share the salad. After the dinner in the Chevaliers' Montmartre apartment, washed down with toasts to their health and "to the confusion of our enemies," Haakon took the Oppenheimers to meet Malraux in Boulogne. The meeting, according to Chevalier, was an extraordinary three hours with a discussion ranging from Einstein to art. Before they left, thirteen-year-old Gauthier and ten-year-old Vincent were introduced to Oppenheimer. Gauthier wanted to be a scientist and when the physicist was out of earshot had asked his father to confirm that this was "the real Oppenheimer." When they drove away, Oppenheimer told Chevalier, "Malraux has some understanding as to what science *isn't,* but he has no concept of what science *is.*[1] It was the last time they saw each other. The next day Oppenheimer flew back to the United States and three months later denounced Chevalier as the man who in 1943 had tried to pry atomic secrets from him for the Soviet Union.

The "trial" before Atomic Energy Commission chairman Gordon Gray had its origins in an obscure official's letter to the FBI calling Robert Oppenheimer a Soviet agent. The charge was incredible, for "the father of the atomic bomb" was one of the nation's most respected scientists. Yet suddenly powerful persons throughout the government rushed to bring him down.

The incriminating conversation, Oppenheimer told the Gray Board security hearing, had occurred in January or February of 1943 in the kitchen of the J. Robert Oppenheimer residence in Berkeley. The Chevaliers had come for dinner. When the host went to the kitchen to get the ingredients for his favorite martini, Chevalier had followed him. Precisely what was said in the ensuing minutes was never to be known, but both agreed their conversation had dealt with one George Eltenton, a British chemical engineer and radiation expert working for Shell Development Corporation in Berkeley. There was no dispute over the fact that Chevalier had said Eltenton claimed he had means of getting technical data to the Russians, nor that Oppenheimer had made it clear he would have no part in such an affair. But had Chevalier actually *asked* Oppenheimer to furnish atomic secrets for transmission via Eltenton to Moscow? Oppenheimer gave slightly different versions of the "kitchen conversation" in congressional testimony in 1949, in letters to *The New York Times* arranged by his lawyers and now at the Washington security hearings that dragged on for nineteen days.

Chevalier first learned of the affair in the carefully orchestrated letters to *The New York Times* in April 1954 and immediately realized he was in danger of losing his job as an American UNESCO employee and perhaps his U.S. passport. Anticommunist hysteria had been running high for a year. After taking on the U.S. Army, Senator Joseph McCarthy had just disclosed that a Harvard physicist, later identified as Wendell Furry,

[1] Haakon M. Chevalier, *Oppenheimer: The Story of a Friendship* (New York: Braziller, 1965).

had refused to disclose his political past. Furry's pleading the Fifth Amendment instantly smeared Harvard, a matter of concern to Oppenheimer, who was chairman of the Harvard physics department's "visiting committee."

When in September Madeleine and André came for dinner at the Chevaliers' tiny apartment, Haakon and Carol tried to explain the *Affaire Oppenheimer* which, in May, had ended with the AEC Board asserting that "the government can search the soul of an individual" and with Oppenheimer losing his security clearance. Oppenheimer, whose motives Chevalier still couldn't fathom, was both symbol and victim of the new and perplexing problem of government—the sudden transformation of the scientist from rumpled, abstracted, ivory-tower figure to a major force in policy making. As they were pondering the implications and ramifications of the case (one witness had shouted "there hasn't been a proceeding like this since the Spanish Inquisition" [2]), André asked whether the Chevaliers had read the transcripts of Oscar Wilde's libel action against the Marquis of Queensberry? Wilde had dominated the scene at the beginning with wit and brilliant repartee, but when the defense lawyer had started to cross-examine Wilde, there had been a dramatic reversal. After a few questions, Wilde suddenly collapsed and became abject and inarticulate. Malraux felt that as long as Wilde had been able to keep the trial on the level of his own hedonistic values, he could retain complete possession of himself. The moment the ground had been shifted by sordid pieces of evidence, he was lost. Malraux's judgment was to be that of posterity. "He should have told them, at the very outset, '*Je suis la bombe atomique.*'"

Time gave Malraux its cover-story treatment a year later—an elegant five-page essay on "the man who, supremely among his contemporaries, has lived the challenges of his troubled times," illustrated with photos of Malraux and the boys at home, with Madeleine at the piano, headshots of France's other "mandarins"—Paul Claudel, Mauriac, Camus and a two-shot of Sartre and Ilya Ehrenburg.[3]

Since the beginning of his association with Gallimard, Malraux had played with the idea of bringing out a series of rich, full-color editions of Bosch, da Vinci, Vermeer, Braque, Ensor, Picasso. Only two books were published. The least successful was the one he worked hardest on—Leonardo da Vinci. Paul Valery's famous 1896 essay, *Introduction à la méthode de Léonardo de Vinci,* served as a preface and Malraux combed world literature for necessary commentaries. What had Goethe, Hegel, Ruskin, Delacroix, Wilde and Chateaubriand said about da Vinci or on any of his paintings. The sumptuous volume was a disaster. A strange bluish-gray cloud seemed to have settled on all the reproductions and, as Payne was to say, "the artist who demands the most careful and cautious

[2] Philip M. Stern, *The Oppenheimer Case: Security on Trial* (New York: Harper and Row, 1969).
[3] *Time* (July 18, 1955).

treatment by the photoengravers was ill-served." [4] For the second volume, *Vermeer de Delft,* the reproductions were especially reprinted and Malraux wrote an inspired essay. Virtually unknown or mistaken for other artists until three hundred years after his death, Vermeer never painted anything except portraits of tradespeople, his wife and children, or views of the street outside his house. Not the least puzzling aspect was his apparent lack of output, an average of three paintings every two years of his adult life, which made it difficult to explain the perfection and facility which were such outstanding features of his work.

Malraux saw new things in Vermeer. No one had previously suggested that *The Geographer, The Astronomer* and other portraits were the same person and that there were excellent reasons to believe they were all self-portraits. Malraux suggested there was no mystery and that far from concealing himself, Vermeer had taken pains to reveal himself by painting his own likeness as a soldier, a geographer, an astronomer. Always a lover of fine books, Malraux designed *Vermeer de Delft* with exquisite care and taste and was rewarded by seeing it become an overwhelming success.

If Vermeer was the sunny face of art—clear colors, immaculate calm, sense of order and compositions of abstract simplicity—Goya was the saturnine side of artistic temperament, the court painter who discovered his genius the day he dared to stop pleasing and who, when he was in his late sixties and stone deaf, drew and painted savage and macabre nightmare scenes to protest the cruelty of war. Malraux had always been fascinated by Goya. He had written about him since 1929, had come to regard him as the true forefather of modern painting. In *Saturne, essai sur Goya,* Malraux found himself in total sympathy with his subject and wrote his most illuminating pages on painting:

> The sparkling freedom of Rubens, of Tintoretto served to create an adorned universe, Rembrandt's freedom served to create a transfigured world. Before Goya, Rembrandt had, better than any one else, managed to escape his own era—the Aix en Provence and the Bayonne portraits and the Old Men in the Prado are simply "modern." But if we compare Rembrandt's *Woman Sweeping* with Goya's *Milkwoman from Bordeaux,* the former is a transfigured Holy Mother or Good Samaritan, the latter a pretext for painting. Until Goya, portraits *also* addressed themselves to the imagination; twenty of his portraits have nothing to do with imagining and are simply art. This man whose dream was his second life—perhaps his first life—freed painting from dreaming. He gave it—not by the sudden shock of a dying Frans Hals, but by perseverance—the right to see in reality nothing more than a primal substance, and to create, not like the poets, an ornamented world, but, like the musicians, an exclusive

[4] Robert Payne, *Portrait of André Malraux,* op. cit.

298

universe. He is the first one to put the model under the domination of the painting; not to subjugate the painting to the model.

During the 1808–14 French occupation of Spain, Goya retained his appointment as court painter, but his activity as society painter decreased as he was torn between his welcome of French liberalism and his abhorrence of foreign military rule. The masterpieces of this period, inspired by the resistance to the French, have the tremendous dramatic force that reached its height in *The Shooting of May 3rd*. Equally dramatic, but much more savage and macabre, are the etchings of *Los Desastres de la Guerra*. After the restoration of the Bourbons in 1814 Goya still remained court painter but he fell out of royal favor. After a second illness (a first acute illness had left him deaf at the age of forty-six), he bought a country house in the outskirts of Madrid, the Quinta del Sordo, and here executed fourteen large murals. Painted almost entirely in blacks, grays and browns, these works were made public only many years after his death. In 1824, when he was seventy-eight years old, Goya obtained permission from King Ferdinand VII to leave Spain for reasons of health and settled in Bordeaux. Here he took up the new medium of lithography and progressed, in the painting of his early eighties, toward a style that foreshadowed the Impressionists.

After *The Bulls of Bordeaux*, he continues to paint, in that impressive light which, as they approach death, unites Titian, Hals, Rembrandt, Michelangelo—old men tired of life but not of painting, finally only bemused by their fellows and filling canvases only for themselves. He works on his last portraits, *The Nun* and *The Monk*. His haunted solitude, now eternal, has joined Beethoven's deafness. But he is exhausting his drawings and he feels he must change their style, and find, perhaps in gouache, the equivalent of the whites of lithography. Still drawings of flying men and dogs, a few belated demons. Spain—he knows that if he hadn't been a painter Spain would not be the same in our dreams—fades away. He almost doesn't see the world he no longer hears; he can almost no longer see his crayons.

Future painters will forget the price this man paid in anxiety for opposing the culture he was born into with a solitary and despairing art. They will retain, however, from his still glittering ashes the proclamation of the individuals' rights and the right to the absurd, his transformation of the world into painting. They will try, with painting as their only passion, what Goya tried—to make us hear a soul both thirsting for, and utterly removed from, the Absolute.

Here, modern painting begins.

When Goya died, he was eighty-two years old.

Malraux also wrote about a revolutionary who died at the age of twenty-six—Louis de Saint-Just, the theoretician of the French revolution during the Terror (1793–94), executed together with Maximilien de

299

Robespierre. To his friend Albert Ollivier's biography on Saint-Just, Malraux wrote a penetrating foreword, showing how modern this "passionate totalitarian" was, this "Mohamed turned lawmaker," with his unyielding logic and his Republic founded on an austere knighthood mixed with secret police methods.[5]

> Saint-Just is not a forerunner of communism and fascism on the level of doctrine, but he is the omen of the all-powerful One Party . . . In him, we see Lenin's little shadow dancing in the Kremlin snow and telling his dumbfounded commissars, "We've now lasted a day longer than the 1870 Paris Commune." . . . Saint-Just's Republic would not have brought about the Perfect State, but Islam's horsemen.
>
> A part of his prestige belongs to his talent, which is not really literary. His speeches and notes are only of interest to scholars; his genius is made up of isolated phrases which his actions have given a reverberating significance because they seem to be what history is made of. He wanted to live inside history as holy men inside their faith, to be confounded with the Republic as saints lose themselves in God . . . Perhaps his *aura* comes ultimately from the glint of the guillotine blade in the evening sun, killing in him not only the murderer of Louis XVI, the accuser of Danton and the architect of the Republic's victory over the Austrians at Fleurus, but also the Revolution's greatest adventurer.

In 1958, Malraux was, not unlike Saint-Just nearly a hundred and seventy years earlier, orbiting toward the central character of precipitous events. The character wasn't Robespierre but Charles de Gaulle, ambiguous fisherman in the troubled waters of a Fourth Republic incapable of either waging war or making peace. In May, a demoralized and near-seditious army threatened to let events in Algeria run away with themselves. A month later, the events swept aside the Fourth Republic itself. The general, now sixty-eight years old, was the towering strongman the army wanted, but he was also a statesman with lofty vistas. Within four years he was to grant Algeria the independence the army and the million *pieds noirs* sought to prevent by bringing him to power.

When in June, de Gaulle began forming his government, Malraux was, again, at his side.

[5] Albert Ollivier, *Saint-Just et la Force des choses* (Paris: Gallimard, 1954).

A political leader is necessarily an imposter since
he believes in solving life's problems without asking
its question.

25

"The most dazzling star in the new government," Pierre Viansson-
Ponté was to write in a history of the Gaullist years, "was André Malraux
who will begin a ministerial career that will be controversial but never
uninteresting, drawn as he is to the general by an admiration and an
esteem that is reciprocal and unfailing." [1] The first four years were to be
the most difficult.

Malraux was in Venice studying Tintoretto paintings when a laconic
statement from Paris announced that a government invested with exceptional powers was undetraking a constitutional revision, to be submitted
to France's voters in an upcoming referendum. De Gaulle was back in
power. Malraux rushed back to Paris. On June 4, two days after de
Gaulle had gone through the motion of having himself elected by the
parliament of a regime he was about to abolish, Malraux was summoned to
afternoon tea at the general's residence. "France needs to be redone,"
Malraux quoted de Gaulle as saying in the *Antimémoires*. "The question
is whether the French people want to build France or go back to sleep.
I cannot do it without them. And we must insure the continuity of our
institutions until I call on the people to choose new ones. For the moment,
they don't want the colonels. So our task is to rebuild the state, to stabilize
the currency and to finish with colonialism."

In public, de Gaulle expressed himself more guardedly on getting
rid of the colonies. Five days before his investiture, the near-rebellion of
Algiers' Europeans had jumped half the Mediterranean to Corsica, revealing both the boldness of the *pieds noirs* and the murky uncertainty
of civil servants. De Gaulle's "restoration" had become possible by the

[1] Pierre Viansson-Ponté, *Histoire de la république gaullienne* (Paris: Fayard,
1970).

301

convergence of three hitherto mutually exclusive tendencies. In him merged the hopes of those who believed—or pretended to believe—that only he could keep Algeria French, of old RPF stalwarts who saw in Algeria the firecracker capable of carrying them to power and of the minority who felt only his immense prestige could make the country accept the inevitable emancipation of Algeria. During the early months of his caretaker investiture, de Gaulle played all sides, but by conviction, he was in favor of independence for Algeria. This nationalist—and contemporary of Mussolini and Roosevelt—had never felt France's grandeur had to be defended in the Mekong Delta or the Maghreb Mountains. Young Lieutenant de Gaulle had never served overseas and during his long military career he had passionately believed in the Rhine, the "revanche," in industrialization and economic independence, in France as a *European* power. He had only discovered "overseas France" during World War II and in Brazzaville in 1942 had first proposed his own brand of decolonization. His postwar government, however, had been too short-lived to allow him to implement his *Communauté*—a Gallic version of the British Commonwealth circa 1950. "The colonies," he now told Malraux, "are finished. Let us come together and create a Community, with a common defense, a common foreign policy and a common economic policy." He didn't mention Algeria, but Malraux gathered the North African territory would also be offered independence along with France's seventeen other colonies and dependencies.

While de Gaulle flew to Algiers to answer the delirious European crowds with his Machiavellian "I have understood you!" (understood *whom*—the Moslem majority fighting for independence or the million *pieds noirs* who, in applauding him, thought they were hailing the guarantor of their *Algérie française?*), Malraux became "minister-delegate" in charge of information. His department was soon enlarged and given the more sonorous title, Ministry of Cultural Affairs, a name more in tune with the Gaullian concept of France's grandeur and civilizing mission. As in 1945, Malraux had expected a more prestigious cabinet post—Interior secretary, according to François Mauriac; the proconsulship of Algeria, according to the younger Mauriac, Claude.

Information Minister with a vengeance then. As in 1945, he started by putting energetic people in key positions and by receiving Cyrus Sulzberger, and calling a press conference where he fielded the taboo questions —Algeria and torture. After appointing Albert Ollivier to the state-run Office de radio-télévision française (ORTF), he told Sulzberger that de Gaulle was preparing a "presidential constitution, something like the American Constitution" as well as social reform but that peace in Algeria was the overwhelming question. The *New York Times* editor found the new minister "terribly tense, pale and electric," and before leaving, said he presumed Malraux was no longer writing. "No," he was told, "this is not a time for literature." [2]

When Sulzberger asked what Malraux's functions were he was told, "I orchestrate." De Gaulle had decided he would rule not through a parliament but through periodic, direct referendums and Malraux was soon out "orchestrating" grandiose rallies on historical dates and sites—a 14th of July manifestation on the Place de la Bastille, a Place de la Concorde rally on August 24, the anniversary of the Liberation of Paris. The first and most important popular consultation was the September 28 constitutional vote which, if passed, would create the Fifth Republic and Malraux was soon on a whirlwind tour of French Caribbean territories on behalf of a "yes" vote for the Gaullian republic and for the *Communauté*. In Martinique he was applauded, but in Guiana an unruly crowd shouted "Down with France" and "Independence now!", to which Malraux answered, "If it is independence you want, take it on the 28th. Who before de Gaulle even gave you the *right* to take it!"

His July 24 press conference in Paris was a journalist's treat. With his staccato verbosity and benumbing rhetoric, the new Information minister twitched and wheezed his way through all subjects with trenchant comments, realistic appraisals and—novelty—candid admissions. He managed to launch his idea of an Algerian "model zone" and to make headlines by inviting France's three living Nobel prizewinners to go to Algiers to investigate the allegations of continued torture of captured terrorists. "A paralyzed France wants to walk again," he began. "The question is not to give the paralysis a new form." Anxious to reassure the Left he launched:

> There are those who want the Republic without the general and those who would like to see the general in power without the republic, but the majority wants both the general *and* democratic institutions. They form the true nation, proud of their liberties but tired of defeat.

Talking about the future of Algeria, he managed to cause vivid fears in European circles in Algiers by saying the very collapse of the Fourth Republic was proof of the limits of integration. When asked whether a May 16 Moslem-European "solidarity" demonstration in Algiers hadn't been organized by *pied noir* integrationists to pressure the previous government into calling de Gaulle back to power, he answered, "It's possible." When the question of torture came up, he said, "As far as I and *you* know, no acts of torture have occurred since de Gaulle went to Algiers." With that he invited the three French authors "on whom the Nobel prize has bestowed a special authority," to form a commission and to go to North Africa to investigate.

[2] Cyrus Sulzberger, *The Last of the Giants.*

303

Nothing came of the Nobel laureates' investigation. Roger Martin du Gard was dying, François Mauriac too skeptical and *pied-noir* Albert Camus not too anxious to associate himself with any open anti-*Algérie française* initiative. Torture was not to go away, but to embarrass and humiliate the author of *La Condition humaine,* the brilliant "left flank" of a régime that took another four years to end the cruel war.

In 1959, the Interior department banned *La Gangrène,* a book written by Bachir Boumaza and three other tortured *Fédération de libération nationale* (FLN) militants, causing an uproar in Leftist circles. French resident Graham Greene wrote an open letter to Malraux to remind the Secretary for Cultural Affairs of what he had written two years earlier when *La Question* had been banned.[3] In September 1960, an imposing group of artists, writers and actors—one hundred and twenty-one in all—signed a manifesto condemning the ongoing war and backing young draftees' "right to disobey." Among the one hundred and twenty-one names was his daughter's—Florence Malraux, filmmaker. A year later, a parachute commando's devastating memoirs of combat was seized at the Editions de Minuit and its publisher, Jérome Lindon, wrote an indignant open letter to "the appointed defender of culture."

And yet. And yet there were also felicitous initiatives—effective interventions on behalf of Camus and other discreet sympathizers to free Algerian militants from the claws of gung ho military commanders and, out in the open, allowing the Theatre de France to stage Jean Genet's Algerian War-themed play *Les Paravents,* which, without the backing of the Cultural Affairs department, Prime Minister Michel Debré would have banned. And the government he was a member of did lumber toward negotiations with the FLN, prodded along by its general-president and underhandedly resisted by Debré. In de Gaulle's Olympian world view, independence was a two-way street. Granting Algeria independence also meant freeing France from Algeria. It meant a stop on the treasure drain, a reordering of domestic priorities and an end to a chapter that tarnished France in the emerging Third World. A strong economy, a franc as solid as gold and regained international prestige were the cornerstones of Gaullian statecraft, the prerequisites for challenging the increasing world hegemony of the United States and for taking bold initiatives in the new era he saw dawning with the end of the Cold War. Not that he—or his Cultural Affairs secretary—had much sympathy for Arab nationalism. De Gaulle knew little about Islam, its history and peoples—Malraux found Moslem culture "formless" and its art unrewarding—but the general knew that what had brought him to power (and so overwhelmingly endorsed his constitutional changes) was a deep desire for peace.

It didn't come easily. In 1958, de Gaulle proposed a *Paix des braves*

³ "Lettre ouverte," *Le Monde* (June 23, 1960).

to the fellaheen which the FLN rejected as being too close to surrender. A year later he offered "self-determination" with three choices—total "Francization" (the very ugliness of the term was, in the mouth of this political esthete, proof that he rejected it himself); outright independence (which he called "secession") and "association," which he obviously favored. The FLN's reaction was far from negative, but the *Algérie française* supporters answered him with barricades in Algiers and a wave of violence in Algeria and in Paris, and a succession of plots on his life.

There were those who saw in Frantz Fanon, the black revolutionary theorist now directing the FLN's pan-African propaganda, a modern Kyo Gisors, and interest in *La Condition humaine* and its urban guerrilla theme picked up both in France and elsewhere. Some of the parallels were disturbing. Like May Gisors, Kyo's wife, Fanon was a doctor who had turned unorthodox Marxist out of hatred of suffering and oppression (and like *Les Conquérant's* Garin he knew he was dying). Serving as a psychiatrist in Blida Hospital in Algeria in the mid-1950s, Fanon had found himself treating both torturer and tortured and required to reconcile both with their fate. He developed the theory that the mental disturbances he had to treat were a by-product of colonialism and decided it was the system, not the individual, that had to be changed. Hunted by French police, he was now traveling all over Africa as the diplomatic representative of what the FLN called The Provisional Government of the Algerian Republic while realizing he was dying of leukemia. In America, interest in *Man's Fate* translated into a project to film the 1934 novel. Director Richard Brooks, who had just adapted *Elmer Gantry* to the screen, came to Paris and met with Malraux. Brooks took an option on *La Condition humaine*. He couldn't get Columbia Pictures behind the project, but was sufficiently captivated by the theme of foreigner-stirring-revolution-in-Asia that he went to Cambodia and filmed Joseph Conrad's *Lord Jim,* with Peter O'Toole in the title role.

On April 23, 1961, a year after the Algiers "barricades," four generals attempted a putsch and during forty-eight hours everything seemed to hang in balance. French commander-in-chief in Algeria Maurice Challe together with Edmond Jouhaud, André Zeller and Raoul Salan had paratroopers take over Algiers in a bloodless coup. To win, the rebellion would have to reach France and at dawn on Sunday, April 24, de Gaulle went on television to awaken every citizen to a sense of historic emergency by asking that all possible means be used to bar the paratroopers should they try to carry the rebellion to the homeland.

Malraux was Colonel Berger again, barricading himself with spontaneous followers at the Ministry of Interior at Place Beauveau near the Élysée Palace. When, shortly before midnight, Debré went on television and in an emotional voice asked every citizen to put himself in a state of legitimate defense and, if the paratroopers would attempt to land, to meet them, "by car, by bicycle, or on foot!" Malraux told an extraordinary cabinet meeting, "I'll hop into the first tank myself."

Within three hours of Debré's appeal, the Interior Department courtyard was full of volunteers. Malraux saw to it that they were provided with arms requisitioned from the Garde républicaine. Inside, Interior Minister Roger Frey and his secretary-general Alexandre Sanguinetti went through the files of known *Algérie française* sympathizers who might be involved in any attempted coup. At dawn, nothing had happened and Sanguinetti pronounced the *mot* of the day, "We've got nothing to worry about; we're defended by Malraux." During the morning new volunteers arrived, many of them bringing their wartime uniforms and guns. Malraux assigned tasks and responsibilities and explained street warfare tactics. Orly and Le Bourget airports as well as military fields near the capital were bristling with stakes on the runways making it impossible for planes to land. "The paratroopers will be here in three hours," commander Malraux said in the afternoon, "or they'll never come!"

When de Gaulle heard "Colonel Berger" was setting up an armed camp in the courtyard of the Interior Ministry, he said, "There's a man who never fails to surprise me." Instead of paratroopers, Paris received an evening downpour that plunged the capital into an autumnal cold and dampened a lot of ardor. The Élysée Palace had lost all contact with Algiers and rumors flew. Some reports had it that Salan had sent an emissary to President Kennedy to explain that independence would mean a communist Algeria. Wilder scuttlebutt had more than a hundred U.S. Air Force fighters streaking toward North Africa from secret bases in Florida. That night, Malraux ordered his volunteers to sleep in shifts.

On Monday morning, he had a hunch it was all over. "Now we can go and sleep like babies; there's no longer any danger," he announced at high noon before he climbed into his ministerial limousine and, with motorcycle escort, had himself taken home to Boulogne.

The putsch caved in that day.

At 1 P.M. on February 7, 1962, four men, three of them carrying machine guns, placed a *plastique* charge on the windowsill of the ground floor of the Malraux residence. Most people were at lunch and everything was quiet in residential Boulogne when the bomb went off and the four men made their getaway. What they should have known was that Malraux rented the top-floor studio apartment and that the ground floor was occupied by his landlord. Instead of killing or maiming Malraux, the bomb blew up in the face of Delphine Renard, the landlord's four-year-old daughter. Surgery saved her life but she remained blind in the right eye and facially disfigured. Two days later, twenty-two-year-old Jean-Marie Vincent, an important member of the OAS in Paris, was arrested as the gang leader and charged with attempted murder.

Personal tragedy had struck Malraux the previous May. After

end-of-the-school-year exams, Gauthier and Vincent were vacationing on the Riviera and visiting with their grandparents Clotis in Hyères. Twenty-two-year-old Gauthier, who had already moved away from home and into a student's garret in the Latin Quarter, prepared to major in political science while Vincent, although only eighteen, was engaged to Clara Saint, the daughter of a South American businessman, and planned to marry during the summer. For Clara's nineteenth birthday her father had given her an Alfa Romeo, which she had lent to Vincent for the brothers' short vacation. They had left their grandparents on May 18, telling an acquaintance they would try to make it to Paris the same night. In the early evening on highway 6 north of Lyons, they were killed. Skid marks on the slippery road showed the driver had lost control and that the Alfa Romeo had careened across the center divider and, with a terrible force, hit a tree on the opposite side of the road. When discovered, the sports car was practically wrapped around the tree. Gauthier, at the wheel, was killed instantly; Vincent, who had been thrown clear, a few moments later. The bodies were taken to the hospital in Beaune, where Malraux arrived the following afternoon. That night, he sat alone in the hospital morgue with his two dead sons. The next day, he had the bodies taken to Paris and buried in the small Charonne cemetery close to their mother's grave.

To still the pain, he plunged into feverish activities—as he had done after Josette's death. While John F. Kennedy, on his way to his historical meeting in Vienna with Nikita Khrushchev, conferred with de Gaulle, Malraux took the American First Lady on a VIP tour of the Louvre, Versailles and Malmaison and promised the enthusiastic Jacqueline Kennedy to have some of the Louvre's treasures go on an American tour.

Malraux was becoming France's "ambassador to the world." After the campaign tour of the Caribbean and Guiana (which had voted to stay French), de Gaulle sent his Cultural Affairs secretary to India, a country that had always fascinated Malraux. Now, two lines of Bengal Lancers, dressed in rainbow colors, saluted him as he made his way to the official New Delhi reception at Prime Minister Jawaharlal Nehru's residence. "I'm glad to see you again," the Indian leader said. "The last time was after you were wounded in Spain. You were just out of the hospital and I was just out of jail." Perception at this level of acuteness would have frightened lesser men. Malraux loved it and in the *Antimémoires* was to spend forty sonorous pages in the company of Nehru, whom he considered, with de Gaulle, the cleverest man he had ever met. Nehru was also charmed by his visitor but perhaps irritated by Malraux's title and role. When he bade him good-bye, he quoted a Gandhi saying: "Freedom must often be sought behind prison walls, sometimes on the scaffold, never in cabinet meetings, courts of law or in school."

After visits to Benares, to the sacred Elloa caves and to Sarnath,

In Washington. Left to right: André and Madeleine, Vice-President Lyndon Johnson, Jacqueline and President John F. Kennedy.

With Nehru in New Delhi, 1958

where Buddha had preached in a deer park, Malraux hosted a luncheon at the French embassy for the prime minister which prolonged itself for hours as the two men talked. Malraux sensed in Nehru an atheist like himself, a man who would like to, but could not—like Gandhi—believe that the Ganges was sacred. Nehru and Malraux wanted to meet a third time and an embassy dinner was arranged before Malraux's departure. Joined by the French ambassador, they talked again for hours. Their subjects ranged from colonialism and atheism to Shakespeare, Phidias and art. To Nehru, the profound question of the times was how to harmonize industrial progress with a civilization of the soul and how to understand Western mechanical frenzy. Malraux told him that each time he had tried to look deep inside man he had found only misery.

The voyage to India led to a French state visit by Indira, Nehru's daughter (who, like Jacqueline Kennedy, was given a personal tour of the Louvre by the Cultural Affairs secretary) and immediately improved Franco-Indian relations. Next, Malraux was in Athens, proclaiming the greatness of Greece from the height of the Acropolis. After closing the 1959 Cannes film festival, which saw the triumph of François Truffaut and the French *nouvelle vague,* he was in Latin America—Rio de Janeiro and the new capital, Brasilia, Buenos Aires, Lima, Montevideo and, a year later, Mexico City.

In May 1962, Madeleine and he were in Washington, the guests of

309

President and Mrs. Kennedy—and learning on American television of the signing of the Evian Agreement ending the Algerian War. Jacqueline Kennedy led him through the National Gallery, where Malraux was impressed by what he pronounced three masterpieces—Domenico Veneziano's *Madonna with Child,* a very young El Greco, *Christ Chasing the Money-lenders from the Temple,* and Rembrandt's *Girl with a Broom.*

"We all want to take part in life's numerous adventures but Mr. Malraux has left us all behind," JFK declared at a White House dinner for the French Cultural Affairs secretary. The banquet was served in two separate rooms. In the State Dining Room, the President had Madeleine Malraux on his right. In the Blue Room, Malraux was at Jacqueline Kennedy's right. The President was in an ebullient mood and cracked jokes about his speech being the first Franco-American relations speech not to include a tribute to General Lafayette. He said Americans, "as participants in a cultural stream and also as admirers of those who travel the far horizons of human destiny," regarded Malraux as their honored guest. When in the Blue Room, Malraux rose to speak, he said it was the first time he had to reply to a speech he hadn't heard. He was brief, saying that:

> The United States is today, outstandingly, the country that assumes the destiny of man. And it is the first time in history that a nation occupies such a place without having sought it. Through the millennia many countries have achieved first place by sustained efforts, at the price of innumerable human lives. There has been an Assyrian Empire, a Byzantine Empire, a Roman Empire. There is no American Empire. There is, however, the United States. For the first time a country has become the world's leader without achieving this through conquest. And it is strange to think that for thousands of years one single country has found power while seeking only justice.

Two days later the Kennedys invited Madeleine and André to spend Sunday with them privately at Glen Ora, their Virginia country home. Kennedy was thinking about economic problems and before he and Malraux broached nuclear politics, they discussed the odd persistence of old issues in modern politics. In the nineteenth century, Malraux said, the ostensible issue in Europe was monarchy versus elected government, but the real issue was capitalism versus the proletariat. In the twentieth century the ostensible issue is capitalism versus the proletariat, but the world has moved on. What was is the real issue now? How to manage a highly complex industrial society, Kennedy replied, a problem, he said, not of ideology but of administration.

The conversation remained in the president's mind. A few days later, when he spoke to a White House conference on economic issues, the "difference between myth and reality" provided the theme. The old debates of Franklin Roosevelt and Woodrow Wilson, he observed, were increasingly irrelevant. With the exception of medical care for the aged, which still aroused "powerful feelings," most contemporary issues didn't lend themselves to party politics solutions. "How can we look at things as they are, not through party labels, but as they are—and figure out how we can maintain the economy so that it moves ahead?" [4]

Their conversation soon moved on to the burning issue of nuclear power. France was on the eve of exploding its first nuclear device in the Sahara and Kennedy was weighing his options. The Evian Agreements granting Algeria independence now freed de Gaulle to seek France's independence from the "Anglo-Saxons," who, in de Gaulle's view, had cast a too ominous shadow for too long over the French landscape. Nuclear warfare research was forbiddingly costly and Prime Minister Harold Macmillan was already dickering for American Polaris missiles so as to be able to scrap the parallel British Skybolt program and Kennedy was now wondering whether to extend the exclusive U.S.-British nuclear relationship to France—something he offered to do in December 1962 when he met Macmillan in the Bahamas and something de Gaulle haughtily rejected. Why? Because he felt the Cuban missile crisis proved *his* point, that to defend its national interest, the U.S. would indeed go to the brink. He felt that if anything, Cuba made it even more imperative for France to go her own way.

For the moment, Malraux tried to explain de Gaulle's nuclear reasoning. French atomic power had two goals: independence from a foreign—*American*—power but also morale boosting for an army badly mangled by Algeria. De Gaulle believed alliances were possible but not that an army could fight, and die, for vague supranational entities. An army, Malraux told Kennedy, must have a "sacred" goal such as the defense of the homeland to be effective.

And NATO? Kennedy asked.

The Atlantic alliance, Malraux answered, was in no way at issue.

In *Felled Oaks,* Malraux was to give his meeting with Kennedy a reverberating dimension by reporting how he told it to de Gaulle in 1969 and by adding de Gaulle's comments. National defense, Malraux here told de Gaulle he had told Kennedy, was a matter of national will, something American presidents should have learned from Mao Tse-tung's final victory over Chiang Kai-shek and something Vietnam would still teach them. Kennedy, Malraux told de Gaulle,

> thought that over, then said, "France is a funny country—with misfortunes *following* victories, which in the seventeenth century had made France Europe's foremost power, then with her rebuilt navy her assistance to us, the Revolution, Napoleon, 1940 and now de Gaulle." I said France

[4] Arthur Schlesinger, *A Thousand Days: John F. Kennedy in the White House* (Boston: Houghton Mifflin Co., 1965).

was a profoundly irrational country which only discovers her destiny when that destiny is also valid for others.

What irritated Malraux, he told de Gaulle, was that Kennedy instinctively wanted to settle European and Asian issues with American solutions. De Gaulle observed that Kennedy obviously wanted to maintain America's domination of the Western alliance, then continued:

> "I am not so sure that despite his exceptional gifts he didn't accept the naive comparison—United States of Europe and United States of America, when in effect the latter was created *ex nihilo* by successive waves of uprooted colons in a kind of green Siberia. Should the United States consciously become the master of the world, you will see how far American imperialism will go."
>
> I remembered President Eisenhower's anxious phrase, "I will not appear before God with blood on my hands."
>
> "Blood dries fast."
>
> I told Kennedy, with an apparent absence of mind: "You are now compelled to have a world policy as Rome was forced to have a Mediterranean policy, but what has been America's policy since the Marshall Plan?" I had the impression that he really wanted to carry on his shoulder both the burden of History and America's enormous responsibility which he felt very vividly. No doubt, he would have done it . . .
>
> "I imagine that it was in telling him he *was* carrying it all on his shoulders that you established the deep relationship which nothing could destroy. When reasons of state prevailed, this clever politician was separated from politicians by a sudden and blunt anger. You remember him on TV: 'My father always told me that when it came to putting national interests ahead of its own, business always behaves like a son of a bitch.' Maybe the danger was already there, but in any case he had decided not to pay attention.
>
> "You know," the general continued, "that to be courageous is to pay no attention to danger. And anyway, we should die assassinated or struck by lightning." He shrugged. "Did his murder destroy a grand design? It is possible, when Caesar was murdered, he held in his hand a list of the conspirators, but he hadn't read it yet. This poor president talked to me about Lincoln in a way that struck me. He wanted to be a president like Lincoln, and, in death, did become like him. Maybe history was bent by an obligingly absent-minded police chief in Dallas."

In January 1963, Malraux was back in Washington—with Mona Lisa. Leonardo da Vinci's masterpiece traveled to America in its own stateroom aboard the S.S. *France,* flanked by curators in a cabin on one side and guards in a cabin on the other, and was trucked from New York to Washington under police escort. At the National Gallery unveiling, attended by Kennedy, his vice-president Lyndon Johnson, their wives, the entire cabinet and Supreme Court, Malraux opened the ceremony with a speech on Leonardo only to have the public address system go dead

312

on him. As National Gallery president John Walker was to write,[5] Malraux continued "heroically," telling his increasingly restive audience that of the many explanations of Mona Lisa's fame, he preferred to believe it was due to Leonardo's transfiguration of a profane face. "The mortal woman with a divine look in her eyes triumphs over the goddesses without eyes." When he mentioned the special nature of the "loan," he magnificently said that the chances France took by letting Mona Lisa leave the Louvre amounted to little compared to the risks American soldiers had faced in France in two world wars, risks that made the humblest of them the true savior of the historic painting.

[5] John Walker, *Self-Portrait with Donors: Confessions of an Art Collector* (Boston: Little, Brown & Co., 1974).

> The government is not in the business of directing art but of serving it.
>
> In interview with *L'Aurore*, December 10, 1967.

26

Malraux's decade in office was both dazzling and—as he himself was to admit on several occasions—disappointing. If, all things told, the government of Charles de Gaulle spent little money on its Ministry of Cultural Affairs it seemingly put no limits on its Secretary for Cultural Affairs. Seemingly, because the main tools of cultural politics—education, radio-television, sociocultural youth training and foreign cultural relations—were all outside his jurisdiction. Malraux was often asked to define culture and his own role but he usually avoided too radiant definitions and called himself a "cultural agitator" or used other witticisms to quip the question away. By a paradox of which he was perfectly aware, the greater reality of his role was personal and symbolic. Now in his sixties, he was a man of world renown, a person of prodigious culture, haunted by catastrophe as much as by tragedy, a lover of art fascinated by glory and transcendence who, moreover, had the ear of the chief of state. Everything should be possible and a lot was accomplished, often in brilliant, daring stabs rather than in sustained efforts. The ending was inglorious, not so much for him as for the aging monarch he was serving.

The Ministry of Cultural Affairs was housed in the Rue de Valois on the site of a palace once occupied by Cardinal Richelieu. Visitors were dazzled, Pierre Galante was to write, "by mirrors, tapestries, gold and white paneling, an air of religious decorum induced by the presence of the frock-coated *huissiers* and by a strange statue of a naked youth in black bronze." [1] But the posh decor was misleading. Most of Malraux's hard-working assistants and secretaries toiled in small cubbyholes. The staff was totally dedicated and subjugated by the minister and the department moved or stood still in unison with Malraux's energies, interests or

[1] Pierre Galante, *Malraux*, op. cit.

314

Secretary for Cultural Affairs, circa 1960

prolonged absences. The department's piece of the national pie never exceeded 0.43 percent of the annual budget. "The most obvious vice of the organizing of the Cultural Affairs was, as we know, its budget," Jean Lacouture was to underline:

> To draw a parallel with the actions of earlier republics and the appropriations the financial services of the Fifth Republic allocated for Mr. Malraux's department is unfair—this undertaking was of a different nature, the man in charge and his position in the government exceptional, and the national and international ambitions without comparison to what had been tried before . . . Who could have changed these things if not Malraux? One of the most serious criticisms that can be leveled against the first minister of Cultural Affairs of the Fifth Republic is his timidity in this area, as shown in 1967 remark by one of the General Accounting director to a Department of Cultural Affairs executive, "These projects are good, but for us to get behind them, they must be argued 'upstairs.' " [2]

The accomplishment of the "Malraux era" that he himself put above all others was the *maisons de culture,* those proto-Marxist multimedia art centers he blew a good hunk of his budget on every year and had erected in Le Havre, Grenoble, Caen, Thonon, Rennes, Firminy, Saint-Etienne, Amiens and in the popular Ménilmontant quarter of Paris,

[2] Jean Lacouture, *André Malraux,* op. cit.

a generous idea stemming from his visits to the Soviet Union, from the *Front populaire* years and revolutionary Spain. In these cultural centers, he invited the people to create themselves. Here, he not only wanted to extend Paris standards of excellence to the provinces but to foster an interpenetration of the arts by combining facilities for drama, music, film and exhibitions. Malraux was convinced that the modern consumer society was profoundly anticultural. An intellectual elite had ample access to the highest quality of art while the masses were flooded with trash. This held true, he was to repeat at many occasions, not only for bourgeois societies where there was no political leadership in the cultural field, but also in Marxist and totalitarian regimes. "Like the right to schools, people have a right to theaters and museums," was one of his happier slogans. The purpose of his *maisons de culture* was to promote, preserve and disseminate culture.

His most famous and most visible enterprise was scrubbing centuries of grime off Notre-Dame, the Louvre and other historical landmarks in Paris and the provinces, and his most lasting legacy an unprecedented inventory of France's artistic wealth and the beginning of new archaeological reserves, both started in the mid-1960s and still in progress a decade later. He pushed fresh subsidies for theater, ballet and cinema through the National Assembly—"for the price of twenty-five kilometers of expressway," he thundered in the Assembly October 27, 1966, "France can, thanks to the *maisons de culture,* in ten years become the world's foremost cultural nation."

After Mona Lisa's trip to America, he sent the Louvre's Venus de Milo to Japan, attending the inauguration in Tokyo himself in 1964. Two months later he unveiled the ceiling he had commissioned Chagall to paint in the Paris Opéra. The idea had come to Malraux during a gala performance in 1960 of *Daphnis et Chloé* with Chagall sets. For the unveiling, Malraux had the Opéra stage a repeat performance of Ravel's "symphonie chorégraphique." On Picasso's eighty-fifth birthday, he inaugurated a huge one-man show in the Grand Palais, which he had renovated for the occasion, and tried to get the Bateau-Lavoir, Picasso's Montmartre studio of his youth, declared a historical landmark. The occasion was marked by a contretemps as busy Cultural Affairs department secretaries forgot to send an invitation to Picasso, who telegraphed Malraux, DO YOU THINK I'M DEAD? To which Malraux wired back, DO YOU THINK I'M MINISTER? *

Malraux continually toyed with new ideas. What about collecting all surviving Vermeer paintings from all museums for one world exhibition? Why not have Egypt ship all of King Tutankhamen's treasures to Paris and why not bring progressive art from China? The Vermeer and the

* Nino Frank says the telegraphic exchange occurred à propos Chagall's Opéra ceiling and that Picasso demanded that he, too, be given a ceiling to paint.

316

King Tutankhamen ideas became reality, the Chinese exhibit didn't, but not for want of trying. In 1966, he was in Egypt, inventorying the Cairo museums and telling Gamal Nasser that to change a people's standard of living without changing its spiritual standards was to lead it to disaster.

At the 1964 inauguration of the Bourges *maison de culture,* he defined culture as "forms that have survived" and wished that the youth of Bourges would come in contact with culture because "there may be immortality in the profundities of the night but surely not in people," a theme he was to amplify in later speeches. Meanwhile, his ministry did what it could with its limited funds to safeguard "forms that have survived." It pushed through an environmental protection law to save ancient sections of cities, such as as Quartier des Marais on the Right Bank of Paris, the Balance district in Avignon and parts of Uzès, Metz and other towns. National monuments that were upgraded included Les Invalides in Paris, the Reims cathedral, Versailles' Grand Trianon and the Chambord, Vincennes and Fontainebleau castles. Less welcome voices of "forms that have survived" were the first volumes of Clara Malraux's memoirs, published in 1963 and 1966. If *Apprendre à vivre* dealt fondly with Clara's coddled childhood in pre-1914 Paris and Magdeburg, *Nos vingts ans* punctured holes in the Malraux legend, retold Cambodia *à deux,* her shipboard adultery and thankless task in rallying support for the accused art thief awaiting trial in Pnompenh. It told ingenuously of André's early misogyny, hurtfully of the Goldschmidts' money and courageously of their breakup. Her books laid claims—as Nino Frank delicately observed, "there are widows who are abusive before their time, some are born that way." [3] The Secretary for Cultural Affairs diplomatically refused comment, except to defend his first wife. When someone suggested it might have been more tactful for her to have published the memoirs under the name Goldschmidt, he snapped, "She has earned the Malraux, you know."

Imperceptibly, he and Madeleine were drifting apart. The death of Gauthier and Vincent had brought an almost natural end to this singular union and although he remained devoted to Alain and saw his stepson through his education, the deliberately forced pace of his ministerial endeavors was a convenient pretext for a growing distance. He had a *pied à terre* built at the ministry in the Rue de Valois, spent the few vacant evenings of his busy week there and thought of buying a co-op apartment in the renovated Marais area. Various viruses brought him back to the Boulogne home during the winter 1964–65. At the weekly Wednesday cabinet meetings, de Gaulle found Malraux pale and distracted and suggested that he take a long rest. Finally, doctors ordered him to get away to a lot of sun. In June 1965, he sailed to the Far East aboard the S.S. *Cambodge* and, in a deck chair off Crete, began to fill legal pads with

[3] Nino Frank, *Mémoire brisée,* op. cit.

317

his tight, nervous handwriting. The result was to be the *Antimémoires*.

Port Said, the Suez Canal, Djibouti, Aden, the Indian Ocean and the first Asian landfall in Singapore—life forty-two years ago with Clara. He was never to mention her in the *Antimémoires*. But the voyage to Asia was to be more than a sunny boat ride into reveries of a fabulous past. It was suddenly to turn into an electrifying event.

In Singapore the French embassy had a coded telegram for him from President de Gaulle. The wire notified him that a visit to the People's Republic was in the offing and instructed him to proceed to Hong Kong without revealing to anyone the nature of his mission or his destination. On July 17, the expected invitation came from Peking and three days later, Malraux-Garin disappeared across the international bridge toward Canton. Legends have long lives. In choosing Malraux for this first mission to Peking—de Gaulle had broken Western ranks a year earlier and established diplomatic relations with China—he thought he was sending the old comrade-in-arms of Mao's revolutionary armies.

In Paris, the journey was shrouded in calculated mystery. To sniffing journalists, Information Minister Roger Alain said Malraux's visit was a private one. In background sessions he admitted contacts might be established that might not be without interest, but, he stressed, the visit had *no* connection with the situation in Southeast Asia, a statement which didn't discourage diplomatic speculation in Washington. Since the Tonkin Gulf incident a year earlier, President Johnson had thrown America's might into the rice paddies of Vietnam and although Defense Secretary Robert McNamara said the enemy would be defeated within six months, it was felt Malraux might help elucidate China's thinking and intentions. Peace feelers from Washington were routinely channeled through Paris, but French officials cautioned not to expect immediate "dividends" from André's mission. "It *was* a private visit," they said. Less reticent, the Chinese announced the visit was official and that Malraux came as President de Gaulle's personal envoy.

The China Malraux disappeared into in the summer of 1965 was *terra incognita* to the West, a totally alien world where one-fifth of humanity was transforming an entire society. After a chaotic decade of pulling the country together, China's leaders had launched the Great Leap Forward, which was materially and spiritually transforming the huge country. Revolution in China meant constant efforts to elevate the standard of living while at the same time preventing relapses into injustice and inequity for man's proper social existence was collective, not individualistic. In the West, this social engineering was not yet admired as the frontier spirit but regarded with horror as the ruthless tyranny of an anthill.

Malraux brought from de Gaulle a message of goodwill to Liu Shao-ch'i, the president of the People's Republic, and was given to understand that he might see Chairman Mao. On his arrival in Peking July 22,

318

he was received by Marshal Ch'en Yi, the foreign secretary. Their meeting lasted two hours and centered quickly on Vietnam. Ch'en Yi told his visitor that if the United States didn't extend the war, China would not intervene. Malraux asked whether by extension, Ch'en Yi meant to Chinese territory, but the marshal wouldn't rule out Chinese intervention on Vietnamese territory. Malraux doubted this because Mao had always followed Lenin's maxim about the defensive tactics of revolutionary armies and, as Nehru had told him, it was a Western obsession to believe that wars of liberation were conducted from abroad. The Vietcong's ideology and its tactics came from Mao as did a number of its organizers and liaison officers but Malraux knew from experience the limits of the help guerrillas could receive, the "advice" they could accept. Ch'en Yi gave a long exposé of American intrigues abroad, from the Dominican Republic to the Congo, and expressed the fear that Washington would escalate the war. "Under the pretext of supporting South Vietnam, they bomb the North," Malraux quoted the marshal as saying in the *Antimémoires*. "Who is to say that tomorrow they will not take the pretext of China's support for North Vietnam to bomb us? They think they can do whatever they like."

Ch'en Yi said de Gaulle was right in resisting the U.S. in Europe and said he hoped France would use her influence to get the Americans to withdraw from Vietnam. Malraux quoted Nehru who had believed colonialism would die when the victory of a Western expeditionary force over an Asian army was no longer a foregone conclusion, and repeated his view of the United States as the only nation ever to have become the most powerful country without seeking to. He added that France's persuasive powers in Washington were probably no more than China's in Moscow, and at the end of the conversation bluntly asked if China would envisage negotiations after an American pledge to withdraw or following an actual withdrawal.

> The Marshal reflects. "The question must be studied; perhaps I will be able to give you a reply in a few days. The decision is one for Ho Chi Minh and Pham Van Dong. As far as I know, they still insist on withdrawal as a prerequisite. Have you brought any proposals with you, minister?"
>
> "None, Marshal."

For the next ten days, the Chinese took Malraux sight-seeing. Their visitor was not content to see the Forbidden City and an exemplary commune, he wanted to travel to Loyang and Sian in Central China—Loyang for its purple-tiled palaces which when Europe was in its darkest Middle Age, had housed the most exquisite art in the world; Sian, which was eleven times the capital of China, for its Summer Palace and the stone animals leading to the tomb of Y'ai Tsung, where the communists had captured Chiang Kai-shek in 1936 only to let him escape again. And further afield to Yenan in the jagged mountains of Shensi province in

319

northeastern China. Yenan was both Sparta and Jerusalem of the People's Republic, the town that had been its capital until the final triumph over the Nationalists in 1949, the town Mao and his army had settled in after the six thousand miles of the Long March, lost to Chiang Kai-shek and recaptured. Yenan had now been transformed into a vast revolutionary museum where the mythological power of Communist China was told in vast socialist-realist murals, in pedantic fetishisms of Mao's inkwell of the Red Army staff room and a shabby red felt tablecloth with candle stains where the Central Committee had deliberated.

On August 2, Premier Chou En-lai received him, "obviously an intellectual, the grandson of a mandarin, Mao's right-hand man on the Long March . . . faultless, urbane and as reticent as a cat." Chou En-lai paid tribute to Malraux's revolutionary past and immediately plunged into the Vietnam question, saying that negotiations were not even imaginable. He reminded Malraux of a Confucian sage faced with those who don't observe the rites. For a starter, Chou said Washington could observe the 1954 Geneva Agreement. He wondered how anyone could negotiate with people who do not respect agreements. He suggested France should advise Great Britain, as China might advise her Russian ally, to formulate a common policy against the aggressive policies of the U.S.

Malraux found the interview disappointing. He felt Chou En-lai was "putting on a record so as not to have to think," while at the same time revealing a world outlook of frightening simplicity. Nuclear war didn't faze the Chinese premier because imperialism numbered six hundred million people, whereas the underdeveloped countries, together with socialists and communist nations, were two billion. In a nuclear attack, China could survive the death of a hundred million people, Chou said. And even if the Americans invaded, sooner or later—perhaps it would take fifty years—one day they would have to go home.

That evening, Malraux was told not to make any arrangements for the following day. Then at 1:00 P.M., August 3, another phone call advised him that "they" would receive him and French ambassador Lucien Paye at 3:00 P.M. In theory, the meeting was with President Liu Shao-ch'i, but Paye translated the "they" to mean Chairman Mao would be present.

Malraux was to devote forty pages of the *Antimémoires* to the meeting with Mao Tse-tung, forty "orchestrated" pages giving the dimension and *frisson* of this historical character who in Malraux's view had influenced the lives of more people than anyone in this century with the possible exception of Lenin. The meeting, at which some twenty people were present, including Lui Shao-ch'i and Paye, was more courtesy call than negotiating session, more visionary history lesson than diplomatic exchange of views. It was a meeting where everybody was seated in wicker chairs with cloths on the armrests, something that reminded Malraux of a waiting room in a tropical railway station, and a convalescing Mao sat

320

against the sun, "the famous wart on the chin, like a Buddhist sign," and retold the waystations of the Revolution.

Mao began by asking what his visitor had thought of Yenan. Malraux answered that the glass-encased mausoleum bareness had reminded him of monasteries and invisible power, an observation that led Mao to recount the epic moments of the Long March from the 1927 Shanghai defeat to the final triumph, his realization that a Chinese revolution had to be a peasants', not a workers', revolution. "Revolution is a drama of passion; we did not win the people over by appealing to reason, but by developing hope, trust and fraternity." He told how, like the U.S., Stalin had backed Chiang Kai-shek to the end and how it would take decades to catch up, how revolution would have to be continuous, how politics came before technology.

Malraux listened and answered, listening to the pauses, watched the others and felt that Mao was also addressing himself to an imaginary opponent. He noticed how the interpreter immediately hit on the word "apostasy" in translating Mao's description of Soviet revisionism. The word made Malraux wonder if she had been brought up by nuns. He felt Mao was more anxious to make China than to make war and that the chairman was positive the United States would not use nuclear weapons in Vietnam any more than in Korea, that what separated him from the Russians was that he still believed in permanent revolution.

Three times a secretary came in to speak to Liu Shao-ch'i and three times the President conferred in a low voice with Mao. Each time, Mao seemed to brush away the interruption.

> He is still holding a cigarette when I get up to take leave. He holds out an almost feminine hand, with palms as pink as if they had been boiled. To my surprise, he accompanied me out. The interpreter is between us, a little to the rear, the nurse behind him. Our companions precede him, the French ambassador with the President of the Republic, who has not said a word. Some distance behind us is a young group—high officials I presume.
>
> He walks one step at a time, as stiff as if he were not bending his legs, more than ever the bronze emperor in his dark uniform surrounded by light-colored or white uniforms.

They reached the front steps, with Mao saying that besides resolute and prudent revolutionaries, China also had a whole generation of dogmatic youth "and dogma is less useful than cow dung." Malraux felt the chairman was struggling against the United States, against Russia and against China.

> He reminded me of the emperors, and he now reminds me, standing there, of the rust-covered shields of the army chiefs which belong to the funerary avenues of the emperors, and are to be found abandoned

321

in the sorghum fields. Behind our entire conversation the hope of a twilight world stood watch. In the vast corridor, the dignitaries have stopped, without daring to turn around.

"I am alone," he repeats. And suddenly he laughs, "Well, with a few distant friends. Please give General de Gaulle my greetings. As for them" (he means the Russians), "revolution doesn't really interest them, you know."

Malraux flew back to Paris, with a stopover in Pnompenh where he hadn't been since he had covered the Bardez Affair for the dying *L'Indochine enchaînée* in 1925. A year later, Mao Tse-tung launched the Cultural Revolution. As he had told Malraux, in turning Chinese society upside down Mao acted to prevent the "apostasy" of Soviet revisionism. The Cultural Revolution began at Peking University, and during the summer and fall of 1966, entire classes embarked on what some American commentators called a "children's crusade." Millions of students began walking through China and setting up revolutionary committees. In theory, these committees represented a grass roots body of people, but they soon challenged Party committees and demanded that initiatives be restored to the people and power be stripped from the cadres, mandarins, apparatchiks and even entrenched professionals.

In May 1968, the youth revolution reached Paris, starting in the suburban Nanterre University with self-styled Maoists demanding grassroots reforms. In a few weeks of accumulated evasion and repression, deception and about-face maneuvers Gaullism miscalculated itself out of power.

Malraux wanted to finish the *Antimémoires* and in early 1966 de Gaulle relieved him of official duties in the evening. In April, however, the Cultural Affairs secretary was again on the move—in Senegal, addressing the Festival of Black Art in Dakar and meeting a tribal queen in the bush, and in Egypt, assessing the wealth of the Cairo museums and meeting Colonel Nasser. "What remains of a civilization if not its art," he told the black arts festival. "Africa must be present in the world. Africa is strong enough to make its 'imaginary museum' on condition that it doesn't stop here."

In early 1967, he managed to finish the *Antimémoires,* where he treated himself as a fictional character. Before de Gaulle flew to Montreal to launch what his Cultural Affairs secretary considered the general's craziest foreign adventure—the *Vive le Québec libre!* endorsement of French-Canadian separatism—Malraux handed the chief of state the pages that concerned him. De Gaulle answered with a telegram from Canada— ADMIRABLE IN ALL THREE DIMENSIONS, but never got around to saying what the three dimensions were. The book was published in the fall and, as Gallimard had expected, was a resounding success, selling 340,000 copies in three months. France's biggest daily, *France-Soir,* published pirated excerpts weeks before the book was scheduled to be released, running no quotes over eleven book lines to remain within the law specifying newspaper excerpts must be under eleven lines. French critics didn't mind Malraux's roaming across his life without regard to chronology and reprinted his enigmatic quote ("I call this book *Anti*mémoires because it answers a question that memoirs don't ask and because it doesn't answer those they do ask").

Despite Malraux's virtually untranslatably dense prose, the foreign rights were sold for enormous sums. Doubleday, *Newsweek* reported,[4] offered $250,000 for the American rights but was outbid (at $350,000) by Holt, Rinehart & Winston. Malraux dedicated the U.S. edition to Jacqueline Kennedy and although the book was not as big a success as Holt had expected, it went through two printings and a paperback edition in two years. With *La Condition humaine,* the *Antimémoires* was to be his most translated book.

He gave "big interviews" right and left. "A man isn't made chronologically, the moments of a life cannot be added up in an orderly accumulation. Biographies that go from five to fifty are false confessions. Experiences make the individual. I think you can rediscover a life through its experiences, not formulate experience as a perfection of narrative. . . . I think of Proust. *Swann's Way* has made it impossible to write memoirs like Chateaubriand's. Proust is an anti-Chateaubriand. I wouldn't mind being an anti-Proust and put Proust's work in a historical perspective."[5] To those who found him too clever in mixing facts and fiction and therefore too little self-revealing, he said, "Why should I care about what only concerns me?" Roger Stéphane interviewed him on national television and in French and English alone, two hundred and eighty-five bylined pieces and reviews appeared in less than two years, including critiques by old comrades-in-letters like François Mauriac, Manes Sperber and Arthur Koestler and by rising stars like Françoise Giraud, Jean-François Revel and Larry Collins-Dominique Lapierre. Unsigned notices appeared in such an exotic journal as *Ward's Automotive Journal* and headlines included "Ecumémoires," "Malraux—l'anti-Mozart" and "Malraux Sidestepping Himself."[6]

Before flying off to Moscow, Malraux had the idea of having Coco Chanel decorate a suite of rooms at the Louvre for an exhibition of forty masterpieces from the museum reserves chosen by him. He also wanted to have her stage her fall collection at the Grand Palais. To discuss the matter, she invited the minister to lunch at her Rue Cambon apartment, together with his old flame Louise de Vilmorin. André and Louise had not seen each other since 1934 when, after their spirited affair she had sailed to America to join her Henry and her daughters while he had gone to

[4] *Newsweek* (Sept. 11, 1967).
[5] *L'Evènement,* Nos. 19–20 (Sept., 1967).
[6] Cf. Françoise Dorenlot, Peter Hoy, Walter Langlois, *Un Evènement littéraire, Les Antimémoires de Malraux, bibiographie préliminaire, La Revue des lettres modernes,* 1972; and Peter Hoy, *Complement, Revue des lettres modernes,* 1973.

Marseille to greet Clara on her return from *her* fling. The lunch lasted all afternoon. Louise had spent most of the war years in Hungary, with her second husband, a Count Pallfy. Now divorced, she lived again at the family château in Verrières-le-Buisson on the southern outskirts of Paris, writing mostly short stories and articles for *Marie-Claire* and other women's magazines.

Louise and André picked up where they had left off. They plunged into a voluptuous if autumnal liaison. On May 1, André moved in at Verrières and at dawn Louise presented her lover with sprigs of lily of the valley, the traditional May Day *muguet.* Together, they bought a couple of floors in a renovated Marais *hôtel particulier,* called it their little Palais Royal. Malraux planned to live on the third floor, Louise on the second. The two entrances were independent of one another. "When he hears my voice on the ground floor he will come down," she said. They were not exactly in the style of the Gaullist regime as they hobnobbed about Paris in André's ministerial limousine.

"What kind of woman is the woman of your dreams?" Louise would ask, according to *Paris-Match* editor Pierre Galante, who was a close acquaintance.

"A woman with whom I am never bored, a bird of paradise who could be told to close her wings when I was intoxicated by colors."

"Do I intoxicate you?"

"You make my head spin with colors, which is not the same thing. That is even the whole difference. Your plumage blends with your language."

She distracted him, poked fun at him and made him laugh with her verbal spark. "Plans were always a part of their conversation and they made them like a young couple," Galante would write. "This pair, both close to seventy and both looking twenty years younger, formed an authentic couple." They lived a precocious and precious intimacy, seeing their "little Palais Royal" take shape in the hands of architects and contractors and repeating to each other Chateaubriand's *mot* that love is incomprehensible to those who don't share it.

In February and March 1968 Malraux was in the Soviet Union. "Have you found any changes since you were here in 1934?" Aleksei Kosygin asked. "Yes," André answered, "but the whole world is changing and changing very fast." "True," said the Russian, "but it is sometimes for the better and sometimes for the worse that the world changes."

After traveling to several cities in the Ukraine, Malraux spent a month in Moscow. His visits began in Lenin's former office. He stood for a long time near the windows, gazing out over the Kremlin and looked at the monkey statuette that an American millionaire had given the Father of the People. "If humanity doesn't stop the arms race," Lenin had said at the time, "it will return to the state of this monkey reflecting on its past and holding a human skull in its hands." At the Union of Soviet Writers, he asked about the present attitudes toward Boris Pasternak, Dostoyevsky and Tolstoy. The ranks had thinned in thirty-four years, but Konstantin Fedin was still there, saying Russians were looking forward to a rapprochement with France, and, for emphasis, adding, "We all know what the alternative is." They didn't talk about those who were missing since they had last seen each other at the 1934 All-Soviet Writers' Congress.

The position of Cultural Affairs minister was not all glory and VIP travel. It also meant dealing with volatile artistic temperaments and mercurial egos. When he created the Orchestre de Paris he made enemies for himself by appointing Marcel Landowski musical director instead of Pierre Boulez and although he bulldozed through the permission of the subsidized Theatre de France to stage Jean Genet's *Les Paravents,* his relations with Jean-Louis Barrault and Madeleine Renaud, the "first couple" of the Theatre, were less than cordial. In 1966, he was in hot water with the serious film crowd. The banning of Jacques Rivette's *La Religieuse,* an adaptation of Diderot's 1760 letter-novel about the moral sufferings of a young girl cloistered against her will, provoked Jean-Luc Godard to write an open letter to "the minister of Kultur." Film censorship fell under the Information ministry's jurisdiction and the banning of this filmization of a two-hundred-year-old classic was apparently undertaken at the personal request of the devout Mme. Yvonne de Gaulle, but, wrote Godard scathingly, "since you are the only Gaullist I know, I must address my anger to you." [7] The *Religieuse* brouhaha was followed by a much more serious incident for Malraux—the attempted administrative removal from the Cinémathèque française of its director and founding father Henri Langlois. The unique Cinémathèque, both film archive and repertory cinema, received an annual $800,000 subsidy from the Cultural Affairs department. The corpulent Langlois spent the money in a fashion that made bureaucrats weep. The attempt to replace him with a proper administrator was a relatively low-echelon decision in Malraux's department.

Langlois, in whose repertory theater the whole "new wave" had spent its youth, had friends around the world and devoted followers in Paris. Telegrams poured in from everyone from Charles Chaplin to Otto Preminger and Arthur Penn, and soon François Truffaut and Godard led a "Keep Langlois In" march from the Champs-Élysées to the Rue de Valois. When the marchers were stopped by police, the affair only exploded into larger demonstrations. Malraux was being pressured by Premier Pompidou and Information secretary Roger Frey not to give in, when suddenly *L'Affaire Langlois* was only a footnote to the May 1968 events. Before the storm, he enjoyed what was to be the apotheosis of his ten years as cultural minister. In April, nearly eight thousand professionals, amateurs and lovers of the theater gathered in the Bourges *maison de culture* for a week of symposiums, debate and theatrical events.

[7] *Le Nouvel observateur* (April 6, 1966).

There is also their nihilism. The co-ed at Nanterre who said, "When you know what you want you're already part of the bourgeoisie," is of course revealing.

Felled Oaks

27

The "May Events" surprised Malraux as much as any cabinet minister. At the height of the events, he called the student riots "an immense lyrical illusion." A few years later, he almost called Gaullism an immense lyrical illusion.

Between May 1 and June 30, 1968, President de Gaulle lost all credibility. The Gaullist establishment managed to surmount the crisis but as myth and as incarnation of a certain heroic projection de Gaulle was not to survive. When he put his politics and personal prestige to a test ten months later, the French people refused to give him its vote of confidence. Hurt, he resigned.

Everything seemed calm, even serene, during the spring of the year Gaullism celebrated its tenth year in power. The headlines of May 1 were concentrated on Czech Premier Alexander Dubcek's May Day speech saying that what his country needed was "socialism with a smile" and on Hanoi's refusal to meet American peace terms and not on the disciplinary expulsion of one Daniel Cohn-Bendit, leader of student activists at Nanterre University in the western suburbs of Paris. Cohn-Bendit, a German national of varied origins, was accused of masterminding sit-in "occupations" of university facilities. The next day, a demonstration of what the government called the "enragés" among the Nanterre students led to the closing of the university. On May 3, students at the Sorbonne, in the heart of Left Bank Paris, took up the cause and decided to hold disruptive study sessions. Rector Jean Roche demanded police action to clear out the "rebels" and for the first time in a century, police invaded the hallowed halls and chased out the students. Three days later, a student march clashed with police in the St.-Germain-des-Prés area resulting in a number of wounded students.

De Gaulle was on the eve of leaving for Bucharest on a state visit

326

and his Premier, Georges Pompidou, scheduled to fly off on a tour of Iran and Afghanistan. "Kids' stuff," the general huffed when Pompidou made a worried remark before leaving for the airport. During the following three days, the government denounced splinter factions fomenting trouble while tens of thousands of students demonstrated in Paris with a three-pronged demand—the immediate reopening of Sorbonne, the pullback of police and the freeing of arrested students. Education minister Alain Peyrefitte almost managed to defuse the situation on May 9 by promising the reopening of Sorbonne. When Nanterre students occupied *their* university, however, he refused to have police evacuate the Sorbonne and the next day students began building street barricades in the Latin Quarter. In the evening, Roche tried to reopen negotiations but refused to free arrested students. At 2:00 A.M. on the 11th, Paris police chief Maurice Grimaud announced on a bullhorn that he had received orders to bring down the barricades. When the smoke cleared two hours later, the streets were littered with three hundred wounded and the wrecks of gasoline-bombed cars. Riot squad police instituted a tactic of hot pursuit and chased demonstrators into apartment buildings to club them, making an indignant bourgeoisie give asylum to bleeding youths. Five hundred demonstrators were arrested.

No one dared to wake up de Gaulle. The next day, Pompidou returned from Kabul and immediately took energetic measures. He denounced police brutality, had twenty-five of the original twenty-eight arrested Sorbonne students set free and announced the university would reopen the following morning. But student leaders had already escalated the confrontation by persuading organized labor to call a one-day general strike that Monday. On May 13, the tenth anniversary of the Algiers coup that had brought de Gaulle to power, eight hundred thousand people marched behind student leaders, liberal faculty members, union chiefs and Leftist political figures, shouting "Ten years are enough." Police had evacuated the Latin Quarter and students reoccupied the Sorbonne, turning the seven-hundred-year-old institution into a neo-Maoist "université critique."

Ignoring the recommendations of several of his advisers, de Gaulle refused to postpone his state visit to Romania. The day after his departure, young workers occupied the Sud-Aviation aircraft plant; the following day, the giant Renault car plant was disrupted by militants. By May 17, the movement had spread to hundreds of businesses. What really frightened the government was that the events were not controlled by big labor or the Communist Party, but was a spontaneous grass roots movement. On the 17th, de Gaulle cut his Romanian visit short and in a public reassessment of the situation managed to insult the whole of France's youth. Had he lost touch? A May 24 appeal in which he offered to hold another referendum in June was mediocre, hesitant and revealed the government's confusion.

327

At the Gare de Lyon where action leaders had called their troops to hear the presidential address, it was greeted with shouts of "He's finished." The brushfire spread to such staid provincial cities as Bordeaux and Lyons, where a police chief was killed—the first and only casualty of the "events" —and to the Cannes film festival where François Truffaut, Jean-Luc Godard, Roman Polanski and other *contestataires* brought the festival to a premature close.

On May 26, Pompidou tried to buy peace with major wage concessions, including a ten to thirty percent boost in minimum wages. When union leaders presented the package to Renault workers, they were jeered. The country seemed to slide toward total anarchy. The president's offer of a referendum was ridiculed, more than generous wage settlements were scornfully rejected, plants and universities were "occupied," the big Leftist organizations, including the Communist Party, seemed out of touch with their rank and file. On May 29, rumors circulated that Pompidou had suggested de Gaulle resign.

The old sovereign appeared dejected and was heard muttering "The French no longer want de Gaulle," but this master strategist knew his people and knew how to give every gesture a dramatic significance. To become legend and myth again, he first disappeared. Cabinet members were told he had left by helicopter for his beloved Colombey but no helicopter landed in the eastern village. Instead, it was rumored that de Gaulle had flown to Germany, to the French armed forces headquarters in Baden-Baden. The rumors were true. The few hours he spent with Supreme Commander Massu—another near-mythical figure, a former paratroop commander of Algiers who deviously had backed legitimacy during the general's putsch—were enough to provoke a reaction. Instead of pitying the aging head of state, a public opinion in disarray divided sharply. Did Massu tell de Gaulle the army was behind him, that not all youths were on the barricades, that despite the strikes that had paralyzed transportation, soldiers on leave were returning to their units? De Gaulle never said what Massu told him in Baden-Baden. Apparently, de Gaulle had expected the communists to stage a coup. When nothing happened, he dramatically resurfaced in Paris at noon on May 30 and told Pompidou he was staying in power. He energetically called his cabinet together and had air time cleared for a major 4:30 P.M. address to the nation. Pompidou agreed that backlash support was beginning to swell but counseled elections instead of a referendum. An election lost, Pompidou told de Gaulle, was not the end of the world, a referendum lost would bring the regime down. He managed to persuade de Gaulle to modify his speech on the dissolution of parliament but not on the referendum.

As de Gaulle no longer had time to learn his text by heart and didn't want to appear to be reading it for the cameras, he canceled TV coverage and, in an echo of his wartime voice from London, chose only to speak on radio. His tone was brittle and threatening as he denounced the communists (who had just saved the regime by confining the brushfire) and announced both the dissolution of the National Assembly leading to a June 30 general election and a future referendum. "In the five minutes the speech lasted," Jean Lacouture was to write in De Gaulle, "France changed masters, regime and century. Before 4:30 it was Cuba; after 4:35 it was almost restoration of monarchy. Immediately everything swung back. The revolutionary force, frozen at the brink of action by its hesitant leaders', by the communist bosses' steadfast decision not to take any chances and by the startling reaffirmation of de Gaulle's authority, saw their gains and alliances melt away." [1]

If Pompidou was the cool head during it all, Malraux was the least painful of the Gaullist stalwarts to listen to (and to reread). Quotations from his works were spray-painted on the walls of colleges and universities, taunting him with his own youth. To many he was a turncoat, to many others—and Man's Fate was part of the whole youth generation's mythology and curriculum—he was the front-rank leader of their dreams. Student leader David Rousset said, "If, at twenty, we had found him still the man whose books we had read at fourteen, a tremendous movement would have rallied us around him. But alas, he was no longer free—he had chosen de Gaulle." The association hurt, insofar as the "events" had shown Gaullist France to have remained a "blocked" nation, as the students said, a country not yet decolonized at home.

If St.-Germain-des-Prés under the tear gas had an evocative whiff of Madrid or Toledo of August 1936, Malraux knew very well he was not meant to lead revolutionary youths against the steel-helmeted riot squads. "To know youth is to be part of it," he said. At a June 20 Gaullist campaign rally, he said, "This chaos believes itself to be fraternal. What the students—the real students—want from us is hope. But on the side of hope we find the most fascinating of negative signs, the old nihilism suddenly reappearing with its black anarchist flag and seeing hope only in destruction. We are not faced with a need for reform but with one of the deepest crises that civilization has known." He had no scorn for the "immense lyrical illusion," but tried to understand it. In speeches and interviews, he insisted on the universal character of it all—from Prague to Berkeley, youth openly displays its beguiling strength. He insisted on the underlying malaise, on the desire for fraternity among the flower children which had led to chaos and on the jolting energy of revolution "which takes convulsion for continuity when only persistence can lead to action."

During the winter 1969–70 when it was all over and he and de Gaulle sat in the general's study at Colombey and watched the snow gently fall outside, the "events" came up. De Gaulle reminded Malraux of the

<hr>

[1] Jean Lacouture, De Gaulle (Paris: Seuil, 1969).

latter's assessment that the problem of youth was a problem of authority. De Gaulle felt there was more to it. According to *Les Chênes qu'on abat* Malraux answered:

> There is also their nihilism. The co-ed at Nanterre who said, "When you know what you want you're already part of the bourgeoisie," is of course revealing. The characters in *The Possessed* would have talked like her.
> "What does she think is the opposite of knowing what one wants?"
> Instinct. The events of May were the conjuncture of a communist revolt—prudent and unionized, and of an irrational youth revolt connected, as elsewhere, with a historical romanticism.
> "Not in Russia."
> Since the [1921] Kronstadt naval mutiny, anarchic romanticism isn't in style in the Soviet Union.
> "The Russian nihilists killed."
> And the czar killed them. Seriousness isn't the same anymore. And besides, the Russians were chaste, they didn't take drugs. In today's adventure there is a whole physical element. For the nihilists the Revolution was really a supreme value which they worshipped, as you just said, through action. The revolution our nihilists dream about belongs to what I call the lyrical illusion. They don't oppose the consumer society with a different kind of society, but with their indignation.

The backlash to the student barricades gave Gaullists in the June 30 general elections their most triumphant victory. But de Gaulle's insistence on the follow-up referendum turned the victory into a suspended sentence. Politically, the April 27, 1969, referendum on the minor and irrelevant issue of increased regional autonomy was an error of judgment and Malraux was, with Maurice Couve de Murville, Edmond Michelet and Maurice Schumann, among those who tried to have the general call it off. De Gaulle hesitated—something he rarely did, but apparently felt the drama had to be played to its last act. Two TV appearances showed him vacillating and perhaps less forgivable, bored. He ended one of them with a plaintive little phrase, "In any case, in three years, I will leave office." His plunging into crowds, always a tonic for him, failed to invigorate him this time and commentators were almost forced to underline the fact that on November 22, the chief of state would be eighty.

The issues didn't "carry" him—why did a believer in a strong executive suddenly want the people to endorse a referendum to decentralize government decision making?—and little campaigning was done. In February 1969, Malraux was in Nice and got paint splattered all over him, but for nonpolitical reasons, it seemed. He went as Secretary for Cultural Affairs to lay the cornerstone—which had been detached from the Louvre—of a building in Cimiez, overlooking Nice, which was to house Chagall's *Biblical Message,* which the painter had given France after

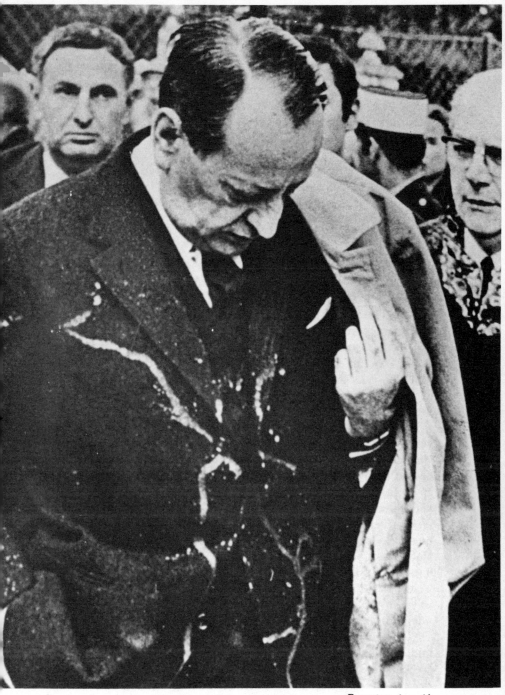

"Simply an esthetic disagreement." Paint-splattered at Chagall
Biblical Message Museum near Nice in 1969.

three hundred thousand visitors had seen a Cultural Affairs exhibit of the murals in the Louvre. Malraux was stepping out of the official limousine with its French flag on the fender when a man stepped forward and splashed him with red paint while shouting, "Down with Chagall!"

Bystanders thought it was an armed attack, but Malraux promptly "disarmed" his aggressor and in turn covered *him* with red paint.

"Simply an esthetic disagreement," Malraux said calmly. "I don't want him arrested; there are screwballs everywhere. But I'm furious at the man for having insulted one of our greatest living painters."

Did de Gaulle obscurely seek defeat to invent his own dénouement? In 1965, a fifty-five percent majority had given him a second seven-year mandate. If the referendum went against him now, he could choose his own exit, a Gaullian possibility whose acrid elegance he appreciated. The April 27 referendum went against him and on the 28th he resigned.

And Malraux with him. Georges Pompidou and he had known each other for twenty-five years but André preferred to be a private citizen and de Gaulle's retirement afforded him a graceful exit. A few years later he would say, "The period in government lasted ten years, there have been others in my life." In interviews he would say it was not politics that drew him to de Gaulle but history. "The times of violence that have now and again filled or encumbered my life have left me with two obsessions— fraternity and the fact that we live in an era where people choose to express their problems in tragedy or comedy, not by making the necessary decisions."

He and Louise wanted to travel—to warm Morocco the following winter—and he wanted to relax before beginning a second volume of the *Antimémoires*. The summer went by in lazy days at Verrières. As minister, he had been in the habit of getting up at 8:30 to be at the Rue de Valois at 10:00; now he got up at 10:00. Louise would wake up at 8:30 and play three games of solitaire, a ritual with her. After getting dressed and making herself up, she would go to André's room to join him as he ate breakfast—tea with lemon and one croissant. She would read the mail aloud and open *Le Figaro;* he only glanced at the morning paper head-lines but read the afternoon *Le Monde* from cover to cover. They would have lunch *tête-à-tête* and at 2:15 leave each other, each going his own way for the afternoon. Before dinner, they would have a drink in the *salon bleu,* where Malraux had moved his precious art pieces.

"My darling, in two weeks we will be flying to Marrakesh," she said one evening in late November when for the first time they had a crackling fire in the chimney. "I can't wait."

"We will stay at the Hotel Mamounia," he told her.

De Gaulle also traveled and wrote the last tome of his memoirs. A Mediterranean cruise included a call at Cádiz and the former chief of state and Mme. de Gaulle went ashore. When in Paris a journalist asked

Malraux's reaction, he was told that if de Gaulle had gone to Spain while still in office, he, Malraux, would have resigned. The author of *L'Espoir* had forgotten nothing. Like Picasso and a dwindling number of men, he had sworn he would not set foot on Spanish soil as long as Franco was still in power.

Malraux was working on the second volume of the *Antimémoires* and stayed out of personal involvement in the planned filming of *Man's Fate,* a Carlo Ponti–Metro-Goldwyn-Mayer production scheduled to roll in Singapore in November. Ponti had bought the screen rights two years earlier and he and director Fred Zinnemann (hot off *A Man For All Seasons*) had assembled an all-star cast—*Hiroshima, Mon Amour* star Eiji Okada as Kyo Gisors, Liv Ullmann as his wife May, David Niven in the role of Baron Clappique, Peter Finch as Ferral and Max von Sydow as Borodin. The screenplay was by Han Suyin.

Three days before principal photography was to start, James Aubrey, MGM's new boss, cancelled the project. An estimated $3 million had already been spent on the $8 to $10-million production, a budget Aubrey simply vetoed as too high since MGM already had David Lean's expensive *Ryan's Daughter* and Michelangelo Antonioni's flop *Zabriskie Point* on its hands. A cliff-hanger meeting at MGM's Manhattan offices tried to save the project, but Aubrey's insistence that Ponti and Zinnemann be personally responsible for any cost overrun was rejected by their lawyers. Later, Zinnemann, von Sydow and Liv Ullmann filed breach-of-contract suits, settled out of court in 1974 when Aubrey himself had been fired as MGM president. Two years earlier, UMC Pictures production chief (and Han Suyin's son-in-law) Sidney Glazier had tried to revive the project and at one point Ponti, still the owner of the screen rights, claimed he was inches away from making *Man's Fate* the first Italian-Chinese coproduction.

On December 11, 1969, de Gaulle received Malraux at Colombey for a "sitting" for the new volume of the *Antimémoires*. Their meeting lasted six hours and in 1971 resulted in *Les Chênes qu'on abat,* which became *Felled Oaks* in English, Malraux's first new book since the *Antimémoires*.*

Louise and André set the date for their departure for December 28. He spent a week going over the notes he had accumulated from the de Gaulle interview. Ten days before Christmas, Louise came down with a flu. André sternly warned her that this year the Hong Kong flu was malign. A raging fever sent her to bed and the family doctor prescribed heavy doses of antibiotics. Agitated by the fear of not being able to go to Morocco, she was up again in three days. On Christmas Day she seemed much better. She did not tell André she was still dizzy and, in a

* Gallimard brought out *Le triangle noir* in 1970, a reprint in one volume of the essays on Laclos, Goya and Saint-Just.

burst of energy went to Paris, to visit her sister, Mapie de Toulouse-Lautrec. The next day, a dizzy spell and a pounding heart made her go to her room to lie down in the afternoon. Two hours later she died of a ruptured intestinal artery.

André's name appeared last on the notifications as the Vilmorin family rallied around him and Gaston Palewski, the former diplomat who had first introduced him to de Gaulle, came and stayed with him. De Gaulle wrote an unusual letter of condolence. To the surprise of her brother André de Vilmorin and everyone else, Louise had left a will, asking to be buried in the garden at Verrières. "I think a tomb would make a sad impression," her will read. "So I have had the idea of a stone bench, with perhaps a bronze table on which children can come and have their tea parties." [2] She asked to be buried beneath a cherry tree under which she had played as a child and asked that her seventeen grandchildren and grandnephews be allowed to come and pick cherries, jumping from the bronze platform. "The cherries will rain down on my tomb. The children will feast on them." With Palewski's discreet intervention, the local prefect gave the permission for Louise to be buried in her garden.

André de Vilmorin, his brother Roger and nephew Sosthène, who with their families also lived at Verrières and were now the coowners of the Château, asked Malraux to stay on in one of the guest apartments. While keeping the Rue de Montpensier apartment he stayed at Verrières.

He was grief-stricken and didn't fly to San Francisco in June 1970 to attend Florence's marriage. His daughter married Alain Resnais, the filmmaker (*Hiroshima, Mon Amour* and *Last Year At Marienbad*), but he met the newlyweds only on their return from America. As an in-joke, Resnais made references to his father-in-law's meeting with Trotsky when he made his Jean-Paul Belmondo-starrer *Stavisky*.

In November, de Gaulle died, two weeks before his eightieth birthday. Malraux had not seen the general since their long afternoon together at Colombey the previous winter. On November 11, the double funeral took place—the state funeral in Paris' Notre-Dame attended by President Nixon and thirty other chiefs of state, and the private ceremony at Colombey for the family, the villagers and his *compagnons*. Malraux arrived late at Colombey, "stooped over, the face ravaged and, during the service, curiously absent-minded," press accounts said.

Had he been a friend of Charles de Gaulle? When de Gaulle's *Mémoires d'espoir* appeared, Malraux was so touched by a paragraph that he rushed to his old friend Manes Sperber to read it aloud to him:

> The cabinet met once a week, rarely more frequently. I always presided and on my right I had, and would always have, André Malraux.

[2] Pierre Galante, *Malraux*, op. cit.

With this brilliant friend at my side, I somehow believed that I would be shielded from the commonplace.[3]

Their long relationship was more an attachment based on lofty complicity than a comradeship of abandon and hilarity, more affinity of views than intimacy of ideas. When asked once why he had become a cabinet member, Malraux had said "because de Gaulle is the first man I have met who demands no less of others than he does of himself." Had he ever been against de Gaulle? He had always refused to give in to the general's demand that he run for public office and he had opposed two of de Gaulle's more controversial foreign affairs initiatives. One was de Gaulle's brusque arms cutoff to Israel following the 1967 Six Day War, the other was de Gaulle's championing of Quebec separatists during the general's Canadian state visit that same year.

Malraux wanted *Les Chênes qu'on abat* to be that unique transcript of a writer-artist's dialogue with a statesman which could have happened many times in history but never did. Diderot had told Sophie Volland about his soirees at the court of Catherine the Great but never jotted down his talks with the czarina. Why hadn't Michelangelo written down his dialogues—and brawls—with Pope Julius II? Why hadn't the philosopher Ibn Khaldun confined to paper his talks with Timur-Lang of Samarkand, or Voltaire *his* with Frederick of Prussia? Why had Chateaubriand gone to Prague to see a minor figure—exiled Charles X—instead of sailing to the Ascension islands to see Napoleon on St. Helena? "He would have written his most powerful chapter," Malraux daydreamed in his foreword and wrote the first lines for Chateaubriand:

> In front of a hovel, a man wearing a planter's hat waited for me. I hardly recognized Bonaparte. We went inside and lost ourselves in the fate of the world. While in a low voice he talked about Austerlitz, the eagles of St. Helena circled in a window opened on eternity.

Malraux wanted to transcribe de Gaulle's way of thinking ("the opening outline, as always with him, sentences he had said or written before, followed by improvisations that allow him to think, then what he says to amuse himself") and to show the facets of him where he was not the historical personage. He wanted to reconstitute the feel of a friendship and a certain angle of history. *Les Chênes qu'on abat,* which in Irene Clephane's English translation, *Felled Oaks,* appeared in 1972, "lights up de Gaulle from the inside and shows the gradients of his mind and soul as he had let a friend see them," Jean Grosjean wrote on the flap of the French edition. In *The New York Times,* Murray Kempton wrote, "To read de Gaulle and Malraux even here together when everything had passed them by is to understand the command that fantasy will forever

---

[3] Charles de Gaulle, *Mémoires d'espoir,* op. cit.

be able to place upon us: both of them are so much more wonderful than anyone real" [4]

The book abounds with acute observations, Malraux remembering, in shaking hands, how small de Gaulle's hands are, like Mao's, noticing de Gaulle's solitaire cards on a table and how de Gaulle's intelligence is determined by the level of his thinking rather than the perspicacity of his ideas. He first finds that de Gaulle's fatigue of the last days in power has disappeared and later, when they interrupt their conversation to have coffee with Yvonne de Gaulle, how he looks aged ("he seems now much older than me: but of course everyone sees only *others* grow old"). Purposely no doubt, it is sometimes difficult to follow who is speaking as the two of them "lose themselves in the fate of the world." De Gaulle comes across as stoically removed and remote, haunted by the limits of his success, assiduously confusing reality and its appearances, soliloquizing if not with death, at least with transfiguration and seeing a twilight descending as much over the West as over his own life.

His judgments are not without generosity as he calls Americans a nation without baseness. He says that by constantly reassuring others of their respect for the democratic process, Western communists have lied so many times they have actually come to believe it themselves. He quotes the ninety-year-old Marshal Helmuth von Moltke when Bismarck asks him whether, after the events of his life, there are still things worth living for: "Yes, your excellency, to watch a tree grow." He cannot understand why intellectuals have never followed him and tells how Stalin's hand contracted itself on de Gaulle's knee each time on the screen of the Kremlin theatre a German soldier died in a close-up. "When I felt he had given me enough blue marks, I moved my leg."

The assessment of de Gaulle's role is the center of their discussion, with Malraux tracing both the outer curvature of the general's feats and the inner limits of *all* political action. Malraux says that in de Gaulle's wartime appeal for resistance, he gave his countrymen a rare gift—the chance to elect the best in themselves, to legitimize their sacrifice. Malraux also says de Gaulle's France has never really belonged to the rational world.

On the steps where de Gaulle sees Malraux to the car that will take Malraux through the now snow-covered village to the railway station, de Gaulle expresses a luminous thought about the future: "True democracy is ahead of us, not behind us—still to be created."

On November 3, 1971, Malraux turned seventy. The occasion was marked by a series of nine, full-hour television specials aired over a seven-month period on the French first network. "Enough to make all French people sick and tired of me forever," he sighed happily as TV crews

[4] *The New York Times* Book Review (April 23, 1972).

Gisèle Freund, Magnum

De Gaulle and his Cultural Affairs secretary

settled in at Verrières. Two intelligent producers, Françoise Verny and Claude Santelli, had asked him, "How about doing a big thing together?" and he had agreed. Over one hundred hours were taped at Verrières, in the garden when weather permitted and in the *salon bleu.* Malraux talked and talked, about the ragged men in Black Périgord harrassing the *Reich* Division, about Trotsky, Mao, Durriti, about the Japanese emperor's geishas, about a lady at Khrushchev's funeral holding an umbrella over the Soviet leader's remains, about meeting in the Spanish skies with bearded fascist fliers, suddenly too human because of their beards to shoot down. The filmed material showed hints of aphasia, but also Malraux's brilliant repartee and his famous presence. The cutting was judicious. When asked about God, he answered that for a "non-atheist agnostic like me," it was hard *not* to end up with religious answers, then suddenly added, "Cut! That's too much hopelessness." Director and crew never stopped the cameras and kept the sequence intact. In 1973, *André Malraux, Une vie dans le siècle* by *Nouvel Observateur* editor Jean Lacouture became a French best seller. The biography was totally political and came down particularly hard on Malraux's association with the just-ended Gaullist era. When asked what he himself thought of the best seller, Malraux huffed that he didn't read books written about him but allowed that he regretted that Lacouture had missed the most important part of his life— art.

Injustice was everywhere in 1971. There were causes to protest and causes perhaps to die for. Together with Jean-Paul Sartre and François Mauriac, he signed a demand to the Bolivian colonels demanding the freedom of the French Marxist and supporter of the late "Che" Guevara, Régis Debray. When asked on television if, at Debray's age, he would have done the same thing, he answered, "I did." And he wrote to President Nixon to protest the continuing bloodbath in Vietnam the day Pakistan realized its defeat and allowed the emancipation of Bangladesh. "If the world's most powerful army hasn't been able to crush the barefooted Vietnamese, do you think the army of Islamabad will crush a country seething with its own independence?" he asked the American president in his open letter, published in *Le Figaro,* before enlarging the scope:

> You remember our conversation with General de Gaulle. You honored me by telling me about American politics. I told you, "The United States is the first country that has become the world's most powerful nation without having wanted it." Alexander wanted to be Alexander the Great, Caesar to be Caesar. You didn't want to be masters of the world. But you cannot allow yourselves to be distracted masters. It is not right that the country of the Declaration of Independence crush misery trying to struggle for its own independence. What I say today, I shouldn't be saying. You should.[5]

[5] *Le Figaro* (Dec. 17, 1971).

For a moment, he thought of seeking his own blazing death in Bangladesh, at the head of another international brigade. Indira Gandhi, however, made him wait for his visa, wiring back that she would be coming through Paris on her way from Washington and London. She knew the victory would be India's and had no intention of giving any part of it, be it ever so symbolic, to a Western brigade of volunteers, especially since China was threatening to supply volunteers to Pakistan. He saw Mrs. Gandhi several times at the Indian embassy and when talking to journalists outside called her "that woman." He appeared sick, the face discolored and the speech contorted in a neighing stammer as he leaned on the embassy fence, apparently barely able to remain standing, before he was led to his limousine. The war lasted only ten days. As she flew home, the Indian Prime Minister gracefully invited her father's old friend to join her and the new nation in the victory celebrations. To a friend, he sighed, "Why go now? They have no longer any reason to kill me."

If he was refused the hero's death at the side of a crucified people in "his" Asia, he was to have the satisfaction of being the man President Nixon saw before meeting the rulers of the world's most populous nation. In preparation for the trip, Nixon had read voluminously about China. One book he publicly praised was the *Antimémoires,* and in February 1972, he invited Malraux to come to dinner in Washington.

"He wants to meet someone who knows Mao," an apparently recovered Malraux told journalists as he took off from Orly Airport. American bombs were raining on Vietnam and most of the world recoiled in horror and anti-Americanism, but, he tartly told the assembled French press, "if the question is to help bring peace, you can contribute more by making a trip to the White House than by writing articles in *Nouvel Observateur.*"

In Washington, he was whisked to the White House and into a closed-door meeting with the president and his adviser Henry Kissinger. Nixon asked questions, Malraux talked and, he remembered, Kissinger took a lot of notes. What did he tell the American president? That in Peking, Nixon would not be meeting revolutionaries but pragmatists. To go and see Mao with the Long March in mind would be like going to see Stalin with images of him as a Georgian holdup artist of czarist banks. Turn-of-the-century Russian revolutionaries had thought they would be saved by a European revolution, but, as Stalin had said, in the fight against fascism it turned out that half of Europe was saved by the Red Army. Mao believed that Asia's revolution would be saved by Chinese potatoes and China rice fields.

For Mao, the Revolution was long ago, and, like Stalin at the end of his life, he was obsessed by one thing—improving the standard of living of his people. Mao's first question to Nixon would be more likely to concern farm aid than Marxian theology because Mao was very conscious of his country's real Achilles' heel—the relative infertility of China's soil. As for Peking's supposed inscrutability and veiled intentions, nothing should be exaggerated. There was, for example, the Canadian ambassador in Peking. If Washington asked Ottawa to instruct its ambassador to ask the Chinese government if it had anything to tell the American government and Peking said no, this in itself was an answer.

Nixon agreed on this point and said he would clear up the whole question of communications once he got to Peking. On the "crucial question" of Taiwan, Malraux said he had seen a Taiwanese diplomat accorded full honors in Peking in 1966 and that he was sure a tacit agreement existed between Peking and Taipei, relative to the status of Formosa after the death of Chiang Kai-shek. At the old Nationalist leader's death, Nationalist China would cunningly become Chinese again—subtly, because when it came to subtleties, nobody could beat the Chinese.

Malraux called Nixon's "journey for peace" noble and courageous, but warned against expectations of instant results. "Nobody will know whether you're successful for fifty years," he told the president. "I know that," Nixon replied, "the American people and I can be patient too." Both quotes were circulated by Press Secretary Ron Ziegler the next day and reprinted in commentaries as the U.S. president set out on his historic journey.

Although Mao's first question to Nixon was not farm aid (but China soon began buying a new strain of U.S. wheat) and the 1975 death of Chiang Kai-shek did not make Taiwan a part of the Mainland (unless the supreme astuteness was to keep it as an Asian "Switzerland" with access to Western technology), Malraux's predictions were largely correct. Nothing "happened" in Peking. The importance of Nixon's journey was the event itself.

When anesthesiologists have put me away, I have
never feared not waking up again.

Lazare

28

Suicidal tendencies, vertigo, hints of aphasia and, out of public
view, convulsive dizziness followed by fainting spells without loss of consciousness (self-analyzed as resembling madness more than disease) resulted in November 1972 in a head-on crash into the glass door of a bookcase. Malraux was rushed to the Salpêtrière hospital and spent the next
seventy-two hours in intensive care with a collapsed peripheral nervous
system and threatened paralysis of the cerebellum.

Seventy-two hours of sliding in and out of consciousness, with
hallucinatory voyages in time and space, near-total amnesia, lancing insights and sensations of an encircling imbalance. Seventy-two hours of
suspended verdict also, with a doctor's first prognosis remembered—total
recovery, death or paralysis—and, somewhere in the middle of a pharma-
cological haze, a doctor's oracular, "Nothing is irreversible," and sensations
of a mind too full, of floating, like an astronaut, toward a void and only
hanging onto life by heavy, leaded moonwalk boots, of sexuality bereft
of any object of desire, of death as a vacuum cleaner sucking like horror
insects in an early illustrated Edgar Allan Poe edition, and, at the end,
a soothing ebb of seismic aftershocks and a long talk with a philosophical
neurologist, recognized as the "Nothing is irreversible" voice, who looked
like de Gaulle and smoked English cigarettes.

Malraux left the hospital in January 1973 to announce a string of
plans: a visit to Bangladesh, attending an "Imaginary Museum" hommage
to him by the Maeght Foundation in Saint-Paul-de-Vence during the
summer and, for the second *Antimémoires* tome, a chapter of yet another
confrontation—not with death but with the intermediary realm of paralysis.

He was in Dacca, Bangladesh, in April. Later the same month
after Picasso's death, he was at Jacqueline Picasso's side in Mongins on
the Riviera helping her to go through the painter's apparently priceless

341

reserves, which he had willed to his adopted country and which the Louvre had accepted with deep gratitude. Very young, Picasso had been famous and rich and for decades had bought his friends' paintings. Together with Jacqueline, André now made a first inventory of the canvases stacked against the walls in room after room of the villa—two little Douanier Rousseau portraits here, a *Figure* by Derain there, one of the most beautiful Matisses Malraux had ever seen—(*Nature morte aux oranges*) yet another, a 1908 Matisse, further on a Van Dongen, plus piles of Picassos of all periods.

Within a year, Malraux had a whole new book on Gallimard's fall list—*La Tête d'obsédienne,* dedicated to Gaston Palewski, and telling about Picasso and the traces an artist leaves behind and about art as lodestar of a continuing human adventure.

Twenty years after *The Voices of Silence,* Malraux says that art is man's fleeting immortality, the permanence of his dream and a part of him he does not completely control. Malraux starts daringly by saying that sacred art not only expresses religious feeling, it *creates* the sacred. In the deep recesses of primitive man, art seems to struggle with itself, entwining man and the unknown which assails him. The history of art is the history of the artist struggling with the human face, with rendering his own likeness.

After the Museum Without Walls, Malraux creates the notion, Imaginary Museum—a museum which can only exist in our minds, a mental storehouse of the arts of all times and all cultures and as such the ultimate metamorphosis of art. The works of art in this Imaginary Museum have chosen us as much as we have selected them. It is no longer esthetics, an inventory of the world's art treasures, nor a triumphant Westernization of all other civilizations. It has become global because it has freed itself from notions of beauty and thereby become a promise of a universal language. Ultimately, the Imaginary Museum is our means of peering into our own future.

Painting here has become its own supreme value—painting, not beauty or genius. Before being a horse in battle or a nude woman, a canvas is a flat surface covered with colors disposed in a certain order. Before being Sumerian goddess, Aphrodite, Holy Virgin or Michelangelo's *Heroic Captive,* a sculpture is a system of forms disposed in a certain order. This notion would have startled the sculptors of the Sumerian Gudea, of archaic Greek statues, of the Elephanta caves and even Michelangelo. They would have said, "Disposed in a certain order to what end if not to become divinity, Virgin or *Heroic Captive.*" It is only today that, escaping reality, the goddess and the Virgin have become masses and volume.

The Imaginary Museum, which may itself end up on the slagheap of mankind's great dreams, is not a tradition but an adventure. All civiliza-

342

tions have carried on a dialogue with the unknown, which includes death, the meaning and origins of life as well as sacrifice and cruelty. The feat is not to choose what is beyond the range of human understanding but to circumscribe it, since what cannot be known merges what we hope to know with what we will never know. From religion, magic and the unconscious, we have come to know the limbos, and the answers to humanity's answerless questions have almost been found in art. The unknowable takes on the forms of what suggests it.

The world's great artists not only converse with men who are no more but are also partners in dialogue with men not yet born. Rembrandt, Baudelaire have obviously helped create their own future audiences. Human life obeys that deep-running conscience which all civilizations have called Destiny—destiny being the opposite of the individual's freedom, of humanity and the world. The creative process therefore upsets this law of fate. Our admiration doesn't so much go to the individual as to his style—to an imaginary artist almost. Ultimately, art is a manifestation of what we cannot see—the sacred, the supernatural, the non-real. The Imaginary Museum may at first glance seem Spenglerian, but at closer examination it is the antithesis of Spengler, "for whom all civilizations are condemned to die." All great art is condemned to metamorphose.

The power of the artist is becoming increasingly enigmatic, less and less limited to any pictorial achievement. Cézanne's influence is not limited to the way he painted. In him exists a certain Western "severity of style," an inner architecture going back through El Greco and Piero della Francesca to Romanesque statues. In Picasso exists a certain power which our grandchildren will define as we have defined Cézanne's and Manet's. This power, which artists have not defined but often recognized (Van Gogh: "In life and in my painting I can very well live without God, but I cannot exist without something bigger than me, something that is my life—the power to create"), runs through all civilizations like a biological force. If we don't yet understand its language, we begin to hear its voice. *The Shepherd and Nymph* is not the crowning of Titian's shimmering colors of 1555, but, in the treasury of our Imaginary Museum, this masterpiece of Titian's last years is inexplicable yet manifestly linked to Rembrandt's last paintings. "We think we elect the members of the jury that decides the survival of works of art, but each is also elected by the others." Even if the nature of art cannot be expressed, it is perhaps possible to transmit it to the civilization that begins with us because there is something deeper than art in art.

The title of this book here takes on its full meaning. The skull is a figure of death, but will we ever understand vanished idols? What makes the obsidian head transcend the ages from pre-Columbian America to the emerging global civilization is not that it represents a skull but that its black quartz represents a skull according to a style. For the Spaniards,

343

it was first a demon, then an imitation of a skull and finally a masterpiece. A metamorphosis prefers to play with images of gods rather than with an image of death. All life created by the gods—religion—is condemned to vanish. What has triumphed over death are forms and ideas created by man—art.

La Tête d'obsédienne, which in English became *Picasso's Mask,* is embued with color, humor and vivid traits of Picasso, here saying that cats, like women, look best disheveled, there saying that he only tried marijuana once because while under its influence he had the impression he would always paint in the same manner. As in the *Felled Oaks* conversations with de Gaulle, Malraux's direct quotes are—he admitted in a *Le Monde* interview—"adapted," based on notes of conversations over the years, but expressing Picasso's character and essence rather than his spoken words. To Malraux, Picasso's genius was his unending self-questioning, his incessant challenging of himself and his creation. His style is both a continuation of styles and his overcoming these styles. Malraux quotes him saying, "Down with style! Does God have a style?" and says that while Picasso was painting *Guernica,* he told him he had discovered what to expect from painting in the Greek Bronze Age Cycladic "frying pan" pottery and, especially, in a flat "violin-woman" terra-cotta fetish.

> Life surprised him. When he was out walking and stopped talking to tear off a branch or to pick up a stone, he wasn't looking for a model but wondering, "What can I do with this?" What he meant—he rarely developed his striking quips and sallies—was probably: "I am wondering how this object can help me shatter painting or sculpture." The branch appeared in [Picasso's 1943 plaster] *Femme au feuillage,* conniving with geometric forms. He hadn't taken the stone home to admire it, but to make an imprint of it. His "I'm looking for things, I discover things," may not express haughtiness but wonderment.

Elsewhere, he has Picasso say that painters should not want to paint canvases that please, but canvases bristling with razor blades.

> A painter should create what he feels, but, Cuidado!, to feel is easily said. It doesn't mean seeing things this way or that way. It's not a question of interpretation. Look (he draws the anxious geometry of *Le Femme qui pleure*): For me, Dora has always been a woman who weeps. Okay. One day I succeeded in drawing her.

Picasso's Mask includes Malraux's address to the Maeght Foundation opening of the prodigious "Musée imaginaire" show in Saint-Paul-de-Vence in the hills above Nice. For the exhibition, which lasted through the summer of 1973, the Foundation had gathered eight hundred documents, from personal Malruciana—manuscripts, letters, photos, corrected proofs and newspaper clippings—to the objects of his life and love.

At Maeght Foundation "Musée imaginaire" exhibition

The highlight was the rooms where, thanks to loans from the Louvre and a half-dozen world museums, an extraordinary Imaginary Museum came to life. Here, classical Europe's foremost paintings—Tintoretto, Titian, El Greco—glowed in the reflection of Wei dynasty and Khmer stones next to the hybrid softness of Greco-Buddhist sculpture. Here, a Takanobu portrait gloried in the magic of stained-glass windows from Beauvais and Sainte-Chapelle cathedrals and a dazzling choice of African and South Pacific carvings grazed Greek and pre-Columbian art. Goya, Picasso and Miró told of the horrors of war and Babylonian statues told of the beauty from the depth of ages. The five-thousand-year-old pre-Babylonian *Ishtupllum* and *Goddess with Protruding Vase* statues had been loaned by the Shah of Iran, the Takanobu portrait by the Zhingaji Temple in Kyoto. El Greco's *Annunciation* and three other classical paintings came from the Baron von Thyssen collection while the African arts were assembled from the Paris Musée de l'homme and La Rochelle Museum.

When *L'Express* reviewed the exhibition (and found Manet, Van Gogh, Toulouse-Lautrec and Douanier Rousseau "a little lost in this eclectic company"), it asked various personalities to come up with the contents of *their* Imaginary Museum. Aimé Maeght said he would begin his with a caveman's carved bone and end with Giacometti's *L'Homme qui marche*. Eugène Ionesco would put in several books and paintings by Andrei Rublev, Vermeer, Giotto. Cranach and Kokoschka. Yves Saint-

345

Mais attention! In front of Tintoretto's Lucretia and Tarquin at
Maeght Foundation show at Saint-Paul-de-Vence

Laurent would include Proust's manuscripts of *A la recherche du temps
perdu* and the Josef von Sternberg movie *Shanghai Express* while Pierre
Boulez said the whole thing was stupid.[1] If the Speech to the Maeght
Foundation was the profound center piece of *La Tête d'obsédienne,* the
Walk Through the Picasso Reserve with Jacqueline proved to be something of an embarrassment. On the first anniversary of Picasso's death,
when illegitimate heirs launched court battles over the estate, a categorical
Louvre let it be known that a lot of the paintings willed to France were
fakes.

A persistent irritant was the flow of thin volumes Clara Malraux
kept publishing. After her childhood in *Apprendre à vivre,* and her meeting
André in *Nos Vingt Ans* came the Indochina Years in *Combat et Jeux*
(1969) and the high 1930s and their breakup in *Voici que vient l'été*
(1973). Pierre Galante had interviewed her in 1970, living "with her
memories and perhaps her bitterness." When he asked her feelings for
André, she had replied, "Admiration and disappointment." [2] In 1973
when *Paris-Match* writer Marie Elbe interviewed her in her little apartment near the Place d'Italie filled with books, paintings and two Greco-
Buddhist heads, survivors of their 1931 Afghanistan expedition and her
World War II flights, she said, "Admiration yes, but also lucidity." Very

[1] *L'Express* (July 23–29, 1973).
[2] Pierre Galante, *Malraux,* op. cit.

346

pro-Israel since the 1967 war, she said that rather than wanting to fight for Bangladesh, "he" should try to help the Israeli cause. "My father died when I was fourteen. I have seen my mother not only the widow but the orphan of a man who had dominated her life to the point of leaving her defenseless and I told myself I'll never be like that." Yes, she had known he would really write one day but had nevertheless been surprised by *Les Conquérants.* "Of course life with a genius is fabulous." No, she no longer saw him. "Now, he has entered History—with de Gaulle." [3] In *Voici que vient l'été* which she said would be the last volume of her memoires, she described herself as being assailed by Malraux PhD writers and Malraux scholars and researchers and after her title page proudly quoted Mallarmé, "We were two, I assert it." Malraux's answer was a continued silence. None of the successive volumes of the second part of the *Antimémoires,* which in 1973 he decided would bear the collective title *Temps des Limbes* (Times of Limbo) would mention her.

With *La Tête d'obsédienne* a best seller in France, he again gave ringing interviews. *Time* described him as remaining "the archetypical questing man, still casting a fiercely brilliant eye on man's fate and mankind's shifting perception of art and politics." [4] In March 1974, he held listeners spellbound for one hour on Radio-Télévision Luxembourg and saw his remarks reprinted in *Le Monde* [5] and, in abbreviated form, in *The New York Times.*[6] He talked about Europe, the absence of American initiative, the Arab oil embargo, Israel's survival and Alexander Solzhenitsyn.

He said the absence of a common enemy made a united Europe a myth and described Henry Kissinger's attempt at "economic leadership" following the Arab oil embargo as nothing more than neocolonialism on behalf of corporate America. As for the oil crisis itself, he felt the West had only itself to blame since it had been criminally slow in developing nuclear energy ("in certain areas we're behind India"). The problem was complex because it also touched Israel's survival. The best way not to understand anything here was to see the Israeli question in terms of sympathy and antipathy. A Jewish homeland in Palestine was carved out of the collapsing Turkish empire, along with thirteen other territories from Rumania to Tripoli, after World War I. When Great Britain decided to make Palestine a Jewish refuge, England was the world's foremost power and British guarantees were backed up by overall control of the whole Middle East, from Suez to India. As the present guarantor of Israel, the United States would not be able to back up its commitment to the hilt. Why? Because domestic considerations following the Vietnam debacle

3 *Paris-Match* (Oct., 1973).
4 *Time* (April 8, 1974).
5 *Le Monde* (March 12, 1974).
6 *The New York Times* (July 27, 1974)

347

would not allow the sending of GIs to the Golan Heights. In expelling "the admirable figure" Solzhenitsyn, the Soviet Union played its hand majestically. At the moment his wife and children were allowed to follow him in exile, "Solzhenitsyn, whose strength was in saying what he did while in the hands of the secret police and knowing himself to be in their claws, becomes an emigré saying things that are in themselves important. The two things have nothing in common, I think. Emigrés with strong characters have existed, and not only in Russia. It's a very noble posture, not necessarily a very important one. The attitude of the martyr—of the man who puts his life and more than his life on the line and who, in putting himself in the hands of those who could be his executioners nevertheless speaks up—has an incendiary power that nothing else has." *

In May 1974, France changed government and era. With the death of Georges Pompidou and the election, with a razor-thin majority, of Valéry Giscard d'Estaing as president, the country moved from Gaullism into the Europe of the pragmatists, for whom the problems of the times were, first and foremost, technical and economic. To survive de Gaulle, Gaullism would have needed another de Gaulle and none existed. For his inauguration, Giscard d'Estaing walked rather than rode down the Champs-Élysées, wore a business suit instead of tails, talked about a "new era" instead of delivering an oration about the glories of the past. His first job, he said, was to help reduce the social tensions of a polarized nation—the privileged, modern and optimistic France and the poor, neglected France burdened with grievances. His premier, Jacques Chirac, said he was less interested in political abstractions than in the technical exercise of governing and his Interior minister, Michel Poniatowski, said he hoped France would not again "catch the Gaullist disease, which is to live on the past, on traditions and dogmas." Less than three months later, the world adjusted to an America without Richard Nixon.

Malraux was in Japan during the French presidential elections. He was no longer close to power although he knew Giscard d'Estaing personally. He saw the new president as a reincarnation of the old Western dream of giving liberalism a political form. "Who is Giscard if not a conservative who wants to be a liberal conservative, a Left-leaning conservative," he said. "This desire to translate liberal ideas into a political reality runs very deep in Europe and in America at the very moment when political forms of liberalism are disappearing." Malraux also altered somewhat his perspective of de Gaulle and his own Gaullism, saying both were the consequences of the historical event of France's fall in 1940. "I was never linked to power," he told the Radio-Télévision Luxembourg listeners, "I was linked to the fact that I could serve a man for whom I had an admiration that everybody knows about. Because of a series of circumstances, this

* Malraux's remarks on Israel and Solzhenitsyn were not included in *The New York Times* reprint.

348

man has played a role absolutely unforeseen and unforeseeable in the destiny of my country." Later, he added that Gaullism was inseparable from historical events and that its rebirth would only be possible in the context of an event.

Lazare appeared in the fall, together with yet another Malraux preface, this time to a new edition of Georges Bernanos' 1936 novel *Journal d'un curé de campagne.*

Lazare is a long meditation on the edge of life. It is the meditation undertaken in the limbo of critical illness, in the closed-circuit world of a modern intensive-care hospital. For the weeks of disease and convalescence, Malraux lived detached from ambient reality and in the twilight of fear of loss his mind relived fundamental experiences of his past. He feels threatened—the peripheral nervous system which comprises the autonomic nervous system and the cranial and spinal nerves—is affected, but he does not want to be sick. Instead, he prefers to face imminent death and in his limbo recounts to himself the grand chapters of his life, almost all moments when death breathed down his neck. Some of the memories are real —episodes of Spain, the Resistance, the Alsace-Lorraine brigade—others are imaginary—the 1916 German gas attack on the Russian front. Malraux hardly makes any distinction. The imagined moments are as powerful as the experienced instances. We are back on the banks of the Vistula in 1916 with Vincent Berger impatiently watching the gesticulating scientist prepare the gas cannisters; we are with Malraux in 1942 discovering "that crucial region of the soul where absolute Evil is pitted against a sense of brotherhood," and we are with Malraux thirty years later meditating on Hiroshima and men's incessant willingness not only to put their individual lives on the line but the future of the planet.

Malraux refuses to write his autobiography. To philosophize is to learn to die, he says, "an ambitious phrase" in an intensive-care unit. When a sixty-year-old intellectual he never meets but hears dies in an adjoining room, he asks his neurologists how people take death. The doctor's answer that Christians die either believing in a Last Judgment or divine forgiveness and that atheists die badly, makes Malraux realize that faith answers death better than science. Yet, he says, he is irritated by the arrogance of religions which all claim only *they* make man unique, but admits that science has only explained life, not given it a meaning. The only answer he can find to fill the metaphysical void that haunts modern man since the collapse of Judeo-Christian civilization is—again— human solidarity.

The neurologist tells him to continue his fabulations and over thirty pages, Malraux remembers instances of fraternal gestures, from the printers in Saigon mutely bringing the *Indochine enchaînée* editors type with French accents, to the cyanide he and other maquis leaders possessed during World War II but which he, unlike Kyo and Katov in *La Condition hu-*

maine, wouldn't have given a comrade if faced with Gestapo torture, to scenes from Spain he had forgotten to write and film, a woman (a mother? he never found out) kissing an airman's mutilated face until the boy dies, the proprietress of the Gramat hotel kneeling in his blood and handing him a bowl of ersatz coffee during the first hours of his German captivity and, finally, the German stretcher carriers in their gas masks carrying stricken Russians to the Vistula field hospital. At the end, Malraux feels death losing its grip. He is on his way to recovery.

For several days, I have meant to write this. Zen texts say that the agony which comes just before illumination provokes laughter. Just before I lost consciousness, I saw my cat, Fourrure, and in the darkness the grin of the Cheshire cat. At the moment of keeling over (I had already left terra firma) I felt death go away. I was invaded and possessed by an alien presence, like the biblical Boaz by the immense goodness of the Chaldean sky—by an irony that somehow became reconciled, an irony fixing for an instant, the wasted face of death.

In November, Malraux was back in India, seeing changes that, in ten years, had been colossal. He felt that an India that neither Nehru nor Gandhi had dreamed of was coming into existence, a new society that was neither neocolonialist nor totalitarian. "China is changing behind closed doors; India out in the open," he said upon his return to France.

When UNESCO votes to cut off Israel's $12,000 cultural allocations for 1975, André joined Stephen Spender and Heinrich Böll in protesting to U.N. Secretary-General Kurt Waldheim. When a Spanish military tribunal condemned eleven terrorists to death, he joined Jean-Paul Sartre, Louis Aragon and Régis Debray in protesting "sentencing without due process of law," a protest which grew to a European-wide cry of indignation a week later when the Franco regime executed five of the urban guerrillas. But during most of 1975 and 1976, he was at his desk at Verrières working eight or nine hours a day to write the last volumes of the *Metamorphoses of the Gods* and to finish *Le Miroir des limbes,* the final overall title of his (anti)memoirs. New meditations included *Hôtes de passage* on Africa, Alexander the Great and the May 1968 Events. He took time out, however, for such mundanities as appearing in a television tribute to Michelangelo in honor of the five hundredth anniversary of the artist's birth, gloomily saying, "There can't be another Michelangelo in today's society because our faith in man is too weak."

La Métamorphose des dieux, which created the expression "imaginary museum," became a three-volume work. The original book, published in 1957, was followed in 1974 by *L'Irréel* and, two years later, *L'Intemporel.* The *Metamorphoses of the Gods* traced the gradual changes, from the Ancient World to the Renaissance, of "the sacred"—statues and temples as solid symbols of a transcendent truth—and "the divine"—the

350

gods of the Greek taking on human forms—through Christianity to fifteenth-century Europe. In *L'Irréel,* Malraux says art is "anti-destiny" and only intelligible through its death and transmutation. Here, he carries the role of the sacred and the divine from the first break with Christian values through the two Italian centuries of the Renaissance, through Masaccio, Piero della Francesca, Uccello, Botticelli, Leonardo da Vinci, Raphael, Michelangelo and Titian to the aging Rembrandt with his "inexplicable" luminosity. He sees in the Renaissance a stupendous turning point in art. Instead of re-creating the world according to sacred tenets, artists begin to re-create it according to imaginary values. "Titian's *Venus of Urbino* is evidently neither reality nor sacred truth; it is what I call *l'irréel"* (in English perhaps not so much the "unreal" as the "non-real").

The Renaissance, he says, is not, as traditional art theorists define it, the progress toward naturalism but the progressive discovery of the power that allows artists to make profane imaginings rival pious dreams, to make the hero a rival of the saint. The Renaissance is a metamorphosis of a society of the soul into a civilization of the mind—in *Voices of Silence,* the transition from the absolute to the relative. The theme running through *L'Irréel* is the autonomy of art, its belonging to its own world, which leads Malraux to reaffirm that there is no such thing as realism, e.g., high-fidelity likeness to nature, and to demonstrate how a work of art always takes liberties with appearances.

Renaissance Florence doesn't try to imitate Antiquity, as art historians keep telling us, but uses classical patterns and forms for its own sake. Pisano, Nani and Donatello "talk" with themselves and with each other. Their figures leave church walls for rich men's houses in order to provoke admiration, not devotion. The knowledge of the Tuscans—anatomy, three-dimensional realism, architectonic space, depth of field—is at the service of yet another dimension, which Flemish painters (Van Eyck at least) have no inkling of. To question the world is to try to reach for another world.

The new artistic power glorifies what is human. Botticelli's *Venus* worships feminine forms; "only the non-real allows the Christian artists of the Renaissance to express profane grandeur." Why are there no Crucifixions, no Annunciations, no Nativities in the Sistine Chapel? Because with the Renaissance the glorification of the mysterious is replaced by the celebration of the powers of the human mind. The Donatello sculpture, *Gattamelata*—a deliberate revival of the classical equestrian monument— frees Renaissance men from St. Augustine's City of God. Style is not nature embellished; it is what allows the embellishment of nature. With the Renaissance, culture is no longer a series of answers but a series of questions. With the Renaissance, a new human being is born—the man-who-asks, later to be called the intellectual.

L'Intemporel—again, in a Malrucian sense, time outside time rather than timelessness—traces the volte-face of modern painting which began with Manet's 1863 *Olympia,* the "realist" version of the reclining Venus motif common to Italian masters. With *Olympia,* says Malraux, painting becomes color arranged in a certain order and escapes poetry, religion and the sacred, thereby reaching not so much immortality as a state of grace outside time. "Manet's discovery is inexhaustible because *Olympia* is not *Venus of Urbino* shorn of Titian's poetry. A painter can extricate the pictorial essence that a masterpiece contains, but he can only re-create it by inventing his own correlation of form and color. This is what Manet did: *Olympia*'s cohesion equals in the world of painting, the harmony of *Venus of Urbino.* Like the passage of souls from one body to another, a painting's essence appears in its reincarnation."

Pictorial essence is always blurred because a painter can only give it body in his own language. The essence that Manet discovers in Titian looks perhaps like the pictorial essence Cézanne extracts from Sebastiano del Piombo, but Manet can only be Manet; Cézanne only Cézanne. With them begins the interiorized museum where paintings escape the gods and saints they portray and where, to a certain extent, they also escape time. What opposed "Independents" (Manet and the young impressionists) and Official Salon painters was not a conflict of representation but of transcendence. The "Officials" believed a painter continued great artists of the past by imitating them; the Independents knew they continued the masters by not resembling them. To the Officials, a painting survived because of its beauty; for the Independents to paint was to exercise a creative power regardless of what was on the canvas. This creative power alone, in a secular world, bestows if not immortality, at least timelessness, the time-lessness Cézanne, Van Gogh, Degas, Matisse and Braque went looking for. "If God had told Cézanne the canvas he was painting was bad, Cézanne would have been saddened; if God had said the way Cézanne painted was bad, Cézanne would have taken God by the hand and shown Him the Louvre. And so would we."

Better than any Louvre, the Imaginary Museum makes us realize the "time of art," a disconcerting time warp which Malraux likens to a saint to whom the devout pray. To the faithful, the saint is here-and-now, a present which bestows eternal life. But the saint also belongs to a historical time—Saint Francis of Assisi lived from 1182 to 1226. Finally, the saint belongs to the chronological time, the duration of the living who pray to him. As the prayer "actualizes" the saint so our admiration of a work of art makes it actual. The work of art belongs to its era, but it also escapes it. By making it intelligible to other periods, the metamorphosis delivers it from the present, from eternity and from immortality. With the exception of religion, art is the only world to escape death.

As Gallimard published *L'Intemporel,* Malraux allowed himself to lean back and, with his cats, Fourrure and Essuie-plume, to take longer

352

walks in Verrières gardens. He was happy because all he still had to do was to put the *Mirror of the Limbos* together, to rewrite certain passages, insert others and delete still others. "The *Antimémoires* from beginning to the end of the second volume is now an unbroken book."

And after art, literature. For 1977, he planned a short volume on metamorphosis in writing. "It goes without saying that totally different things happen in literature. If we don't see the Parthenon as the ancient Greeks did nor do we read *The Iliad* as they did."

When asked *which* Malraux—the writer, editor, revolutionary, statesman or art critic—future generations will put first, he smiles and with an impatient gesture says, "The writer, obviously."

"As Gide would say, 'Writer, *hélas!*' But I accept neither the *'hélas'* nor the exclamation point."

The true painter strives to paint what can only be seen through his world.

L'Irréel

29

"It is interesting of course that prehistoric art experts and anthropologists have now come to the same conclusion—that around 40,000 B.C. man discovered at the same time how to draw, how to make fire and how to bury his dead. If that is true, homo sapiens is contemporary to his art and his sense of death." [1]

Malraux is approaching old age still in love with the beautiful and tragic dimension of man's fate, as André Gide said thirty years ago, and watching his own metamorphosis with bemused detachment. "When you have seen several schools come into existence and die, you realize that a body of work, not to talk about human life, undergoes a metamorphosis," he says. "I know what *La Condition humaine* was when it was published and I'm sure it's not the same thing now. It would be interesting one day to analyze the odd inner life of a work of the mind."

One day. He has made his peace with the past and with the memory of that past. In *Lazare,* he wrote:

My memory has a hard time remembering personal detail. I have read what has been written about my books, not about my life. I don't remember my childhood; I don't remember, except by deliberate attention, the women I have loved, or believed I have loved; nor friends who have died. If I really try, do I remember three birthdays? Will I one day study the mechanics of memory, which has intrigued me for so long? Psychoanalysis is only interested in content, yet the *capacity* for happy memories leads us in different directions than enemy memories. Did Freud ever write the word happiness? When I will be able to talk to my fellow-patients, I will ask them whether their memories are often linked to the elements, to clouds, to trickling rivers, to night—on the evening of my eighteenth birthday I crossed the Châtelet Bridge and the emotions

[1] *Newsweek* (Nov. 12, 1973).

354

of *Oresteia*, which I had just discovered in the theater in Leconte de Lisle's translation, mingled with the sun sinking below the Trocadero towers—or whether memories are linked to life in general as much as to life in particular. "My memories are bunched together by sensations of heat and cold," Hemingway told me.

He has proved that an individual can reach further than himself. He has written fiction that is totally modern, novels in which violent action is underpinned by profound intellectual themes. He has found meaning in art—art, not as beauty but as transcendence—and in culture has discovered not answers but questions. "To transform experience into conscience—that's what it means to be a man," someone exclaims in *L'Espoir*. "You can learn to handle a machine gun in two minutes. What takes longer is to learn to reject the past in favor of the future you're fighting for." He has wanted to make his life the expression of his ideas and has done so. He has wanted glory and has achieved it, even if his long service as his country's Secretary for Cultural Affairs—it is common knowledge—stands between him and a crowning Nobel prize. To some of the professors in Stockholm de Gaulle's France was tainted, and Malraux with it, but as *Newsweek* said in 1973, Nabokov, Borges and Graham Greene, it seems, may also die unrecognized "by the amiable Swedes."

One day. What interests him is the future. His latest dada, he says as we sit down on a rainy afternoon in the *salon bleu* at Verrières, is audio-visual technology to further revolutionize art concepts. He compares audio-visuals to the print media revolution and wonders, *en passant,* if Marshall McLuhan didn't stand the Gutenberg revolution on its head. What was revolutionary, he feels, wasn't so much the invention of the printing press as the insistence of the Century of Enlightenment that everybody learn to read. "Think of the possibilities of televising the world's art treasures every day or putting them on video cassettes. Something enormous will happen because people still think of painting in relation to its model, as true or idealized rendition of 'something.' But when you have an African fetish follow a classical statue, follow Miró, follow Michelangelo, you'll be forced to realize that the importance isn't between canvas and model but between one canvas and another. I mean, when you see Christ you will want to know what the relation is to Buddha, not to the 'actor' in the canvas—it was the eighteenth century which invented theatrical staging in painting. All this means that in art, we will have learned to read in twenty years."

His typed-up crib sheet, he says, contains interesting statistics. Between 1960 and 1970 the number of books sold have doubled, the number of records tripled, he reads. The percentage of French people who never buy a book has fallen from forty to twenty-nine percent and in six years the number of books each person reads has nearly doubled. According to UNESCO, there are 17,630 television stations and three hundred million TV sets in the world—one set per fourteen persons. Ballet audi-

355

ences in the United States have increased seven fold in ten years. Nearly one Frenchman out of three visits a museum every year, two out of three visits take place during travels and the number of individuals attending special exhibitions has doubled in ten years.

To metamorphose works of art into electronics, he says, is yet another function of the Imaginary Museum, which of course only exists since the invention of modern reproduction techniques. "The Imaginary Museum is a giant step because all future art will be judged against it, against what is acceptable to our collective sensibility which in itself is the sum-total of a past made present. And it means that a real museum is, in a sense, episodic."

"You mean that if the Louvre burned down tomorrow it wouldn't be the end of the world?"

"That is what is extraordinary. If the Louvre burned to the ground it would no longer have the same importance. Before, art would have disappeared; today, what would disappear would be the film negative, so to speak."

He pours mint tea with a slightly shaky hand. "One of the things that even our clever century failed to recognize is that the *function* of art could change." He leans forward and forgets his tea glass. "I think the era that began with Manet ended with Picasso. Why? Because contemporary artists, post-object, conceptual, earth artists, work in a temporal, consumer world, whereas, Attention! Picasso and Braque, at the time of their cubism, were perfectly aware that they were taking on the whole Louvre. So we're on thin ice when we identify art with its objects. In 1890, Huysmans said that to be modern was to paint laundresses like Degas, but in 1890 the future was not in Degas' laundresses but in Cézanne's apples. When Seurat died he was probably, in the deep sense of his time, the most modern painter, yet his subjects weren't particularly modern. Artists don't necessarily find their genius where they look for it."

The newest acquisition in the *salon bleu* is a fourteenth-century ashtray-sized turquoise and silver vase from Tibet. It stands under the Greco-Buddhist sculpture, "the only example of Indian art with a bowed head," he smiles, maliciously explaining the reason for the inclined head probably isn't a mark of genius but the fact that this figure stood in a particularly low-ceilinged grotto. He adds that evolution has no meaning in art, then corrects himself. Metaphysically, the question of time can be formulated, but not resolved in art.

"If the weather had been better, we could have taken a walk in the garden," he says. "Verrières was the first formal Japanese garden in France. It hasn't been kept up and it is interesting to see nature revert to nature." Through the windows he points to the cherry trees. "You rarely find a civilization become the master of the world while searching for its own values."

356

"The only example of Indian art with a bowed head," the Greco-Buddhist sculpture on the chimney in the *salon bleu*

His ellipses are sudden. There is again talk of turning *Man's Fate* into a movie, this time with Paramount Pictures financing and Karel Reisz directing, possibly in China. He regards a film version of his most famous book as of little contemporary interest and doubts whether Chinese authorities will collaborate. "Nothing remains of the 1920s Shanghai and China's rulers have now thoroughly canonized the revolution. The presence of the Russians in Canton—Gallen, Borodin are no chimera!—the whole international, Trotskyite core has been carefully removed."

His achievement as a novelist has been to write about metaphysical implications of violent political action. His characters are ethnologists, art dealers, archaeologists, but he has never tried to draw the portrait of a great painter, a fictitious Braque. When one asks why, he intimates that the novel declined before he could get to it and cites the examples of unfinished novels by Sartre, Mauriac, Hemingway and Faulkner's painful last book. He might also say that the painters who fascinate him, the great solitary figures like Goya and enigmatic like Vermeer, possess, like all Malraux heroes, a visionary sense. They, too, glow and burn themselves out for a vision. No writer has looked so rationally on the darker sides of man and, in both novels and nonfiction, come up with the same world view. Men's readiness to torture and to murder each other—themes present in all his novels—seems to have fascinated him very early. Later, he found that man's noblest endeavor is also achieved through struggle and that the creative process is a tortuous advance toward illumination.

As one listens to the expressions of his lucid synthesis, one realizes that he has lived his entire life in a country in decline, from that 1914–18 bloodletting first glimpsed on a class outing where funeral ashes from battle pyres wafted onto the box lunches, through the liquidation of an empire to the loss of a continent's momentum. Like a Roman under Diocletian, he has lived with money and values always worth a little less. Is there a connection? One ventures into the subject obliquely, by asking why the United States lost the Vietnam War.

"It is always Rome that wins and Carthage that loses," he begins. "If the United States had wanted to conquer Vietnam it would of course have done so. It *is* ironic that America's own War of Independence was fought by the British with the same lack of vigor and the same formidable opposition within the government. If the British had put the energy into defeating the colonial rebels they had put into defending England against the Spanish Armada—because against Spain, against Napoleon, they fought!—I'm not so sure the Americans would have come out so well."

America brings him to a new and "essential" idea—that modern nations live on an abstraction of their political institutions and that the sense of manifest destiny has disappeared everywhere, even in communism.

"We are now accepting the caricature of democracy with those one or two percent election majorities—Kennedy, Schmidt, Trudeau, Palme, Wilson—forgetting that when the ballot box was invented two hundred years ago, the Third Estate was, when opposed to nobility and clergy, a crushing majority. We have kept the words, but with a one percent majority, governments don't govern; they make deals. Democracy has become its own abstraction and is therefore unlikely to last another two hundred years."

He looks for the deeper reasons for modern malaise beyond other "dazzling appearances," old ones that won't go away and new ones that seem substantial. He thinks we are losing energy combatting fascism—fascism in the precise Third Reich totalitarian meaning, not in the loose sense of Leftist rhetoric. "We are all the victims of the memory of fascism. I mean, all intelligent people agree fascism is, literally, backward looking; Hitler wanted to restore a nineteenth-century Germany, but everybody is also afraid of it. Antifascism was one of the most important political realities when the Russians were fighting alongside the democracies—a brief but extraordinary period. Fascism was defeated but antifascism persists. The oil crisis is another mirage. If all cars suddenly stopped it would of course have a lot of effect, but the crisis has not profoundly changed the profound fact that historical will has disappeared everywhere.

"It has never happened before that the world's most powerful nation has no sense of what it wants. Yet the United States has no longer

358

any manifest destiny; nor does Russia. The Chinese don't have any either—domestically, yes; the national willpower is very real but when they say they want to change Tanzania, they're talking propaganda. Brezhnev doesn't know Europe and no longer believes in international communism. We once feared the Red Army on the Rhine, but Moscow no longer thinks of even sending it there. Nevertheless, of all this remains a certain Marxist idea which is that, in a century, the contradictions within capitalism will have ruined capitalism. But as we go along, Marxists are beginning to realize that something totally unforeseen is happening inside capitalism—the third-force phenomenon, both as the Third World and as service industries and technocracy in developed countries. The Russians don't call this an anti-Marxist phenomenon, but they realize that the demarcation line of the class struggle is becoming exceedingly thin. Instead of ever-contracting capitalism and proletariat, you now have capitalism and the working class undergoing their own metamorphosis and between them something Marxists refuse to admit—an emerging third force whose future is unpredictable yet is likely to become a decisive factor in the new century."

It is here that he sees India as alternative and synthesis. It is the new India with its "Indo-American" architecture—"you'd have guessed Hong Kong's high-risers; not Bombay's"—which is much more complicated than an Americanized India. It is a perplexing India because totally unforeseen by Gandhi and Nehru, an India unique among nations insofar as it alone can pretend to give others a spiritual lesson. "The main difference between all we can say about the West, communism included, and traditional India is that Indian thought is inseparable from a series of psychic states. For you to be Kantian or Hegelian is a matter of point of view, of preference because you feel one is closer to the truth than the other, but to the traditional Hindu the union with the Eternal is not a concept; it is a state of being. Having said this, it *is* curious that a caste system should coexist with universal communion. It is odd that the Hindu who has no trouble imagining himself born as woman or bird in his next life treats women and birds as inferior. Societies who believe in metempsychosis should not have hierarchies, but they do."

A Western spiritual revolution is hard to foretell, he says, because profound change is, by definition, subterranean and because we have a tendency to take problems for examples. "If no one really talks about deep influences, it is because it is in the nature of such influences to be concealed. So? So we continue to play the same game until something happens and that something *should* happen because we feel very intensely that the political system is drawing to a close. The question is not one of morality but of destiny; we're not looking for a new Moses to give us new laws, we're trying to find out what we can be."

He wonders if science cannot become that new fuction, if science, which so triumphantly has formed the world, cannot take on the added challenge of forming man. He finds it stupefying that the era which discovered nuclear physics and true genetics is satisfied with conceiving man somewhere between Marx and Freud. "Is it too much to ask of science?" he asks with a broad gesture. "It wasn't that easy to discover modern biology, was it? Isn't it characteristic of science to discover more than it is looking for?"

He drinks his tea with dramatic effect. He has no concrete suggestions, he says, plunging forward again, but thinks a new methodology can be invented, as other systems of principles have been invented. He doesn't fear any awesome power of science. He thinks the risk of having science turn future generations into robots is worth taking considering that Rome already felt the formation of the individual was too important to be entrusted to politicians and that the whole world is today in their hands. "Modern medicine and biology have created an image of man which would have dumbfounded nineteenth-century scientists—the possibility of finding in its disciplines our next myths. If science cannot give us a future, we will have had the honor of conquering the moon in order to commit suicide on it."

A life is also quieter voices. The unknown and the unthinkable have neither forms nor names, he says calmly, only contours. One of his cats grazes his crossed legs. He reaches down, but the cat walks on, indifferent. One of the stylistic devices of his writing is his use of sensory images— alternating light and darkness, sound and silence, elevated to almost structural significance, still there in the last pages of *Lazare,* recollections of a childhood hedge of mimosas full of mayflies next to memories of the first winter cold in Spain and of silently watching a soldiers' campfire. Hindu metempsychosis, he says, cannot be faked because all conversation with death is irrational and an agnostic West has not yet accepted *its* irrationality. To live long enough, he also says in *Lazare,* is to see the grand moments of one's life become conscience, nothing more.

And fraternity? one asks, thinking of the fidelity to the self of his long life.

"One doesn't exclude the other, conscience and fraternal sentiments."

Thirty minutes later one is back at rainy Antony station, courteously dropped off in the black Citroën. One is moved, thinking of the fussy yet unsentimental leave-taking, the two minutes' wait for the chauffeur to appear from somewhere in the big house, two minutes fleshed out with comments on the Mexican folk art which adorns the cavernous entrance. One thinks of the inner coherence of a life that has had its vicissitudes, its inconsistencies, but contains no rancor, no hate. The trains run every four minutes in the rush-hour rain, crowded outbound commuter trains on the opposite track. "At least we know that we call those artists for

360

Paula Porter

In the salon bleu at Verrières

whom art is a necessity—whether creator or not," he has said. "To love someone is not to hold that someone for marvelous, but for indispensable."

The inbound train is empty except for an adolescent in a window seat plunged in a book. Paliseau, Bourg-la-Reine stations. Haunted by a feeling of being isolated in a universe where people lead alienated lives whose essences cannot be transmitted, Malraux has invented fraternity as a state of grace and art as necessity. A life isn't created in chronological order, isn't years but experiences added up, he has said. Nino Frank has wondered about the little-known adolescence, the time before Clara, "the age when dreams are born," and one wonders with him—an adolescence fled and denied, yet remembered at the edge of life for its hedge of mimosas full of mayflies.

The boy at the window looks up. Fontenay-aux-Roses and denser suburbs; other stations and a slowly filling railway car. A life created like a piece of art, deliberately, and remembered for what is "anti," for what is imagined, amplified, transcended, for what is intelligence imposed, for what is challenge to the indifference of the starry night.

The boy looks through the raindrops at the fleeing high-risers. The book in his hand is *La Condition humaine*. One smiles to oneself in gratitude for the coincidence and thinks of the elephant in the *Anti-mémoires* who stands motionless for long periods of time and contemplates his former lives.

Books by André Malraux

In French

(Editions in French in order of publication; all books published in Paris unless otherwise noted.)

Lunes en papier. Galérie Simon, 1921.
La Tentation de l'Occident. Grasset, 1926.
Les Conquérants. Grasset, 1928.
Le Royaume du farfelu. Grasset, 1928.
La Voie royale. Grasset, 1930.
La Condition humaine. Gallimard, 1933.
Le Temps du mépris. Gallimard, 1935.
L'Espoir. Gallimard, 1937.
Les Noyers de l'Altenburg. Lausanne: Editions du Haut-Pays, 1943.
Oeuvres complètes. Geneva: Skira, 1945.
Scènes choisies. Gallimard, 1946.
Esquisse d'une psychologie du cinéma. Gallimard, 1946.
Le Musée imaginaire. Tome I, *La Psychologie de l'art,* 1947; Tome II, *La Création artistique,* 1949; Tome III, *La monnaie de l'absolu,* 1950. Geneva: Skira.
Saturne, essai sur Goya. Gallimard, 1950.
Les Voix du silence. Gallimard, 1951.
Vermeer de Delft. Gallimard, 1952.
Le Musée imaginaire de la sculpture mondiale. Tome I, *La statuaire;* Tome II, *Des bas-reliefs aux grottes sacrées;* Tome III, *Le monde chrétien.* Gallimard, 1952–54.
Le Miroir des limbes. Tome I, *Antimémoires,* 1967; Tome II, *Les Chênes qu'on abat,* 1971; Tome III, *La Tête d'obsédienne,* 1974; Tome IV, *Hôtes de passage,* 1976. Gallimard.

La Métamorphose des dieux. Tome I, *Le Surnaturel,* 1957; Tome II, *L'Irréel,* 1974; Tome III, *L'Intemporel,* 1975. Gallimard.
Oraisons funèbres. Gallimard, 1973.

In English
(Editions in English in order of publication; all books published in New York unless otherwise noted.)

The Conquerors. Translated by Winifred Stephens Whale. Random House, 1929.
Man's Fate. Translated by Stuart Gilbert. Smith and Haas, 1934.
The Royal Way. Translated by Stuart Gilbert. Smith and Haas, 1935.
Day of Wrath. Translated by Haakon M. Chevalier. Random House, 1936.
Man's Hope. Translated by Stuart Gilbert and Alistair MacDonald. Random House, 1938.
The Psychology of Art. Translated by Stuart Gilbert. 3 vols. Pantheon, 1949–1950.
The Walnut Trees of Altenburg. Translated by A. W. Fielding. Limited edition. London: John Lehmann, 1952.
The Voices of Silence. Translated by Stuart Gilbert. Doubleday, 1960.
Anti-Memoirs. Translated by Terence Kilmartin. Holt, Rinehart and Winston, 1968.
Felled Oaks; Conversations with de Gaulle. Translated by Irene Clephane. Holt, Rinehart and Winston, 1972.
Picasso's Mask. Translated by June Guicharnaud with Jacques Guicharnaud. Holt, Rinehart and Winston, 1976.

Bibliography

Agee, James. *Agee on Film: Essays and Reviews.* New York: Grosset and Dunlap, 1969.

Aub, Max. *Sierra de Teruel.* Mexico: Editorial ERA, 1968.

Audoin, Philippe. *Les Surréalistes.* Paris: Seuil, 1973.

Baker, Carlos. *Ernest Hemingway: A Life Story.* New York: Charles Scribner's Sons, 1969.

Bazin, Germain. *A History of Art.* Translated by Francis Scarfe. New York: Crown Publishers, 1969.

Blend, Charles. *André Malraux: The Tragic Humanist.* Columbus: Ohio State University Press, 1965.

Blumenthal, Gerda. *André Malraux: The Conquest of Dread.* Baltimore: Johns Hopkins University Press, 1960.

Boak, Denis. *André Malraux.* London: Oxford University Press, 1968.

Boisdeffre, Pierre de. *André Malraux.* Paris: Classiques du 20è Siècle, 1957.

Chevalier, Haakon M. *Oppenheimer: The Story of a Friendship.* New York: Braziller, 1965.

Crespelle, Jean-Paul. *Chagall.* Translated by Benita Eisler. New York: Coward-McCann & Geoghegan, 1970.

De Beauvoir, Simone. *The Prime of Life.* Translated by Peter Green. Cleveland: World Publishers, 1962.

De Gaulle, Charles. *Mémoires d'espoir.* Paris: Plon, 1970.

De Montherlant, Henri. *Carnets.* Paris: Table Ronde, 1947.

Deutscher, Isaac. *Trotsky,* Vol. I, *The Prophet Armed: 1879–1921* (1953); Vol. II, *The Prophet Unarmed: 1921–1929* (1959); Vol. III, *The Prophet Outcast: 1929–1940* (1963). London: Oxford University Press.

Doyon, René-Louis. *Mémoire d'homme.* Paris: Connaissance, 1953.

Duthuit, Georges. *Le Musée inimaginable*. Paris: Corte, 1953.

Ehrenburg, Ilya. *Memoirs: 1921–1941*. Translated by Tatania Shebunina. Cleveland: World Publishers, 1960.

Flanner, Janet. *Men and Monuments*. New York: Harper and Row, 1957.

―――. *Paris Was Yesterday:1925–1939,* ed. Irving Drutman. New York: The Viking Press, 1972.

Frank, Nino. *Mémoire brisée*. Paris: Calmann-Lévy, 1967.

Frohock, Wilbur Merrill. *André Malraux and the Tragic Imagination*. Stanford: Stanford University Press, 1952.

Galante, Pierre. *Malraux*. Trans. Haakon M. Chevalier. New York: Cowles, 1971.

Gannon, Edward S. *The Honor of Being a Man: The World of André Malraux*. Chicago: Loyola University Press, 1957.

Garnier, François. *Max Jacob: Correspondance*. Paris: Éditions de Paris, 1953.

Gide, André. *Journals*. ed. Justin O'Brien. New York: Knopf, 1951.

Green, Julien. *Journal*. Paris: Plon, 1972.

Hoffmann, Joseph. *L'Humanisme de Malraux*. Paris: Klincksieck, 1972.

Horvath, Violet M. *André Malraux: The Human Adventure*. New York: New York University Press, 1969.

Jenkins, Cecil. *André Malraux*. Boston: Twayne Publishers, 1972.

Kazin, Alfred. *Starting Out in the Thirties*. Boston: Little, Brown & Company, 1962.

Keats, John. *You Might as Well Live: The Life and Times of Dorothy Parker*. New York: Simon and Schuster, 1970.

Koestler, Arthur. *The Invisible Writing: An Autobiography*. New York: Macmillan, 1970.

Koltzov, Mikhail. *Diario de la guerra de España*. Paris: Ruedo iberico, 1963.

Lacouture, Jean. *De Gaulle*. Paris: Seuil, 1969.

―――. *André Malraux: Une Vie dans le siècle*. Paris: Seuil, 1973; translated by Alan Sheridan, New York: Pantheon, 1976.

Langlois, Walter. *André Malraux: The Indochina Adventure*. New York: Praeger Publishers, 1966.

Malraux, Clara. *Le Bruit de nos pas,* Tome I, *Apprendre à vivre,* 1963; Tome II, *Nos vingt ans,* 1966; Tome III, *Les Combats et les jeux,* 1969; Tome IV, *Voici que vient l'été,* 1973. Paris: Grasset.

―――. *Memoirs,* trans. Patrick O'Brian. New York: Farrar, Straus & Giroux, 1967.

Marion, Denis. *André Malraux. Collection Cinéma d'aujourd'hui*. Paris: Seghers, 1970.

Matthews, Herbert L. *The Yoke and the Arrow*. New York: Braziller, 1957.

Mauriac, Claude. *Malraux et le mal du héros*. Paris: Grasset, 1969.

366

————. *Un autre de Gaulle.* Paris: Hachette, 1970.

Mauriac, François. *Journal.* Paris: Grasset, 1937.

————. *Mémoires politiques.* Paris: Grasset, 1967.

Morand, Paul. *Papiers d'identité.* Paris: Grasset, 1931.

Mounier, Emmanuel. *Malraux, Camus, Sartre, Bernanos.* Paris: Seuil, 1953.

Ollivier, Albert. *Saint-Just et la force des choses.* Paris: Gallimard, 1954.

Payne, Robert. *Portrait of André Malraux.* Englewood Cliffs: Prentice-Hall, 1970.

Picon, Gaëtan. *André Malraux.* Paris: Gallimard, 1945.

————. *Malraux par lui-même.* Paris: Seuil, 1953.

Prévost, Jean. *Les Caractères.* Paris: Albin Michel, 1944.

Rebatet, Lucien. *Les Décombres.* Paris: Denoel, 1943.

Righter, William. *The Rhetorical Hero: An Essay on the Aesthetics of André Malraux.* New York: Chilmark, 1964.

Sabourin, Pascal. *La Réflexion sur l'art d'André Malraux.* Paris: Klincksieck, 1972.

Sachs, Maurice. *Au temps du boeuf sur le toit.* Paris NRC, 1939.

Schlesinger, Arthur. *A Thousand Days: John F. Kennedy in the White House.* Boston: Houghton Mifflin Company, 1965.

Serge, Victor. *Mémoires d'un révolutionnaire.* Paris: Seuil, 1951.

Shirer, William. *The Collapse of the Third Republic: An Inquiry into the Fall of France in 1940.* New York: Simon and Schuster, 1969.

Spender, Stephen. *World Within World: The Autobiography of Stephen Spender.* New York: Harcourt, Brace, 1951.

Stéphane, Roger. *Chaque homme est lié au monde.* Paris: Sagittaire, 1946.

————. *Portrait de l'aventurier.* Paris: Sagittaire, 1950.

————. *Fin d'une jeunesse.* Paris: Table Ronde, 1954.

Stern, Philip. *The Oppenheimer Case: Security on Trial.* New York: Harper and Row, 1969.

Struve, Gleb. *Russian Literature Under Lenin and Stalin: 1917–1953.* Norman: University of Oklahoma Press, 1971.

Suarès, Guy. *Malraux, La Voix de l'occident.* Paris: Stock, 1974.

Sulzberger, Cyrus L. *A Long Row of Candles: Memoirs and Diaries, 1934–1954.* New York: Macmillan, 1969.

————. *The Last of the Giants.* New York: Macmillan, 1970.

Vandegans, André. *La Jeunesse littéraire d'André Malraux.* Paris: Pauvert, 1964.

————. ed. *André Malraux: Du "farfelu" aux Anti-mémoires.* Paris: Revue des lettres modernes, 1972.

————. ed. *André Malraux: Visages du romancier.* Paris: Revue des lettres modernes, 1973.

Viansson-Ponté, Pierre. *Histoire de la république gaullienne.* Paris: Fayard, 1970.

Vilmorin, Louise de. *Poèmes.* Préface d'André Malraux. Paris: Gallimard, 1970.

Walker, John. *Self-Portrait with Donors: Confessions of an Art Collector.* Boston: Little, Brown & Co., 1974.

Werner, Eric. *De la violence au totalitarisme.* Paris: Calmann-Lévy, 1972.

Wilson, Edmund. *Shores of Light: A Literary Chronicle of the Twenties and Thirties.* New York: Farrar, Straus & Giroux, 1952.

Wilkinson, David. *Malraux. An Essay in Political Criticism.* Cambridge: Harvard University Press, 1967.

Index

Beach, Sylvia, 54
Beauvoir, Simone de, 212, 213, 224-225, 269, 272, 273
Becher, Johannes, 41
Béguin, Albert, 275
Belgium, 54-55
Benda, Julien, 170
Berenson, Bernard, 289, 290
Bergamín, José, 175, 181, 182, 201, 202, 221
Bergson, Henri, 43
Berl, Emmanuel, 118, 127, 138, 233, 234
Bernanos, Georges, 100, 259, 349
Bernard, Marc, 110
Berthelot, André, 135
Bible, the, 148
Bidault, Georges, 293
Bifur, 109
Billy, André, 110
Bloch, Jean-Richard, 156, 158
Blok, Alexander, 40
Blum, Léon, 154, 155, 177, 180-182, 203, 212, 260, 263
Blumenthal, Gerda, 290
Boak, Denis, 202, 229*n*, 232
Bockel, Pierre, 244-248, 259, 266
Boleslavskaya, Señorita, 207
Böll, Heinrich, 350
Borodin, Mikhail, 80, 90, 91, 108, 109, 123, 124, 164
Botticelli, Sandro, 351
Bouchor, Jean, 82
Boulez, Pierre, 325, 346
Brandin, Marcel, 33, 34
Braque, Georges, 13, 14, 17, 41, 42, 44, 140, 285, 352, 356
Bredel, Willi, 163, 165
Brentano, Clemens, 39
Breton, André, 72-76, 102, 126, 127, 220
Breton, Simone, 72, 73, 74
Brezhnev, Leonid I., 22, 359
Briand, Aristide, 101
Brod, Max, 170
Brothers Karamazov, The (Dostoyevsky), 19
Buckley, Henry, 207

Buddhism, 12, 107, 124-125, 383
Bukharin, Nikolai, 158, 161
Bunin, Ivan, 158
Buñuel, Luis, 203

Cahiers du Sud, 110
Cahiers verts, 104, 105, 245
Cambodia
    Bardez Affair, 95
    Khmer art affair, 57-75, 84, 116, 121, 224
    native conditions in, 78, 81
Camus, Albert, 53, 111, 167, 242, 246, 247, 251, 269-270, 272, 293, 295, 297, 304
Candide, 76, 121, 127
Capa, Bob, 207
Carnet intime (Tailhade), 40
Caravaggio, Michelangelo da, 284
Causeries (Baudelaire), 40
Caves du Vatican, Les (Gide), 53
Cecil, Lord Robert, 126
Cendrars, Blaise, 40
Cerf, Bennett, 135
Cézanne, Paul, 14, 18, 282, 284, 286, 288, 343, 352, 356
Chagall, Bella, 48
Chagall, Marc, 14, 16, 48, 76, 316, 330-332
Challe, Maurice, 305
Chamson, André, 105, 170, 245
Chanel, Coco, 14, 140, 141, 323
Charpentier, John, 121
Chauveau, Jean, 272
Chauveau, Leopold, 228, 272
Ch'en Yi, 319
Chênes qu'on abat, Les, see Felled Oaks
Chevalier, Carol, 295
Chevalier, Haakon M., 13, 135, 195-196, 295-297
Chevasson, Germaine, 233
Chevasson, Louis, 30-31, 32, 34, 42, 114, 213, 233
    Khmer art affair, 48, 59, 61-66, 70, 71, 74-75, 84

372

Espoir, L' (motion picture), 210, 267, 270
Esprit, L', 275
Esquisse d'une psychologie du cinéma (Malraux), 270
Ethiopia, 152, 173-175
Etincelle, L', 271-272
Evian Agreements, 310, 311
Express, L', 293, 294, 345

Fanon, Frantz, 305
Fascism, 136-137, 174-175, 254, 275-276, 358
Faulkner, William, 114-115, 136, 357
Fédération de libération nationale (FLN), 295, 304, 305
Fedin, Constantin, 155, 325
Felled Oaks (Malraux), 17, 37, 219, 256, 292, 311, 326, 330, 333-336
Fels, Florent, 40, 41, 43, 47, 49, 56, 57, 73, 74, 272
Figaro, Le, 332, 338
Fischer, Louis, 194, 207
Flanner, Janet, 115, 266-267
Flaubert, Gustave, 19, 148, 149
Fleuret, Fernand, 42
Foch, Ferdinand, 34
Fogg Museum, 58
For Whom the Bell Tolls (Hemingway), 188, 202
Forces françaises libres (FFL), 221
Forster, E. M., 135, 169, 170
Fortune, 221
Fouchet, Christian, 264, 272
Francesca, Piero della, 343, 351
France-Soir, 322-323
Franco, Francisco, 172, 176, 182-184, 187, 192, 203-204, 208, 257
Frank, Nino, 45, 54, 105, 157, 168, 259, 266, 316 *n,* 317, 362
French Somaliland, 59
Freud, Sigmund, 43
Frey, Roger, 264, 306, 325
Frobenius, Leo, 228
Frohock, Wilbur Merrill, 290
Fry, Varian, 219-221
Furry, Wendell, 296-297

Gabory, Georges, 38, 40, 42, 43, 45, 58, 70
Galaction, Gala, 170
Galanis, Demetrios, 40, 42, 52-53
Galante, Pierre, 314, 324, 346
Gallimard (publishing house), 15, 42, 103, 115, 118, 138, 140, 144, 148, 197, 213, 219, 269, 322
Gallimard, Gaston, 18, 20, 74, 114, 127
Malraux and, 102, 111, 114, 125, 135, 139, 146, 196, 223, 242, 273
Gallimard, Raymond, 74, 114
Gambert, Paul, 151
Gandhi, Indira, 17, 309, 339
Gandhi, Mohandas K., 16, 79, 359
Gauguin, Paul, 282, 284
Genet, Jean, 304, 325
Georges (Dumas), 30
Germany, 51-52, 55, 136-137, 141, 144-146, 175, 176, 182, 188, 212-215, 225, 238-242, 257, 258
Giap, Vo Nguyen, 292, 293
Gide, André, 20, 43, 53, 104, 115, 117, 126, 165, 170, 172, 198-200, 215, 221, 222, 225, 259, 273, 277, 353, 354
literary influence of, 53
Malraux and, 10, 52, 53, 58, 74, 118-119, 135, 137, 141, 144-145, 153, 183-184, 226, 242, 267
Gilbert, Stuart, 13, 137, 279
Giotto, 282, 286
Giral, José, 179-180, 187
Giraud, Françoise, 323
Giscard d'Estaing, Valéry, 348
Gleizes, Albert, 48
Godard, Jean-Luc, 325, 328
Goebbels, Joseph, 145
Goethe, Johann Wolfgang von, 114
Goldschmidt, Clara, *see* Malraux, Clara
Goldschmidt, Madame, 49, 50, 51, 52, 57, 72, 103, 107, 127, 347
Goldschmidt family, 50-52, 66, 72, 103, 127, 138, 317
Goll, Claire, 41, 48, 54, 105

375

376

377